D1025096

UNREPENTANT RADICAL

ALSO BY SIDNEY LENS

UNREPENTANT RADICAL

An American Activist's Account of Five
Turbulent Decades

Sidney Lens

BEACON PRESS Boston

Copyright © 1980 by Sidney Lens

Beacon Press books are published under the auspices

of the Unitarian Universalist Association

Published simultaneously in Canada by

Fitzhenry & Whiteside Limited, Toronto

All rights reserved

Printed in the United States of America

(hardcover) 9 8 7 6 5 4 3 2 1

Library of Congress Cataloging in Publication Data

Lens, Sidney.
    Unrepentant radical.

    Includes index.
    1. Lens, Sidney. 2. Socialists — United States — Biography. 3. Socialism
in the United States. 4. Radicalism — United States.
I. Title.
HX84.L37A35   335′.00973   79-53757
ISBN 0-8070-3206-9

FOR
SOPHIE
SHIRLEY
IDA

Contents

Chapter 1
First a Rebel

I

What a pity to waste childhood on the follies of children!
Think of those great happenings we are unaware of during
those formative years while studying the three R's, playing
baseball, stealing apples from the corner food stand, and
groping slowly toward an inchoate *Weltanschauung.* It is like
living two lives, one of them prehuman, and being cheated
out of the intellectual insights of half a generation. In my
own case, World War I broke out when I was two, the Russian Revolution when I was five, the strangled German
Revolution and the national steel strike in the United States
when I was seven, the Palmer Raids when I was eight, and the
La Follette third-party campaign for president when I was
twelve.

My only vivid memory of anything having to do with
radicalism during all those years was a small incident when I
was seven or eight. My mother, already widowed and back in
the garment factories from which she had escaped to marry
my father, took me to a huge indoor rally in New York.
There were double doors leading to a large hall, and outside
the hall proper — in the foyer — tables set up with all kinds of
literature. At one of these my mother bought me two postcards that, I discovered much later, pictured the two martyred

German revolutionary leaders, Karl Liebknecht and Rosa Luxemburg. I treasured those cards for a number of years without knowing exactly why.

Neither the cards, the meeting, nor the vague political views of my mother — which were more pro-Russian than pro-Communist and were never central to her life anyway — had anything to do with my becoming a leftist. But they were a gentle reminder that we live in the stream of history before our minds are prepared to accept history. Though millions of my generation were not consciously aware of it, developments in the quarter of a century before the Great Depression had already established our status as psychological outsiders; the slump reinforced our alienation and institutionalized it. In my specific case, there was the additional factor that I was a fatherless only child.

My father, Charles Okun (I changed my surname to Lens in the mid-1930s when I was blacklisted for union activity and couldn't find a job under my own name), seems to have been, from what I can reconstruct, an intelligent man, but not political and certainly not lucky. Like so many other young Russian Jews, he came to the United States around 1907, at the age of twenty, to dodge the draft. He was moderately successful in business for a while; "love letters" he wrote to my mother (then his fiancée) in 1910 show he was a partner in a "trunk, bag, and suitcase handles" factory located at Hamilton Street in Newark, New Jersey. From what I can gather he skipped through grammar school, high school, and the necessary curriculum for a degree as pharmacist in just a few years. His letters, cleanly typewritten, were remarkably literate for a man whose acquaintance with the English language was so short. "Dear Sophie," he wrote on the eve of Yom Kippur, the Jewish day of atonement, "I beg leave to inform you that I will be over to see you tomorrow evening after the feast and find out how you are getting along without eating a day. We are all well and hope that you are the same. Trusting that God will put you and all of us down for a Happy, Healthy and Prosperous New-Year and will seal same, I remain, Your nearest friend, Charles

Okun." It wasn't much of a love letter, but for a man in the country so short a time it was a literary masterpiece.

Beyond the few "amorous" notes I found in my mother's papers after she died in 1954, I know very little about my father. He went broke, I understand, as a pharmacist, did moderately well running a newsstand in Newark, but died suddenly in April 1915 at age twenty-eight from cirrhosis of the liver.

My father's luck seems to have rubbed off on his family — one of his brothers, whom I know only from a portrait, committed suicide; another died of the same illness as my father; a sister died before she was thirty, leaving two children behind. Only the youngest brother, Louis Okun, survived into his fifties and lived a normal, moderately affluent life.

I have only one recollection of my father, a dream that my mother claimed was accurate recall. In the dream a tall man is tossing me to the ceiling, and as I come down I am screeching with joy. I put my arms around him for a second, then detach them, and he throws me to the ceiling again. I scream but don't wake up. The dream recurred frequently until I was perhaps twelve or thirteen, accompanied by a daytime fantasy I constructed in which my father was still alive, living in another country as a great potentate. In due course, I became reconciled to the reality that there was no father in my family — except for a few months in my tenth or eleventh year when my mother married a former Jewish burlesque straight man.

My mother — Sophie Horowitz — came from the same village near Minsk as my father — phonetically, as she pronounced it, it would be spelled *Rebshevitz*. Her parents evidently had never heard of birth control, for they sired twenty-seven children, sixteen of whom died at birth or before they reached the age of one. Of the remaining eleven, four emigrated to the United States, seven stayed behind. Many years later, in 1968, I asked the Soviet peace committee whom I was visiting in Moscow as part of an American peace delegation if they would arrange a trip to my parents' birthplace. Unfortunately, they were distressed with our opposition to the Soviet invasion of Czechoslovakia a few months before, so they refused. Chances are, however, that most of my mother's family perished in Nazi camps after the western part of the Soviet Union was overrun in World War II.

Sophie, one of the four sisters and brothers who came here in that cascade of immigration that brought 13 million aliens to the United States from 1900 to 1915, was a beautiful woman, five feet tall, 102 pounds dripping wet, oval-faced and rosy-cheeked — until the bloom wore off after decades in New York's dress factories. She made the long trek a few months before her future husband, in part to prepare the way for him, in part to escape an unwanted marriage being arranged by her parents. As she told the story, it was a harrowing trip. Along with a group in similar circumstances, she had to cross a border (I don't know which) guided by a man who constantly remonstrated one woman to keep her baby from crying. The child was dead, my mother said, by the time they reached safety. Then came the multiweek trip in steerage, and, finally, Ellis Island and the Statue of Liberty.

In New York, Sophie settled on the East Side with her family. The patriarch, an uncle who owned a shoe store on Hester Street, insisted to all and sundry that he could have been a millionaire if only he had bought the land offered him many years before in a far away place — now Times Square — that he thought would never be inhabited. Mama went to work in a nearby dress factory, a sweatshop where her first pay — this was before the union — was $2.05 for a sixty-hour week.

The bare-bones story of my mother's life is tragic. She lost one husband after four years of courtship (I don't know why they didn't marry sooner, unless it was because of my father's business failures) and four abbreviated years of marriage. After my father's death, there was a big hassle over custody of the child, me, with my grandfather charging in court that Mama was unfit to bring me up and my mother hastening to a rich relative (one of the Schiff family) who lived on Park Avenue in New York for legal reinforcements.

(To my mother's everlasting embarrassment her three-and-a-half-year-old wonder boy took his shoes off at the Schiff table, and no amount of reassurance from the millionaire relatives ever won me forgiveness in her eyes.) Mama's second trip to the altar was a boon to me. I loved being in a big house in Elizabeth, New Jersey, with three step-brothers and -sisters who idolized me, and a big Hupmobile car in which my stepfather always permitted me to sit up front, but as far as Mama was concerned the marriage didn't take. In less than a year it was over. We moved in with some relatives in Roselle, New Jersey, then returned to New York. Mama's day-to-day existence before and after the two marriages consisted of a long day at the sewing machine; perennial quarrels between the union and the boss over piecework rates; home to a single room in which we boarded with some family or other until we finally got our own three-room apartment; and to bed exhausted after making dinner, washing clothes, and preparing the next day's breakfast. I recall one place we lived on the fifth floor of a big tenement on Henry Street in New York; the toilets were outside in the back yard, and there was no bathtub. To bathe you either had to go to a bath house a few blocks away, or make do in the washtub at home.

With all that, however, life was not entirely bleak, and never desperate. My mother always had a few hundred dollars in the bank for a rainy day, and it never rained hard enough — not even during the Depression — to wipe her out. We were poor but we knew we would never go hungry or have to appeal to charity. She turned out the electricity "to save money" — the memory of which still causes me to turn on every light switch I can get my finger on — but she always sang. At work, at home, day or night, in a small, barely audible voice, seldom remembering the right words, Mama rendered one song after another. A couple of times a month she would buy two standing-room tickets at the opera and listen as if mesmerized. (I still am lukewarm to opera, never having recovered from standing through two and a half or three hours of *Aïda, La Traviata,* and others.)

On Saturday afternoons Mama went for an English lesson to Mr. Edelstein's apartment on Rutgers Street, in Lower Manhattan. Mr. Edelstein wrote with the beauty of a practiced calligrapher, which made my mother very proud — she was studying with the best there was. At home, in between her chores, she would do her English homework, invariably turning to me — when I was old enough — for the correct spelling of a particular word. Beyond work, taking care of her son, the opera, an occasional union meeting (though I don't remember too many of those), and English lessons that went on for years, Mama's life was filled with the usual comings and goings of a typical family. Every few Sundays we would make the trek to Uncle Dave's general store in Whitestone, Long Island, where I would play with a namesake cousin and gorge myself on ice cream at the candy store across the street, which was owned by Dave's brother- and sister-in-law, two generous people whom I loved as much as my blood relatives. On the subway to Flushing and the bus to Whitestone Mama would invariably recall how Dave had "forced" her to stay with him during the great flu epidemic (in about 1919 I think), to take care of his wife — Aunt Mary — who almost perished. Nonetheless Mama always kept coming back, not to get a pair of shoes wholesale or borrow money — she never borrowed a cent from anyone — but just for a change in scenery — trees and flowers. Less frequently, she visited her sister Annie, who owned a candy store in Whitestone (which Uncle Dave had helped finance), and a brother Jake, who had a similar emporium in Brooklyn (also partly financed by loans from Uncle Dave and, oddly enough, by my poor mother). In addition, there were Mama's dentist, with whom we hobnobbed in the Bronx, and assorted relatives in Elizabeth, Newark, and Roselle, New Jersey. Mama was on the go almost every weekend.

Except for a brief flirtation with the Russian Revolution Mama was apolitical. Like many émigrés she was overjoyed with the ouster of the czar in 1917, and attended meetings celebrating the Bolshevik victory. But Mama's flirtation with leftism — more properly her expression of Russian pride —

ended quickly. I suspect it was because of the raids by Wilson's attorney general A. Mitchell Palmer, which resulted in the imprisonment of thousands, the deportation of thousands more, and above all a climate of fear.

With this small digression, there was nothing in my mother's routine to predispose me toward Marxism. We were poor but, as already noted, never hungry or in fear of hunger. I wanted for nothing. My clothes, sewn by an expert seamstress — my mother — were excellent. Every now and then someone bought me a toy. It was enough. Before I reached school age I was placed in a nursery every morning, then collected by Mama at the end of her workday. When I reached school age Mama placed me in a Jewish parochial school — not out of religious conviction, but simply to keep her beloved son off the streets until she came home. At Rabbi Jacob Joseph School (RJJS) on Henry Street, we studied Hebrew, the Bible, and related subjects from nine to three, then took an hour recess, and spent three hours with the three R's of the English curriculum.

Many people believe that parochial schools stifle the dissident spirit, but the religious orthodoxy at RJJS had the opposite effect on me. The demand for unquestioning acceptance of our teachers' interpretation of the Bible, and the constant recourse to corporal punishment — with a heavy ruler on our rumps or the backs of our hands — for slight infractions of discipline, turned me into an anti-establishmentarian. I felt a rapport with the English teachers, who didn't practice these black arts and who allowed more free discussion, but I disliked and distrusted the rabbis.

Two incidents stand out in my stay at RJJS. One occurred in the third grade. A little fellow named Jakie Mikie Cohen — almost a midget — informed on one of the students about something and the rabbi beat Jakie's victim with a ruler on the back of his hand until he drew blood. During the punishment I got up — spontaneously — and emptied my soul of every dirty word and epithet I had ever learned, to characterize Jakie Mikie Cohen. It brought me a beating and a summons to my mother to come to school. Mama took off an hour from work to discuss my errant deportment, but neither she nor the rabbi were sympathetic to my lecture on the immorality of squealing.

Despite a few similar outbursts against the RJJS authoritarian structure in ensuing years I remained a fairly good Hebrew student — close to the top — until another argument cut me adrift entirely. In the sixth grade, we were studying Rashi — the commentary and interpretation of the Bible and Talmud by a legendary rabbi — when a question of judicial punishment came up. As I remember it, Rashi held that if a master knocked out a servant's eye or broke his nose, he was liable for financial damages, but if he beat him and ruptured a kidney, he was not. The justification for this inequity was that the Bible speaks of "an eye for an eye, a tooth for a tooth," both external organs, but makes no mention of internal ones like kidneys. It didn't seem fair to me, and I said so — loudly. The rabbi rebutted that it was not for me to determine what was fair and what wasn't. One word led to another until I was called up to the front of the room for the usual punishment, a thick ruler over the knuckles. When I refused to submit, the rabbi chased me around the aisles, ordering one boy after another to grab me — in vain. So many big brawlers in the class were beholden to me for copying my homework or copying from my test papers (on the rare occasions when I made a mistake in arithmetic there were eight identical errors) that no one dared catch me for fear of a beating later on. Given this immunity, then, I was able to elude the rabbi, and, regrettably, make him look a little silly. Ultimately, I ran to the roof, where the police — and my mother — had to be called to coax me down. Never again, however, did I actively study the Hebrew courses.

Parochial school was probably not the cause of my rebellious spirit, but it clashed with an active mind always probing for answers. Since there was no one at home to teach me the ABC's or help with homework, I had a tendency to ask questions about everything. "You are always asking questions," my mother would say, not always with pride. I didn't read much — there was little time after nine hours in school, dinner (which we called supper), homework, and an hour in the street with other kids. What I did read, however, I read slowly, constantly asking myself questions about the content and allowing my mind to run off in rumination and daydreams. Today I read incessantly, but I still do it slowly, and I consider speed-reading the enemy of intelligence.

I graduated from RJJS English school a year early, at age thirteen, having been double-promoted twice. I delivered the valedictory speech, and a few days later was bar-mitzvahed — the last time I ever set foot in a synagogue for religious purposes. There was nothing venal or deliberate about this decision; I didn't discuss it with anyone or weigh its long-term consequences. I just didn't believe.

Going to a public high school — De Witt Clinton, then on 59th Street on the West Side — was a liberation of sorts, though after a year or two I regretted that I hadn't enrolled in a co-ed school. I was only a fair student, except in mathematics and history, and in subjects like Latin, which seemed to have no practical purpose, a poor one. The post-school routine was simple: a little milk and a cookie, out to the school yard where I played a tolerable second-base in baseball games during the summer and a poor, often bloodied, tackle in football games during the fall. Hank Greenberg, who was to become one of the great home-run hitters in professional baseball, sometimes played in the same Bronx school yard (we had moved out of the East Side by then), but I didn't know him and of course I wasn't in the same league. After dinner I did homework for fifteen minutes or half an hour, then off to the street corner where a small group of boys met and joshed. After a year or two, I also hung out with a clique in a nearby pool room. So far as I know no criminal gangs made their headquarters in that pool room, the only illicit activity was talk about seduction — most of it an exercise in imagination. On Saturday afternoon two or three of us went to the Luxor theater on 170th Street, either with our own girl friends (I had a steady girl beginning at age thirteen) or in search of new ones. At night, as per the tradition of the times, we went to parties or crashed weddings where we danced to the wee hours. Beginning with the last year of high school two friends and I started going to the theater every Wednesday night. We would buy cut-rate tickets in the basement of Gray's drug store on 43rd Street, and enjoy the world of culture from way up in the second balcony.

At the age of seventeen, I graduated from high school, a bright young lad but only a so-so student. My mother urged me to go to college, and all of my relatives seconded her efforts by repeatedly assuring me I would make an excellent lawyer. I don't remember how I arrived at the conclusion because I had read nothing as yet of a radical nature, but I was convinced that the planet would soon explode in another world war, and it was therefore useless to waste one's time in college. Oddly enough, though I was wrong by a decade, Joseph Stalin had shifted the political course of the Communist International toward what became known as the *Third Period* a year or two earlier for exactly the same reason —namely the belief that the West was about to spark a second world conflagration by re-invading the Soviet Union.

In any case, I didn't proceed to college. Instead I went to work on a drill press in a fountain pen factory, where my hands became raw from revolving a machine by hand. After a few months of this grueling exercise I decamped to Wall Street because my closest friend, Manny Rich, told me of an opening for a runner at a brokerage firm headquartered just a few whispers from that great tomb on the corner of Broad and Wall that housed J. P. Morgan & Co., and directly across the street from the stock exchange itself.

It was a heady experience, living in a financial milieu where millions changed hands like match sticks. One of my duties after I'd been there a while was to borrow money from the bank where our firm, Adler Coleman & Co., did business. In the morning I would present to the bank a long piece of paper, duly signed by a broker, and borrow a million dollars; five hours later, at 3 P.M., I would arrive with a check for a million, plus—if I recall rightly—$60 or $90 interest. One could become mesmerized playing this game, and not a little greedy. Once a bank teller gave me an extra $10,000 when I drew cash for our payroll; it was a behemothean task for me to give it back, setting in motion a three-cornered war between my conscience, the desire for better things, and fear of being caught. Every payday I received a piercing shock as I pocketed $15 (later $17) just after delivering a million-dollar repayment on the morning's bank loan. But it excited dreams that sums such as these might be my own someday. Once, another runner and I, having received a tip from one of our brokers, pooled $13 each to buy a hundred shares of a stock selling at twenty-five cents a share. A week later we sold our holding for $1.37½ a share — a cool profit of more than a hundred dollars. Alas for our financial ambitions, however. That night we lost the profits in the biggest crap game I've been in before or since. I never again gambled on the stock market. Subliminally I must have understood the kinship between these two games; intellectually I decided somewhere along the way that I ought not invest money in a system that I was working to overthrow.

My days as a Wall Street tycoon ended a couple of months after "Black Thursday" (October 24, 1929), when the brokerage house let me go, ostensibly in an economy move, but actually for a small disagreement. During those tumultuous days when the market was sliding to oblivion our crew of twelve or fifteen runners worked scores of hours overtime. The firm, we all knew, had made enormous profits selling stock short — in fact, it had made so much it gave us double pay one week and triple pay ($51) another. Early in November when the exchange closed down and we runners had caught up with our work (in large part confirming purchases and sales by having other firms stamp duplicate sheets of paper called comparisons) we sat in our long office twiddling our thumbs. By this time I had been promoted to assistant head runner and from that hierarchical perch urged the head runner, a short bald-headed man in his forties, to send the tired boys home. He refused. "Suppose a broker wants a sandwich," he said, "who's going to get it for him?" That remark brought out all my rebellious fury. "He can bloody well go downstairs," I said, "and get it himself." For this subversion I was never forgiven, and at the first opportunity was severed into perdition. I hadn't yet read *The Communist Manifesto* and only barely knew what the term *class struggle* meant, but I had been initiated into its secrets and, in an existential sort of way, had learned something about historical materialism.

II

A couple of months before the crash the widely acclaimed economist Irving Fisher was boasting that the United States was at "a permanently high plateau" of prosperity; and President Herbert Hoover was telling the nation that "we in America are nearer to the final triumph over poverty than ever before in our land. The poorhouse is vanishing from among us."

Soon the poorhouses would be more than full, but most people could not reconcile themselves to the fact that the Jazz Age, with its lurid prosperity, had ended. The Great Depression was an insidious affair — like water torture breaking the spirit a drop at a time. There was always the subliminal hope, fed by synthetic optimism from Herbert Hoover's White House, that the nightmare would soon end. Hoover, who was more capable and less venal than the image he left for history, could not admit that his vaunted free enterprise system was disintegrating. It was simply "readjusting"; prosperity was "just around the corner." To question "the basic strength of business," he said in November 1929, "is foolish." It wasn't, of course, but constant presidential reassurance preserved a thin thread of optimism.

As the days and years passed, however, the weight on the human spirit either caused collapse or left a permanent scar that, at least in my case — and I'm sure in millions of others — remains unhealed even today. When I eat, I finish every last snippet as if it were my last meal. When I map a peace campaign or a strike or when I send a manuscript to a publisher — even one who has published me many times or who is bound by contract to do the book or article — I grapple with the kind of anxieties I experienced in Depression days when I went door to door seeking a job. Most Depression people ultimately recovered their self-confidence, but not intact or unblemished; and some just gave up.

At noon on February 14, 1933, for instance, just a few weeks before Roosevelt took the oath of office, a fifty-one-year-old man in overalls entered a bank at Garden City, Kansas, drew a revolver and told the assistant cashier: "I've got to have some money . . . I'm sorry but I'm desperate. I'll pay this back when times get good." Scooping up $1,838, the farmer, a man named Ross Mundell whose farm was being foreclosed, repaired to the home of a friend and asked him to hide the money for the use of his children. "I'm going down the road now and kill myself."

The statistics of economic decline after the stock market crash can only be described as macabre. From October 1, 1929, to August 31, 1932, according to Frank A. Vanderlip, former president of the National City Bank of New York, 4,835 banks failed, costing depositors more than 3.25 billion dollars. A share of General Motors fell from a high of 91¾ to 7 5/8; Radio Corporation of America from a peak of 114¾ to as little as 2½; United States Steel, 261¾ at its highest in 1929, 21¼ at its nadir in 1932. The consequence, of course, was a malevolent merry-go-round: loans called in because stocks put up as collateral were plummeting, cuts in industrial spending and manufacture, layoffs of workers, further cuts in spending, more declines in business, further loans called in. The full effects were not felt immediately, but by late 1932 industrial production had fallen by one-half, construction by six-sevenths. Farm prices, already depressed, fell another three-fifths by March 1933, and a million more families abandoned their homesteads.

Wherever one turned there was a wasteland of shattered lives. By March 1930 there were 4 million out of work, a year later 8 million, and, when Roosevelt took office in March 1933, 13 million. Some estimates were as high as 16 or 17 million, with a similar number working short hours. As of 1934, a year after the New Deal applied its magic, there were 2.5 million who had not been employed for two years or more, and 6 million who had been out of work at least a year. Those still lucky enough to hold jobs had their pay cut by 20, 30, or more percent, as payrolls dropped by 60 percent in just four years. The number of city dwellers who were dispossessed from their apartments ran into hundreds of thousands. "This depression," commented Colonel Leonard Ayres in *The Economics of Recovery*, "has been far more severe than any of the twenty depressions that we have experienced in this country since 1790." Jobs were so scarce that when the Soviet trading firm Amtorg announced it had 6,000 skilled jobs available in Russia, it was swamped with 100,000 applications.

If there was one feature that lent a distinction of sorts to the Great Depression it was its universality. As Helen M. and Robert Lynd expressed it in their classic *Middletown*, "The great knife of the depression . . . cut down impartially through the entire population, cleaving open lives and hopes of rich as well as poor." It was no longer the urban immigrants who held the citadel of poverty almost as a monopoly, or the working class and farmers. Caught in the web was a majority of every class, including professionals, academics, and businessmen. The man selling apples on the street corner (for a nickel) was as likely to be a former certified public accountant as a drill press operator. This was, future sociologists would say, a "majority" poverty. Thus Langlan Heinz, forty-four years old, could tell a Brooklyn court trying him for vagrancy in May 1932 that he was a graduate of the University of Colorado and had held responsible jobs in China, Panama, and Venezuela as a civil engineer. But his resources were gone and for the past forty-six days he had been sleeping on a cot in a vacant lot near Flatbush Avenue. Of the 455 qualified chemists registered for employment at a New York relief agency, 109 were said to be destitute, 130 others in need, and 158 had funds for a brief period.

The glow of the 1920s faded; the tune of the day was "Brother, Can You Spare a Dime?" Marc Connelly, in his 1930 play, *The Green Pastures,* summarized it pithily:

"Everything nailed down is comin' loose." A joke making the rounds had it that applicants for hotel rooms were asked by clerks whether they wanted the rooms "for sleeping or jumping."

III

Finding a niche for oneself at age eighteen — resolving the problems of love, sex, marriage, career, and education — is a difficult venture for sensitive young people of any generation. But it was compounded during the Depression by a pervasive sense of futility; it was as if you were threshing in quicksand with no rope in sight. After I was dismissed from Wall Street, I would pick up the next day's newspaper in the evening, make a list of potential jobs, then next morning betake myself to the most likely prospects, only to find that there were a dozen or two dozen people already on line waiting to be interviewed, that the job was taken, or — worst of all — that the employer rejected me because I had so little experience. After that, I would pick a block of garment factories or office buildings, take the elevator to the top floor, and go door to door, down to the first floor, soliciting work. It was depressing beyond belief, not because I was unable to find something but because I anticipated, as I entered each establishment, that once again I would be turned down. I developed a feeling of worthlessness — and loneliness; I began to think of myself as a freak and misfit, particularly when I confronted my mother each evening with the bleak news, and watched those questioning eyes accuse me of not looking hard enough, being lazy. By Wednesday or Thursday I was looking less and goofing off more, visiting the library, walking the streets or slipping into a movie with my conscience nagging that I had wasted a few pennies. Had the times not been so dire I might have married before my twentieth birthday, but the young woman of my affections (an émigré from the Soviet Union) could not be induced to take the fling with an unemployed dreamer whose talents were uncharted.

Periodically, of course, I did find work but it was usually

of short duration and seldom held promise. One day I blundered into a job in a basement lamp factory with eight foreign-born workers; being the only one who spoke English adequately I was designated foreman and paid a munificent $8 for a six-day, seventy-two-hour week. The others received only $6. Unfortunately the boss went broke after some months and I was again on the prowl for work. Through a friend I found a job in a garment factory packing dresses for shipment. The hours were excruciatingly long, till 7 P.M. or 8 P.M. most nights, sometimes till midnight — with no overtime pay, and only a dollar supper money. Some evenings, when most people had left, a prostitute would sneak into the lofts to service regular customers; occasionally a Communist union organizer (the Communists then had their own labor organization, the Trade Union Unity League) would come by for a chat, but received little encouragement — except from me. That job too faded ultimately as business continued to slump.

If it hadn't been for summer jobs as a busboy or waiter in the Adirondacks or Rockaway Beach, my situation would have been desperate, especially when I moved away from home (to Greenwich Village near New York University) in about 1932. My first such position was at a hotel north of Saratoga Springs, where I organized a dozen waiters and five busboys into a "union," and led them in a strike the night before the Fourth of July. It was an exhilarating experience, but not a fruitful one. The hotel survived its crisis by impressing office workers and athletic directors to waiting on tables; and along about midnight my first adventure as a labor leader came to an abrupt end when the county sheriff unceremoniously shook me out of bed, took me for a thirty-mile ride into a wooded area, slapped me around a bit, and left me miles from nowhere with my suitcase for company. I should have felt pained and angry, and I did to an extent, but I also felt exalted — I had joined a great fraternity.

Despite this abortive experience I found other summer hotel jobs, and usually — though not always — came away with a few hundred dollars for the lean months ahead. There were no expenses, food and shelter were free, and the tips, plus occasional winnings from playing poker with guests, added up to a fair bit of change after ten or twelve weeks.

Makeshift — like my summer jobs — was the order of the day for many millions in the first years of the Depression. Under the prevailing philosophy of free enterprise and rugged individualism, it was considered indecent, immoral, and probably illegal for the federal government to help hungry people. As expressed by President Grover Cleveland in 1887 when he vetoed a $10,000 drought relief bill: although "the people support the Government, the Government should not support the people." So ludicrous was this notion of self-reliance that the same Herbert Hoover who had dispensed millions of government funds to relieve the starvation of Russians and other Europeans a decade before was opposed to using government funds to relieve starvation at home. "Works of charity," he said, were the proper — and "loftiest" — solution. "A voluntary deed by a man impressed with the sense of responsibility and brotherhood of man," Hoover insisted, "is infinitely more precious to our National ideals and National spirit than a thousandfold poured from the Treasury of the Government under the compulsion of law." Ironically, during a drought in Arkansas (in December 1930) he urged Congress to allocate $45 million to save the animals, but was patently displeased when the Senate added $20 million to feed human beings.

For Hoover (whom I hated with a passion at the time), as with so many others, the theorems of laissez-faire were a religion. Indeed, even the president of the American Federation of Labor, William Green, went on record against federal relief and unemployment insurance on the ground they were "a hindrance to progress," a "dole" which affronted "the dignity of the workingman" and would only "subsidize idleness." Voluntarism and charity were the answer, not government aid — which the middle classes and many labor leaders still stigmatized as "socialism." In October 1930, Hoover appointed the Committee for Unemployment Relief, headed by Walter S. Gifford of American Telephone and Telegraph, to raise $175 million through sporting events and theater benefits that would be used for charity. Unfortunately the drive coincided with a 10-percent wage cut announced by Ford, U.S. Steel, General Motors, and others who were represented on the committee. Equally distressing, what Gifford and his copywriters called "a great spiritual experience" netted less than $100 million, or $3 for each of the 30 million people estimated to be in need. When Senator Robert M. La Follette cut through the nonsense of voluntarism in 1931 and proposed a bill for direct federal relief, a senator from Oklahoma denounced it, amid applause, "as the beginning of the dole. . . . Of all the diseases known to pathology, the passion for a pension such as this is the most debilitating."

Private initiative, taking its cue from the president, did perform, it is true, with characteristic American ingenuity. The most poignant symbol of the day, apart from the breadlines one saw everywhere, was the man on the street corner selling shiny apples for a nickel apiece. Some promoter at the International Apple Shippers' Association had thought of the idea of supplying the indigent with apples on credit, to be hawked from boxes on the sidewalk; and within a short time there were 6,000 apple entrepreneurs in New York alone eking out a few dollars daily. In 1931, someone thought up the Give-a-Job campaign, urging working neighbors to employ the jobless in their community to whitewash a ceiling or clean a yard. Another fashion in relief was called Block Aid — dwellers in the same block made weekly collections for less fortunate friends. Additionally, a million or more people seceded from the economy to form 154 barter associations in 29 states, exchanging products directly or through the use of special scrip. One such group in California numbered 200,000. All such schemes, however, including those of the president's committee, were garden hoses against a forest fire. Cynics had adequate proof that the "brotherhood of man" was chimerical without a federal warrant or an unemployment demonstration, or both, behind it.

Localities did try to dole out relief funds, but by 1932

their efforts had all but collapsed. H. L. Lurie, director of Jewish Social Research in New York, told Congress: "Relief has been gradually reduced so that whole families are getting an average of $2.30 a week relief in New York City, with $3 and $4 and at the most $5 a week . . . in other cities." The agencies, he said, were unable to pay for rent, gas, or electricity. On the average, they gave succor to 32 percent of "the totally jobless." In Chicago there were 700,000 unemployed — 40 percent of the work force — but the city didn't have the money to pay its teachers, let alone its paupers. New York, Detroit, Boston, and Philadelphia were similarly at the brink of bankruptcy, all trying to borrow money from corporations. Detroit automakers made one such loan to the city on the condition that it grant no more than seven and a half cents a day for food for each needy person. Two university professors, Henry Bamford Parkes and Vincent P. Carosso, estimated that one million people were living in "Hoovervilles" — huts made of discarded tin and cardboard, without any amenities, on vacant land. A half million people had moved in with relatives, and there were two million "homeless migrants," 200,000 of them children.

IV

In an interview with the *New York Graphic* during the 1932 election campaign, Franklin Roosevelt recited a conversation with "an old friend who runs a great western railroad. 'Fred,' I asked him, 'what are the people talking about out here?' 'Frank,' he replied, 'I'm sorry to say the men out here are talking revolution.'"

That the old order should even appear to be crumbling was remarkable considering that the crisis had lasted only three years and that there was really no leftist force with substantial grass roots following. The Socialist Party had reached a nadir of 7,793 members in 1928, and, though it doubled in size to 17,000 during the slump, it never re-established itself as the formidable force it had been in 1912. The Communist Party, approximately the same size when the Depression began, added only 8,000 new members during the cataclysmic period from 1929 to 1933 — despite the fact it led nation-wide unemployment demonstrations on March 6, 1930, involving — by its count — almost a million jobless, and despite the decisive role it played in the highly publicized bonus march of 1932 (violently suppressed by Army Chief of Staff Douglas MacArthur aided by Dwight D. Eisenhower).

There were three other leftist groups with a few hundred adherents each: the Conference for Progressive Labor Action, an independent leftist force headed by A. J. Muste, and two spin-offs from the Communist Party, one led by its expelled leader, Jay Lovestone, another by James P. Cannon, a follower of the Russian exile Leon Trotsky. But though the left was minuscule in 1932, people spontaneously talked of revolution, without knowing how it would come about or who would lead it.

Inevitably a young rebel like myself became embroiled in this talk. Spurred on by a chap my own age who was politically more astute (he later became a dentist and joined the Lovestoneites), I began to read the traditional tracts of the Marxist movement, most of which I bought at a communist bookstore — Marx's *The Communist Manifesto, Wage-Labor and Capital,* Lenin's *What Is to Be Done?,* and *Imperialism.* "Marxism," I recorded in a diary, "is a venture completely new in civilized thought. . . . Marx's scheme, like Plato's, is something logical, with a dispassionate analysis of truth." It would succeed, I told myself, where Christianity, Buddhism, and democracy had failed. I occasionally scanned the *Daily Worker* — the communist publication — and attended a few communist social events. I found myself, also, hanging around Union Square at 14th Street, then the mecca of revolutionary soapboxing, much like Hyde Park in London or "Bughouse Square" in Chicago. I recall vividly one speaker in particular, a veteran of World War I who mounted his box every day at about noon, pointed his finger at S. Klein, the big women's clothing store across the street, and shouted: "You see that man over there, S. Klein. He makes more Communists in an hour than I've made in a lifetime."

Intrigued though I was, however, with Communism and the

Soviet Union (the Socialist Party never interested me because it was the "party of Noske and Scheidemann" that had suppressed the German Revolution in 1919, and it was too moderate anyway), I didn't join the Communist Party. Three or four factors inhibited me. One, of course, was the commitment it required — all one's spare time and money. Another was the danger: the newspapers were filled with reports of demonstrators being clubbed, beaten, shot, jailed. (A humorous anecdote that made the rounds somewhat later was about the little postman who stops by a Communist rally at Union Square out of simple curiosity. A cop on horseback wades into the crowd and as he raises his billy club over the poor postman's head the postman cries out, "Look officer, I'm not a Communist, I'm an anti-Communist." The cop swings savagely, shouting as he does so: "I don't give a damn what kind of a Communist you are.")

Another difficulty was philosophical. Almost immediately after graduating high school I became what I had never been at school, a voracious reader. For three, six, or more months at a time I would immerse myself in books on a particular subject — philosophy, psychology, economics, literature. In slow, plodding style, often having trouble with "big" words or heavy thoughts, I waded through Plato, Aristotle, Schopenhauer, Hegel, Bishop Berkeley, Kant, Henri Bergson, Freud, Adler, Jung, the pragmatists, Adam Smith, Ricardo, and innumerable plays and novels, especially by Dostoyevsky and Chekov. Bergson's theory of creative evolution and Freud's psychoanalytical doctrine left me wondering whether the solution to humankind's problems was individualism or collectivism. In an untutored mind there was an inevitable seesaw in ideologies — at one point I thought of myself as an anarchist, on other occasions I concluded that the whole business of fighting oppression was futile.

Still another impediment to joining the Communist Party was an intense desire to become a writer. Writing is an occupation for rebels and introverts, and I fit both categories. For an indecisive two semesters, as I passed my nineteenth birthday, I took noncredit night courses in economics, marketing, and journalism at New York University. Evidently I still had hopes of making it in the business world, but by the spring of 1931 I had given up such notions, and the journalism courses were uninspiring, concentrating as they did solely on craftsmanship. I gave up night school and began to write on my own. I published a few columns in the *Sunday Mirror* magazine on "Things You Probably Never Knew About Your World," an imitation of *Ripley's Believe It or Not* — without cartoons. A sample item: "There's nothing new under the sun! Not even the invention of gunpowder. The bombardier beetle, when pursued, ejects a volatile fluid that explodes noisily and knocks the pursuer either cold or dead."

The columns, however, didn't pave the way for a career as a journalist — at least no one knocked on my door — and, after two or three tries with city editors, I gave up the quest. My first play, however, almost launched me on a literary career. *Yours Is the Earth* (after a phrase in a Kipling poem) dealt with an unemployed intellectual (partly autobiographical) and an unhappy woman wedded to a successful lawyer. The Theater Guild considered it for a long time, asked me to rewrite it, and then rejected it on the grounds that it was only doing a few plays that year and had just received an opus from a star writer — I believe it was Eugene O'Neill — it had to perform. By the time I had finished my second play, *Yellow Grass* — a sad play in imitation of Chekhov — and sent it to a couple of agents, I had lost all interest in writing.

Hitler was now ensconced in Germany, suppressing leftist critics and labor unions with methodical efficiency, and preparing to re-arm even while calling war an "unlimited madness." The swirl of fascism from Italy to Germany also engulfed some of the smaller central European states, and the turbulence in Austria, where the semifascist regime of Chancellor Engelbert Dollfuss was murdering socialists in the Karl Marx Hof, spread a feeling of gloom throughout the world. It seemed obvious to many, including me, that these separate madnesses would coagulate not long hence into a single world war. One could no longer languish in the luxury of disengagement. I had made up my mind to join a leftist group, the only question being whether it would be the communists or Trotskyites.

For a few months I gorged myself on books dealing with the Stalin-Trotsky dispute. There wasn't much on the Stalinist side, except for bitter diatribes by men such as Moissaye Olgin that referred to Trotsky as a counter-revolutionary, and a volume of long essays by Zinoviev, Kamenev, and Stalin that was decidedly unimpressive. The communist movement was then in Stalin's Third Period — the first one, from 1918 to 1923, being a time of revolutionary upsurge; the second, from 1923 to 1928, one of democratic pacifism and the relative stabilization of capitalism; and the third one, from 1928 on, a period in which the capitalist states were preparing war against the Soviet Union and the working masses were poised for a new stage of proletarian revolutions, even in the United States.

As part of the third period dogma, Stalin elaborated the strange concept of social fascism. Socialists (and Trotskyites and Lovestoneites) he averred were not brothers in a common struggle who disagreed on strategy and tactics, but "twins" of the fascists, to be despised and fought against with the same fervor. "During the war and since the war," wrote the American Communist leader Earl Browder, "the capitalist class has placed its main reliance for holding the masses in support of its class dictatorship upon the parties of the Second International. . . . Today the social fascists are the main prop of capitalism among the working class masses." Naked fascism, he said, would be used only when "the declining capitalist class sensed the approach of a revolutionary crisis." In other words, the only difference between socialists and fascists was that the hated enemy relied on each for different purposes in different periods. From this incredible thesis it followed that other leftists were not, in fact, revolutionaries but counter-revolutionaries.

The practical effects of this conclusion was a self-granted license to break up socialist, Trotskyite, and Lovestoneite meetings.

Typically the April 11, 1929, issue of *The Militant,* organ of the Communist League of America (Trotskyites), reported "another Stalinist pogrom in New York, the story of the bloodiest and most criminal attack in the record of the terrorist campaign against the opposition . . ." A couple of nights before, it seems, "an organized mob of Stalinist gangsters raided the weekly meeting of the Hungarian opposition group at Hungarian Hall" where fifteen comrades were present, six of them women. "A gang of fifty more Stalinists invaded the home of Bonnie Dulong with blackjacks, brass knuckles, knives, lead pipes and clubs . . . Comrade Basky whose life had been threatened repeatedly was struck across the face with a rubber hose wielded by Lusty. The speaker's 75-year-old father looked at Basky who had been in the revolutionary movement for decades, jumped to the defense of his son, only to be struck over the head and knocked to the floor. Six stitches were later taken for the wound . . ." When the police arrived they arrested fifteen people, both from among the victims and victimizers. Max Shachtman, one of the Trotskyite leaders of that day, records that there was hardly a "meeting that I spoke at from coast to coast, and the same held true for other speakers, that did not suffer from the same threats of violence at communist hands." Perhaps the most ironic event in the third period was the 1934 invasion of a socialist meeting at Madison Square Garden, called to pay homage to socialist workers of the Karl Marx Hof in Vienna who had given their lives to forestall fascism in Austria. Hundreds of American communists, led by a party official and armed with the usual bats and brass knuckles, made a shambles of the affair.

I was not yet conversant with all this — and I didn't fully believe it when Trotskyite friends told me about it — but the Stalinist theoretical arguments left me with doubts. Why should Leon Trotsky, the man who was second in command of the Russian Revolution, be in exile? Why the strident attacks on him and his followers? I read Trotsky's autobiography and his three-volume history of the Russian Revolution. I was immensely impressed with his book

Problems of the Chinese Revolution, which argued that Stalin had betrayed that revolution by entering into a "bloc of four classes" with Chiang Kai-shek and the Kuomintang. Stalin's theory of "socialism in one country" seemed to me a withdrawal from revolutionary obligation. Trotsky's theory of permanent revolution seemed to be the only clear clarion in a world consumed by depression and military preparation.

I didn't have to be recruited into the Trotskyite movement. I made the decision intellectually, based on my readings; and one day — in late 1934, I believe — I went to the Trotskyite office and joined up. The person who enrolled me was taken aback that someone should enlist in this fashion, but I was taken in hand and assigned to a branch in the Bronx. It was an exhilarating feeling, assuaging a sense of guilt that I had stayed on the sidelines while others had made the commitment. The simple act of joining had a certain finality to it, washing away doubts and indecision; I was on a one-way trip toward the beautiful tomorrow.

Chapter 2
Trotskyism

I

The American Trotskyite organization was a quixotic outgrowth of the same Sixth Congress of the Communist International (August 1928) that sired the theory of social fascism and elaborated strategy for the so-called Third Period. James P. Cannon, its founder, claimed in a series of lectures given in the spring of 1942 that he became a convert when he accidentally came upon a document by Leon Trotsky (who was already in exile) that had been routinely (and mistakenly) rendered into English. After reading the former Red Army chief's manuscript, "The Draft Program of the Communist International: A Criticism of Fundamentals," Cannon said "I knew what I had to do . . . Our doubts had been resolved. It was as clear as daylight that Marxist truth was on the side of Trotsky. We made a compact there and then [Maurice] Spector [a Canadian communist] and I — that we would come back home and begin a struggle under the banner of Trotskyism."

This may in fact have been how Trotskyism was born in the United States, but I've always been a little suspicious of that story. Cannon was a handsome man, with great charm and a bright sense of humor. I knew him only casually after I joined the Workers Party — he was too high in the hierarchy for the likes of me to draw closer — but it is inconceivable that this seasoned warrior, the head of an enduring faction of the Communist Party in the United States, would have made this compact with Spector without weighing Trotsky's potential for coming back to power. I know from Paul Scheffer, the editor of my first book, who was then the Moscow correspondent for the *Berliner Tageblatt,* that the Trotskyites in the Soviet Union were confident their leader would soon return. Karl Radek, a member of Trotsky's inner circle, pointed out to Scheffer that Stalin's shift to the left and his espousal of rapid industrialization (which Trotsky also espoused, though not as rapidly as Stalin) would cause the rank and file of the party to realize that the fallen leader had been right all along.

In any case it is of no great importance. Cannon didn't utter a word in defense of Trotsky while in Moscow, and was silent about his conversion after returning to New York, content for the time being to show the precious document he had brought out of Russia to a few close associates. It didn't take long, however, for the two other party factions — the one in the saddle headed by Jay Lovestone, the other by William Z. Foster — to uncover Cannon's heresy. Along with Max Shachtman and Martin Abern, Cannon was expelled from the Communist Party in October 1928 for being — of all things — "counter-revolutionary." A few months later, in May 1929, forty-eight delegates and alternates from twelve cities — representing, according to Cannon, "approximately 100 members in our national organization" — formed the Communist League of America, "Left Opposition of the Communist Party."

Though they published a biweekly newspaper, *The Militant,* it was almost a year before Cannon's small band was able to rent a rundown headquarters on Third Avenue in Manhattan. And two years before they could buy a mimeograph machine. (As late as 1933 they still didn't have a telephone in their office.) Meanwhile they labored assiduously to win over comrades from the bigger pond, the Communist Party, which they continued to consider the vanguard of the working class. Eschewing independent existence or the role of a rival party, they thought themselves simply "an opposition faction" — the Left Opposition — to the old party. Presumably they hoped to win over a major — or at least a substantial — portion of that vanguard.

They didn't; in fact they couldn't. Many communists who sympathized with Trotsky or were distressed with the new monolithicism in the Communist Party nonetheless were emotionally incapable of disassociating themselves from the bastion of world socialism, the Soviet Union. But if the Communist League of America was unable to attract the bulk of the vanguard, it was inevitable that it would attract other forces, especially during an economic slump. Its leaders were simply too capable to be sidelined entirely. Cannon, I'm sure, could have become an outstanding lawyer (he was studying law three nights a week when he joined the communist movement a decade before). Shachtman was an outstanding orator, more adroit in using irony and humor than almost any speakers I've ever heard. Over the years, I have debated such right-wing figures as William Buckley, Fulton Lewis III, Russell Kirk, M. Stanton Evans, and many others; none, including Buckley, could turn a phrase or devastate an opponent like Shachtman. And in Minneapolis the Trotskyites had a group of unionists — the three Dunne brothers, Vincent, Grant, and Miles; Karl Skoglund; and Farrell Dobbs — who were unexcelled as labor strategists. Without the Minneapolis Trotskyites, the teamsters union could never have grown to its present size. Even Jimmy Hoffa admitted to me, many years later, that his organization would not have attained the power it had and he himself, Hoffa, would not be "sitting where I'm sitting," if it hadn't been for Dobbs.

After five years as an unwanted appendage to the Communist Party, the Communist League of America decided to break out of its isolation. Cannon issued a call for a new political party and urged his comrades to activate themselves in unions and other mass organizations. On the international front, Trotsky struck the clarion for a new Fourth International, as a rival to Stalin's Third International.

Initially, this turn away from what was essentially a parasitic existence, oriented to nibbling at the Communist Party's trough, showed considerable promise. The first effort at winning a mass following was the unionization in 1933 of 10,000 hotel workers in New York, under the guiding hand of a talented intellectual, B. J. Field—a statistician and economist by trade, who also spoke a number of languages, including French, which endeared him to the French cooks. Assisting Field was a man who would play a big role in my life for the next decade, Hugo Oehler. Oehler, who was a shade under medium height, thin lipped, and balding, was a dull speaker—given to malapropisms—and a poor writer. But he was that unique personality who on the one hand had an immediate rapport with workers, and on the other could hold his own with anyone on the most abstruse philosophical discussions. His apartment and his person, unlike the stereotype of radicals, were always immaculate. His small piercing eyes gave the impression both of distance and warmth, of a man to whom almost no one drew very close but who exercised a mesmeric influence on followers. I lost contact with Oehler after World War II; I can't say why he never struck a lode of fame, but it was certainly not for lack of talent.

Unfortunately, despite Oehler's help the hotel workers strike disintegrated—according to Cannon, because Field sought a deal with government officials and the employers. For this dereliction Field was expelled while the strike was still on, and he formed a rival Trotskyite group (later called the League for a Revolutionary Workers Party), which left no enduring mark but did provide a number of interesting personalities for the post–World War II period—including an Eastland Committee spy, a Rand Corporation theorist who, today, is among the leading exponents of the nuclear arms race, and on the other side the late Paul Jacobs, a writer of some prominence who once edited *Ramparts* magazine and was part of a group that launched *Mother Jones,* another leftist publication.

While fretting over the debacle of the hotel strike, Cannon's small legion was soon embroiled in one of the most important labor wars in American history — three teamster strikes in Minneapolis which helped change the face of the American trade union movement and incidentally added meat and marrow to Trotskyism.

II

The communists, of course, were also gaining supporters in this hectic period — much more than other leftists in fact. But Cannon and his cohorts in the Communist League of America executed a tour de force in 1934 that led many of us to believe they might soon rival the communists. They effectuated a merger with A. J. Muste's American Workers Party, an unaffiliated radical group that was neither Stalinist, Trotskyite, nor Norman Thomas socialist, but had a true American flavor, a sizable following among the unemployed, and a few score trade unionists with experience and talent.

Muste, who was to be one of the prime influences in my own life, was universally respected in radical circles, even by some communists. Tall, spare, with a long nose and thin lips, Muste could melt into any crowd without being noticed. He spoke in a quiet, low voice, always waiting for the other person to finish before he began. He wrote in a lackluster style, and to most people — as I noted in his 1967 obituary that I wrote for *Liberation,* the magazine of which we were both editors — he seemed terribly inconsistent: "He had been a churchman and presumably, as a Trotskyist, an atheist. He had moved from pacifism to Marxism and back again. His career was so varied — minister, labor organizer, leader of the unemployed, educator, Marxist politician, pacifist — that he seemed to be flitting from place to place without central purpose." Yet in all these incarnations Muste was exactly what he had been from the beginning — a humanistic revolutionary. He was a humanist in the revolutionary sense that he never — absolutely never — deliberately denigrated another person. He believed not only in physical nonviolence, but, more important, in psychological nonviolence — and he practiced it. I was with Muste on occasions when he argued with political adversaries ranging from traditional conservatives to Stalinists, but no one ever walked away from such an "argument" feeling hurt or demeaned. He was always careful not to trample someone else's ego — not only as a matter of principle but because he had so much inner self-confidence (more than anyone I've ever known) that he didn't have to. One of Muste's famous catchphrases was "if I can't love Hitler, I can't love at all." Outlandish as that sounds, he meant that if a revolutionary cannot understand the insecurities that cause people to commit horrible deeds, he or she cannot really understand or sympathize with other human beings. We must oppose the ideas and the actions of such people, Muste argued, but always give individuals — as Gandhi did — the opportunity to retreat by not challenging their self-respect.

Born in Holland and brought up in Grand Rapids, Michigan, where his parents settled when he was six, Muste was the all-American boy — basketball star, second baseman, valedictorian. Like so many first sons in a Dutch Reformed family he studied for the ministry and in 1909 at age twenty-four was duly ordained and assigned a pulpit in New York. Calvinism, however, was too confining for a young man who had listened to William James lecture at New York University on pragmatism; had been befriended by another great philosopher, John Dewey; and had begun to immerse himself in socialist and pacifist literature. Transferring to a Congregational Church at Newtonville, Massachusetts, a suburb of Boston, Muste again ran into intellectual difficulties. His congregation was pro-war; he was anti-war. Muste resigned his ministry, did volunteer work for the American Civil Liberties Union and on behalf of conscientious objectors, moved to Providence where he served as a minister for the Society of Friends — Quakers.

Unlike most radical leaders, Muste came to his radicalism through the ministry — and in stages. After the war, he and other Quakers raised relief funds for 30,000 textile workers on strike in Lawrence, Massachusetts, where a previous walkout in 1912 had made international headlines. Before long Muste had become the strike leader, and when the stoppage ended in a surprise victory (a 12 percent raise), he became head of an independent national union, the Amalgamated Textile Workers of America. After two years, however, trying to flesh out his organization — with the help of Sidney Hillman and the more enduring Amalgamated Clothing Workers — he was forced to give it up during the 1921 depression.

Typically — as I was to see in joint efforts with him decades later — Muste was able after a setback to involve new people in new ventures. He was, I think, the most unsectarian radical since Eugene V. Debs. Aided by such trade union luminaries as James Maurer, a socialist who headed the Pennsylvania Federation of Labor; John Fitzpatrick, the humanistic president of the Chicago Federation of Labor; Fannie Cohen of the ladies' garment union; and a number of educators, including John Dewey, Muste established a labor school, modeled after the British labor education movement, in Katonah, New York. The Brookwood Labor College, supported at its peak by thirteen national unions, was something unique and exciting in American labor history. Many young people who would later become secondary leaders of the CIO (Congress of Industrial Organizations) drive in the 1930s graduated from Muste's labor college.

By 1929 Muste had decided that both he and his friends were inadequately involved; they needed to be active, he thought, not only on the economic front, as a left wing within the AFL (American Federation of Labor), but in radical politics as well. The AFL leadership under William Green was a relic of antiquity in its "stodgy class collaboration" and its phobic opposition to industrial unionism. The Socialist Party, Muste felt, was too timid and not really revolutionary. And though he hailed the Russian Revolution and called for defense of the Soviet Union, he felt little affinity for an American Communist Party that was tied to Moscow's apron strings. If there had been an "intelligent" Communist Party, he once said, he could have joined it, but the existing one was not of that genre; it lacked an American flavor. In May 1929, therefore, Muste mobilized 151 delegates from 31 cities in 18 states — including socialists James

H. Maurer and Harry Laidler, and independent leftists such as Louis F. Budenz — to lay the keel for a new movement, the Conference for Progressive Labor Action (CPLA).

Originally, CPLA was a hybrid of an assemblage of left-wing unionists dedicated to the reform of the AFL, and a political party. In that form it could attract many Socialist Party members, including Norman Thomas who served on its executive board, but no communists. Its program was compatible with both sides of its dual personality — it urged formation of a labor party, as well as "a complete system of social insurance against the hazards of unemployment, sickness and old age," and a labor movement that would help "put an end to imperialism, militarism, and war." But as the months passed the Musteites functioned more like a political party than a hybrid. Late in 1933 they converted their "conference" (CPLA) into a party — the American Workers Party. Among its leaders were, in addition to Muste and Budenz, such intellectual figures as J. B. S. Hardman, editor of *Advance,* the official paper of the Amalgamated Clothing Workers; Ludwig Lore, a columnist for the *New York Post* who had helped found the Communist Party; and philosophers Sidney Hook and James Burnham. A year and a half later, with the approval of Leon Trotsky, James Cannon arranged a merger with the American Workers Party and thus, in December 1934, the Workers Party of the United States was born, with Muste as secretary and Cannon as editor of its newspaper, *The Militant.* The headline in *The Militant* announcing the marriage indicated some of the lavish expectations of the united group: NEW PARTY LAUNCHED INTO ITS TREMENDOUS UNDERTAKING: THE OVERTHROW OF CAPITALIST RULE IN AMERICA AND THE CREATION OF A WORKERS' STATE.

III

Cannon let himself get carried away with that headline. But in fact there were great possibilities for the Workers Party out there in America, if only we could remain cohesive and not frit away our opportunities. There were millions of desperate workers waiting to be enrolled in unemployed organizations or trade unions. And there was no one more willing or able to do it than the socialists, communists, Trotskyites, and Lovestoneites, for whom "organizing the unorganized" was the noblest of revolutionary duties. The territory was virgin; only a tiny fraction of the "injured and oppressed" belonged to mass organizations. A radical could become a leader of a group of unemployed or a trade union (as I did ultimately) just by making a rabble-rousing speech or taking the first steps to unionize fellow workers. Unlike today — where the unions are institutionalized, their leaders are middle aged or older, and it is virtually impossible for a young person to become a part of the hierarchy — the situation in the 1930s was fluid. Opportunity beckoned everywhere, and we Trotskyites had as good a chance as any — probably better — to assume the leadership of working-class organizations in their gestation stage.

My own first effort at organizing was perhaps typical of what was happening on a broad terrain. Like the vast majority of such efforts it ended in failure, but each failure somehow built toward future successes. Shortly after I became a Trotskyite, I tried to unionize the Hecht Bros. department store on 14th Street and Sixth Avenue in New York. I had been working for some time as an assistant to the fur buyer at Hecht's, a job with a glowing title but only $15 a week in pay. Part of my duty was to take in old fur coats for storage during the summer months, an operation that had cost the company thousands of dollars in losses because of inept record keeping. I didn't particularly care about minks and muskrats, but like many leftists I had a compulsion for efficiency. I introduced an almost foolproof record system that endeared me both to my boss and his boss. The store manager bought me a suit so that I would look presentable; gave me a raise; and, when I expressed an interest in writing advertising copy, put me to work composing tracts to promote the store's installment buying plan. I did well enough to win the promise of a full-time job in advertising at the phenomenal ultimate wage of $75 a week.

Alas, I had already convinced seven or eight people to form a secret union cell and had affiliated them with an AFL department store union that was typical of many AFL unions at that time. It had virtually no members and no contracts with employers, but the two men who headed it held a charter from a legitimate national union, which under the right circumstances could be turned into a profitable "business." Apart from these two hoodlums (they wore shoulder holsters and guns under their jackets) the viable membership consisted of two or three mini groups like the one I had assembled and a somewhat larger communist faction. The communists, who had belonged to another federation until then, the Trade Union Unity League, were in the process of liquidating that organization and returning to the AFL. Thus "swamped" by an unexpected influx of recruits, the two hoodlums decided to set up an executive committee composed of themselves, a few communists, and the lone Trotskyite — me. Suddenly, with hardly an effort I had become one of the leaders of a labor union. The same thing was happening to thousands of young radicals who were either joining "paper" unions or forming new unions. If they succeeded in completing the organization of the unorganized, they became full-time officials; if they failed, they usually were fired and went elsewhere to try again.

Unfortunately for me, there was a spy in that local union. The store manager at Hecht's called me into his office one day: "Sidney," he said, "I don't want you to admit or deny it, but we know you're organizing a union here. Someday probably all the department stores in New York will be unionized, but we don't intend to be the first. Anytime you walk into this office and tell me you've quit the union, your promotion will be waiting for you as if nothing happened." I didn't get fired — that day — but another member, a young communist whom I had recruited to the union and was trying to proselytize for Trotskyism, was dismissed within the hour.

When I informed the two gun-toting leaders of my union

about the discharge they expressed regret, but said there was nothing they could do about it. This was before the Wagner Act, which allowed a union to litigate before the National Labor Relations Board on discharges for union activity. But the disposition of radicals — then and now — was to take our issues to the streets; my communist friend and I hit on the idea of a one-man picket line. He paced in front of the store five or six hours a day, carrying a sign that read FIRED FOR JOINING A UNION, DON'T PATRONIZE HECHT BROS., and gave out a leaflet I had written and mimeographed, explaining what had happened. During my lunch hour I would run about madly to the Workers Party office lining up relief pickets to spell my communist friend; often one of his own comrades also would come by. It was a futile effort, however. The one-man picket line lasted a few weeks. Instead of drawing workers in the store closer to the union, as we had hoped, it had the opposite effect — workers were more terrified than ever. A few weeks later I too was given a pink slip; I never did walk into the store manager's office, even to say good-by. Eventually of course the big New York department stores — Macy's, Gimbels, and others — did agree to bargain with a union of their employees, but by that time I was long gone.

IV

The big question of the 1930s was not whether the workers were "ready" — but ready for what? "In traveling around the country," wrote a left-of-center writer, Mauritz A. Hallgren, "I talked with thousands of jobless workers. I found them increasingly sympathetic with the activities of the Communist Party, at least to the extent that those activities dealt with their own immediate problems. In large cities like Chicago and New York the communists experienced no difficulties at all in persuading entire neighborhoods to take part in demonstrations against evictions and relief cuts. Yet a vast majority of the unemployed with whom I talked were utterly cold to communism as a way of life." Leftists must have sensed this dichotomy in rank-and-file attitude because they seldom openly proclaimed their membership in the Communist Party, the Workers Party, or whatever. Members of the working class — especially the jobless — were ready to follow radical tacticians, unions, and unemployed organizations; they were willing to listen to arguments for socialism; but they were not ready to accept socialism as their future — at least not yet.

Like it or not, the New Deal had a stronger impact on the American psyche than we radicals realized. Prior to Roosevelt's inauguration, writes historian David A. Shannon, "fear of a revolution was very widespread . . . and much of the politics of the period can be understood fully only by viewing political events against the background of anxiety about violent revolt. The vigor with which the army dispersed the Bonus Expeditionary Force from Washington in the summer of 1932, for example, had its roots in revolutionary fear." But Roosevelt introduced reforms that, though inadequate by leftist standards, did mute talk of revolution. In just four or five months during the first year of the New Deal, 2.5 million unemployed were provided with jobs. The banks were closed, then reopened, and a new law went into effect insuring individual savings deposits up to $5,000. The Federal Emergency Relief Administration, under Roosevelt's closest advisor, Harry L. Hopkins, funneled $3 billion in grants to the states over a two-and-a-half-year period for direct relief to the indigent. Hopkins's description of his objective — "feed the hungry, and Goddamn fast" — indicates the mood of urgency that permeated the new administration. Within a short time America swelled with new alphabetical institutions — the NRA (National Recovery Administration), which imposed government controls on production, prices, wages, hours; CWA (Civil Works Administration), which initiated 180,000 projects within four months; PWA (Public Works Administration), which ultimately allocated $3.3 billion to revive the construction industry; CCC (Civilian Conservation Corps) to place young people in camps at $30 a month plus food and lodging; AAA (Agricultural Adjustment Administration) to reduce farm acreage and thereby increase prices; and many others. In due course

Congress also approved such "socialistic" measures as unemployment compensation and social security.

All of it together did not solve the crisis of capitalism. The number of unemployed was trimmed by only 3 million from 1933 to 1939. The job situation did not improve appreciably until the following year when the nation began selling vast amounts of war material to the Allies and cranking up its own war machine. The economic crisis of the 1930s was simply converted into the military crisis of the 1940s. What the New Deal had failed to accomplish through Maynard Keynes's "compensatory spending" and "deficit financing" in peacetime was accomplished through far vaster expenditures and deficits during World War II. It was the war that put America back to work, and the Cold War thereafter that kept it at the work bench in the ensuing decades. It was not the New Deal welfare and job reforms. I'm aware that in making this point I collide head-on with the Roosevelt legend and the hero worship that surrounded this charismatic and, in many respects, humane man. But it is a fact; the New Deal mitigated but did not terminate the Depression.

Until Roosevelt's first term was half over, all sections of the left, except the moderate social-democrats, expected the New Deal to lose its popular support and the working class to move in a direct line toward revolutionary consciousness. According to the May 27, 1933, issue of *The Militant,* "the working class will only sink deeper into its misery unless it sees clearly the hypocritical nature of the Roosevelt program . . . " The Revolutionary Policy Committee, the left wing within the Socialist Party, openly advocated "armed insurrection," and many of its comrades in March 1935 believed it was not far off. Earl Browder, secretary of the Communist Party, was calling the New Deal "a policy of brutal oppression at home and of imperialism abroad." Roosevelt, he said, was "carrying out more thoroughly, more brutally than Hoover, the capitalist attack against the living standards of the masses." The Blue Eagle, symbol of the NRA, was dubbed the "*fascist* Blue Eagle," and as late as ·February 1935 a Communist Party manifesto carried the caption: "Against the New Deal of Hunger, Fascism, and War."

But capitalism in the United States was more resilient and Franklin Roosevelt more popular than we had expected. The result was an anomalous situation in which workers and the unemployed were ready to accept our leadership in unions and strikes — but not in politics. We were like a magnet, positioned too distant from the piece of metal we were trying to attract. We were right in our analysis of capitalism — but we were right too early, and our analysis was incomplete.

Many years later, in 1966, Earl Browder (having long been expelled from the Communist Party) reminisced before an audience at the University of Illinois that the New Deal "had put America on the road to the welfare state and thereby cut the ground from under both the socialist and communist parties. . . . No mass discontent with the economic system existed except such as provides the basis for *reform* movements." Left-wing socialists and Trotskyites reacted to this preemption of the center by the New Deal by turning on the spigot of revolutionary phrases. "The Communist Party, on the other hand, rapidly moved out of its extreme leftist sectarianism of 1930 toward the broadest united front tactics of reformism for strictly limited aims. It relegated its revolutionary socialist goals to the ritual of chapel and Sundays on the pattern long followed by the Christian Church. On weekdays it became the most single-minded practical reformist party that America ever produced."

If the 180-degree turn in communist strategy brought snickers from rivals, it nonetheless opened wide many new doors for the Communist Party. The Socialist Party, embroiled in factional disputes and splits, saw its membership reduced to a pitiful 6,488 by February 1937; but the Communists grew steadily to 70,000 by 1939. "Americanization" made the Communist Party acceptable to many who had shunned it before. By tying itself, if only tenuously, to New Deal coattails the party gained an aura of respectability, which made recruitment far simpler. Looking back with the hindsight of forty-five years, I don't think I would have surrendered to reformism, as Browder did, but I think Trotskyism could have found a happy compromise between its ultimate revolutionary goals and the need for creating single-issue groups for immediate reforms.

The Trotskyites, unfortunately, failed to match abstract theory with living reality. I don't recall, for instance, a single discussion of Keynesian economics, though Keynesianism was responsible for capitalism's recovery. There was a tendency to think of events in absolutist terms: things were going downhill, they would continue to go downhill; workers were organizing and striking, they would continue on a militant course until they became revolutionary. Perhaps this rigid stance was due to the garrison mentality of a small movement. Each of us spent an enormous amount of time in party meetings — weekly meetings of the branch, weekly meetings of the branch executive committee, trade union faction meetings for those involved in union work, faction meetings when there was an internal party dispute. In addition, once a week when the weather was tolerable, each branch would hold an outdoor meeting, much like those at Hyde Park in London or Newberry ("Bughouse") Square in Chicago, except that the speakers were all from our own party. Even fledglings like myself learned the time-honored trade of soap-boxing, of turning a heckle — either by a right-winger or a communist — into a counterpunch.

Again, however, as with our trade union or unemployed work, we touched the outside world for a moment, then retreated into our cloister. Our whole lives revolved around the party. We gave it inordinate shares of our earnings — 10, 20, 30 percent or more. (In Washington, D.C., we had a comrade named Tommy who raised money for the movement by panhandling three or four days a week.) Our girl friends and boy friends were party members (and if they weren't, they were invariably recruited); our Saturday night socials were with other comrades or sympathizers. Our political discussions were either with party members or potential recruits who were close to our position.

We seldom exchanged views with liberals or conservatives

(on the rare occasions that we did, it was a shouting match, not a discussion), and never with government officials. Our contact with Stalinists, Lovestoneites, and socialists was in an adversary relationship — less concerned with joint intellectual probing than with demolishing the positions of people we considered opponents. Sometimes this could take bizarre forms. I recall a confrontation I had on the 42nd Street side of the New York Public Library with a wild radical of one of the other tendencies who accused me of supporting capitalism. "Look at the tie you're wearing," he said. "Where did you buy it?" "At Macy's," I said. "You see," he sneered, "that proves my point." Being a radical, but especially a radical of one of the smaller groups, induced parochialism and catered to the beleaguered mentality. From there it was a small jump to unrestrained factionalism.

The Workers Party had barely been formed — and I had just joined it — when a dispute arose over what became known as "the French turn." The French Trotskyite group, it seems, had decided to join the socialist party of that country and work within it as an organized faction. It was like a fly joining a brigade of elephants, since the Trotskyites numbered 200, whereas the S.F.I.O. counted its adherents in hundreds of thousands and would soon head a French popular front government. Trotsky, who was the architect of the French turn, believed he was taking a quantum leap, transforming, as he put it, "a propaganda group . . . into a revolutionary faction directly and indirectly exercising an influence upon the working class movement in the country." But whatever luster the idea had for France (actually it was an abject failure) it was an embarrassment in the United States — and all the more so because an anti–French turn faction had coagulated in Cannon's own Communist League of America, headed by Hugo Oehler and Tom Stamm, a New York intellectual with great verve.

What ensued for the next year, therefore, was a debilitating faction fight that immobilized Trotskyism at a critical juncture when opportunities for growth were most propitious. Four disciplined factions pelted each other with charges and countercharges. Oehler, Stamm, Louis Basky, a veteran of the struggle in his native Hungary, and Paul Eiffel, a German émigré, denounced the Cannon group as "capitulators" and "betrayers of the Fourth International," who were secretly planning to join the American Socialist Party; Muste agreed with Oehler that it would be wrong to join the Socialist Party, but was not so vehement in labeling it a "principled" issue that must lead to split; the Weber group had some esoteric differences, which I no longer remember; and of course the Cannon-Shachtman forces defended the French turn but denied that they were going to repeat that experiment here. When the smoke cleared, the Oehlerites and Musteites left the Party (or were expelled) and the Workers Party liquidated into Norman Thomas's Socialist Party with unseemly haste. There is no doubt in my mind that Cannon had intended to do this all along, his merger with the Musteites being merely a stratagem to absorb and eliminate a possible rival on the left before executing the delicate marriage with Norman Thomas. Cannon, despite his charm and wit, was more than capable of such complicated deceptions.

V

The Revolutionary Workers League, born in the backwash of the faction fight over the French turn, was a small force of 200 persons, reassured by the same dogma that reassured other leftists, namely that history was riding on our shoulders and that zealous adherence to the "correct line" would lead to the ultimate victory. All the RWL had to do was hold on, working within the "class struggle" where it could, and build capital for the future. When the workers were ready to move they would pay homage to the RWL's farsightedness and integrity. That's the way it had happened in Russia; it would happen here, too.

Clearly the RWL misjudged its potential, yet it was made up of a remarkably competent group of people. Dozens of RWL members who later drifted away became immensely successful in the outside world. Two became editors of *Fortune* magazine. My good friend Joe Fox became head of a large cafeteria union in New York; another ex-comrade is still vice president of a national union with almost half a million members; a sympathizer from Southern Illinois who briefly joined the RWL became the secretary-treasurer of another good-sized national union. At least half a dozen became college professors, an equal number well-to-do businessmen, one a top civil servant in New York; and I'm sure a scientific survey would reveal many other "success stories."

But if the RWL was a group made up of able individuals, collectively it was a total failure. As I assess it nearly four decades later, it suffered from the same irremediable maladies as Trotskyism and kindred groups. It based its strategy on the axiom that revolution—resulting perhaps from war—was close at hand. It was a reasonable assumption from existing circumstances; world war did in fact break out a few years later and the most extensive revolution in all history engulfing six dozen nations followed. But the war did not lead to the collapse of American capitalism—on the contrary—or to social revolution in any of the major capitalist countries. Our portrait of impending catastrophe, therefore, was not a saleable commodity, and, since we did not grow, we turned inward—to personal diatribe and factionalism.

All the small leftist groups suffered decimation or death in the next decade. The League for a Revolutionary Workers Party, headed by B. J. Field, the man who had led the hotel strike, disintegrated in 1936 while Oehler was negotiating to unite with it. The Communist League of Struggle, led by Albert Weisbord, one of the most accomplished men I've ever known—a linguist, a fine writer, an excellent teacher, a good thinker, a magna cum laude from Harvard, and a distinguished union strategist as shown by his role in the heralded Passaic and Gastonia textile strikes—limped on for a while and also fell apart. Weisbord wound up for a time on the organizing staff of the AFL. (In 1941, when a group of us tossed Capone gangsters out of our retail clerks union in Chicago, AFL president William Green asked me if I would accept Weisbord as his, Green's, representative to our union.)

The official Trotskyites fared somewhat better, but by no means well. They liquidated their party after a convention in March 1936 and joined the Socialist Party where they functioned as a disciplined faction and published their own paper, *Socialist Appeal*. The uneasy marriage lasted little more than a year, ending on New Year's Day 1938. Then a few years later the reborn Trotskyist Party suffered another schism, as Cannon and Shachtman fell out over the Russian question — was the Soviet Union a "warped workers state," as Cannon averred, or a "bureaucratic collectivist" one, as Shachtman insisted. Shachtman and his allies slipped away to form the Independent Socialist League — also short-lived.

The official Trotskyites, now called the Socialist Workers Party, still exist and after half a century — according to Cannon whom I talked with a couple of weeks before his death in 1974 — had grown to approximately 1,200 members.

For the RWL — my group — it was all downhill, almost from the start. We were unable to proselytize even a tiny fraction of the people who followed us to trade union and other mass activity. The gap in political understanding was just too great to breach. What worker, for instance, could make sense out of an item in the March 1, 1936, issue of the *Fighting Worker*, which claimed the Weisbordites didn't understand "the relation of revolutionary strategy to the uneven development of capitalism in the imperialist epoch, in connection with the transformation of revolutionary situations into successful revolutions"?

Considering our size, we covered a wide range of labor activities. In the first half of 1936, for example, I was involved in four campaigns. Early in January Leonard Levy and I unionized May's department store in Brooklyn; the ensuing strike was bitter, resulting in at least five arrests. I recall vividly the young red-headed woman who manacled herself to a telephone pole, and while police were sawing away at the chains, drew a large crowd to whom she conveyed the story of management abuses. Then in February I participated in a strike called by an independent utility workers union at the Mellon-owned Koppers Coke plant in Brooklyn. The two leaders of the union were inundated with problems. They had to find pickets for a facility that was a mile or two in circumference, and it was so bitter cold and windy that none of us could take more than half an hour on the line at a time. The communists supplied some, so did the Lovestoneites, and we, in the RWL, a handful. I became editor of a daily mimeographed strike sheet that for a while fortified morale. But it was a losing game. We couldn't stop sixty strikebreakers from entering the plant and we couldn't halt its operations. After a while, strikers began to slink back to their jobs; the company had won. On the last day, when the stoppage was called off, the two union leaders, each blaming the other for the defeat, engaged in a bloody fist fight, one of them drawing a knife. It was all we could do to separate them and prevent a murder.

In June, I participated in a hunger march to Trenton, New Jersey, in which hundreds of unemployed took over the legislative chamber at the state capitol demanding greater relief payments. The communists ran this show but I was able to make a few impassioned speeches (which were attacked in their press), and a few friends. For some reason or another the police didn't try to oust us; my faded memory is that some kind of compromise was worked out with the Governor.

A month later, in Chicago, I was involved in a more sensational action. The city had cut off cash relief to 83,000 families. The Illinois Workers Alliance, then headed by Frank McCulloch, a socialist who would later become administrative assistant to Senator Paul Douglas, decided to bring a couple of thousand of its adherents to the city hall chambers to put pressure on Mayor Ed Kelly and his machine aldermen. For us in the RWL this was not militant enough, the issue had to be taken to the streets. Thirteen of us, barely scraping up the seven-cent streetcar fare to go downtown, began picketing outside city hall —and, as we expected, the rank and file of the Workers Alliance joined us. Our placards called for "nationalization of industry under workers control," for "jobs at trade union wages," and similar planks, but what attracted Workers Alliance members was simply a desire to express themselves through some form of action — rather than sitting placidly in council chambers. Soon the line numbered in the hundreds, then, as the *Fighting Worker* reported, 2,000. At the peak of the picketing we decided to invade the building. Pushing our way past the police to the entrance of the visitors gallery we interrupted the orderly proceedings of the city council. One of our comrades, I think it was Joe Fox, shouted for quiet below and introduced me to make a speech. While the mayor and the aldermen gaped, I berated the city for its callousness. When I finished we took our "troops" back to the streets, where picketing continued. It was a great victory; the council, which had claimed it didn't have any money, somehow raised the funds to send out food boxes that were six days overdue, that very day.

I was certainly not the only RWL member working in what we called "the class struggle"; in fact we were a whirlwind of activity, unionizing auto and WPA workers in Detroit, the unemployed in Cleveland, cab drivers in Washington, touring the country end to end to make contacts with coal miners in Scranton or in Southern Illinois, steelworkers in Gary. These were all eye-opening and gratifying experiences for me personally, even though my mode of transportation was always the thumb, hitchhiking; and if perchance I got stuck after dark in a town where there were no comrades I found lodgings in a church, crept into a car on a side street, or — on one occasion, with another fellow I had met on the road — slept in the local police station. Such efforts by half a dozen of us paid some dividends. The May 1, 1936, issue of the *Fighting Worker,* for instance, reported thirty new members recruited (and four expelled). But we didn't catch on, certainly not in the way we should have in a period of industrial upheaval and social uncertainty. And as the months and years flitted by, we were afflicted by the same frustrations that had consumed the official Trotskyites — splits over issues that as often as not were insignificant or irrelevant. The first to break away, taking a good segment of the organization with him, was Tom Stamm. Ostensibly the schism was over political differences, but I'm convinced that the true cause was Stamm's unwillingness to move from New York to Chicago, where we had transferred our headquarters to be near the heart of American industry. Invariably, personal differences burgeoned into political disputes, Stamm's being simply the first of half a dozen.

Each schism of course sapped our strength, not only because we lost members, but because we wasted so much time and energy in torrid debate. We continued to believe, however, that some great trauma would propel the working masses in our direction — another economic slump, an international war, or what have you. There was a brief slump in 1938, to be sure, and a world war in 1939, but none of it sparked a surge in our direction. And so we labored in routine and primitive fashion, while our ranks steadily diminished. In time, our main activity became publication of the *Fighting Worker* and a few hundred mimeographed copies of a theoretical magazine *International News*. Some of our prose, especially Oehler's — he had an excellent mind but an awful pen — was less than inspiring, and our mimeograph had a devilish knack of printing unreadable lines. What matters, we told ourselves, however, is "the line"; it had almost a religious connotation. And so every month we assigned, wrote, and edited our copy; then had it printed in a manner almost as rudimentary as when printing was discovered hundreds of years ago. Linotype was set at a commercial printer (a former anarchist), but a couple of us set the headlines by hand, made up the pages, and put them two at a time on the bed of a proof-press, which we kept in a tiny store on Ashland Avenue near Grand in Chicago. Then, with one of us feeding and the other turning the drum, we managed in a few hours to run off a thousand copies of the *Fighting Worker*.

VI

If some of this sounds a bit grim, I should point out that the life of a young radical, though it was bisected by serious and often unhappy events, was not necessarily solemn or dour. Even living in penury sometimes had its compensations. When I first came to Chicago in 1936 to set up headquarters for the RWL and prepare the way for Oehler and Stamm, my friend Bill Streeter and I rented a room from Mrs. Davis, the mother of one of our comrades. We paid her a dollar a week, which was a bargain in itself. But Mrs. Davis, who was not particularly political, loved to listen to Bill and me talk. She would wait up for us every night, with a pot of tea on the fire, and all the Jewish rye bread and prune jelly we could eat. Sometimes that was all the food we had for the whole day, but, even if it wasn't, it was more than welcome. We repaid Mrs. Davis by washing the sinkful of dishes she had accumulated since breakfast. When we really got hungry we could visit the wife of a North Side druggist who was always generous with meals and a dollar or two.

Our social lives were better than adequate; there were parties and picnics, and the normal joys of associating with the opposite sex. Then there were the endless discussions, debates, and arguments which set the adrenalin running as much as a football game. Early after our split from the main body of Trotskyism, I was assigned to Washington to build a branch there and help organize cab drivers. Two of our comrades — one a chiropractor who was saving his dimes to reopen his professional office, the other a sometime writer who later became the publisher of books on dianoetics, were driving taxis — and unionizing the drivers of Diamond Cab, the company with whom they all contracted for gas, insurance, and the like. I would ride around for hours with Doc or Art, seeing the city, meeting interesting people, some of them moonlighting government workers. It was far from a hardship. At night Doc would take me to one or another of the Marxist discussion clubs that many government workers were attending at that time. (I was amused in the 1950s to hear charges of complex spy plots during the New Deal days. You could have picked half the secrets in Washington just by attending one of these Marxist discussion meetings. Everyone talked quite freely, and if there was any agency gossip withheld from the ears of the participants it was solely by oversight.)

On Friday evenings we would drive to Baltimore for a big splash at the lavish home of V. F. Calverton, one of the prominent leftist editors of *Modern Monthly*. The discussion and the arguments and the drinking would go on to early morning, unless the party was broken up by a fist fight, which sometimes happened. There was excitement to all this, and, even more than the stimulation of political exchange, the subliminal exhilaration of feeling that we were on the side of history. In time, we finished organizing the cab drivers, but were forced out on strike prematurely and lost. I was transferred to other parts, where the routine was much the same.

It was at one of the social affairs in New York that I met my first wife, Lillian. She was in the process of divorcing her husband in Boston and had come to the big city for a little relaxation. I didn't see her for some weeks after that — I was on a trip to the Midwest — but when we met again it was to enter into what today would be called a relationship. Both of us considered it a full-fledged marriage, but without the blessings of the state or the clergy, neither of which were high on our list of favored institutions. Apart from the tendency to get married without marriage licenses, the moral code of radicals I knew — including myself and Lillian — was somewhat sterner than that of most people. Our relationships were emotionally strong, and, though there were no legal ties or taboos on sex, infidelity was probably less frequent than it was among the public at large.

The day-to-day work in the movement was mundane, except on rare occasions when something sensational was happening — a demonstration, a strike, a formal debate. The biggest slice of time was spent getting from one place to another, either from one city to another (I hitchhiked at least 40,000 or 50,000 miles between 1935 and 1940) or visiting someone's home for a discussion. The trips to other cities were interesting because you met old comrades who would regale you with stories of the past, coal miners in Scranton, Pennsylvania, or Staunton, Illinois, steelworkers in Pittsburgh, colorful Southerners like Sam Garrett in Detroit (whom we ran for president in a write-in campaign in 1936), and Thomas H. Stone, an attorney in Richmond.

That routine continued from the time we formed the RWL

into World War II. We worked in private industry on and off — since there never was enough money to support full-time functionaries — or, if we didn't, our wives worked. Oehler occasionally took a job as a commercial artist, sometimes as a factory worker — he was quite competent in both — but usually he depended on his wife's, Anne's, earnings. In my case, Lillian and I alternated working in restaurants, she as a waitress, I as a short-order cook. Afterward we would write articles, attend meetings, edit our little paper, distribute leaflets, visit contacts.

We were held together by a sense of history that made the most mundane and dull tasks tolerable. Certainly we were aware of the paucity of our numbers — could a few hundred people and perhaps a thousand sympathizers change the face of a nation of 125 million, stretching 3,000 miles ocean to ocean? Our answer, one we never doubted, was why not? Didn't a few thousand Bolsheviks change the face of an even larger nation, Russia, because a man named Lenin had galvanized a whole people around the simple slogan "peace, bread, land"? And what of Bela Kun in Hungary who was released from jail by the old authorities when their nation was in total disintegration, to set up — temporarily, it turned out — a Communist government? We were living in a setting — difficult for most people today to grasp — in which history was ready for quantum leaps. And in that setting all that was necessary, we felt, was to have the "correct line." The smallest group could grow like wildfire at the propitious moment if it had the "correct line," the correct analysis of present events, and the correct strategy for meeting a historic challenge; at the appropriate moment the masses would follow a revolutionary party whose program was simple and clear, just as the Russian masses had followed Lenin in the critical days of 1917.

In our day-to-day tasks, then, whether it was the drudgery of running an antiquated printing press or the drama of a union campaign, we felt the exhilaration of being on the side of the future. It was not a religious feeling, but it had a comparable characteristic — religiosity. Doubts vanished, defeats were dismissed as episodic, isolation was deemed a way station toward the final victory. Sometimes this stance deprived us of objectivity, but it also inspired us to work endless hours for the movement and to take risks that we would not have taken otherwise. This was especially true when the strikes, revolts, and unemployment demonstrations rose in crescendo during the mid-1930s, tearing severely at the fabric of the American establishment.

Chapter 3
The Labor Wars

I

When I first came to Chicago to set up headquarters for the RWL, I joined an existing unemployed group in the district where I lived—Branch 26 of the Workers Alliance. Except for a single month, my wife and I never went on the relief rolls ourselves (we always found some sort of work to support ourselves, usually in restaurants), and I never took a job with WPA. My credentials as an "unemployed," therefore, could have been questioned; my true occupation was a full-time revolutionary. But no one did question my credentials. I could speak, I could organize, I could administer — Branch 26 was glad to have me, and soon I was its secretary. The president, a short, dark man whose name, I think, was Gold, was a communist, but we got along well. Like so many communists he was not "heavy" on theory, he just believed that capitalism was moribund and should be overthrown, and he didn't know enough about the Trotsky-Stalin fight to be concerned about my dissidence. He just recognized in me a kindred spirit — and I in him —and we collaborated exceptionally well.

Our activity in Branch 26 was fairly routine, not unlike that of a union business agent. A jobless worker would come to us for advice on how to apply for relief. Our role was to point out the pitfalls facing him: "Make sure your rent records are straight, and if you don't have receipts for some payments make sure you work out the details in your mind so that you are not caught in a discrepancy. You lived in such and such a place for two years and three months, in the next place for seven months, and so on. Under no circumstances say 'I don't remember.' If you haven't been in the city long enough to be eligible, lie about it, but don't get mixed up on your dates. The case worker will try to declare you ineligible for picayune reasons. If your wife has a diamond ring, be sure she isn't wearing it. If you have a bank account or a car don't tell the case worker; and if he or she asks, say you don't have any." Invariably the people we coached got relief checks without undue delay. For the most part it was people who hewed to the truth — say, that they had $300 in the bank from an old inheritance — who ran into problems.

Periodically, the officers of Branch 26 visited the relief offices to take up a "grievance," say, that an applicant was being kept off the rolls or was not getting enough or had missed a check; and more often than not we won our case. When we didn't, we would put a picket line around the relief office and distribute leaflets in the neighborhood. Sometimes we would sit inside the office and a few of our people would submit to arrest, much like the civil disobedience of antiwar and civil rights groups in the 1960s and 1970s. Our secret weapon in these confrontations was a big 300-pound fellow by the name of Stickles, whom I remember most fondly. He had a bull-horn voice and ten or eleven children, plus a wife who was as militant as he. If everything else failed, we sent Stickles and his brood into the relief station to occupy it; when the police came, he and the family would resist removal like tigers, causing chaos for an hour or two. On occasion we could win our demands simply by telling the director we were going to unleash Stickles and his kids for another sit-in.

But although these small victories gave us a big lift and made it possible to recruit more members to our branch, there were also cases of stark tragedy that we were unable to prevent. One I recall poignantly is that of a man and woman who lived in a basement on Damen Avenue. They had applied for an allotment of coal to heat their apartment that winter, but were turned down repeatedly. We were in the relief station with the wife arguing the issue and finally had won our protest just at the time that the husband put a rope around his neck and jumped off a chair in their living room. He was dead when we arrived to give him the "good news." I had never seen a man hang like that before; it was a gruesome experience.

Organizing the employed was somewhat more difficult than organizing the jobless, but again the radicals had the advantage — a militant message and organizational adroitness. Standing on improvised soapboxes at factory gates or on platforms in meeting halls, we made thousands of impassioned speeches condemning the moguls of industry. In urging workers to join a union to win a nickel-an-hour raise or end speedup, we also reminded them how evil was the capitalist system, how it led to poverty amidst plenty, how it spent millions for war but little for the working class. We appealed to the insurgent impulse, not just the desire for more. We passed out leaflets, held meetings, led strikes with a zeal no other force could muster. And we were willing to make personal sacrifices in a way that the staid leadership of labor was not. Whatever one may think of communist political foibles, individual members faced hardships, beatings, and the threat of jail with great courage. During a New York restaurant strike the courts issued 110 injunctions against a communist-led union in a vain attempt to dampen its ardor. From late 1929 to 1932 twenty-three men and women were shot in strikes and unemployment demonstrations led by communists.

The RWL's experience with autoworkers in Detroit was fairly typical of what was happening in many places. We had a comrade, Zygmunt Dobrycinski (I think that is how it was spelled), who worked for NAFI (National Automotive Fibres Inc.), a firm with 1,500 workers that fabricated the material for automobile seats. Quietly "Ziggy" recruited a nucleus to unionize the shop, but after more than a year he had the support of only three others — his brother, whom he also recruited into the RWL, plus two other brothers. Traditional union "porkchoppers" would probably have given up at this point, but Ziggy persevered — and even more so when he was fired. He prevailed on a UAW (United Auto Workers) local at Chrysler to subsidize him at the rate of $10 a week and began distributing leaflets at plant gates every other day. Now the trickle became a small torrent as, for some reason or another, workers overcame their fears. Though management formed a company union to counteract Ziggy's efforts — and hired a number of industrial spies — there were soon 400 members in Local 205, and when NAFI took the next step of firing members on Ziggy's committee, a short strike ensued during which 600 more people joined the union. After a six-hour bargaining session, management granted a nickel-an-hour raise and agreed to negotiate for more once the plant was back in operation. It reinstated all strikers, abolished Sunday work, and — more important — recognized the union shop committee. It was a great victory for Ziggy, showing how a single leftist could turn things around without much help from the UAW (which had few staff members and even less money at the time), or the CIO itself, which was putting little effort in the motor centers because its central focus was on the steel workers.

Moreover, once a leftist got a foothold in one corner of the industrial world it was relatively easy to expand it. The most sensational instance I know of was that of Walter Reuther, then a member of the Socialist Party. Walter had just returned from a trip to the Soviet Union where he and his brother Victor had worked two years at the Gorky auto plant. Though he had once been employed by Ford, at the moment he had no job or base in the auto industry. Nonetheless, socialist comrades who held a UAW charter for the Ternstedt plant designated Walter as their delegate to the UAW convention in South Bend. Reuther had never worked at Ternstedt and the charter was actually inoperable since the local had not yet enrolled the fifteen members required by the constitution. But with the help of the communist faction at the South Bend meeting (Reuther was on good terms with the communists and worked closely with them for a number of years) he was seated as delegate. He went on to build a large local, and was elected vice president, then president, of the UAW, and finally president of the CIO itself — all on the foundation of a questionable credential plus the uncanny knack of a radical to deal with rank-and-file problems.

Comrades in the RWL had that same knack, and given a small base they too expanded their influence. Three or four of us, including myself, were sent to Detroit to help Ziggy. One of us, a young woman from Brooklyn, took over as office secretary. She was the sloppiest typist I have ever seen, and her filing system consisted of throwing anything and everything into a cardboard box. But as a picket — a job she had to perform constantly — she was unsurpassed, altogether the best union secretary we could have had in that period. The rest of us did whatever was needed, acting as props to Ziggy. We wrote and distributed leaflets, hired halls, and went to organizing meetings, made contacts with nonunion workers at taverns or visited them in their homes, and published a local union paper.

Before long Local 205, which barely had four members a short time before, mushroomed to four thousand. We unionized some of NAFI's competitors in the fiber industry, such as Arvey's and Woodall's, then branched out in unrelated fields. I recall one occasion when we hired a hall that seated thirty people and gave out leaflets inviting workers of a certain shop to a meeting. Of the 275 employees more than 200 showed; we had to adjourn to a nearby parking lot, where all the workers present signed application cards for Local 205. Within a day or two, we were able to wrest from their employer a substantial wage increase.

It was an exhilarating time for young radicals. When I got on a bus, strangers were talking freely with each other, exchanging information about how the union drives were going in their shops. I have never seen anything like it before or since. "This must be," I thought to myself, "how things are during a revolution." When I first arrived in Detroit, I stayed with a big, hulking comrade, George Saul, and his wife, who was as short and slender as he was tall. They were good and kindly people, but they sometimes couldn't squeeze me in with the rest of their family. Frequently, then, after a day at the union office I would rake up a dime for an all-night movie downtown and sleep there. On other occasions, I would stretch out on a desk in the office, but apart from the fact that it was uncomfortable, sleep was often interrupted by night-shift workers who came by to make a report or get information.

One of the strangest interruptions I had, one that happened a number of times, was small groups of union members trekking into the office during the wee hours proud as punch that they had just disarmed a cop. They would unload a billy club, a badge, and a gun on my desk and give me the gory details of how they had acquired them from one of Detroit's finest. Once they came by with an inspector's badge. This wasn't the kind of "class struggle" we were preaching, and we ultimately talked them out of this practice, but it testifies to the strange operation of working-class minds. Just weeks before, many of these workers were hesitant about joining the union; now they had gone full circle to one of the most revolutionary of all activities, disarming the state. Years later when I published my first book on labor — *Left, Right and Center* — I explained this strange phenomenon on the theory that workers undergo a saturation process — they silently absorb one affront after another until a moment is finally reached when they are saturated with the abuses heaped on them. At that point they strike back with all their pent up anger. That is what happened in the red decade and why we radicals were so in tune with the times. "The workers take to our line," read an item in the RWL internal bulletin, "like ducks to water." It was true.

We did what the workers wanted done. Once Ziggy uncovered a couple of industrial spies at NAFI — they had left on a desk a memo that a worker read and confiscated. We shut the plant down, called a meeting in the factory yard, and, while the spies turned eight different colors, berated them and the company with militant speeches. It was a lesson in the realities of industrial strife and it greatly strengthened the sense of union solidarity inside the plant. The spies were allowed to take their belongings and leave the shop untouched, though they were roughed up a bit on their way home.

On another occasion, we had a confrontation with the police that set my adrenalin running. One of our comrades had secured a job at a sheet metal plant that employed fifty-five or sixty workers, had enrolled everyone into Local 205, and was now leading them in a sit-down strike. The RWL policy, hammered out after considerable debate, was to have some of the workers sit inside the factory and some picket outside; in that way the police would have greater difficulty invading the plant. Thus we had about thirty workers inside and a picket line outside of about an equal number over which I was in charge. The police, harried by sit-down strikes from one end of Detroit to the other, were hoping to put an end to the practice by evicting sit-downers as an example to the others. This small sheet metal plant seemed ideal for their purposes, and before long we were looking at an army of more than one hundred cops, with mounted guns, helmets, tear gas, and other paraphernalia of the trade. "Who's in charge here," the captain asked. I said I was. He gave me fifteen minutes to clear the strikers out of the factory. I took him to a window, looking inside where piles of sheet steel, weighing sixty or seventy tons, were stacked. I pointed to a crane operator moving his crane about. "If you attack us," I told the captain, "he's going to push those piles of metal through the building (which sloped downward and directly into the police lines). If you don't take your men and guns out of here in ten minutes, that crane starts moving." I doubt that we would have carried out that threat unless the cops started shooting, but the captain decided that perhaps this wasn't the best place to have a showdown after all; he withdrew. We won our strike a few hours later.

Ultimately, though, the police did have their victory. A group of 144 women sitting-in at a metal products plant — Yale Towne — were given an ultimatum to get out. During the night, Walter Reuther climbed in through a window to show his support for the embattled women, and scores of local unions waited for a signal to come to their defense. By an odd happenstance, which was probably not so odd, one union after another suddenly found its telephones out of order. By the time we got the word that the authorities were poised to attack, the plant was surrounded by police. Even so, thousands of union members, the largest contingent coming from the nearby Kelsey-Hayes plant, showed up for a mass picket line. We shut down a couple of our plants and gave workers picket "signs" that read LOCAL 205 and were attached to short two-by-two pieces of wood, beveled on one side. In case of attack, the "sign" could be torn away and the stick wielded like a club. When our contingent of automobiles reached the scene Vic Reuther, Walter's brother, was in a sound truck talking to the assemblage. For a while it looked as if the police might back off, but then it began to rain, the crowd thinned out, Vic Reuther urged us to leave, and the cops attacked mercilessly. I wasn't hurt, but the chap next to me was laid low by a crack on the head and we had to take him to a hospital. The young women — and Walter Reuther — were evicted.

Despite such setbacks, radicals were immensely successful from 1934 to 1937 "organizing the unorganized." The problem for leftist groups was taking the next step, moving from control of a single local union to leadership of an effective force within the national unions already in existence or in the process of being formed. The Trotskyites had succeeded for a while in building a good-sized base within the teamsters union throughout the Midwest, but they lost that base within six or seven years under the slashing attacks by teamster president Dan Tobin, which culminated in prosecution of their leaders and the national Trotskyite leaders by Franklin Roosevelt's Justice Department, under the Smith Act. Harry Bridges and his communist allies fared much better on the West Coast after the 1934 longshoremen's strike, extending their influence far and wide in the Pacific states.

The RWL, too, had a rank-and-file base from which to start and we developed good personal relations with many of the noncommunist officials in the UAW — men like Dick Frankensteen, a national vice president and leader of the Dodge workers; Morris Field, his assistant; Francis Henson, administrative aide to UAW president Homer Martin, a man with whom I had become friends when Oehler sent me into his left-wing Socialist Party caucus in 1935; and quite a few others. And we also became allies of a number of local union leaders, such as those of a Chrysler local involved in the sit-downs, who were not members of any political group. We were far from being pariahs, but we vitiated our potential by self-isolating purism on the one hand and by imposing such rigid discipline on the president of Local 205, our comrade Ziggy, that he finally deserted us.

We stood apart from the other radical groups in the UAW because we were convinced that rank-and-file militancy would reach beyond the limits set by CIO president John L. Lewis — which it did — as well as the limits set by the communists or Lovestoneites — which it didn't. In the name of Local 205, for instance, we printed and distributed 25,000 copies of a one-page union paper calling for recruiting squads to organize other factories, and a closed shop in the auto industry. Those were understandable goals and met with warm reception from UAW members. But as a political group, the RWL distributed a newspaper — also a one-pager — at a demonstration of 50,000 UAW members at Cadillac Square in the center of town, calling for a general strike to win the six-hour day, five-day week, as well as demanding workers' control of production. I felt instinctively, as a dozen of us were giving out this sheet, that we were too advanced for the circumstances; I fully expected to have our papers torn from us and be beaten up. The workers, to my surprise, were most friendly, many of them taking stacks of the paper and helping us distribute it; yet, if given the opportunity, not 1 percent of that crowd would have opted for a general strike to win the six-hour day, and not even that number felt that workers' control of production was a realistic demand for the foreseeable future.

Another example of purism was our attack on the settlement made by John L. Lewis with Governor Frank Murphy and the General Motors hierarchs to evacuate the sit-down strikers from GM plants early in 1937. The main demand of that sit-down strike (organized and led by the communists) was a single word, *sole* — sole collective bargaining rights. GM had offered bargaining rights to any and all unions, as a ruse to retain and strengthen its own company unions. The UAW and the GM workers therefore demanded *sole* bargaining rights — to exclude the company unions. Lewis's agreement did not contain that word, and we of the RWL distributed a leaflet to the delegates called together in Detroit to ratify the agreement, urging that they reject the pact and return to the picket lines. We called the agreement a sellout. In the strict sense, viewed in a vacuum, it was. In fact, however, it was one of the most important victories the American labor movement has achieved in this century. For, even though the word *sole* was not won in the written agreement, the sit-down had shaken GM. Hundreds of subsequent mini-sitdowns — over local grievances — shook it further. Sole collective bargaining became a reality, and was written into the next agreement. Had we been a little less intemperate, our leaflet would have stated that it was unfortunate that the word *sole* was not included in the agreement, but acclaimed the strike itself as a victory that would pay dividends in the future if its spirit of militancy were retained. The GM workers *felt* they had won; for us to say that they had lost isolated us from them and from many secondary union leaders to whom we could have drawn closer.

The other side of this purist attitude was a growing tension between the RWL leadership, which insisted on further "politicalization" — that is, raising the issue of a six-hour day, worker control of production, and so on — and Ziggy, who was pressed by the mundane problems of serving his membership. A middle ground could have been found, perhaps, but it wasn't and the recriminations became ever sharper until Ziggy resigned from the league, leaving us with nothing but a memory for our efforts. We had recruited almost no one into the RWL itself, and we had no base in Local 205 capable of doing an end run around Ziggy. Though our small group was made up of competent tacticians, writers, and organizers, we lost an opportunity to root ourselves in the most important union of the day — the UAW — and with it the best chance to overcome our isolation.

II

By 1934, it was no longer a question as to whether the millions of unorganized workers would form unions — but under whose auspices they would do it. Hundreds of important strikes broke out in the first two years of the New Deal, most of them spontaneously. Attesting to the fierceness of the strike wave were the figures on casualties. From August through October 1933 fifteen strikers were killed on the picket line, another forty were slain in 1934, and forty-eight in the next two years. From mid-1933 to the end of 1934 troops were called out to quell strikes in sixteen of the forty-eight states.

The impulse for unionization did not come from the leadership of the AFL; more often than not it was a spontaneous action. A group of workers enraged over wages or an unresolved grievance would be taken in hand by a leftist fellow worker who knew just what to do under the circumstances, or, if not, where to get the best advice. The radicals brought to their task a number of a priori concepts, which were immensely helpful in organizing the unorganized. They opposed in principle any collaboration with business. They considered the government an implacable enemy to be fought without restraint. And they were unequivocal about the "labor fakers" — heads of the established unions — whom they thought of as concubines of the employers and the state, to be opposed with equal vigor.

So sizable was the influx of workers into the labor movement that from July 1933 to July 1934 the AFL, then led by William Green, issued 1,300 federal charters — charters for unions affiliated directly with the AFL itself rather than to national unions of their trade. This was five times as many as in the previous five years. In 1933, 1.2 million workers went on strike and, in 1934, 1.5 million, five times the number two years before. There were so many federal locals being formed and so many independent unions outside the AFL that Charles P. Howard, a founder of the CIO, was constrained to say at the 1935 AFL convention: "I don't know, there is no one at this convention who knows . . . how many workers have been organized into independent unions, company unions and associations that may have affiliation with subversive influences during the past few years." The number, he said, was "far greater than any one of us would grant."

In 1934, four pivotal strikes — three startlingly victorious, one defeated — pointed the way. The West Coast longshoremen's strike that began in May had its roots in the rank-and-file Committee of 500 formed by an Australian dockworker, Alfred Renton ("Harry") Bridges a year earlier. By the end of that month, it had spread to other maritime unions, embracing 35,000 workers from Vancouver in the north to San Diego in the south. "It is a different strike from any the Coast has ever known," reported Evelyn Seely in *The Nation.* Bridges, though not a Communist Party member himself, was close to the party and surrounded by many of its members. True to the tradition of the left he did not trust the U.S. Department of Labor, which twice tried to have the strike postponed (so that "a plentiful supply of student scabs might be obtained" by the employers when the college semester ended, according to communist longshore leader Sam Darcy), the employers, or "King" Joe Ryan and William Lewis, leaders of the International Longshoremen's Union, who had a strange habit of signing agreements with the companies without the advice or consent of the membership.

Bridges introduced three creative tactics in the strike. The first was mass picketing. One thousand men stood watch at the Embarcadero in twelve-hour shifts, day and night, weekends and holidays, to guard against strikebreakers. No sensible person would have tried to cross that picket line without a few squads of police to shepherd him through, and even then might have hesitated. Similar tough picket lines existed elsewhere. In Portland one day twenty-five strikebreakers were tossed into the Wilamette River. In San Pedro, pickets stormed a stockade housing strikebreakers, leaving one of them dead. The second novel aspect of Bridges's strategy was the expansion of the strike to include marine workers and teamsters. As each ship came to port, its crew was met by longshoremen as well as representatives of Marine Workers Industrial Union, and urged to declare a sympathy walkout. And despite the original opposition of the teamsters union leadership, Bridges was also able to win the support of truck drivers who hauled cargo from the piers to warehouses and railroads, and vice versa. Michael Casey, president for forty years of the teamsters in San Francisco, at first refused to help the longshoremen, but rank-and-file drivers, approached by pickets on the docks, overwhelmed his opposition. The third distinctive feature of Bridges's strategy was the formation of a Joint Strike Committee of fifty members, five from each of the ten unions on strike, with Bridges as chairperson. The committee was pledged not to end the stoppage or return to work until *all* the unions had won individual agreements they considered satisfactory.

Events showed that it was the radical distrust of employers, the government, and the "labor fakers" that finally guaranteed victory. A secret agreement made in mid-June by Assistant Secretary of Labor Edward F. McGrady with King Joe Ryan was repudiated by the workers; then on July 3 the police and employers tried to run five loaded trucks through the picket line at the Embarcadero. For four hours a battle flared, while tens of thousands of San Franciscans watched from nearby hills. One picket was killed, a couple of dozen badly hurt. Two days later the entire city police force charged the pickets, hurling vomiting gas and shooting off revolvers — the pickets were dispersed. The "war" however was not yet over — large numbers of workers from other unions joined their beleaguered longshore brothers. Again the casualties were high. Two strikers were killed, two subsequently died; hundreds of pickets, police, and onlookers were injured, at least 115 of them requiring hospitalization. The incident so outraged San Francisco unionists that for three days 127,000 of them — defying an order of AFL president William Green — struck in sympathy with the longshoremen. After three months, the strike ended in arbitration and a substantial victory.

The strike called by AFL Federal Local 18384 against the Auto-Lite company and two of its subsidiaries in Toledo, Ohio, was led by George F. Addes, a swarthy young man who would eventually become secretary-treasurer of the UAW. The first job action at Auto-Lite was quickly terminated by AFL officials, who under AFL rules had total veto rights over a federal local. A month and a half later, however, after a disenchanting experience with another one of Roosevelt's wonders, the Auto Labor Board, 4,000 Auto-Lite workers took to the streets again. This time their strike fell into disarray when a judge issued an injunction limiting the number of pickets to twenty-five, and the company recruited 1,800 strikebreakers. At this point, the Lucas County Unemployed League, headed by two Musteites, Sam Pollock and Ted Selander, decided to take over the picketing duties, in open violation of the injunction. On the first day, 1,000 unemployed were mobilized, the next day 4,000, and the day after 6,000. The league's leaders were arrested, tried, and released with a warning, only to go back from the court room to the picket line.

There was a stalemate for a while, but a couple of weeks later a small incident shattered the calm. A strikebreaker inside the plant hurled a bolt that hit a woman picket and hospitalized her. By the time a hundred police arrived to escort more scabs through the lines tempers were out of control. Scabs lofted tear gas bombs from upper factory windows, pickets responded with bricks as they choked from the gas fumes. But they would not yield as police with swinging clubs tried to clear a lane for the scabs. Fifteen hours later 900 National Guardsmen arrived to rescue the men inside. For the next six days the combat continued, this time against the guardsmen. The confused troops, subjected to taunts and attempted proselytizing by women pickets, finally shot into the crowd killing two and wounding two dozen. The pickets retaliated, attacking guardsmen in a six-block zone. In a few days, the state government ordered the troops removed, the company closed its plant, and, after a demonstration of 40,000 people in a city of 275,000 and a strike threat by 98 of the 99 local unions, the company caved in. The Auto-Lite strike had a major domino effect in unionizing the whole auto industry.

The three Minneapolis strikes followed the same pattern as the other two, except that they were, if anything, conducted with greater military precision. The saga began when a middle-aged Swede, a Trotskyite named Karl Skoglund, organized drivers of 67 coal companies and led them in a successful strike. The campaign then widened as four other Trotskyite leaders, the three Dunne brothers — Vincent, Grant, and Miles — and Farrell Dobbs recruited 3,000 inside warehousemen to Local 574 of the teamsters. When employers balked at granting them recognition the warehousemen and 2,000 drivers "hit the bricks." The Dunnes and Dobbs adopted a unique tactic to assure that the walkout was total. They organized "flying squadrons" to roam the area and close down operations. The fleet of automobiles used by the flying squadrons found opposition only among gas station owners, but after pickets in a hundred cars demolished a few gas pumps the gas stations too were quiet.

The nerve center of the strike was the garage headquarters at 1900 Chicago Avenue, with a great Local 574 banner under its rooftop, which served as a refuge where thousands slept and ate, an auditorium for union meetings, a hospital and first-aid center, and a dispatch center for the flying squadrons. Here, as with the West Coast waterfront strike, the strategy was to spread the strike as far as possible. On the second day, cab drivers left their taxis; a few days later 35,000 building trades workers joined the strike, to be followed by 10,000 streetcar employees.

The denouement came in a violent confrontation between strikers and a so-called Citizens' Alliance on May 21 and 22, as police and deputies prepared to move perishable goods from the closed-down central market. Local 574 was ready. It had secreted 600 men in the Central Labor Union office and held another 900 in reserve at the garage. Small squads spread inconspicuously inside the market. At the appointed time, the Central Labor Union contingent marched from one side and the headquarters group from another, completely surrounding the police and 1,000 deputies. They swung pipes, clubs, and bricks. At the peak of the fight a driver with 25 pickets on his truck drove headlong into the police to prevent them from using guns. The winner this day was the union: 30 police hospitalized, no trucks moved. The next day — called the Battle of Deputies Run — there was less planning but there were more people involved, 20,000 workers against 2,000 police. By nightfall the deputies had been routed, two of their people killed, including the lawyer for the Citizens' Alliance, and hundreds were injured. Governor Floyd Olson effected a truce and called out the Guard, but the union had won its main demand, recognition of both the drivers and the inside workers. An ambiguity over the term *recognition,* unfortunately, led to a third strike in July — more violence, 55 pickets shot and two killed, a raid on union headquarters by the National Guard, but total labor solidarity in Minneapolis. In the end, after five weeks, the employers conceded defeat.

Dan Tobin, head of the national teamsters union — which then had only 95,000 members — berated the strike leaders as "radicals and communists," but in fact they built his union as it had never been built before. Every time an out-of-town driver came to a dock or warehouse in Minneapolis he was forced to show a union card or was turned back with his truck unloaded. In this way, the union in Minneapolis, and then in other cities, brought into the fold the intercity drivers, without whom the present teamsters union would have been — as Jimmy Hoffa admitted to me a number of times — a shell.

The one big strike that was defeated in 1934 involved operatives in the textile industry, who were protesting the fact that the NRA minimum wage of $12 to $13 a week was being violated and a "stretch-out" was increasing workloads by 25, 50, and even 100 percent. The strike affected 364,795 workers, from New England to the deep South. Flying squads shut down one mill after another and challenged tens of thousands of National Guardsmen, police, sheriff's deputies, private police, and vigilantes. Governor Eugene Talmadge of Georgia declared martial law and opened a concentration camp for "disorderly" strikers. Thirteen strikers were slain, six in a confrontation between deputies and a flying squadron near Greenville, South Carolina. No one can tell what might have happened if the stoppage had followed a normal course. On September 22, however, though the strike was by no means crushed, its leaders Francis Gorman and Thomas McMahon decided to accept a Roosevelt offer to end the walkout and turn over the matter of enforcement of the NRA wage codes to the Textile Labor Relations Board. As might have been expected, the board proved to be either impotent or disingenuous or both. In any case the workers gained nothing. Fifteen thousand of the more militant unionists never got their jobs back, and in some factories returning laborers had to sign "yellow dog" contracts, stating that they would not join a union. The stretch-out remained unchanged, wages continued at $10 a week or less, and the union's roster fell to 79,200 by August 1935.

III

The strikes of 1933 and 1934, sensational as they were, were essentially a prelude to greater events. The road was now open to storm industrial fortresses like United States Steel, which had resisted unionization for decades. The immediate obstacle was the craft-minded AFL leaders —

lurking in fear that a new generation of militants would swamp them. Green and his friends reacted with transparent guile. They couldn't turn their backs on what was happening; what they did, therefore, was grant *federal* charters to industrial workers who asked for affiliation. Since the federal charter vested in Green all power over the locals, their treasuries, and their right to call strikes, the new unionists were effectively controlled. When the tempest died down, Green intended to dissolve those locals and divide their members among the appropriate craft organizations.

Opposing Green in these calculations were a group of middle-of-the-road leaders like John L. Lewis of the miners and Sidney Hillman of the Amalgamated Clothing Workers (a former socialist), who decided that the way to checkmate the radicals was to assume leadership of the movement themselves. The issue came to a head at the 1935 AFL convention. "I stand here," Lewis told the delegates, "and plead for a policy . . . that will protect our form of government against the isms and the philosophies of foreign lands that now seem to be rampant in high and low places throughout the country." What he wanted the AFL to do was to charter vertical (industrial) unions in mass-production industries, such as auto, rubber, packinghouse, and steel, so that control would rest with the moderates rather than the far left. If the AFL itself took the initiative, he reasoned, the radicals would be relegated to secondary roles. When Lewis's advice went unheeded (it was turned down by a vote of two to one), eight national unions, with approximately one million members, formed a caucus, the Committee for Industrial Organization — and later, after they were expelled, adopted a name with the same acronym, the Congress of Industrial Organizations.

The break came at a favorable time. The communists had made a shift in policy, giving up their dual organization, the Trade Union Unity League, and agreeing to work within the established labor movement. In 1932 William Z. Foster had called Lewis and the other AFL leaders "practically open fascists." Now party members were willing to work for them, and scores of communists were put on the CIO payroll.

Though at the top the CIO was run by old-line officials like Lewis, Hillman, and Philip Murray, one notch below was an assortment of leftists, with the communists predominating, who actually did the grass-roots work. In a book published years later, Foster claimed that of the staff of two hundred hired by the CIO Steel Workers Organizing Committee, sixty were Communist Party members, including Gus Hall, future secretary of the party. How many were sympathizers is not known, but it must have been a substantial number because, according to labor historian Bert Cochran, thirty-one or thirty-two of thirty-three Steel Worker Organization Committee staff members in Chicago attended communist caucuses. When Lewis was asked why he hired so many communists, he quipped: "Who gets the bird, the hunter or the dog?" The CIO succeeded, as Lewis had hoped, in containing radicalism, but not before the communists had secured control of such unions as the electrical workers (headed by a noncommunist, James B. Carey, but run by a communist, Julius Emspak), the transport workers (headed by a man who was then a fellow-traveler, Mike Quill), the maritime union (headed by another fellow-traveler, Joseph Curran), the shipbuilders, fur workers, packinghouse workers, Bridges's longshoremen, and more. Most important, the communists, in alliance with the Reuthers and George Addes, predominated in the key organization of that period, the UAW; and its faction leader, Wyndham Mortimer, probably could have taken over the presidency of the UAW had the party willed it.

The use of the sit-down strike technique was also important in forging unions in the mass-production industries. Picket lines outside a plant were vulnerable to attack by police or troops. But by seizing a plant and sitting-in, strikers gained a measure of immunity, since corporations were loath to have police battle workers in the vicinity of expensive machinery. The sit-down was an old technique that had been used by the Wobblies as far back as the 1906 strike at General Electric in Schenectady. It was now applied on a broad front. In the nine months from September 1936 to

June 1937 almost a half million American workers seized their factories. There were 150 "quickie" sit-downs in the rubber plants alone, lasting from half an hour to four days. All told, from 1935 through 1937 there were at least 900 sit-downs.

Things had a way of happening almost by accident in the red decade; the bitterness underneath came to a surface after what would ordinarily be considered minor provocation. Thus in January 1936 there was a small flare-up at the Firestone rubber plant in Akron, Ohio. One of the company's pacemakers — one who speeds up operations, forcing all those behind to keep pace — was forcibly slowed down by his fellow workers. A fight ensued and one of the union men (the union was small and not yet recognized) was fired. Usually such incidents ended at this point; this time the other workers demanded that the discharge be rescinded. When the company refused, the workers stopped work and sat down near their machines. No one planned this; it just happened. The machines shut off one by one; by 2 A.M., January 29, the whole plant was in absolute silence. "Jesus Christ," yelled out one worker, "it's like the end of the world." The sit-down lasted three days and was a complete success; the union man was reinstated, the company agreed to reduce speedup. Four hundred triumphant Firestone workers, who had previously drifted away from the union, rejoined.

Not long thereafter, in mid-February 1936, the CIO met its first major test at the Goodyear plant, also in Akron. The immediate cause of the trouble was the discharge of 137 workers on the third shift. Under the NRA code for the rubber industry, the work day had been set at six hours, but Goodyear decided to raise it to eight, thereby reducing the number on the staff. This was the last straw for the men who had taken two wage cuts — in November 1935 and January 1936 — from a company that earned a profit of $5.5 million. Management was confident it could contain any protest — there was a pliant company union on the scene as well as the thugs of the Pearl Berghoff detective agency. The Rubber

Workers Union on the other hand had only 200 members in a plant with 14,000 workers. But on the night of February 17, in bitter cold with temperatures reaching nine below zero and a forty-five-mile-an-hour wind blowing, thousands of men poured out of the largest rubber plant in the world to establish an eleven-mile picket line around the company's fences and gates, and build sixty-nine shanties of tin, paper, and wood as picket stations. By the second day, 10,000 employees had joined the walkout — and rejoined a union they had deserted the previous year when William Green refused to sanction a strike. Now Lewis sent in some of his best people — Powers Hapgood, Leo Krzycki, McAlister Coleman (all Socialist Party members), as well as other firebrands — to manage the strike, not call it off! War veterans in the union's ranks began regular military drills for the expected showdown with a vigilante group called the Law and Order League. On the day the attack was expected CIO officials leased a radio station all day so they could inform workers in the area when to mobilize. The showdown never came, but after four weeks Goodyear entered into negotiations and a week or so later agreed to recognize the union, reinstate the discharged workers, grant seniority rights, and reduce the workweek to thirty-six hours.

Everywhere similar dramas were underway — in the radio and electrical, packinghouse, glass, transport, office and professional, oil, shipbuilding, even newspaper industries. Unlike Green and the AFL, John L. Lewis and organization director John Brophy (another old radical who had fought Lewis in the miners' union), encouraged these efforts with money and organizers. The CIO's main concentration was in the steel cities where Murray opened thirty-five regional offices. I was in Detroit at the time, working with Local 205. The CIO office was so starved for organizers — because most were assigned to the steel drive — that when I asked someone to come out to the plant I was unionizing — a fire extinguisher factory — I was told that all the office could do was give me a few hundred application cards to pass out.

Contrary to Lewis's expectations, however, the critical

moment for the CIO came in auto, not steel. The single event that everyone concedes gave wings to the CIO was the sit-down strike at General Motors from late December 1936 to February 1937. It was not on John L. Lewis's agenda, for he was concentrating on steel and was opposed to sit-down strikes as a matter of principle. But Mortimer and one of his protégés Robert Travis had worked out the meticulous details for shutting down GM, the largest auto company in the world. They planned to immobilize the company by striking the Fisher Body factories in Cleveland and Flint, "mother plants" that produced three fourths of the body stampings for the entire GM empire. The strike was to begin after the new year, 1937, but as luck would have it a trivial disagreement in Cleveland — management's postponement of a meeting to discuss wage-cutting with the union committee — caused 7,000 workers to walk out and 1,000 men and women to sit-in. GM, not unaware of the union's strategy, would have been happy to resolve the Cleveland dispute at this point, but Mortimer decreed "no settlement without a national agreement."

Two days later, on December 30, the strike spread to Flint. Travis received word from John "Chink" Ananich of Fisher One that the company was moving dies out of the plant — obviously to carry out its operations elsewhere. Travis ordered the plant seized, and while he, Roy Reuther (the third Reuther brother), and Henry Kraus waited outside 3,000 workers completed the occupation. A few hours later, a grievance over the transfer of two employees at Fisher Two led to a sit-down in a smaller GM shop two miles across town.

Organization of the forty-four-day stay-in by Travis, Reuther, Kraus, and others (mostly communists) was as impressive as it was complicated. The 500 to 1,000 men holed up at Fisher One (women were sent home) had to be molded into a disciplined force. A plant committee was enlarged to include representatives from each department, and its word was law — subject to review by the membership, which met every night. The workers themselves were divided into "families" of fifteen, each headed by a captain, each finding its own nook in which to set up house. Sleeping facilities were either car-cushion wadding placed on the floor or the inside of unfinished auto bodies, which were lovingly referred to as the Mills Hotel, Hotel Astor, and so on. Food — hot meals — was prepared by a women's auxiliary outside the plant and brought in. Every man was required to shower each day and put in six hours of work — in the kitchen, on patrol duty at the gates, sweeping the floor. For relaxation there were Ping-Pong games, books, magazines, even some boxing. Two UAW educators taught classes on labor history, how to conduct a meeting, and other relevant union subjects. Each evening before the regular meetings there was an hour of entertainment and singing, most of it provided by sympathetic artists outside. What had begun as an unformed mass was thus converted into an effective community. Clubs of wood and Leatherette were manufactured to defend the premises against police or National Guard invasion — I got one of them after the strike and kept it for fifteen or twenty years until someone made off with it from my home. Special patrols saw to it that there was no drinking and no rowdiness that might destroy property. (On New Year's Day company police smuggled in liquor and two prostitutes, causing a severe deterioration of discipline — but only temporarily, until the strike committee tightened it again.)

As Mortimer had anticipated, the simultaneous strikes at the two Fisher plants had a paralyzing effect on all GM operations. As of January 11, 1937, three quarters of all blue-collar employees at GM were idle, either because they had joined the strike or because the company had been forced to close operations where they worked.

Stunned, the colossus of the auto industry, which earned profits of $228 million in 1936, struck back early with time-tested methods. GM attorneys secured an injunction ordering the sit-downers not only to leave the plant but to refrain from picketing outside as well. The sheriff had trouble serving the papers; then it was discovered that the judge who had issued the injunction owned $219,000 worth of GM stock. Back-to-work efforts were similarly unsuccessful. The next gambit was more direct, an amazingly maladroit effort by GM and the police to evict the sit-downers in the small Fisher Two shop — resulting in the most famous skirmish in CIO history, the Battle of Bulls' Run or the Battle of the Running Bulls. There was no need to evict these strikers because Fisher Two had no strategic significance, but GM wanted to hammer home an object lesson. The eviction plan was simple: deny heat and food to the strikers, then find a pretext for the physical siege. In sixteen-degree weather on January 11, 1937, and with the temperature due to fall further, the company shut off the heat. A few hours later, union supporters carrying the evening dinner to sit-downers were denied entry to the plant — for the first time. Anxious to avoid a fight the pickets raised a twenty-four-foot ladder to the second-floor windows and tried to haul the food in that way. But the guards formed a phalanx and captured the ladder.

All this, of course, brought union reinforcements from all parts of the Midwest. Meanwhile a minor skirmish occurred in which twenty tough strikers, armed with clubs they had manufactured, descended the stairs, broke down the locks of the gate that the guard captain had closed, and drove the guards on the ground floor into the women's washroom. This was the pretext for police and deputies to invade the plant — to rescue the "kidnapped" guards. Victor Reuther, microphone in hand, stood nearby exhorting the unionists not to yield. Women alternately argued and pleaded with police to let food into the plant. Early in the morning pickets temporarily broke through police lines, but were met with tear gas and buckshot. "We wanted peace," shouted Vic Reuther, "General Motors chose war. Give it to them." The war went on for three hours, with the strikers inside turning a water hose against their tormentors and using slingshots to hurl door hinges at them. Police responded with buckshot and bullets. Bob Travis was carried off to Hurley Hospital with gas burns from a tear gas grenade. Fourteen union men were wounded, thirty-six police were taken to the hospital. At midnight, five hours after the fighting had begun, the police made another attempt to rush the plant and were again driven off by the strikers' high-pressure water hose and a rain of missiles. The Battle of Bulls' Run was over — the Bulls had run. GM made no further effort to retake any of its plants, even when Travis and his subalterns arranged the seizure of additional factories in Flint early in February, including the indispensable Chevy Four plant where motors were made. Governor Frank Murphy, considered an outstanding liberal, threatened to put state militia around Chevy Four, but Walter Reuther, who was at the scene with his Detroit West Side local members, threatened to start a bonfire in the plant if the governor turned off the heat or called out the troops. At the same time, at Fisher One, 5,000 pickets armed with pipes, clubs, and crowbars were gathered to ward off an expected attack following the UAW's ignoring of a judge's injunction and the threat of a $15 million fine to halt the strike on February 2.

Under these tense circumstances the strike was settled by Lewis without winning the precious word *sole* — sole collective bargaining rights. The company agreed only to bargain. Fortunately, however, the spin-off of the sit-down strike was such that the union gained its major objective in short order. Just after the settlement there were eighteen additional sit-downs in GM plants within twenty days. A few months later, a larger stay-in occurred involving 59,000 Chrysler workers in Detroit. This time the atmosphere was less tense, as thousands of workers sat peaceably inside the Chrysler shops. One or two of my comrades and I climbed through the windows of one of the plants periodically for a few hours at a time, but there was no feeling of danger. At one point, when a rumor spread that the National Guard might make an effort to eject the strikers, 50,000 people congregated in front of the Dodge Main plant in Hamtramck (an independent community completely surrounded by Detroit). No confrontation came, however, even the most headstrong employer or politician realized by now that the third strike wave during the New Deal could not be set back. On the lips of innumerable workers in countless industries was the mystical word *sit-down*. A month after the conclusion of the GM war there were 247 stay-ins involving 193,000 workers, from Chrysler to dime-store employees, Western Union messengers, glass blowers, hotel workers, and even garbage collectors. Only two dozen sit-downs were smashed by police in the period from 1936 to 1937. The number of work stoppages in 1937, including sit-downs, was double what it had been in 1936 — 4,470 as against 2,172 — and embraced about 2 million unionists. The reign of the open shop had been halted; the morale of American workers was never higher.

On March 2, 1937, less than two months after the Battle of Bulls' Run, the nation heard the electrifying news that U.S. Steel had granted bargaining rights to SWOC (the Steel Workers Organizing Committee) for its major plants, had raised wages by 10 percent, reduced the workweek to forty hours, and granted time and a half for overtime. Without fanfare the big corporation had been negotiating with Lewis and Murray behind the scenes. According to "two financiers closely identified with Morgan interests," said the New York *World-Telegram*, the House of Morgan, which controlled U.S. Steel, had recognized "that complete industrial organization was inevitable . . ." Rather than face the prospect of long, violent sit-downs, and "hotheads" like the young labor leaders in auto, the Morgans accepted collective bargaining with Lewis and Phil Murray as the lesser evil. By the time of the Little Steel strike in May 1937 (in which eighteen workers were killed during the Memorial Day Massacre and 160 wounded), 140 firms with 300,000 workers had appended their names to SWOC contracts.

It is difficult to impart on ordinary paper the magic that surrounded the letters *C-I-O* in 1937. Millions were attracted to the union fold in just one year. John Brophy could report to the CIO conference in Atlantic City in October that the CIO had grown from a million members two years before to 4 million. There were thirty-two national unions in the new federation by that time, including sizable forces in rubber (75,000), textile (400,000), oil (100,000), transport (80,000), and in fur, municipal workers, longshore, aluminum, and of course in the two pivotal industries, auto and steel.

"It is inevitable," Nobel Prize–winning novelist Sinclair Lewis had said earlier, "that the Commitee for Industrial Organization will do to the American Federation of Labor what the Federation did to the Knights of Labor — namely put it out of business. Sinclair Lewis was wrong. We in the RWL, however, also believed that after 1937 there would be another big wave of strikes. We were present in Flint, Hamtramck, everywhere there was a picket line or a demonstration, talking, picketing, trying to proselytize, holding meetings — confident that there would be a new spurt of labor activity.

It didn't come. Nineteen thirty-eight was a Depression year. Lewis had already pledged an end to sit-down strikes, and as economic conditions slumped during that perilous year, the momentum of labor also slowed down. It had reached a peak of militancy that would never be duplicated in the next four decades.

Chapter 4
A Backlash of Defeats

I

The victories gained by American radicals for the working masses in the United States were more than counterbalanced by four catastrophes in Europe — a backlash of proletarian defeats. The worst, of course, was the 1933 ascension to power of Adolf Hitler in Germany. That tragedy could have been averted, I believe, if the communists and socialists had formed a united front and issued the call for a general strike. The two parties together were measurably stronger than the Nazis. But Stalin's position at the time was that fascism and social-democracy were not enemies but "twins." "Fascism," he said, "is the bourgeoisie's fighting organization that relies on the active support of Social Democracy. Social Democracy is objectively the moderate wing of fascism." With that as the basic premise it was obviously impossible to unite with the socialists to defend elemental democracy. In fact, so paranoid were the communists about the kinship of fascism and socialism that on August 9, 1931, they joined with the Nazis in a referendum against the socialist government of Prussia. Many years later the communists admitted that their policy had been wrong. Wilhelm Pieck, the post-World War II East German leader, pointed out that among the errors his party had made was failure to put "in the forefront the fight to defend democracy and the political rights of the masses," and the attack on "the Nazis and Social Democracy at one and the same time." Hitler was by no means certain of victory in 1933. There was serious opposition within his own party from Gregor and Otto Strasser who commanded thirty or forty deputies in parliament and were scheming to prevent Hitler's takeover. The Nazi steamroller seemed to have passed its peak in November 1932 when it polled 2 million *less* votes than in the previous election. In retrospect, it is obvious that it wasn't so much a matter of Hitler outmaneuvering the left, as the left outmaneuvering itself.

A second catastrophe was the defeat of the Austrian socialists by the neo-fascist Heimwehr forces and Chancellor Engelbert Dollfuss in February 1934. The socialists, under Otto Bauer, controlled the unions and the government of Vienna, but when they decided to resist the Heimwehr's seizure of power, everything seemed to go wrong — including a partly aborted call for a general strike because the socialist electrical workers union had failed to provide electricity for socialist printing presses when they walked off the job. The battle in Vienna, mostly in the area of the Karl Marx cooperative housing project, resulted in a thousand deaths, the hanging of nine socialist leaders, and still another defeat for radicalism in central Europe.

A third catastrophe, this time committed by the left itself, or more specifically the communist segment of the left, was the execution of innumerable leaders of the Soviet regime as "counter-revolutionaries." The Moscow Trials began in January 1935 with the conviction of nineteen people, including Zinoviev and Kamenev, two of Lenin's closest associates. The frame-ups — since confirmed as frame-ups by Khrushchev himself at the 20th Congress of the Soviet Communist Party in 1956 — continued through 1938, drawing into their maw virtually every leader of the Russian Revolution still alive, with the exception of Stalin, Molotov, and a handful of others. Trotsky, though not in the dock — he was in exile — was condemned to death in absentia and assassinated on Stalin's orders on August 20, 1949, by a Spanish communist and NKVD agent, Ramon Mercader. So far-reaching was Stalin's dragnet that as of the beginning of 1939 110 of the 139 members and candidates elected to the Central Committee of the Russian Communist Party less than five years earlier had been arrested.

It was difficult to explain all this to the average American. We were asked to believe that the generation of leaders that had made the revolution and led it in its first decade — Trotsky, Bukharin, Kamenev, Zinoviev, Radek, Piatakov, Rakovsky, Rykov, to mention a few — were spies for foreign powers, traitors, and counter-revolutionaries. Though there were some people who put credence in Stalin's charges, many lost faith in the very idea of socialism because "socialism was killing its own children." At open meetings where I spoke during this period the trials were cited repeatedly as proof that socialism doesn't work.

The fourth catastrophe of the 1930s was the victory of General Francisco Franco and his Phalangists in Spain after a bloody civil war that lasted for three years, from 1936 to 1939. Spain, a semi-feudal country, had removed its monarchy in April 1931 and after five years of indecisive Republican rule had just elected a popular-front government — with the support of socialists, the unions, communists, Trotskyites, syndicalists, even anarchists — when a mutiny in the army that began in Spanish Morocco spread to the mainland and erupted into civil war. Before the end of the year, Germany and Italy were supplying Franco's so-called Nationalists with weaponry, ships, advisors, pilots, and planes. While the Axis forces were for all practical purposes belligerents in the internal conflict, the Allied powers, for their own reasons, adopted a policy of neutrality and nonintervention. After a short period, during which France permitted men and supplies to cross into Spain, the borders were closed. Of the great powers only the Soviet Union sent appreciable aid to the Loyalist forces, and communists from many countries (including the 3,000-man Abraham Lincoln Brigade from the United States) went to Spain to fight against fascism.

There is no quarreling with the determination and courage of the communists, but we in the RWL and two groups in Spain with whom we established close relations — the left wing of the POUM (Workers Party of Marxist Unification), and a militant anarchist group called Friends of Durruti — differed fundamentally with communist policy in Spain. The communists and their socialist allies, we said, were fighting to save the Republic, not to make a socialist revolution. They argued that if there were to be a revolution it would have to take place *after* the war. We thought, on the other hand, that the two processes — war and revolution — had to go together because it would be impossible to sustain the fighting spirit of the Spanish people needed to defeat Franco unless workers and peasants could see immediate benefits for themselves, benefits such as the distribution of land to peasants — burdened for centuries by landlordism — the nationalization of key industries, worker control of production, and the like. In a pamphlet I wrote toward the end of hostilities, I drew a parallel between the popular-front government under socialist F. Largo Caballero in Spain and the Kerensky regime in Russia in mid-1917. The workers in Spain, I noted, had armed themselves "against the orders and wishes of the Peoples Front," seized control of segments of industry and the land, "established Soldiers Committees at the front" and "Anti-Fascist Committees" (Soviets) in the rear — most dramatically in Catalonia. "In this period, the first three months after the July uprising," I wrote, "the working class could and should have taken power and destroyed the remnants of the Capitalist State. But the 'leaders' of the masses instead put forth the idea of first winning the war against Franco." We criticized the communists and socialists for liquidating the independent committees.

We were especially critical of the communists for their suppression of the anarcho-syndicalist uprising in Barcelona in May 1937. As Hugh Thomas points out in his history *The Spanish Civil War,* "the real executive organ in Barcelona, and therefore of Catalonia, was the Anti-Fascist Militias Committee, which had been formed on July 23 [1936]" by the syndicalist CNT and the anarchists, with support from the POUM. "Barcelona thus became a proletarian town as Madrid never did. Expropriation was the rule — hotels, stores, banks, factories were either requisitioned or closed. Those that were requisitioned were run by managing committees of former technicians and workers." The anarchists were truly a formidable power, with their own radio station, eight newspapers, and many weeklies. Moreover they were quite successful militarily as well, their militias seizing and dividing landed estates in Catalonia as well as penetrating far into Aragon. But the socialists and communists considered them enemies and tried to liquidate their militias and integrate them into the regular army. The friction continued for the better part of a year until a civil war within the civil war broke out on May 3, 1937. It lasted for a week, under the leadership of the left wing within the anarchist movement, the Friends of Durruti, and the POUM, but was suppressed by the national government and the communists, at a cost of 900 dead and 2,500 wounded.

A few months after the shooting had started in 1936, the RWL sent one of its members, a cartographer named Russell Blackwell (he used the name Rosalio Negrete), to Spain to make contact with left-wingers in the anarchist and POUM movements. Negrete, a thin man with a delightful sense of humor, was not one of our theoreticians but he spoke Spanish fluently and could be depended on to mix easily with the comrades in Barcelona. Early in 1937, the RWL also dispatched its leading figure, Hugo Oehler, to the scene, hoping that the two could help forge a new political center. "There are no Workers Councils in Catalonia and in Spain as a whole that anyone knows of," Oehler wrote in his first report from Barcelona, February 18, 1937. "They have been destroyed by the leadership. In the factories the embryos exist. With proper line and party these embryos can again be brought to blossom. This is also true in the Peasants and Soldiers Sections." Oehler and Negrete made a good team; along with a Chicago professor and a couple of American Trotskyites and ex-Trotskyites they established excellent rapport with Spanish leftists. But they were foreigners and many of the Spaniards who might have promoted their version of a Marxist program were either killed at the front or executed — most notably Joaquin Maurin, leader of the POUM. Also, there really wasn't enough time to turn matters around, especially after the communists defeated the anarchists in Barcelona. In the wake of that defeat the authorities (with the communists in the van) arrested POUMists and anarchists with abandon, also clapping Oehler in jail — a sure sign that his activities bothered them — on the charge of being a "Franco spy." It took a good part of our energies and most of our money back home to win Oehler's release. Subsequently we had to mount a similar campaign for Negrete, who was held in jail for a considerably longer period.

When 200,000 Franco troops marched into Madrid on March 28, 1939, they wrote finis to the Spanish Revolution and set back the radical movement everywhere else. I think James P. Cannon was right when he wrote years later that "The Spanish revolution had within it the possibility of changing the whole face of Europe if it should succeed." Alas, it didn't.

II

There was no counter-revolution in the United States like those in parts of Europe, but after a few brief years the labor and leftist surge of the mid-decade spent itself, and the nation again veered to the right. The brief depression in 1938 caused production to tumble by 20 percent in just a few months — a sharper downturn than that at the onset of the Great Depression. Then on January 4, 1939, Franklin Roosevelt gently laid his New Deal to rest. "We have now passed the period of internal conflict," he told Congress. Henceforth the task would be to preserve rather than expand reforms. The New Deal, as historian William E. Leuchtenberg observed, "never demonstrated that it could achieve prosperity in peacetime"; nor did it solve the problem of joblessness. Unemployment dropped from about a quarter of the workforce in 1933 to a fifth in 1939; even as late as 1940 the unemployment rate was 14.6 percent. But by this time the agitation in the streets and factories was modest; WPA strikes, eviction struggles, and rural violence were episodic; and the various reform panaceas like the Townsend Plan (which promised $200 a month for the aged) were on the road to oblivion. The communists were safely on Roosevelt's bandwagon — at least for the time being — and though the labor movement was three times as large as in 1933 and ensconced in the mass-production industries for the first time, the sit-down strike that sparked that growth was a thing of the past, and the conservative AFL, which many thought would be inundated by the CIO, was making a surprising recovery. Roosevelt, as he once boasted, had saved capitalism; he could back away from the New Deal with little fear of popular retribution.

Most of us on the left had an uneasy feeling that the "class peace" Roosevelt had achieved was the planned prelude to America's participation in a new and far worse conflagration than the one of 1914–1918. "Roosevelt primes for war," read the lead article of the *Fighting Worker* on June 1, 1938, a warning repeated constantly. In January 1939, the prestigious firm Lloyds of London was giving odds of 32 to 1 that there would be no war in Europe that year, but Lloyds was very wrong. What had been an economic crisis was about to metamorphose into an international military crisis. Capitalism did not solve its domestic problems; it simply transferred them from one arena to another.

Toward the end of August 1939 Americans picked up their newspapers to learn that Soviet Russia and Nazi Germany had signed a "nonaggression" pact. It was unbelievable. An arrangement with the Nazi butcher, Hitler? Impossible. Six weeks earlier Earl Browder had stated at an institute in Virginia that "there is about as much chance of such an agreement [between Germany and Russia] as of Earl Browder being elected president of the American Chamber of Commerce." In an interview with the press after the pact was announced, Browder insisted that there must be an "escape clause" that would give Stalin the right to repudiate it if Hitler invaded Poland or Rumania. Another Communist Party official went further, predicting that if Poland was attacked by Germany, the Soviet Union would come to its aid. Shortly thereafter the Wehrmacht seized the western half of Poland, the Red Army the eastern half.

On September 3, the day Britain and France declared war on Germany, Roosevelt told the American people: "I hope the United States will keep out of this war. I believe that it will. And I give you assurances that every effort of your government will be directed toward that end." The Democratic Party platform on which FDR ran the following year for an unprecedented third term was even more forthright: "We will not participate in foreign wars, and we will not send our Army, naval, or air forces to fight in foreign lands, outside of the Americas, except in case of attack." Speaking in Boston during the 1940 campaign, Roosevelt repeated a theme he referred to often: "I have said this before, but I shall say it again and again and again: Your boys are not going to be sent into any foreign wars."

Except for moderate socialists, the whole American left including the communists reacted negatively to World War II. A month after it began the AFL declared: "As for our country, we demand that it stay out of the European conflict, maintaining neutrality in spirit and act." The CIO seconded this theme: "Labor wants no war nor any part of war." The auto workers union distributed 100,000 copies of an antiwar pamphlet titled "Soldiers Get Free Graves." It was written by a sympathizer of the RWL. Republican candidate Wendell Willkie, like Democratic candidate Franklin Roosevelt, asserted that he was "for keeping out of war." Norman Thomas continued to preach the gospel of pacifism he had preached so long.

Of all the forces on the left, from September 1939 to June 1941, the communists were the most visible opponents of both the war and Roosevelt's policy of aiding the Allies. At a meeting of the national committee on September 19, 1939, the party called the conflict "a war between rival imperialisms for world domination." During the 1940 presidential campaign, candidate Earl Browder caustically commented that "Mr. Roosevelt has studied well the Hitlerian art and bids fair to outdo the record of his teacher." Communists attacked Roosevelt furiously for his conscription bills, lend-lease aid to the Allies, and the gift of fifty destroyers to Britain. A pro-communist union official described the conscription law as "a death sentence on the trade union and all democratic institutions." Whenever they could, communists called strikes in plants associated with military preparations, such as Vultee Aircraft, North American Aircraft, and Milwaukee's Allis Chalmers. The favorite party slogan was: "The Yanks are not coming."

But in June 1941, when Hitler launched his surprise attack on the Soviet Union, the American communists performed a complete volte-face. Six days after the invasion the party issued a statement calling for "full and unlimited collaboration of the United States, Great Britain, and the Soviet Union to bring about the military defeat of Hitler." "The Yanks are not coming" slogan disappeared and was replaced after Pearl Harbor with "All out for the war effort." Yesterday's "imperialist war" became a "peoples' war."

The Trotskyites, the RWL, and other leftist splinter groups took the traditional Marxist position—and did not alter it throughout the years of hostilities. This, like World War I, they said, was an imperialist war for markets. It was true that the Axis powers were tyrannical regimes, greedy and ruthless. But the fact that they took the initial military offensive was not due solely to their fascist character, but to the circumstance that they were "have-not" states more desperate for markets than were the "have" states. American concerns were no different from those of the Axis powers, only not quite as urgent. "Foreign markets must be regained," said Franklin Roosevelt early in his administration. "There is no other way if we would avoid painful dislocation, social readjustments, and unemployment." Secretary of Agriculture Henry A. Wallace called foreign economic expansion vital if the United States were not to lapse into either fascism or socialism. Every industrial nation had the same idea, to expand or recover markets, lest the economic crisis at home become intolerable. Each of the great powers developed its own way of doing this: through barter trade (in the case of Germany), through manipulation of the value of money (Britain), and through bilateral trade agreements (the United States). Then, with increasing frequency, the interests of the great powers clashed. In July 1940, for instance, Roosevelt cut off the supply of oil, scrap iron, and aviation gasoline to Japan — all vital to the economy of a nation woefully lacking in primary materials. The Japanese responded by sending troops into Indochina, by consolidating their influence in Thailand, and by threatening the Dutch East Indies and Singapore. Whether the methods used by the United States were fair or unfair, moral or immoral, compared to those of Germany, Japan, and Italy, was an irrelevant question, for it was the *intensification* of the trade and money wars between nations that tipped the scales toward military war.

This was the essence of our analysis, and it was — and still is, I think — credible. Few people, however, were willing to listen to it. I was working on our proof-press on Ashland Avenue in Chicago putting out a special issue of our paper shortly after learning that the war in Europe had begun. The headline read: WORLD WAR. FIGHT AGAINST ROOSEVELT'S WAR PLANS. NOT A MAN, NOT A PENNY FOR BOSS WAR! The anxieties of a lifetime coagulated within this one twenty-seven-year-old radical. That vague, subliminal hope I cherished against all my intellectual beliefs, that the world would somehow avoid another bloody conflict, was shattered that moment, and I wondered whether others would now be ready to listen to our message. They wouldn't; our paper, as might have been expected, made no impact. Neither would anything else we said or wrote about the worldwide cataclysm in the next five and a half years. The thin voice of a few Marxist groups and the pacifists, who came to their position from another focal point, had little effect against the strident sounds of chauvinism. Americans felt that "Hitler had to be stopped," no matter how. It was useless to tell them that there were other ways of stopping him; that, in fact, as Hans Rothfels points out in his incisive book *The German Opposition to Hitler,* Chief of Staff Colonel General Ludwig Beck had been actively plotting, a year before hostilities, with the commanders of the Berlin and Potsdam garrisons, the Berlin chief of police, the general in charge of an armored division in Thuringia, and a wide range of others, to overthrow Hitler. He wanted only an assurance that "the Western democracies would oppose Hitler's designs on Czechoslovakia." The plotters even sent an emissary to 10 Downing Street to advise Lord Halifax that if Britain opposed the Nazi venture "the German army would refuse to fight against Czechoslovakia." This, "at least by implication," writes Rothfels, "meant a promise to overthrow the Hitler regime."

While waiting for a British reply, Beck was dismissed from his post, but his successor General Franz Halder "was prepared to go ahead, and orders were about to be issued for the action [a takeover of the government by the military] to take place on the morning of the twenty-ninth" of September 1938. At midday on September 28, however, "word came that Chamberlain and Daladier had accepted an invitation for a conference at Munich." Two weeks later Carl Friedrich Goerdeler, one of the plotters, wrote in sorrow to an American friend, "the German people did not want war, the army was ready to do everything to prevent it . . . the world had been warned and informed in time. If these warnings had been heeded, and if one had acted accordingly, Germany would be free of her dictator today and could turn against Mussolini. In a few weeks we could begin to shape a lasting peace based on justice, reason and decency. Germany with a government of decent men would have been prepared to solve the Spanish problem together with France and England, to remove Mussolini and to create peace in the Far East in cooperation with the United States." Similar plots were hatched in 1939, but were again given short shrift in London. Throughout the war, military conspirators, including Admiral Wilhelm Canaris, head of the

Intelligence Division of the War Ministry, tried on more than one occasion to remove Hitler.

The argument that with a little encouragement the Germans themselves might have overthrown Hitler was seldom made during the two years before the United States joined the fray, and would have changed few minds anyway. Unlike World War I when President Wilson called on the people to be neutral in thought and deed, this time there was not even a pretense of neutrality. The vast majority of Americans prayed for an Allied victory — while simultaneously urging that the United States keep out. There was no hue and cry when Roosevelt effected a modification of the neutrality laws to allow "cash and carry" sales of war material to Britain and France. Nor did many object when Roosevelt adopted his "short of war" policy after France was overrun.

Public opinion was so nearly unanimous — and chauvinistic — that this time there was no frenzy of arrests, jailings, and lynchings such as those that punctuated World War I. A month or two after hostilities began in Europe, Browder was convicted for a passport irregularity on the flimsy charge he had failed to inform the authorities that he had used a pseudonym when he applied for a passport in 1934. He was given the unusually harsh sentence of four years in prison and a $2,000 fine, but was released by Roosevelt after America's entry into the war. Another reprisal was the revocation of the citizenship of William Schneiderman, Communist Party secretary in California, who was accused of having withheld the information of his communist affiliation when he had applied for citizenship in the 1920s. Schneiderman was defended by the Republican standard-bearer, Wendell Willkie, who secured a reversal from the Supreme Court.

The only radicals seriously penalized were members and friends of the Socialist Workers Party — Trotskyites. In October 1941, twenty-nine of them, including their leader James P. Cannon, went on trial on two counts. The first charged them, under an 1861 statute, with conspiring to overthrow the government by force and violence. The second, under the

Smith Act passed in 1941, accused them of conspiring to *advocate* such overthrow. After a five-week trial in which the government quoted long and laboriously from Trotskyite writings, eighteen of the defendents were adjudged guilty on the second count and given prison terms of twelve to sixteen months. Since the Trotskyites (unlike Browder and Schneiderman) did not recant their antiwar position, they served full terms — with time off for good behavior.

The RWL made minor preparations in 1941 for going underground should the need arise. We rented a room on Huron Street where we stored files. Oehler moved to Denver where he kept his address a secret, even from me. And a couple of other comrades went into hiding, for both personal and political reasons. It was all unnecessary, however, for there were no arrests or convictions of radicals after Pearl Harbor. The only problem we in the RWL had to contend with was the periodic refusal of the Post Office to mail our paper, the *Fighting Worker.* Even that was rectified, however. Our fears of arrests and raids on our homes and headquarters never came to pass. For that matter, neither did any trace of defeatism develop in the nation per se. Leaving aside the deaths and injuries on the front, which brought tragedy to hundreds of thousands of families, the rest of the country lavished in synthetic prosperity, suffering no greater travail than looking for black-market cigarettes, meat, and gasoline coupons. Never before or since has the U.S. government had such thorough support for a war policy.

III

In these unfavorable circumstances — for the left — it was obviously difficult for any force that opposed the war to function. Pacifists gave personal witness to their antiwar beliefs by refusing induction and either going to jail or doing alternate service. Marxists had no such alternative; they opposed the military in principle, of course, but their strategy called for accepting induction so that they could work within the armed forces to organize soldiers into antiwar cells.

From September 1939 to mid-1941, RWL activity, as well as my personal activity, was in low gear. There just wasn't much we could do except publish our paper sporadically, hold meetings (attended by a few dozen people), and occasionally become involved in a civil liberties or trade union campaign.

In the fall of 1940, one of our comrades, Thomas H. Stone, a lawyer in Richmond, Virginia, took on the murder case of a sharecropper named Odell Waller.

Stone, born to an upper-class Southern family, was a warm and colorful figure who could add a column of six-digit figures in his head as fast as they could be written, and spin yarns by the hour. One of those tales always delighted me. During World War I, it seems, Tom had joined the Socialist Party, and as befits a young man who believes what he is preaching, posted a notice in the city hall asking all those who were opposed to the imperialist war to contact him at such and such an address. No recruits came, of course, but the police did. Stone's father, an upright Bourbon, was furious and forbade his son to have anything to do with those "damn socialists." A year or two later the Communist Party was born and Tom naturally joined it. Unfortunately he didn't have the money to go to its convention up North, but he devised a scheme of squeezing it out of his parent. "Dad," he said, "you know those socialists you hate. Well, I've just joined an organization that pledges to fight them to the death. All I need is money to attend its convention." Stone senior jubilantly supplied the funds, never suspecting that the cure was worse than the disease.

Twenty years later, now a graduate of Stalinism and an RWL member, Tom Stone heard of the Waller case and immediately offered his services. Odell Waller, a twenty-three-year-old black, born and raised around Gretna Village in southwestern Virginia, was an intelligent young man with three years of high school behind him, but not much future ahead of him. In January 1939, he had arranged with a white man named Oscar Davis to work an acre of tobacco on shares, but had only earned $60 net the first year. In 1940, his cash income fell to zero, in large part because the land-owner reneged on promises to pay for such items as fertilizer, and because Davis decided to plow under Waller's land in order to earn a federal subsidy for conservation. To add to Waller's woes, his mother was cheated out of monies due her for midwifery and nursing, and when — in desperation — the young sharecropper went to Baltimore to work in a factory, Davis evicted his mother and wife from their shack. Waller returned, confronted his landlord, demanded wheat and money due him, and in the course of a furious argument shot and killed his tormentor.

Stone visited the young man, took his case, enlisted another lawyer to help, and put the RWL to work organizing a defense campaign. Despite our meager resources we held meetings, sent petitions to the Virginia authorities, and later to President Roosevelt to stay Waller's execution. Obviously we didn't condone murder, but there were extenuating circumstances here and we knew that punishment would not be limited to a jail term. Our fears were confirmed when a jury convicted Waller, and the judge sentenced him to death; it was all that a black man could expect in a bigoted South those days.

We were able to contact Eleanor Roosevelt and win her support for the case, and we secured a number of stays of execution. But despite Mrs. Roosevelt's selfless endorsement we could not prevail on her husband, President Roosevelt, to commute the sentence. In 1941, Odell Waller was electrocuted; we distributed a bitter leaflet: "Waller Murdered by Capitalism." The jargon was raucous but the charge was valid. The killing of the landlord was not premeditated; had Waller been a white movie actor like Fatty Arbuckle instead of a black Southern sharecropper, he would have received a few years at most, perhaps even been let off with probation.

While I was involved with the Waller case I had to deal with another problem that affected me more directly. For a number of years I had been taking jobs in restaurants when my wife was jobless or when we couldn't make ends meet. Now I hired on to manage a luncheonette in a small department store, Meyer Bros., on Ashland Avenue and 48th Street in Chicago. Within six months I turned a big loss into a handsome profit, and my bosses rewarded me with four wage increases. The compulsion to be efficient even while working for a capitalist was one of those characteristics I could neither explain nor overcome. But I did not forget my revolutionary duty.

On the second day of my employment I went downtown to the offices of the Department Store Employees Union Local 291, signed an application card, and paid my dues and initiation fees. Local 291 was then a fledgling organization trying to organize one store, Marshall Field & Co., and not doing particularly well. Walter (Scotty) Deans, a short stocky Scotsman who would eventually work for me and become one of my closest friends, advised me that "you don't have to pay initiation or dues until your store has a union contract," and must have thought I was a spy or something when I insisted. In a few weeks I had formed a nucleus of eight or nine members at Meyer Bros. and Local 291 began distributing leaflets openly every few days or so. Unfortunately there was no flood in our direction — only a few more workers joined — and in due course, by a process of elimination, management concluded that I was the culprit responsible for the union drive. Despite the flourishing business and the four wage increases, I was summarily fired.

Local 291 didn't have the organizers or the money for a full-scale strike, nor was there any hope that we could pull out enough workers to shut down operations. In that circumstance I polished off the strategy I had utilized years before at Hecht Bros. in New York — a one-man picket line. For a few weeks I manned the line by myself, with help from Deans, Martin Heckmann (another chap with whom I was associated for a long time), and members of the Packinghouse Workers Union, who relieved me for a few hours each day. Once the police dragged me off to jail, charging that I had threatened a customer. The one-man line unfortunately didn't stop teamster deliveries — in part because I couldn't picket in front and in back of the store, where deliveries were made, simultaneously; and in part because my international union, the CIO Retail, Wholesale, and Department Store Union (RWDSU) was on bad terms with the teamsters, then affiliated with the AFL.

The only hope of getting my job back was to institute a boycott and, since there was a strong Back of the Yards Council in the neighborhood headed by Saul Alinsky, a man who would soon become nationally renowned for his theory of fomenting conflict, that seemed a promising channel. I met with Alinsky and a few priests, but was surprised to find them unsympathetic. Alinsky, whom I got to know moderately well in later years, was acerbic. At any rate, I was not helped by the council and without it a boycott was doomed. A week or two later, I might add, Meyer Bros. carried a two-page ad in the council's newspaper, which may or may not have been coincidental. Months later the vice president of my international union, Leonard Levy, an old comrade with whom I had worked in New York, arranged a settlement with the company's lawyer, Stanford Clinton. In lieu of presenting charges to the National Labor Relations Board, which would have been of little value since our organizing drive was no longer viable, I took a hundred dollars and called it a day.

My trade union career was far from over, however. It was about to receive new adrenalin.

Chapter 5
Stickin' with the Union

I

Soon after the debacle at Meyer Bros., I was to reacquaint myself with the socialist lawyer, Francis Heisler, whom I had known casually for a number of years. As one listened to Heisler in a courtroom one might wonder whether he had ever read a law book. "Are you going to connect this up?" the judge would ask him as he went on one of his legal fishing expeditions. With roguish charm and a delightful Austrian accent, Heisler would say "Yes, your honor," but he never did. What he was trying to do was produce a newspaper headline the unionists he represented could use in a leaflet, not win legal points. The job of a socialist or labor lawyer, Heisler used to say, was not to accept a law (or an interpretation of a law) that was unjust, but to make "new law."

He was slightly taller than average, thin, and distinguished looking, and an effective lawyer despite the Viennese accent. When Leonard Levy, who was, as noted, a former comrade with whom I had been involved in a few strikes, came to Chicago as director of the Midwest office of the Retail, Wholesale, and Department Store Union, he selected Heisler to represent the organization. And when five young workers at the Hillman's grocery chain were fired for challenging a

Capone syndicate mobster, they inevitably gravitated to Levy, who referred them to Heisler for legal and other advice.

Heisler told me some of the details of this fight as we stood on the sidewalk not far from his office building early in June 1941, and asked me to wade in. "None of those people," he said, "has any previous union experience. Why don't you get a job with Hillman's and help them out." I agreed — this small decision changed my life dramatically for the next quarter century. Within a day or so I was working at one of the supermarkets of this middle-sized chain, as a soda jerker. A day or two more and I was making speeches at the dissidents' meeting and being drafted to their Temporary Working Committee. A humorous incident occurred after I had made my maiden talk and had been given a great ovation. "How do we know this guy isn't a company spy?" one worker asked. I took off the jacket of the only suit I owned, turned it inside out, and showed the 700 people present the torn lining. "Would a spy wear anything like this?" I asked. To which the suspicious young man replied: "Yeah, those could be your working clothes."

The story of Local 1248 of the AFL's Retail Clerks International Protective Association (RCIPA), the union that the five young men at Hillman's had challenged, bears telling if only because it reflects a widespread phenomenon that served to mute, then immobilize the "CIO revolution" of the 1930s. Innumerable people thought, after the sit-down strikes, that the CIO would inundate the moribund AFL. But the AFL didn't die, it grew steadily, enjoying the largest advance it had ever known. What happened was that corporate America, though reeling from its defeats at the hands of the CIO mavericks in the mass-production industries, caught its breath and devised a new strategy to undermine militant unionism. One of the techniques it adopted was to prod company unions and paper unions to apply for AFL charters — and then recognize them as legitimate.

The AFL was not an unwilling accomplice. "Since the Supreme Court decision upholding the Wagner Act," wrote

A. O. Wharton, president of the AFL machinists, to lower line officials on April 20, 1937, "many employers now realize that it is the Law of our Country and they are prepared to deal with labor organizations. Those employers have expressed a preference to deal with A.F. of L. organizations rather than Lewis, Hillman, Dubinsky, Howard and their gang of sluggers, communists, radicals, and soap box artists, professional bums, expelled members of labor unions, outright scabs, and the Jewish organizations with all their red affiliates. We have conferred with several such employers and arranged for conferences later when we get the plants organized. The purpose of this is to direct all officers and all representatives to contact employers in your locality as a preliminary to organizing the shops and factories." Needless to say the employers were most cooperative in lining up their employees for moderate AFL unions as a means of bypassing the more militant CIO. The machinists tripled their membership in the six years after Wharton wrote this letter.

In many instances, crossing many industries, union leaders went in to see employers without a single member and came out after a few hours' conference with the right to collect dues from hundreds, sometimes thousands, of working people. The next day company supervisors would walk around the plant and get workers to sign application cards. Organizing the employer and back-door contracts became widespread phenomena. Sometimes they involved outright gangsters.

RCIPA Local 1248 was the product of two interesting back-door deals. In 1937, a small group of warehousemen at the National Tea Company, led by a member of the RWL, became weary of their company union and formed an independent union that affiliated, after a while, with the CIO, and enrolled most of the 600 employees at the warehouse. The company, however, steadfastly refused to recognize the legitimate union, provoking a strike that lasted almost six months. There were the usual arrests, beatings by police (including a couple at the police station where the men were hit with rubber truncheons), and mass picket lines.

For a few weeks the company was unable to open its warehouse; soon, however, as if by miracle, the company union reappeared with an AFL charter and announced that a contract had been signed with National Tea. The corporation took the tack that it was an innocent bystander, that the strike was really a jurisdictional dispute. With the aid of the AFL, it recruited a new staff and in due course smashed the strike. Long afterward, the National Labor Relations Board reinstated about 150 strikers and awarded $51,000 in back pay, but the agreement between National Tea and the AFL was not revoked.

In the course of the warehousemen's strike, our RWL comrade had put pickets around fifty of the larger company stores in the hopes, among other things, of recruiting the clerks to join the strike. They didn't join the strike, but they did take the initial steps to form a union, and National Tea started looking for a means of checkmating that effort. At this point a man named Max Caldwell entered the picture with just the insurance management was looking for. Caldwell's career was undistinguished except for the fact that he was the son-in-law of the advertising manager of the Chicago Federation of Labor newspaper. In Prohibition days Caldwell had been the proprietor of a nightclub and was frequently in the clutches of the police for infractions of the Prohibition law. In 1925, he had been sentenced to six months in jail on a liquor violation charge, but mysteriously never served his term. In 1932 he insinuated himself into a waiters' union and two years later was indicted with two officers of the union on the charge of trying to extort $10,000 from the owners of the French Casino — but was acquitted. He had also tried to organize hatcheck girls, but again his efforts brought him into trouble with the police and proved unsuccessful.

By any standards, this was an unsavory character, with known links to the Capone crime syndicate and with a record available to any self-respecting corporation that cared to look it up in the newspapers. But Caldwell was able to get a charter in the RCIPA — though he didn't have any members —

and was able to meet with the grocery chain officials and sign an agreement, again without having organized a single clerk. In fact not a single worker even knew him. Yet his deal with National Tea was so alluring that A&P, Hillman's, and a host of smaller grocery outfits signed similar pacts. Years later — in 1941 — when we threw Caldwell out and were able to have the Local 1248 office and safe opened to us, we finally were permitted to see the precious contract: it contained two provisions — closed shop (everyone must join the union) and no wage increases for two years, renewable on demand, if I recall correctly, to five years. All in all Caldwell built a thriving union business for himself. In time he obtained six charters from the RCIPA, AFL, covering 12,000 workers. Initiation fees varied from $3 to $100, dues — for clerks earning $14 and $15 a week — were $2 a month, payable a month in advance. Many of the companies, knowing how their workers would react to a union that provided them with no benefits, paid the dues and initiation fees out of their own funds. One firm paid a set figure of $1,000 a month to the Caldwell treasury as "permit money," even though the number of its employees varied from month to month.

Generally, however, workers paid their own dues — a month in advance, subject to a fine of 5 cents a day if they were late. Business agents — appointed, not elected — kept a share of the dues and initiation fees, stewards were given their dues free, and workers who were delinquent were fired. An old woman who went to the union office to ask for a copy of the contract to see if she was entitled to sick benefits was thrown down a flight of stairs. There were complaints to the AFL in Washington, to the Chicago Federation of Labor, to the newspapers, but, except for the fact that Caldwell was expelled from the Chicago Federation of Labor after his men had slugged women demonstrators who refused to liquidate their local union and join his, no other reprisals were exacted against him. He functioned in a lucrative business, with strong employer and official support, and evidently made himself a bundle. When Heisler put Caldwell on the witness stand in our law suit after the revolt began, he admitted that he had never received more than $125 a week in wages, had no other income, was broke when he took the job, yet owned a residence on Winchester Avenue and had bought another one in Florida from mobster Frank Nitti at what was then the hefty price of $45,000. Though he had received no money from his wife or any other source, Caldwell now owned at least two buildings, bonds, diamonds, and an automobile purchased by the union. On $125 a week he frequently flew to Florida with his wife, baby, and baby's nurse as well as various relatives and friends. The union's treasury, which Heisler estimated had taken in $910,000 in almost four years, was empty, except for $62.18 in petty cash.

In June 1941, a minor incident wrote finis to the grocery industry's collusion with Max Caldwell. At one of the seven Hillman stores, the steward was taken sick early in June and therefore unable to collect the monthly dues. On return, he insisted that every one of the 125 or 150 employees pay a 25-cent fine for being five days "late." Five young people, including two — Frank Socki, a signpainter, and Russell (Kelly) Pratt, a stockman — with whom I would be associated for the next quarter of a century, refused. They were immediately fired, but, instead of slinking away, they went through the store and took everyone out on the streets with them. In less than an hour management capitulated, reinstated the discharged men, and one of their number — a leftist who knew his way around — contacted Levy, who referred them to Heisler. Under Heisler's tutelage they prepared a petition removing Caldwell from the union, and not only signed up most of the Hillman workers but many hundreds in the other chains. They formed a Temporary Working Committee, rented a headquarters on Wells Street, and called a meeting at the Midland Hotel, where, as already related, I became involved in the campaign.

The technique we used in getting rid of the gangsters was simply to read them out of the organization. Since practically every Hillman worker had signed a petition to that effect and 700 or 800 of the 1100 employees attended our meetings, the company got the message. And just in case the parties concerned intended to wait us out until the publicity was over then resume the sweetheart relationship, Heisler went into court ostensibly to get an accounting of the funds Caldwell had squandered, but more important to make a daily headline so that the issue might be kept before the public. We were most fortunate that, for reasons of its own, the Chicago *Tribune* assigned a competent reporter named George Hartmann to dig beneath the surface. I'm sure that without the *Tribune*'s headlines and Heisler's antics in the courtroom, one of us, probably me, would have been killed. The father of one of our RWL comrades — a man with eleven children — was murdered under similar circumstances a year or two previously, when he led a revolt in another gangster-controlled union. I was not unmindful of this man's fate.

As our court case and Hartmann's revelations continued we learned some amazing things about how deep the strain of corruption runs through our society. Not a single one of the great corporations that had signed back-door contracts came to our aid or showed the least willingness to deal with us. Neither did the parent RCIPA, or for that matter the AFL and its president William Green. With the concurrence of C. C. Coulter, secretary of the RCIPA, Green sent John Van Vaerenewyck from Boston to supervise our activities, but refused to give us the Local 1248 charter. Instead of retaining the union as a single unit, Green and Coulter established separate locals of National Tea and A&P workers under their own control. When we tried to attend meetings of these units, the AFL officials called the police — a wise move from their point of view because the rank-and-file clerks of these chains were shouting that we be let in.

Van Vaerenewyck turned out to be a personable chap, but he made it clear that Green wanted to get rid of Heisler and me. My friend Frank Socki was offered a $75-a-week job (a bonanza for a $22-a-week signpainter) as a bribe if he would desert us. After two months of this sort of thing I put a mass picket line around the Drake Hotel (one of the fanciest in Chicago) where President Green was holding a meeting of the AFL executive council. A.F.L. LEADERS SHUT THEIR EYES WHILE NEW CALDWELLS TAKE OVER OUR CLERKS' UNION, read one of the signs. Green was furious when he met with our delegation. "What the devil do you want?" he shouted at me. "Do you want me to send in a Trotskyite to work with you? I'll give you Albert Weisbord." But we never did get Weisbord, a charter, or anything else from the AFL factotums, and we finally had no alternative but to affiliate with the CIO. I personally would have preferred to remain somewhere in the AFL where we would have the vital support of butchers, bakers, and teamsters. But Heisler was so intent on drawing us into the CIO organization he and Levy represented that we really had no opportunity to do any shopping.

Once in the CIO, as Local 329, we ran into immediate problems. Hillman's attorney, Leonard Woods — a man who had recently broken a long strike against a Hearst newspaper — signed a quickie contract with a local of the AFL Amalgamated Meat Cutters. Under Woods' inspired direction a number of store managers had been issued a Meat Cutters charter as Local 643, and of course had no trouble signing up clerks who were their subordinates. The company now proclaimed that it was caught in the middle of a jurisdiction fight, but was willing to sign contracts with both unions. It offered AFL members a $2-a-week raise; those in CIO Local 329 one dollar. This was a clever ruse aimed at wooing members away from a militant union to a "soft" one. Apart from being illegal, it was certainly unfair and impractical. The workers understood instinctively that their situation would be hopeless unless they forced management to deal with a single organization. When this proved impossible, they were left with no recourse but to strike.

In September 1941, then, a vast majority of the clerks were out on the streets in a stoppage that lasted six and a half bitter weeks. Our picket lines were effective and our ranks held together quite well for most of that period, but we had no money for strike benefits and in the end our forces simply disintegrated. I put out a strike bulletin every day or two (twenty-four in all) and frequently visited all the locations to sustain morale. But the AFL teamsters, butchers, and bakers went through our lines, and management was able to operate. For the next year we argued our case before the NLRB, and held monthly meetings of twenty-five or thirty ex-strikers to retain a nucleus for the next phase. Periodically I took a job as a counterman in a restaurant to keep body and soul together, and was able to wangle $300 from the United Mine Workers District 50 to work on the campaign. Finally, in September 1942, a year after the strike, the company and AFL Local 643 acceded to an NLRB settlement by which thirty people were put back on the job with $10,000 back pay, and an election was called for five weeks later. (One of the provisions we had to agree to was that Pratt, Socki, and I — I had been fired a few weeks before the strike — would not be reinstated.) To everyone's surprise — including that of our regional director, Leonard Levy — we won that election by a margin of 61 percent. I became the full-time director of Local 329 (the only staff member) at a salary of $35 a week. (The local couldn't afford much more, but, even if it could, the bylaws that I drafted provided that no one working for the union was to be paid more than the highest-paid worker under contract.) I remained in that post, elected annually, then biannually until the 1960s, when I decided to work only part-time.

As for Caldwell, his star dimmed only slightly — attesting to the corruption of American politics. He not only never served a day in prison, but resumed his union career — in Florida. One of the Caldwell appointees, secretary-treasurer Michael Savachka, was a draft evader. Early on he was sent south by Caldwell on a long "vacation," but in due course the FBI found him and along with Caldwell had the two men indicted for conspiring to evade the draft. Savachka was permitted to join the army; Caldwell was convicted, but the Circuit Court of Appeals set aside the verdict. Meanwhile he carved a niche for himself in the bartenders' union in Miami,

and a few years later in the American Guild of Variety
Artists.

The significance of this small saga in a single local union goes
beyond the event itself or its effect on my career. It reflected
the American establishment's recovery of the strategic offensive against labor. Contrary to our image of the system as a
helpless giant buffeted by the winds, it regained its compo-
sure after the sit-downs, took stock of its potential, and
elaborated a double-pronged strategy. The back-door and
sweetheart contract was one of these prongs, a means by
which management, in effect, chose the "right" union for its
employees — rather than have them choose one for themselves. The imposition of corrupt leadership on helpless
workers not only retained for the employer the unhindered
rights of management and shielded him from taking up
worker grievances, but was extremely profitable in most
instances — saving as little as a nickel-an-hour raise can mean
$10,000 a year for a plant with 100 employees, $100,000
for a plant with 1,000 employees. Though the back-door
practice has been on the wane in recent years, even today
there is at least one unsavory union official in every major city
with whom an employer can "make a deal."

I had many unhappy experiences with the technique
while I headed Local 329. Once, for instance, we organized
an optical company, but when we presented the application
cards to the NLRB, as required to secure an election, we were
told that a contract already existed with a teamster local — a
contract that evidently provided no benefits because not a
single worker had ever heard of it.

I'm not suggesting that corporate-racketeer collaboration
was a rule in the labor movement, but neither was it an incidental aberration. Thomas E. Dewey, when he was district
attorney in New York, denounced those employers who
"invite the racketeers to organize their industries to increase
their profits at public expense." New York *Times* writer
A. H. Raskin detailed in an article for *Commentary* the

"sordid story of employer collaboration" with the International Longshoremen's Association over a quarter of a century. He charged that they had "subverted the union . . . kept its president, Joseph P. Ryan, in automobiles and expensive clothes," and had subsidized the hooligans Ryan recruited from Sing Sing to hold the rank and file in subjection. When Harry Bridges finally established a democratic organization of longshoremen on the West Coast, Ryan was called in by management in the Pacific ports to work his backdoor magic there — but this time in vain.

The most widely publicized back-door deal of recent years was between the teamsters union and California's large farms. In 1970, 200 lettuce growers of Monterey County concluded a quick agreement with the teamsters to avoid dealing with Cesar Chavez and the militant United Farm Workers. In effect, they were imposing leaders on their employees even though — according to the California Supreme Court — "probably the majority of the applicable field workers wanted to be represented by the United Farm Workers Union." Einar Mohn, retired director of the Western Conference of Teamsters, conceded that his union's base amongst the laborers was tenuous. He told the Los Angeles *Times:* "It will be a couple of years before farm workers can start membership meetings. . . . Maybe as agriculture becomes more sophisticated, more mechanized, with fewer transients, fewer green carders, and as jobs become more attractive to whites, then we can build a union that can have structure . . . and membership participation." What was organized in this instance was not the employees but their willing bosses.

The back-door technique, harmful as it was to legitimate unionism, was in fact the lesser prong in the corporate arsenal, and became less significant with the passage of time. Of much greater import in business's strategy to roll back labor militancy was the institutionalization of the collective bargaining process itself. Employers, to a large extent, reconciled themselves to the fact that unionism was here to stay and worked out a classic trade-off, offering security for labor's *leadership* in return for containing rank-and-file militancy. Employers (and especially their lawyers) found that the Wagner Act was not so terrible after all; indeed it could be turned to advantage. The more security you granted a union *official* the less likely he was to stir rank-and-file militancy. Moreover, in the larger industries the costs were negligible, because, as John Kenneth Galbraith pointed out, "the characteristic firm of the industrial system eschews price competition" — the three or four top companies in auto, steel, rubber, and cereals passed on wage increases to the consumer.

In short order capital recognized that granting security to the labor officialdom in the form of the union shop, check-off of dues, longer-term contracts was a sounder policy than permanent confrontation. The less a labor leader worried about where his own next paycheck would come from the less likely he was to stir a hornet's nest. I recall one company attorney, negotiating for a Chicago firm, who made it a condition of our negotiations that we accept the union shop and check-off. "I don't want a situation," he said, "where you guys try to win over the non-union people by soliciting grievances and behaving as super-militants." Ford Motor Company, which fought unionism with unparalleled determination in the 1930s, surprised everyone in 1941 by granting the first national union shop and check-off of dues in the auto industry.

The tradeoff of security for "labor peace" became increasingly evident just before and during World War II. In 1941, Sidney Hillman, then functioning as associate director of the Office of Production Management, reached an understanding with the AFL building trades unions (bastion of labor conservatism) giving them *sole* jurisdiction in all defense construction. The CIO had been trying to organize the building trades into an industrial union, and while its campaign was limping, it might have caught on in time. But the government's decision cut the ground from under the CIO and gave the AFL leadership the stability it could not have enjoyed otherwise. In Detroit, a corporation that handed in the lowest bid for defense housing was turned down — because it recognized the CIO — in favor of a company that dealt exclusively with the AFL. That this was no small factor in the revival of AFL business unionism is indicated by statistics of union membership. From 1938 to 1944 the boilermakers' skyrocketed from 28,000 to 336,900, the bridge and structural iron workers' from 41,300 to 105,600, the hodcarriers' from 147,700 to 333,100, and the plumbers' from 37,700 to 130,000.

The World War II understanding between government, labor's officialdom, and business was based on a simple quid pro quo: the AFL and CIO leaders (without consulting their members) gave up the right to strike for the duration; in return, the War Labor Board (WLB) and other federal agencies prodded or ordered recalcitrant corporations into the fold. Though the board refused to grant a union shop, it did order "maintenance-of-membership" — an individual worker was not required to join the union, as under a union shop, but if one did one had to maintain membership and pay dues. Again this gave union leaders a measure of security and helped them add 6 million members to their rosters — slightly more than had been added by the turbulent strikes of the 1930s. The three Little Steel companies, which had refused to come to terms in 1937, were brought aboard, and hundreds of workers discharged during the strikes were reinstated with back pay by the NLRB. Master agreements were signed in the packinghouse industry. Goodrich was eased into the Rubber Workers' Union. To make this partnership between government, business, and labor's hierarchy stick, Roosevelt seized forty factories and establishments twenty-three times during that four-year period because employers refused to accept a government order and twenty-six times (there were overlaps in nine cases) when unions refused. Militants chafed at the bit under the War Labor Board's Little Steel formula, which held raises to 15 percent above the January 1941 levels, but the union ranks grew from 9 million to 15 million, and union leaders gained a sense of power and security they had never had before. Hundreds of socialists, Trotskyites, and communists by now were former socialists, Trotskyites, and communists, drifting perceptibly from radicalism and, in many instances, their militancy.

Abandoning the right to strike was, in my opinion, a classic mistake, and as a delegate to the Chicago Industrial Union Council I made that point over and over again. The employers, I argued, had not abandoned their right to profit. They weren't even willing to invest their own money for war plants — the government was building and equipping the new ones, and letting the corporations run them. If this was a war to save civilization, why wasn't big business willing to make sacrifices to save its own system? If the employers intended to treat labor fairly there would be no strikes, with or without a pledge. But to give up labor's most potent weapon in advance was simply to put working people at the mercy of management — which certainly didn't have an exemplary track record for industrial justice.

Unfortunately, the whole leadership of the labor movement, with the exception of John L. Lewis, was caught up in the wartime chauvinism, which held that to strike while "our boys" overseas needed war materiel was akin to treason. Even if one agreed with that thesis, of course, most economic activity — the manufacture of shirts and shoes and cigarettes — had nothing to do with the war; the least Murray and Green could have done was to confine their no-strike pledge to military production. The mood of the hour, however, was blind, super-patriotism. The communists carried this super-patriotism to its ultimate limits, sometimes advocating programs that could only be called anti-union.

The communist-controlled United Electrical, Radio and Machine Workers went so far as to suggest a 15-percent speedup by "the direct additional expenditure of energy and effort" as a gesture of national unity to win the war. Harry Bridges of the longshoremen called on the officers and the grievance committee of his union to spend "the majority of the time" to increase production. "I'd rather say speed-up," he said, "and I mean speed-up. . . . To put it bluntly, I mean your unions today must become the instruments of speed-up of the working class of America." Even Phil Murray, no great militant, accused the communists of "excessive appeasement of anti-labor forces."

I had some direct experience with this "excessive appeasement" during the Montgomery Ward strike of 1944. A sister local of ours, Local 20, had unionized the big Chicago warehouse of this mail-order company and won an election in February 1942 affecting 5,000 workers. Sewell Avery, stern-faced president of the company and a class-conscious capitalist to the tip of his toes, refused to sign an agreement until President Roosevelt personally wrote him in December. A year later, however, Avery categorically defied a War Labor Board order to renew the agreement. On April 12, 1944, Local 20 called out its members in the first authorized CIO strike since Pearl Harbor. I recall that morning vividly. Along with my sidekick Frank Socki and an organizer from New York, I was there early organizing the picket lines, getting leaflets mimeographed, training pickets in how to approach truck drivers to keep them from taking goods in or out. Thousands of people were present, and the press was giving the stoppage major coverage because the entire labor movement, AFL and CIO (all except the communist faction), had endorsed the walkout, and the federal government was giving it covert support. A few hours after the picketing began there was a scuffle and Captain George Barnes of the Chicago labor detail took a swing at me, missed, and hit Mike Mann — secretary of the Chicago Industrial Union Council — square on the jaw. Barnes curbed his enthusiasm after that; it didn't make for good press to lay low one of the top CIO officials in town.

A couple of days into the strike, regional vice president Leonard Levy asked Harold Gibbons, a former socialist and vice president from St. Louis (he would later become executive vice president of the teamsters under Jimmy Hoffa), and me to go to Minneapolis where Ward's had another good-sized warehouse. We didn't expect the local union there to join the strike because its leaders were close to the Communist Party, but we hoped we could convince them to refuse to fill orders that normally would be filled in Chicago. Gibbons and I spent hours talking to a woman who was a top official of the union in the Twin Cities. She was taken with Gibbons personally, a tall and exceptionally handsome man, but his charm availed little against communist politics. She insisted her members would pack Chicago orders because "we have to win the war." Our trip was a total failure.

Meantime, back in Chicago the strike won near unanimous support, with AFL teamsters, independent railroad brakemen, and engineers respecting our lines. Finally after fourteen days Roosevelt ordered the federal troops to seize the warehouse and carry Sewell Avery, corporate president, out of his office — arms folded, grim, still sitting on his swivel chair. It was a great newspaper picture. Unfortunately our "victory" was an illusion, as was another one, on May 9, when the union won a second War Labor Board election. The company refused to come to terms; Local 20 won every case before a government board, but lost the union. Discouraged workers dropped away in droves, seeing no direct benefits from union membership.

It would be wrong to say that labor made no gains during the war. All the jobless were absorbed into the economy, millions with no skill or with lesser skills were upgraded into higher-paying positions, overtime padded pay checks, many wives entered the labor force adding another paycheck to millions of families. For those back home the war was an economic boon. Employers who operated on a "cost-plus" basis — the government reimbursed for all expenses plus a guaranteed percentage of profit — hired redundant help (a friend of mine, a highly paid tool and die worker, spent six months in the washrooms doing nothing because there was no machine for him), and were lavish with overtime. Yet wage increases under the Little Steel formula were not only limited to 15 percent over the January 1941 figure, but were subject to arbitrary decisions and incredibly long delays by the War Labor Board. The board usually erred on the side of conservatism; you had to argue, cajole, beseech, scream to get approval for modest raises. Once I filed for a $1-a-day raise I had negotiated for sixty food demonstrators — the women who give you a sample of a new bacon or biscuit — and was turned down. Then, at a Midwest conference called by the board to explain its policies to union officials, I delivered a scathing speech against the board members for being on the side of management. Next morning I called the chairman of the WLB in Chicago and introduced myself. "I know who you are," said the chairman. "What can I do for you?" I explained my frustration. "No problem," he said. Next day I received an official letter reversing previous decisions and granting the $1-a-day raise — "based on new evidence received," the letter said.

Many workers asked, "Why do we need a union when the War Labor Board decides everything anyway?" Had it not been for the fact that many were working overtime and that there were now two and three breadwinners in some families, the resistance to official policy might have been greater. Even so, groups formed in quite a few cities to fight the no-strike pledge — including one I helped organize in Chicago with the help of Max Weinrib, chairman of the union committee at the General Motors Electromotive Plant. At the International Harvester plant in Melrose Park, Illinois, where Frank Socki was working, I collaborated with the Progressive Union Group of Local 6 UAW-CIO, which was able to wrest control of the Local on a program of "rescinding the no-strike pledge," "withdrawing labor members from the War Labor Board," "smashing the Little 'Steal' formula," a thirty-hour five-day week, and similar planks. In Flint, Michigan, in 1943 UAW locals called together a save-the-union conference to rescind the no-strike pledge, and at a subsequent national UAW-CIO convention a resolution to cancel the pledge carried by a vote of 5,232 to 4,988. But clever parliamentary maneuvers and a questionable ruling from the chair reversed this position. So hostile were rank-and-file workers to the no-strike pledge and to the WLB that by 1945 there were long strikes in the rubber industry (forcing the United Rubber Workers' president Sherman Dalrymple to resign from his union post). And Emil Rieve of the textile union resigned from the WLB when it refused to raise minimum wage rates from 50 to 55 cents an hour. Nonetheless the struggle against the no-strike pledge and the wartime industrial relations mechanism never attained the dimensions of a crusade, nor did it provide sufficient adrenalin to revive the militancy of the 1930s.

III

The institutionalization of industrial relations — providing security for the union leadership in return for damping rank-and-file militancy — continued after the war had ended. Four and a half million unionists "hit the bricks" in 1946, but as *Fortune* observed "the strikers of 1945–46 were not desperate men. On the public platform their leaders sounded off with booming phrases directed at the enemy Capital; but privately they, like the strikers, were calm, cool, even friendly warriors." Walter Reuther, by that time president of the UAW, threw a few novel and progressive ideas into the hopper; demanding, for instance, as a condition for settling the long 1946 strike that General Motors pledge not to raise prices, or calling on the great corporations to open their books so that the public could see what their true profits were. But such proposals were rejected almost with disdain. The pattern became that after each raise the big corporations boosted prices apace — or more. In 1946, Phil Murray, negotiating with the steel barons, insisted that prices were not his domain, and sure enough after a pact was negotiated for an 18½-cent raise, Murray made no objection when the government's price control officials allowed the corporations to hike steel prices $5 a ton.

Employers, especially those listed on the *Fortune* 500, lost their anxiety over the collective bargaining process. It not only cost them nothing to deal with a union, but in many cases — because of *administered* prices — they could turn an additional profit from a wage increase. As for the labor officialdom its quid pro quo was security. "When anti-unionism was abandoned in the Forties and Fifties by significant segments of American industry," writes professor

George Brooks of Cornell (once an educational director for the Paper, Pulp and Sulphite Union), "a new world was created for the unions. For it now turned out that the *imperative* requirements of the union, that regular flow of new members and dues, could be underwritten by the *employer* with considerably more reliability than was possible under earlier arrangements."

In time, union contracts with management previously signed for a single year were negotiated for two- and usually three-year periods — periods in which the officialdom did not have to worry much about being challenged by the rank and file. CIO dues, a dollar a month originally, were raised to $2, $5, and $10. The term of office for union leaders was similarly modified; instead of elections each year they were spaced to two, three, and four years — ordinarily three years. The UAW, where a healthy factionalism prevailed during its first decade, has not had a challenge for any top post for about thirty years. When Reuther was killed in an airplane accident the choice of Leonard Woodcock to replace him was made — for all practical purposes — by a handful of vice presidents and the secretary-treasurer. The same was true when Woodcock retired to be replaced by Doug Fraser. And the UAW still has more inner vitality at the local union level than the vast majority of other labor organizations. For all practical purposes, it has become next to impossible to remove leaders of national unions; they are self-perpetuating. More, they have failed — just like the old AFL — to keep pace with the imperative of the times. As a percentage of the labor force, they are declining in number, and the benefits they win annually are becoming pedestrian — exceeding the rise in the cost of living only insofar as the stronger unions are concerned, and even then not always.

The corporate establishment has won its war against labor — at least for the time being. It has come full circle since the mid-1930s, and unless there is a turnaround in labor strategy, militancy, and organization, management will record further victories. For an example of how the relationship of forces has been reversed, consider the strike weapon. Since 1886 it has been the movement's basic instrument, a means of meeting power with power. But in an age of conglomerates and multinationals, the strike weapon is blunted. Labor's present structure was hammered together at a time when corporations generally functioned in a single industry, in a single country. The CIO industrial union — say in auto or steel or rubber — matched power with corporate power. A single union could shut down the operations of a whole company, General Motors for instance. But that is no longer the case.

International Telephone and Telegraph, with a billion in assets in 1961, had almost all its money concentrated in telecommunications. In the next decade or so it spread its wings to include a hundred corporations worth four times that much — here and in seventy other countries. Only one sixth of its investments are now in telecommunications. It deals with at least fifteen major unions — auto, teamsters, communication workers, electrical workers, bakers, plumbers, machinists, steelworkers, hotel workers, etc. And its bargaining power far outstrips that of any individual union it confronts. A strike at any one of its facilities — say Wonder Bread — is hardly more than an irritant; its costs can be absorbed elsewhere. My own Local 329 once organized forty workers in a cafeteria run by Canteen, an ITT subsidiary. Collective bargaining and grievance machinery were a farce; we had no levers to make such a vast corporation concede anything more than it wanted to. I often thought to myself as our organizers met with Canteen's negotiators that ITT probably doesn't even know this small unit exists, and wouldn't care if it went down the drain. Similarly, we once unionized a small cellophane plant with 150 workers that was later taken over by a multinational conglomerate, Gulf Oil. We had to take what was offered. There was no way to "put the muscle" to Gulf; a strike would have been useless.

Nor has the AFL-CIO kept up with the transformation of capitalism itself, from laissez-faire to controlled capitalism under Roosevelt, and now to state-managed capitalism. Government — federal, local, and state — today generates a third or more of the national income. Its decisions on money, on regulation, on subsidies, on taxes and a hundred other matters, including military policy, are determinative of the state of the economy as never before. If it cuts the military budget, workers at tens of thousands of prime and subcontractor plants lose jobs; if it permits the price of gasoline or natural gas to rise, workers' paychecks shrink accordingly; if it pursues policies that raise interest rates, it produces unemployment in the building industry, which depends on available mortgage funds. Government, moreover, sets the wage standards for 15 million workers directly employed by itself, as well as cities, counties, or states.

The labor movement's techniques for dealing with government are hopelessly antiquated. Labor is merely *another* lobbying force on the Hill or at the White House, a supplicant seeking favors through the Democratic Party. Though it constitutes far and away the largest single force in the nation, its political influence does not begin to match its political needs. It has failed to win social reforms that were won many decades ago in Europe — national health insurance, for instance. Without a labor or socialist party to speak for it, and without a coherent understanding of the present crisis of capitalism (much like the myopia of the AFL in the 1930s), labor today wallows in relative — and increasing — impotence. It certainly has not been the center of social protest — let alone revolutionary action — for three decades.

IV

When I signed on as a full-time union official in 1943 there didn't seem to be much else to do. I remained, in Hugo Oehler's absence from Chicago, the acting national secretary of the RWL but there was no sizable antiwar sentiment to capitalize on. Political work, apart from writing and publishing, was minimal; union activity seemed to offer greater promise for the moment. It was my view then and for years afterward that the labor movement would soon enjoy another upsurge like the one in the 1930s. I believed, as did most of the people I associated with, that capitalism's days were numbered, that economic and political crises impended, and that working people everywhere, including in the United States, would soon be challenging the system. Being a union official therefore was not just a job, but a pivotal perch from which a radical might give guidance to the impending upheaval.

My first task as director of Local 329 (we called the top post director rather than president, allocating the latter title to a working member) was to consolidate a weak organization. Technically we had won our fight against the hoodlums, the AFL, and the Hillman company, but in fact we were decimated and enervated. Instead of the 12,000 members that had been in Caldwell's Local 1248, we were able to salvage only 800, at one supermarket chain. While we were preoccupied with strikes, raids, and explosive negotiations the AFL quietly selected "safe" leaders for the other chains, and handed them charters. These men were for the most part rank-and-file workers, but not very militant, and they were willing to accept orders from Harry O'Reilly, the ranking local AFL official. Our own contacts at these chains were bypassed. In addition, Local 329 CIO was isolated from the craft unions it needed to strengthen its hand in collective bargaining—the teamsters, butchers, bakers, all of whom were in the AFL. And, to make matters worse, we had to grapple with a 100- to 200-percent turnover in the workforce. Jobs were plentiful and workers in low-paying industries tended to drift elsewhere. To keep the allegiance of our members in these circumstances was more than Herculean; it was next to impossible. How could a single official (myself) and a dozen stewards hope to overcome deeply implanted prejudices in 800 or 1600 people? The average new employee came to the job with a bigoted bias: unions were rackets, union officials crooks. How could one sit down with hundreds of such people and break through those prejudices: explain that in *our* union the leaders were chosen from the rank and file, that *our* constitution provided that no one working for the local be paid more than the highest-paid worker under contract, that all *our* contracts were negotiated by a committee of rank-and-filers and ratified by the whole membership? It couldn't be done. We had to have a union shop — if the union was to survive even as long as a year or two. The company and its new attorney Stanford Clinton (partner in a law firm with the wealthy Pritzker family) understood our weakness well, and exacted a heavy price for granting the union shop — an inferior wage increase. I agreed to it with a lump in my throat, but as I explained to our membership at an exceptionally well attended meeting, we either had to retreat to fight again another day or resign ourselves to liquidating the union in the near future. I was afraid, as I spoke, that the membership would reject my reasoning and turn down the agreement. To my surprise they approved it with enthusiasm, almost unanimously, they knew we were bargaining from weakness and that this was the best we could do.

The average worker has a lot more common sense than most intellectuals admit, and what the average worker wants from a union is not just more pay and better conditions, but a sense of belonging, knowing that someone is interested in him or her. I remember one occasion when a janitor came to my office at five minutes to midnight, just before we were scheduled to go out on strike. I didn't know him and was somewhat startled to find a worker who had walked off on his own before being approached by his steward. I asked him what made him do it. "You remember that grievance of mine you took up two years ago when I was hurt on the job?" he asked me. I didn't recall it. "How did we make out?" I asked. "We lost," he replied, "but you fellows were willing to go to bat for me. That's why I'm here now."

In the absence of a good contract, and because it was the kind of unionism we believed in anyhow, I set about developing a strong steward and grievance system for Local 329. We took up scores of complaints every week on all kinds of issues, minor and major: a worker being docked fifteen minutes for being late *two* minutes; the discharge of a worker who the company claimed was *probably* stealing; deliberate misclassification of employees in order to reduce their pay, and so on. We won an overwhelming majority of these disputes, if only because the company's supervisors were so accustomed to having their way under the Caldwell union, they were inept in implementing a written contract. We also instituted a program of steward training classes, softball teams, theater parties, and community services. The latter took a good part of my time: typically a member would call to say that his brother had just been picked up by the immigration service for deportation to Mexico — could the union supply a lawyer; or a member's father had grown senile, did we know a home where he could be placed free or at low cost; or a member had just bought a second-hand car which fell apart, could we help get his money back. By the time we negotiated our second and third contracts (those days they were usually for a single year) our ranks were more solid and we were able to win considerably better conditions — though not as good as we did after returning to the AFL fold (with another international) in 1946.

Apart from the normal servicing of Local 329, holding down a union job propelled me — almost automatically — into a host of other activities. Our victory against the Capones sent ripples through the ranks of unions whose members were also shackled to hoodlums, unscrupulous dictators, or both. A number of those forces contacted me for help. In 1943, for instance, a small group of men who repaired streetcar tracks trooped into my office. They were members of Local 1009 of the hodcarriers' union, who claimed that their self-perpetuating president Sam Luzzo had never given an accounting of a million dollars collected in dues over the previous twenty-four years (we later learned there was $135.73 in the treasury), had failed to hold the elections scheduled for the previous December, and had been negotiating sweetheart contracts with the Chicago Surface Lines with depressing regularity. "What can we do about it?" asked Angelo DeIulis, the rank-and-filer who headed the delegation. The only answer of course was for them to take matters into their own hands.

I drafted and mimeographed a petition that informed the district leadership of the hodcarriers' and the Chicago Surface Lines that Luzzo and his fellow officers were "no longer officers of Local 1009." I urged DeIulis and his group to take the petition to each worksite, but to make sure they had two or three husky friends nearby just in case the Luzzo people attacked them. Within a couple of days they had amassed 900 signatures — out of a total of 1,300 members. The next step was to establish a new structure and give the members a sense of physical solidarity. A leaflet calling tracklayers to a meeting brought 700 members to the Midland Hotel — and the press. In the interest of security, I had our people form a defense squad of 100 of the toughest members, who stood at the back of the hall guarding against an invasion. The meeting went off smooth as silk. The older leaders, including Luzzo, were read out of the organization by thunderous voice votes, DeIulis was installed as temporary chairman of the Temporary Reorganization Committee of Local 1009, the dues were reduced from $2 to $1 a month, and plans were made to meet with the company to secure recognition. Francis Heisler, whom I had introduced to the dissidents, served as their lawyer and in short order prevailed on the company to deal with the Temporary Reorganization Committee — or face an immediate work stoppage. It was a quick bloodless and satisfying victory.

My memory of the 1940s is of random activities that seldom formed a pattern or created a permanent constituency. The tracklayers' success, for instance, did not spark a wave of rebellions against entrenched bureaucracies in the same national union — or elsewhere for that matter. Neither did a number of internal fights against communist union leaders that I helped along produce many results. The communists, I was convinced, deserved to be removed from their posts in the labor movement because they were the most fervid supporters during the war of the idea of "anything to increase production," including speedup, piecework, and strikebreaking. But they were exceptionally capable people, and they had a lot of capital to draw on because of their outstanding services in the 1930s. It was no easy task, therefore, to fight them in the 1940s, but occasionally we succeeded.

Russell (Kelly) Pratt, one of the three people who had formed the triumvirate of leadership in Local 329, was employed at a plant that belonged to Local 453 of the United Auto Workers. Soon after being hired Kelly was embroiled in a fight with the communist leadership of the local, which he accused of failing to handle grievances adequately, and negotiating below par agreements. With the help of a dozen leaflets I wrote for him, Kelly was able to consolidate a majority of the plant behind his position. There was a considerable amount of violence — a worker was tossed down the shaft, presumably by forces favorable to the Local 453 leadership, mice were found in lunchboxes, there were shoving matches and fights — but Kelly's group won out and was able to sever from Local 453 and secure their own UAW charter. There was a humorous epilogue to this tale. Kelly, a charming Irishman who could talk most people out of their shirts, convinced the employer that I was an impartial arbitrator. I never met the employer but I arbitrated dozens of grievances over the phone with him. Kelly would toss in two meaningless grievances that no union would ever expect to win, and I would arbitrate all three in one package — invariably ruling against Kelly, of course, on the two extraneous issues, but with him on the one he needed.

Another group of Local 453 members I helped were not so lucky as Kelly Pratt. Their leader, Joe Zrust, a tall, lanky foundry worker, came to see me one day — he knew of me, I think, because he had read RWL literature — to help him and his friends at a shop called Illinois Malleable secede from Local 453. They had once had a separate UAW charter (Local 758) but their communist leaders had dissolved it and affiliated with 453. In the prewar period that didn't matter because Party stalwarts did an excellent servicing job. Now, in wartime, it was another matter. I suggested to Zrust that he form a caucus and begin putting out leaflets. The first one, signed by twenty-two rank-and-file workers was headlined WE NEED OUR OWN LOCAL and gave the reasons: "Local 453 has done practically nothing for us. It hasn't kept its promise of organizing the foundry workers in the city. . . . Local 453 is run by a group who work with the employer against us workers. . . . The 453-Buckner crowd raised our dues even though we voted against it three times. . . . Local 453 has fought against the welfare of its members and has done such things as strike-breaking and getting workers who opposed them fired. It has a policy of no-strike, no wages, no working conditions, no settling of grievances — only collecting dues." The mere airing of such charges brought some improvements (and charges by the 453 leadership of red-baiting), but 453 had enough clout with the national union to prevent Zrust from securing a separate charter.

We had better luck with a black friend of mine named Bennie Banks, who challenged the communist leadership of the Mine, Mill and Smelter Workers union. Banks, who worked in a predominantly white foundry with 300 employees, was elected president of the union repeatedly. His troubles began, he said, when he was asked but refused to join the Communist Party. The leaders of the national union had him fired from the job, forcefully broke into the local headquarters to seize its books, negotiated a back-door contract that provided for no wage increases, and ultimately forced Banks and his by now independent union out on strike to overturn a sweetheart deal. (I know that communist friends become uneasy when one brings up their record of this period. But these are historical facts and no one should rewrite them, if only to learn from them.) In any case, eight of Banks's people were arrested on picket line duty and the city of Chicago was treated to the unedifying spectacle of a communist lawyer and a Mine-Mill organizer asking the judge to raise bail on eight strikers. The judge obliged by tripling the sum. Nonetheless Banks's group won the strike and saved their union.

Through the years I was to become involved in many internal union fights, most of them against entrenched bureaucrats. The one that perhaps commanded the most attention was against James Petrillo, president of the Musicians' Union nationally and of Local 10 in Chicago as well. Sometime in 1961 five members of the Chicago Symphony Orchestra traipsed into my office at the suggestion of Lee Leibik, a lawyer friend. One was a percussionist, another a trumpet player, the third a violinist; what the other two played I no longer remember. Anyway, they had been fired by the orchestra, they said, for having fought too militantly for a raise, and Petrillo was doing nothing to have the firings revoked. (Fired was not the right word, more accurately they were given a year's notice that they would not be rehired.) The five men had been to see a prominent labor lawyer to whom they paid $2,000, but all they got for their money, they said, was the advice to file a charge with the NLRB that they had been dismissed for legitimate union activity. They had filed but the board refused to take jurisdiction of their case; so they went to another lawyer — Leibik. Leibik told them that he too could take their money but there was no legal solution to their problem; what they needed was advice from a unionist on how to deal with the Orchestra Association and Petrillo.

It was a simple campaign. I wrote a leaflet explaining the issues to the symphony musicians and drafted a petition stating that we the undersigned members of the orchestra will not renew our contracts unless the five discharged men are reinstated. The next day 90 percent of the symphony put their names on the petition, including such key musicians as the bassoon and tuba players, and the fight was over. The decision not to renew the five contracts was reversed.

Heady with the taste of victory the discharged musicians now suggested that I run in the coming elections against Petrillo. "You're crazy," I said, "not only am I not a member of Local 10 but I don't know how to play any instrument; I can't even read a note." Sam Denov, the percussionist, assured me that was no problem — any member of the symphony I chose would come to my office each day at my convenience and teach me to play whatever instrument I liked. "And as far as becoming a member," said Denov, "don't worry, we control the committee that will test you and pass you." It was a flattering offer but I made the counterproposal to teach them about unionism, instead of them teaching me about music.

The upshot was that Denov and his friends formed a caucus and ran a slate against Petrillo in the December 1962 elections of Local 10. Unfortunately my old friend, Francis Heisler, injected himself into the campaign at this point, demanding that the caucus run a dance band leader, Barney Richards, for president (he was the father of someone associated with Heisler), or Heisler and Richards would field a third slate. Grudgingly I advised Denov to compromise, because I was confident Petrillo — well-known throughout the country — couldn't be defeated, but that Denov and his friends could take all the other posts. Alas, Petrillo did lose to Richards, and though the progressive slate won all other jobs as well, the one that eluded them was the recording secretary post for which Sam Denov was running. Richards, who knew nothing about unionism, was a disaster, lasting for only a short period, to be replaced by one of Petrillo's former supporters. But the symphony musicians subsequently won conditions they hadn't even remotely anticipated back in 1962 and they still represent a major force in the local.

Chapter 6
Scattershot Politics

I

The postwar world baffled most of us on the left; it did not conform to our preconceptions. We had been predicting for years that the war would lead to revolution, and in fact it did. Beginning with the upheaval in Madagascar in 1944, six or seven dozen national revolutions — depending on how you counted them — upset the old colonial order in Asia and Africa. But these were not the revolutions forecasted in the Leninist scenario; they were in the arteries of capitalism, rather than in the heart of the system. There were, it is true, revolutionary situations in such key countries as France and Italy. Two leaders of the Communist Party of France, Andre Marty and Charles Thillon, had been urging since August 1944 that their party — the largest force in the French Resistance — seize political power. In Italy the communists had formed a partisan movement known as the *Garibaldini,* and in March 1944 organized a general strike in the northern part of the country which historian Hugh Seton-Watson described as "the most impressive action of its kind that took place at any time in Europe under Hitler's rule." In both France and Italy on the morrow of liberation, armed resistance fighters seized the factories, and only relinquished them grudgingly on orders from Stalin — who had his own reasons for not rocking the boat, the expectation of American credits for reconstruction. In addition there were revolutionary opportunities in Greece, where at one time the royalist government was confined by the leftist EAM to patches of real estate in a few cities.

Nowhere, however, did socialism sweep into any of the so-called advanced countries. The core of the capitalist system was only slightly in jeopardy from 1945 to 1948, and then out of danger entirely for the next three decades. It was in the peripheries, in the underdeveloped states, that the old order was toppled — in Yugoslavia, China, Cuba, Guinea, Vietnam, Laos, Cambodia, Angola, Mozambique, Ethiopia, where one or another type of leftist regime was installed; and in India, Indonesia, and scores of other countries where moderate regimes confined the revolution to nationalist objectives.

Another one of our wartime expectations, as an RWL article put it, was "that Stalinism would not outlast the military phase of the war" — it would be overthrown by democratic socialists within Russia. But Stalinism, like the major capitalist leaderships, also retained its power.

The American establishment, I should note, was no more clairvoyant about the future than we leftists. Not Roosevelt, Truman, or anyone else in high places anticipated the ferocity of national revolution in Asia, Africa, and parts of Europe. Most of Roosevelt's advisors assumed that a Pax Americana could be arranged with a modest effort, involving only monetary measures, international relief (via the United Nations Relief and Rehabilitation Administration, for instance), a mechanism for resolving international disputes (the United Nations), and judicious loans to certain nations. Social turmoil, if there was to be any, would be contained by Stalin as the price for coexistence, just as Stalin had contained the communist movement in the United States, France, and elsewhere as the price for diplomatic recognition and the France-Soviet pact in the 1930s.

But Stalin's proferred hand was turned aside by the United States after Roosevelt's death in April 1945 and even more vigorously after the explosion of the first atomic device in July 1945. The bomb "gave Truman," Secretary of War Henry Stimson recorded in his diary, "a new feeling of confidence." Future secretary of State James F. Byrnes told the president that "the bomb might well put us in a position to dictate our own terms at the end of the war." There was no longer any need, the Trumanites felt, to coexist with the Soviet Union — it could be put in its place without much ado. Many years later, in 1976, Clark Clifford, a Truman aide in the early postwar period, showed me a document he had prepared for the president in 1946. The sixty-two-page study, based on conversations with the secretaries of State, War, and Navy; the attorney general; the joint chiefs of staff; the director of intelligence; and Fleet Admiral William D. Leahy, concluded that "the U.S. must be prepared to wage atomic and biological warfare" against the Soviets. Truman felt there was no need to curry Stalin's help against impending national uprisings, or to pay the price of coexistence for it. That was a miscalculation, for in the end Washington had to devise a far more elaborate scheme for saving the system than it had ever thought would be necessary.

The myopia of the establishment, unfortunately — which was irremediable in any case — was small comfort to us on the left. It is true that the worldwide system could not have survived without American aid, and that the American economy itself would have foundered without a form of Keynesian "compensatory spending," which Lord Keynes had never advocated, almost 2 trillion dollars of military expenditures from 1945 to 1979. It is a fact, however, that the system did survive and produced levels of prosperity in the advanced nations such as the world had never seen — or anticipated: more than 100 million automobiles in the United States alone, per capita income upward of $8,000, 2 million new dwellings every year, and so on. The poor were still there but it was now a minority that was poor; not the majority, as in the 1930s. In 1946 Eugene Dennis, general secretary of the Communist Party, talked of "the next cyclical crisis" of capitalism as if it were predestined. Most of us believed that a depression on the order of 1929 or at least 1921 was inevitable, and that in the process the American masses would swing leftward.

It did not happen that way, however. As the federal budget had skyrocketed from $12.8 billion in fiscal 1941 to $100 billion in fiscal 1945, the government not only drained away scores of billions in higher taxes but instituted what amounted to a forced savings plan in the form of Series E and other wartime bonds. Corporations had subscribed $102.2 billion, individuals $43.3 billion, all of which was now available after the war for new investments and consumer purchases. Though there were severe economic tremors all over the world, in the United States, bastion of capitalism, the transition from war to peace was made without serious dislocation.

The titans of business who had fought labor bitterly in the 1930s learned that accommodation could usually be more profitable than irrepressible conflict. For one thing business soon was practicing a form of monopoly that made it possible not only to pass on all additional costs to the public but even to make a profit on wage increases. The two, three, or four leading companies in each of the major industries "administered" prices — set them in tandem, and invariably higher. Along with military spending this collusion was to be a decisive factor in inflation, and it was certainly a violation of many laws including the anti-trust laws. But the government winked an eye at this social dereliction, so that in due course practically no one attacked the practice.

By a conscious decision of big business the class struggle in America was toned down. General Motors accepted the escalator (cost-of-living) clause in 1948, a modified union shop in 1950, and supplementary unemployment benefits in 1955. Union agreements in the mass-production industries had generally been of a single year's duration, but in 1948 the UAW signed a pact with GM for two years, in 1950 for five years, and in 1955 for what has become fairly standard since then, three years. Long-time agreements had the effect of building up union treasuries, because in the interval of peace there were no expenditures on strikes.

Of course, abatement of the class war in the United States was not due only to the determination of management to abate it, but to the more basic fact that the United States had found a way to stabilize its own as well as the world's capitalist system. It was synthetic, built on the quicksand of militarism and a sort of international Keynesianism — but it worked for a quarter of a century. The formula for Pax Americana was not conceptualized in advance; like Topsy it "just grow'd," as the United States was forced to react to specific events.

In January 1947 a great snowstorm, the worst since 1894, hit Britain like an avalanche, leaving as much as twenty feet of snow in some places and, after a thaw, blocks of ice. By February more than half the factories were out of production, coal pits were shut, electricity was cut off to industrial consumers for several days and to the population at large for three hours daily. Before it was over Britain had lost $800 million in export sales and the drive to close the dollar gap had collapsed. Millions were out of work, demoralized, disillusioned. The financial editor of Reuters called the crisis "the biggest crash since the fall of Constantinople," and warned that the Empire itself was about to founder.

It was obvious even to the average citizen that England could no longer support a large navy, station 1.4 million troops around the world, and police an empire on which "the sun never sets." Some of the colonies and spheres of influence would have to be cut adrift. The decision to get out of Greece, where guerrilla warfare against a reactionary monarchy was flaring for the second time, was implemented just a month after the snowstorm. The United States was in a dilemma. If Greece were to go communist (at one time the monarchy controlled barely a square mile of Athens), the surrounding areas of Europe and the Middle East might also be in jeopardy. Truman therefore stepped into the breach with $400 million in economic and military aid for both Greece and Turkey (also considered in danger) in order, he said, to "insure the peaceful development of nations . . . free of coercion." The term *free of coercion* could be taken with a grain of salt that year when a National Security Act was being passed providing, among other things, for a Central Intelligence Agency that coerced, bribed, overthrew governments, and killed adversaries to shape foreign governments to the needs of Pax Americana. The Truman Doctrine, however, was the blueprint for the future: The United States gave economic and military aid to governments it hoped to keep within its orbit, entered into "entangling alliances" with them (for the first time during a peace period since George Washington had warned against them), and, in emergencies, when this nostrum failed, intervened militarily to save its clients.

The new pattern became clearer as Secretary of State George Marshall formulated his famous plan to rescue the Western European states, where disaster was imminent. Under the Marshall Plan $12.3 billion (a very large sum at the time) was granted seventeen governments over a four-year period, lest — in the words of Undersecretary of State William Clayton — "the Iron Curtain . . . move westward at least to the English channel" and the United States itself suffer "a blackout of the European market [that] could compel radical readjustments in our entire economic structure." The Marshall Plan was not exactly eleemosynary, since the United States received significant concessions in return — acceptance of the dollar as the world medium of exchange, agreement to a more open world market so that American goods and investments could penetrate it, as well as specific concessions such as granting the Rockefeller interests the right to buy 600,000 shares of Tanganyika Concessions in Africa. The American hammer lock on Western Europe, won with dollars and military aid, was so firm that governments held back sales of strategic materiel or arms to Soviet Russia and Eastern Europe under the threat they would lose American monetary support. Popular front governments in France and Italy were replaced under pressure from the United States by regimes more pliable to U.S. interests.

Both the dispensation of aid with strings attached and persistent interference in the internal affairs of foreign nations — sometimes openly, sometimes subtly — were to become fixtures of America's global imperialism. They replaced the standard British-French technique of occupying colonies with home troops — not because the United States was averse to military occupation, but because it had become impossible to police the world with a few million American troops in an age of revolution. At one time Britain could conquer India with 50,000 troops and France could take over Indochina with just a few thousand, but, as the French war against Algeria and the U.S. war against Vietnam would soon indicate, that sort of thing was no longer feasible. A victorious campaign against guerrillas, if possible at all, consumed far more resources than the capitalist states could afford. Nonetheless military force was a prerequisite of Pax Americana, for it made no sense to emplace or retain in power governments friendly to the "American way" unless those governments could be kept at the helm. The Truman Doctrine applied to Greece and Turkey was a beginning: American arms were supplemented by American "advisors" who did the training and played the decisive role in working out strategy. NATO (the North Atlantic Treaty Organization), conceived in 1947 and fleshed out in 1949, was the counterpart of Marshall Plan economic aid. The treaty involving fifteen nations had, as an interdepartmental foreign military assistance coordinating committee of the U.S. government stated it, a "two-fold objective . . . *first* to protect the North Atlantic Pact countries against *internal* aggression inspired from abroad," and second to "deter aggression" (emphasis mine). It is interesting that defense against internal forces, i.e., revolutionaries, is listed first. American guns saved the Greek monarchy, and American-subsidized rearmament helped France combat the Indochinese and Algerian revolutions, and Britain to fight the people of Malaya and Kenya.

The grand design, as it evolved, was to grant military help to the imperial powers — to save them per se and in some instances to save part of their empires — then to give help to the new nations that had broken away from the old empires. Few of them were in danger of attack by neighbors; the only threat to their survival was their own people, and it was this threat that the United States wanted to guard against. If economic and military aid was sufficient, that was the end of it; if not the United States often intervened directly through the CIA (by overthrowing the governments of Arbenz in Guatemala and Mossadegh in Iran, for instance); or U.S. troops were sent in directly, as in Lebanon and the Dominican Republic; or, in extreme cases, the United States came to the aid of clients incapable of defending themselves adequately by trying to do the job for them, as in the Korean and Vietnam wars.

For all this the Pentagon needed a network of bases around the world, and a force ready to jump into any fray anywhere at a few hours' notice. Even more, it needed to immobilize the Soviet Union, the one nation capable of giving substantial aid to peoples seeking to secede from Pax Americana. A military machine was fashioned, complete with nuclear weapons and launchers, to threaten the Soviets with disaster if they became too frisky. During the Korean War, for instance, measures were taken in Washington out of fear that the Russians would counter America's invasion of North Korea with seizure of West Berlin and perhaps a sector of Western Europe. General Eisenhower was dispatched to Europe to beef up NATO, since it didn't make much sense to win in Korea while losing more important bastions in Europe. Thus, while the trigger in postwar international affairs was a great national revolution, it expressed itself also as a conflict between two superpowers, and in the most extensive arms race in history.

The scope of Pax Americana and its potential effectiveness were not clear to us on the left in the mid-1940s. We continued to think of capitalism in stereotypic form — it was doomed to depression, war, and collapse, and we set the date for these dire happenings earlier rather than later without allowing for possible resiliency in the old system. Just as we failed to gauge the effectiveness of Keynesianism in ameliorating domestic economic problems in the 1930s, so we misjudged the effectiveness of what can be called "international Keynesianism" — the $170 billion used to prop friendly foreign economies — and militarism. It was not evident to us that the 2 trillion dollars the United States would spend on its military establishment in the next three decades would prime not only the economic pumps at home, but abroad. The militarism that sustained Pax Americana beyond our shores also sustained the U.S. economy, indeed kept it at amazingly high levels of prosperity.

II

A political movement that foresees depression when prosperity is imminent and defeatism and revolution when class peace is on the agenda obviously will not react as it should. That is what happened to the radical movement of the postwar period. Looking down the long pike of history we leftists were — and still are — correct in our evaluation of capitalism as an exploitative, war-promoting, and inhumane social system. We were and still are correct in prognosticating its ultimate demise — assuming the human species can survive the major threat of this generation, nuclear war. But to be ultimately right is of restricted value in formulating a political strategy for the here and now. You could talk revolution until your tongue was paralyzed, but the average worker or middle-class intellectual was not ready to put his sights beyond realizable reforms. There was no sense of desperation in American society as there had been fifteen years before, and, contrary to our expectations, the nation was soon veering determinedly to the right.

Under the circumstances the only kind of leftist politics that was feasible was either a reformist movement, or what might be called "scattershot politics," organizing campaigns around single issues, usually, though not always, for limited periods. Instinctively, without formulating it to myself in just that way, I made the transition from the intensely purposive activity of the previous dozen years to a looser form of political activity — unrelated to centralist parties or grouplets.

It was in fact a period of transition for me in many ways — personal, political, and in my trade union work. In the personal sphere my first marriage had broken up early in 1944, and my second one was consummated in October 1946. I was driving to Detroit with an official of another union, and Shirley, a recent widow whom I had known in the movement, asked if she could come along to meet a blind date. The blind date never showed up, but I took his place and we both knew within hours — we didn't have to discuss it — that we would soon be living together. It turned out to be an enduring union.

The transition in my trade union activity was a genuflection to reality — the reality of impotence. The local union I headed, Local 329, was affiliated with the CIO Retail, Wholesale, and Department Store Union, one of the smaller national unions, with no roots other than ourselves in the Chicago supermarket industry. That left our members isolated not only from workers in the same occupations but from the AFL teamsters, bakers, butchers, and maintenance workers who would be indispensable to victory if and when we went on strike. If we were to remain in the CIO, we would have to reconcile ourselves to a weak bargaining position and to helter-skelter organizing outside the supermarket field — in factories, offices, department stores, warehouses, and what have you.

That might have suited me fine, except that there were three additional problems. One was that RWDSU was embroiled in a national faction fight, and Local 329 and I were on the wrong side insofar as regional director Leonard Levy was concerned. We lined up with an anti-administration faction headed by Harold Gibbons of St. Louis, who had built one of the most dynamic local unions in the country and was challenging the national president Sam Wolchok and Levy for a variety of mis- and malfeasances, including lackluster leadership. Since our views coincided with his, we joined Gibbons in a campaign to topple Wolchok. Another problem was that Levy planned to merge all the locals in Chicago into a centralized joint board, which would deny us autonomy. Third, and flowing from the other two, Leonard was coldly unsympathetic to granting Local 329 money to mount an organizing drive. Since our own cupboard was bare and our staff limited to one woman and myself, the only new members I had been able to enroll between 1943 and 1945 were 550 previously unorganized candy factory and restaurant workers at Hillman's. That was not enough to give us viability; I wanted to build a union sufficiently diverse that a long strike in any of its segments would not jeopardize its survival.

We didn't succeed in ousting Wolchok and Levy just then, and the threat to abolish Local 329's autonomy forced us to a new course somewhat earlier than we had hoped. When Frank Socki was mustered out of the navy at the end of the war, Levy offered him a job on the international union's staff if he would work to get rid of me. The AFL had made him a similar offer four years earlier, but Frank didn't allow himself to be bought off then either. It wasn't merely that he was close to me personally — and to my political views — but he had a healthy suspicion of bribes. Instead of taking the job with Levy, Socki became the point man for finding a new haven within the AFL that would suit our twin needs for greater bargaining power and expansion. We investigated the possibility of joining the teamsters but found that door closed. Returning to RCIPA, from which we had fled a few years earlier, was impossible. Our choice narrowed to the AFL Building Service Employees International Union (BSEIU), which had already absorbed a sister CIO local, Local 291, representing department store employees.

The president of BSEIU was a Chicagoan, a smooth operator named William L. McFetridge, with solid connections both to the local teamsters (which was the deciding factor in our choice) and to the Democratic political machine. He was one of the closest friends of Richard J. Daley, who was destined to become — with McFetridge's help — mayor of the city within a decade and one of the nation's best known politicians. We were fully aware that McFetridge was not our idea of a trade unionist. He had started as a chauffeur and body guard to an uncle, Bill Quesse, president of the Chicago Janitors Union, who was subsequently convicted for extortion and pardoned by a Republican governor. In due course McFetridge, though hardly a janitor by profession, worked his way into Quesse's job as well as that of vice president of the national union. In that post he served — evidently without discord — under an East Coast gangster named George Scalise, who was ultimately sent to prison by New York's prosecutor Thomas E. Dewey for looting welfare funds. McFetridge's connections in and out of the labor movement clearly were not exemplary; in fact only two years previously I had written leaflets for James Leonard O'Grady, president of the elevator operators union, Local 66, whom McFetridge was trying to oust on the flimsy charge that he was not a citizen. But McFetridge was a power in Chicago and we needed that power, Socki and I felt, to augment our collective bargaining muscle and organize the unorganized. Anyway there was no other national union we could join that held the promise of greater support, and we had to go somewhere. It was, as they say, a marriage of convenience.

Early in 1946, then, Socki and I proposed — and the Local 329 membership agreed — to secede from the CIO and join McFetridge's BSEIU. After the usual NLRB election, which we won with negligible opposition, we found ourselves in a new home. The first benefits of our shift were impressive. We handed the Hillman company an ultimatum to fire its industrial relations lawyer, Stanford Clinton, or face a strike. This was an unusual step, but Clinton had been particularly difficult to deal with. It was a refreshing feeling for a change to have the company accede to our demand without argument. In our negotiations with the new lawyer, Sol Dorfman, we won benefits that would have been impossible had we remained under CIO tutelage — a one-year wage increase of about 20 percent, a three-hour reduction in the workweek with no loss in pay (it had been six days, forty-eight hours), thirteen weeks back pay and improved vacations. Subsequent contracts were also above par. It was a sad commentary on the state of the labor movement that we had the support of AFL teamsters and butchers only because Local 329 now carried an AFL label rather than because of concern for the principle of labor solidarity. But it is a fact that support would not have been forthcoming under a CIO shield.

McFetridge of course knew that I was a radical and that Socki shared most of my political views. But he evidently was confident he could make life so attractive for me that I would give up those "foolish" notions and settle into the establishment. One day he phoned: "What is Shirley doing this Saturday?" A half hour later his secretary came by with tickets to the football game that weekend, where Shirley and I sat between McFetridge and Richard Daley, with half a dozen ushers and politicians fawning on us. On another occasion, I returned from New York to find my name at the head of a list published by all four Chicago newspapers of eleven union officials who allegedly had endorsed the Democratic candidate for mayor, Martin Kennelly. McFetridge had used my name without consulting me, testing the waters to see if I would object. I did; I had each of the papers publish a retraction. Another time he called me to a meeting at his office where the heads of local BSEIU unions were being asked to pledge funds for the Democratic Party. Everyone said $500 or $1,000, but when it came my turn I parried the request with the observation that "my executive board will have to make the decision." Needless to say we never contributed anything to the Democrats (or Republicans) as long as I was the Local 329 director, but though McFetridge constantly tried to get me involved in his politics he never chided me when I refused. In 1948 he endorsed the Republican, Thomas Dewey, for president — I suspect because Dewey had stopped the prosecution of BSEIU officials (after convicting Scalise) before it embraced too many others. The rest of the house of labor of course was supporting Harry Truman, and when McFetridge appeared at a statewide AFL convention he took an awful booing. To remove the heat from himself he asked me if I wouldn't put in a resolution to support the Socialist candidate, Norman Thomas. "Sure," I said, "if you will speak for my resolution." He smiled and walked away.

McFetridge had that characteristic so many men of power have: He was generous as long as he felt there was a chance you might serve his purposes; but when it became apparent he wouldn't succeed, he could become a fearsome enemy. For the first six or eight years after our affiliation to BSEIU he was helpful to our local and me in many ways. He had me placed on the seven-man executive board of the metropolitan BSEIU council — 55,000 members — and I served as its publicity and educational director for years. When Daley periodically came to address the council he usually sat next to me at the far end of the table since he was invariably late. I had a number of interesting conversations with him on these occasions; once I asked how he was able to "live with the crime syndicate in the Democratic Party." "Well," he said, "to be practical about it you can't get rid of that element. The trick is to let them have a little power but never enough so they can threaten you."

McFetridge was also helpful with staff and money. The international union subsidized the salary first for Socki, then another good friend of mine, Walter A. (Scotty) Deans, and later others. With that kind of help we unionized a small department store — South Center — with 100 black workers, a lamp factory, a cellophane printing plant, and others. The local grew from 600 or 700 to four times that size for a while, and if it hadn't been for the fact that we refused to buckle to McFetridge's purposes we could have grown many times that large. Chicago was and is heavily unionized, but getting a foothold in new — and particularly un-unionized — fields was difficult without political clout. For instance, Local 329 conducted a campaign in 1954 and 1955 to unionize Michael Reese Hospital, with something like 800 or 1,000 nonprofessional workers. We got application cards from 90 percent of those eligible, but the hospital and the Jewish Federation of Chicago, which ran it, refused to bargain. I found myself once again in the office of Stanford Clinton, the same lawyer whom I had had fired by Hillman's, who was now representing the hospital. Clinton got an especial pleasure telling me — with a broad smile — "we ain't going to recognize you, Sid." I went from there to McFetridge's office to ask for strike sanction as required by the international's bylaws, but he refused to grant it until he discussed it with Dick Daley. Daley, politically beholden to many of the rich patrons of Michael Reese, thought it was a bad idea to jeopardize the health of patients. I offered to rent a dozen ambulances and transport any patient to the hospital of his choice, but that did not appease McFetridge — or Daley. Sanction was denied, Clinton had his way, we had to give up the drive or face the lifting of our charter.

Subsequently I printed 100,000 leaflets recounting the story of our abortive drive and urging Chicago's Jewry to withhold contributions from the Jewish Federation until it recognized our union. We distributed the circulars far and wide in Jewish neighborhoods (for which one of the federation leaders denounced me as an anti-Semite), but it evidently didn't hurt enough to make the hospital or the federation change their minds. A friend of mine, Victor Gotbaum of the American Federation of State, County and Municipal Employees who now heads AFSCME's district in New York but was then nursing a tiny organization in Chicago, also tried to unionize hospitals some years later and was forced to strike the Mount Sinai Hospital. McFetridge, who despised Gotbaum, not only gave him no support, but probably arranged with the teamsters to go through the strikers' picket lines. Here again Daley played a role behind the scenes, in support of McFetridge's position. The two men didn't want unions to grow if they could not control them. The bottom line to this saga is that when a large teamster local and a large service employees local in McFetridge's good graces initiated a joint organizing drive years later, no obstacles were put in their path. They hedge-hopped from one hospital to another — including Michael Reese and Mount Sinai — without much difficulty.

At the time we joined the BSEIU, there seemed to be two channels for breaking out of our isolation. One was to organize the department store industry together with two other locals — 291 and 242 — which had footholds on State Street, the retail mecca of Chicago. Local 291 had contracts with the Fair and Boston stores; Local 242, headed by Martin Heckmann a former book salesman, represented about 1,000 nonselling employees at Marshall Field's. But these were only a small portion of the tens of thousands of department store employees throughout the city and its environs ready for union cards if we could only enroll them.

Our first effort, under the aegis of my own Local 329, was directed at two of the big stores on the Street, Mandel Bros. and Carson, Pirie, Scott. While this campaign was sputtering along, making only modest progress, Heckmann and I initiated a more ambitious drive — in the name of Local 291 — among employees of the Goldblatt Bros., its ten stores, and a warehouse in the Chicago area. Every couple of days we would distribute a leaflet, usually written by me or sometimes by Heckmann, and wait for a cascade of application cards (which were stapled onto the leaflet). They came return mail in droves, far beyond our expectations, indicating there would be no problem enrolling the workers. There were other hurdles we had to contend with, however. One was the existence of a rival national union in the AFL — the Retail Clerks — which claimed jurisdiction over department store employees and which in fact had succeeded in unionizing Goldblatt's store in Gary, Inidana. To meet that problem Heckmann and I — with McFetridge's approval — worked out a deal with the Clerks for a joint drive. There was to be a single staff under my direction, a sharing of expenses, and a division of the membership after the drive had succeeded. The Clerks would take the salespeople, we in BSEIU the nonselling employees. Further, in order to guarantee the newly organized men and women effective bargaining power, we set up a Department Store Council, with its own elected officers separate from either national union, which would have overall direction of the organizing campaign and subsequently would negotiate contracts. It was a complicated structure, but the best possible under the circumstances, and fully protective of rank-and-file interests.

Our second difficulty was the company — and its attorney, our old nemesis, Stanford Clinton. Clinton was no old-fashioned union buster; he was the modern type who would gladly bargain with a union if he had a sub-rosa assurance in advance that it would settle for a meager wage increase or, better still, nothing. Otherwise he might try a subtle bribe (once he offered to pay Shirley's and my expenses for a two-year trip to Latin America), or he could revert to industrial Neanderthalism. In this instance, once the joint drive began, he had a couple of hundred of our key members fired on the flimsiest pretexts, and when I called him on it he said — with typical relish — "Well, Sid, you've got your recourse, you can take it up with the National Labor Relations Board." We could, of course, but it would take at least a year or two to adjudicate the discharge issue, and even if we won and had our people returned to the job the campaign momentum would have been lost.

There was, as Clinton knew, only one alternative — strike — and he was prepared for it. We, too, tried to prepare. With the approval of everyone concerned — the Retail Clerks, their local leader, Jack Cullerton, the rank and file in our working committee, and McFetridge, we set a date for the stoppage and began alerting our members. The strike was my responsibility and I must say it looked promising. I assigned one or more staff persons to each store, had picket signs printed, as well as thousands of leaflets aimed at the public, asking it to boycott Goldblatt's during the stoppage. But at 4 A.M., just an hour or so before the pickets were to take their places, I got a phone call from McFetridge. Shirley and I were then living in a single room at the Lord Manor Hotel on the near North Side, without a private bathroom, let alone a telephone. The only phone was in the hallway about fifteen feet away, and it was that number I had given McFetridge in case of an emergency. Sure enough, there was an emergency. "You've got to call off the strike," said my national union president. "The teamsters don't want us to go out." It was impossible, I told him, even if we wanted to because there was no way to contact all our key people. Anyway I was furious. McFetridge was supposed to have a strong relationship with the teamsters; one of his closest friends was Bill Lee, a teamster and president of the Chicago Federation of Labor. His biggest selling point was that he could deliver teamster support; now, where was it? We were told a little later — through a high official at another department store — that $50,000 had changed hands that day, and with that little bribe went the hopes of department store workers in Chicago for finding a haven in the trade union movement for years to come.

I told McFetridge the strike would have to proceed regardless of what the teamsters wanted, and went off to the union headquarters. By 11 A.M., however, the strike was over. The trucks refused to go through our lines for a few hours, then they disregarded the pickets as if they didn't exist. Later that morning McFetridge called Heckmann and me to his office, where we met with two Goldblatt officials and a top representative of the teamsters. They had a paper ready, which they asked us to sign, stating that Goldblatt's would put no obstacles in the way of an immediate NLRB election. Needless to say they were only covering their flanks; the election was delayed and sidetracked into oblivion on one excuse after another — despite the agreement. The drive fizzled. We had to turn, in future organizing campaigns, to an occasional small department store, such as South Center in the black ghetto, to factories that did not fit the jurisdiction of the larger industrial unions, then fleetingly to the hospital industry. In Chicago, unless you had political clout or were willing to sign back-door contracts, this sort of union drive was, in the parlance of our present generation, a hassle. Each one had its unique features, some, in retrospect, were amusing.

The South Center Department Store workers — about 100, all but four of whom were black — chose Local 329 rather than another union in our international which was headed by a black man. Their loyalty was to Scotty Deans and me for the help we had given them in strikes when they were in the CIO. They were truly wonderful people who, to this day, many years after the store has closed and long after most of them have reached retirement age, still look to me for advice. Once when the South Center committee, Frank Socki, and I were negotiating at the office of our BSEIU vice president, Tom Burke, I left word that if the members didn't hear from me by noon they were to stop working. We came to an agreement at 11:30 A.M., but instead of phoning, as I should have, I took the committee to lunch. When I arrived at the store at 1:30 P.M., the workers were still standing near their cash registers, with brown change bags in their hands, refusing to wait on customers until they had the word directly from me. Company supervisors swore on a stack of bibles that everything was settled and "Sid will be here soon," but the workers wouldn't budge.

At Crystal Tube, a cellophane printing plant with about 150 employees, we had few problems with the owner, Harold Goldring, or his attorney, settling grievances between contract negotiations. But once every two years we were forced on strike to win a new agreement — and invariably it was in the most bitter part of winter with below-zero temperatures, sometimes a dozen days in a row. There were seldom more than a couple of scabs and we almost always got approximately what we wanted at the end of six or eight weeks on the picket line, but for some reason or another Goldring never was able to come to an understanding early enough to avoid a confrontation. After five or six weeks I would search him out, butter his ego a little (a vital function in collective bargaining with most entrepreneurs), bring our committee in, and come to terms. I learned a little about Chicago's police during these strikes. Invariably they would take me aside: "You know it's customary to take care of the cops." "Why should I pay you anything," I would ask, "you haven't brought us a bit of information about what's going on inside, and you're probably getting more from Goldring than

I can give you, anyway." I never gave a policeman a penny during the Crystal Tube strikes.

I did pay off policemen during a strike we had at another plant, Bradley Mfg., a lamp company with 100 or 150 employees. The factory had to be picketed around the clock because a large part of its shipments went by rail, and the company's shipping dock was flush against a railroad siding. The railroad workers respected our picket line religiously, but if we didn't have any pickets around they would accept the lamps. One of the cops made me a proposition: "You can take your pickets off at night," he said, "and if the company plans any shipping I'll call you at home (about five blocks away) and you can hustle down with a picket sign." The policeman was as good as his word, he phoned when a sneak shipment was about to be made, and I came down — sometimes with Shirley — armed with a picket sign that kept the railroad car from the dock. For this service, which saved us many hours of aggravation and picket scheduling, I gave the policeman and his partner each $25 a week.

In the course of time, Local 329, Socki, Deans, and I became known for militancy — a circumstance that sometimes plunged us into strange organizing drives. Two of them in particular stand out in my mind. I was visited one day by a tall, stately woman in her eighties, Clara Rubovitz — who I learned later was the aunt of Chicago's best known independent alderman, Leon Despres — and another woman in her late thirties or early forties, who introduced herself as Madame Andree Ridoux. They were teachers at the Berlitz School of Languages, which they wanted to unionize. It was not the kind of venture we savored, because the teachers were too transient and there was little leverage for forcing the company to bargain if we had to strike — no shipments to halt, for instance. Nevertheless, we mimeographed some leaflets, gave the women a pile of application cards, and within a week most of the teachers had joined the union and a half dozen of them, including the beautiful Madame Ridoux, had been fired. Now we had no alternative but to file an NLRB charge of unfair labor practices — and call a strike.

Mme. Ridoux was an absolute whirlwind: she pulled students out of the elevators, she shouted at the owners in a delightful French accent, and picketed endlessly. She also prevailed on the elevator operators, who belonged to a local, to refuse service to and from the Berlitz floors, though students and staff got around this difficulty by going to the floor above. When the strike was a few days old I had the teachers paint picket signs in eleven languages, including Chinese, and we received an enormous amount of publicity not only in the local press but in national weeklies, including *Newsweek,* for the "picket line in eleven languages." The strike, however, could not halt Berlitz operations; it petered out. Months later we accepted a $1,254 back pay settlement for Ridoux and reinstatement to her old job, but as far as I know Berlitz in Chicago is still not unionized.

Another group that approached us was one of handsome young dance teachers, male and female, who worked for Arthur Murray Dance Studio on Jackson Boulevard. Again, we didn't boil over with enthusiasm but we couldn't turn the dance instructors away, especially since most of them had been made to pay for additional lessons, costing thousands of dollars, to get jobs as teachers. Ultimately we forced Arthur Murray to refund more than $50,000 to these instructors, but as expected we couldn't force management to bargain. One noontime on a cold winter day I had a few dozen instructors, in bathing suits and short pants, dancing on Jackson Boulevard, holding up traffic and drawing a vast crowd. One of the teachers walked with his dog on whom he placed a picket sign: MY MASTER LEADS A DOG'S LIFE AT ARTHUR MURRAY. After a week or two of picketing we adopted a supplementary tactic. I rented an office around the corner from the studio and offered free lessons to Arthur Murray students. At first it was, as they say, a ball; many of the students contributed a few dollars to pay for the rent. But the strikers drifted away, as did the students, and before long the fun and games were over. I never was entirely sure in my own mind whether we were right to expend time and energy on such peripheral campaigns, but in unionism as in life itself one sometimes has to play long odds. Anyway, it just seems wrong in principle to tell a worker, whatever his occupation, "I don't have the time to help you."

IV

Another possible avenue for broadening the base of Local 329 was suggested when Harold Gibbons, my old cohort during the Montgomery Ward strike, and his union were looking for a home in 1947–48. Gibbons, a former Socialist Party member who had migrated from the coal mines of Pennsylvania to Chicago, then St. Louis, built an amalgamated local of warehouse workers that had won plaudits far and wide. The local was, to begin with, a model of democracy, with the stewards council acting as the highest body, subject only to decisions of the annual conference of elected delegates. The local's health center, established during the war, took care of virtually every health need, including psychiatry, and was a model that many later would follow. And its militancy, sparked by such men as Lou Berra and Pete Saffo, two of Gibbons's associates, was in the best trade union tradition. Gibbons himself was rangy, charismatic, an excellent strategist, and a sound, logical speaker who always had the audience's attention. He was often criticized for womanizing and living high on the union expense account, charges that were true — a fact he never tried to hide — but no one ever accused him of taking money from an employer. My wife and I used to go out with him on occasion when he was in Chicago, but not too often because his spending habits became an embarrassment to us. Once at a party in our apartment Gibbons literally had to sneak out a back door to escape a married woman who was begging him to take her away from her husband. He was a man of many contradictions, but when it came to a trade union issue or, later, the Vietnam War, he was usually sound. I involved him in the antiwar movement years later with just a telephone call — one of the first top union leaders to be so recruited.

Thus, with Gibbons and his union seeking new affiliation, I posed the possibility to McFetridge of setting up a special department within our international that would include eight or ten locals from RWDSU, with Gibbons as the head of the department. It would be, in effect, an international within an international, with full autonomy. Gibbons was receptive when I brought him to Chicago to speak with McFetridge, and so were the leaders of a number of locals in New York, Toledo, and Detroit whom I visited to discuss the matter. But the plan foundered on two shoals. If the CIO warehousemen of St. Louis were to join the AFL, McFetridge would have to guarantee that neither the teamsters nor any other AFL affiliate that claimed warehouse jurisdiction would raid them. McFetridge sought to assure Gibbons that he could give such a guarantee but it was obvious that though he had clout in Chicago his influence did not extend nationwide. Nor could McFetridge offer support against gangsters who threatened both Gibbons and members of his staff. In any case, Jimmy Hoffa, then a teamster vice president but already recognized as the power behind the scenes, entered the auction at this stage, and he had more to sell than I did. He offered to merge a larger warehouse local into Gibbons's union if Gibbons would join the teamsters, and do the same thing for Larry Steinberg in Toledo, George McLean of the dairy workers in Detroit, and others in New York and elsewhere. Hoffa undoubtedly had unsavory associations, but he also recognized a need for brainpower if he was to take control of the teamsters international — and flesh it out. He sent a big bruiser to St. Louis to defend Gibbons against the hoodlums, and he helped Gibbons ease out the old officers of the teamster local — 688 — with which he merged. In due course Gibbons became in effect Hoffa's executive vice president when the latter replaced Dave Beck as president of the union.

I got to know Hoffa moderately well in the ensuing years. I would see him while visiting Gibbons at the national office on Louisiana Avenue in Washington, and I also interviewed him a number of times for articles in the *Nation* and *Ramparts.* The piece I wrote in the *Nation* was a challenge to Attorney General Robert Kennedy for "pursuing a man" rather than "a crime." Hoffa could have been everything Kennedy said he was, but it was illegal and unconstitutional to open Hoffa's mail, and shadow and wiretap him and his staff, waiting to pounce on him if he so much as spit on the sidewalk. An attorney general, I wrote, should pursue a crime — to find out who committed it — not a man, on the off chance he might commit a crime in the future. I didn't write the piece as a favor to Hoffa or Gibbons; it simply represented my beliefs concerning due process. Hoffa reprinted the piece in hundreds of thousands of copies.

Jimmy was a strange man, short, squat, tough, fearless. He didn't drink, smoke, or, according to Gibbons who should have known, run around with other women. He didn't have a particularly keen sense of humor either, but on the other hand he had one of the fastest brains I've ever confronted; you could almost hear the computer working in his head. He reacted quickly and firmly within the context of his practical philosophy. In an interview I taped in about 1965 or 1966, he stated his opposition to Lyndon Johnson's invasion of the Dominican Republic and to the war in Vietnam (though he asked me not to publish his remarks on Vietnam because it might cause him problems in a pending trial). On the other hand, when I asked him whether he felt the United States should stop bullying China, he gave me an adamant no. "You know how it is in the trade union movement, Sid," he said, "unless you can show the boss you have the strength to knock his brains in he won't yield. The government needs the same kind of strength with China, otherwise they'll never respect us."

Hoffa had a down-to-earth quality about him. Most union officials would give their right arms for an invitation to the White House, but Hoffa was completely indifferent to such bogus honors. If he liked or admired you he would give you the shirt off his back. On occasion he insisted on driving me to the airport, and when I pleaded I could take a taxi he cut me short with "nothing doing." Once I asked him if he would let the Women Strike for Peace use his union's meeting room.

I expected him to say it might embarrass him during his legal difficulties; instead he said sure. One of the people he admired most, as I've said, was Farrell Dobbs, the Minneapolis Trotskyite whose leadership in the 1934 trucker strikes laid the foundation for the great surge toward the teamsters union.

But the pressures of our society — in particular the drives to get ahead, make money, be somebody — penetrate everywhere, including the union movement. With the rarest of exceptions, everyone is seduced by it to one extent or another — and the opportunities are there almost for the asking. Hundreds of leading labor leaders forgot their socialism because that would have meant going back to the shop and giving up positions that gave them power and access to men of power. Hoffa was never a socialist, but he wanted to be where he was, at the epicenter of things, and he wanted to be there so much he was willing to enter into alliances with gangland figures and unsavory politicians to stay there. This sort of thing, let it be noted, could happen only in the United States, first because there is no effective socialist movement to guard against it, and second because the minions of law and order, as well as employers, are as often as not in league with crime syndicate figures too.

In any case, Hoffa had more to offer Gibbons and his associates than McFetridge, and my plans for an international within an international died aborning. It is a pity it didn't come about. It would have been an interesting experiment and it might have offered Harold Gibbons a better stage from which to operate than as adjutant to Hoffa. Hoffa benefited immensely from that relationship, but the two men broke with each other at the time of the Kennedy assassination in 1963 (over a picayune issue, seemingly — whether to fly the flag at the teamster headquarters at half mast — but really over deeper division), and when Hoffa went to jail a few years later he chose as his "temporary" stand-in his alter ego from Detroit, Frank Fitzsimmons, a man of far lower stature than Gibbons.

Concurrent with all this, I became involved in a host of activities that were "scattershot" in the sense that they were not related to each other, but were done solely for a good cause, with no ulterior motive of proselytizing for a political movement. The first one of major importance was the Hickman case.

James Hickman was an intensely religious Southern sharecropper who emigrated to Chicago with his wife and eleven children in search of the good life. There he found a job with a steel company which netted him a fair income, but adjusting to the big city, in particular to its housing patterns, was a problem. Wartime restrictions on housing construction made apartments as scarce as hens' teeth. Hickman, a short black man with a pleasant face, finally paid $100 to a black landlord named David Coleman, as an under-the-table bribe to rent an attic in a three-floor building on the near West Side, one of Chicago's ghettos. It was a monstrous living space for the nine people who crammed into it, the two parents and seven of the eleven children. There was no gas or heat, the water was often turned off, the toilet was outside the "apartment." "We lived like rats in a hole," Hickman later said. And to make matters worse the landlord ultimately decided to get around rent-control restrictions — rent controls were imposed during the war — by dividing the apartments into "kitchenettes" that would be freed from control and net more profit. In order to start conversion, however, he had to get rid of the present tenants. Unfortunately for Coleman they didn't want to move — and under the law couldn't be made to do so.

According to Hickman, his landlord tried to burn them out of the attic — and there was much evidence that Hickman was telling the truth. A number of small fires occurred on the stairway leading to the attic. Then, one day, Coleman was explicit about his intent: "I'll get you out of here," he told Hickman, "if I have to burn you out." Sure enough, in January 1947 a great fire broke out on the top floor and attic of the building — and four of Hickman's younger children were burned to death. Hickman, called home from his job, was absolutely shattered. Exactly six months to the day after the fire James Hickman loaded the pistol he had brought with him from the South, took a trolley to the home of the landlord, pumped six bullets into him, took the trolley back, and surrendered to the police.

Left to his own resources Hickman might still be in prison — or dead. But the tenants in the building where he lived had been periodically contacted by the Chicago Tenants League, a group under Trotskyite influence, and they turned to the Tenants League now for help. In short order Hickman had a lawyer, Mike Meyer, who was attorney for the League, and the Hickman Defense Committee was formed by Mike Bartell of the Socialist Workers Party, which included along with Bartell and a young chap named Frank Fried, three unionists — Willoughby (Bill) Abner, a black staff member of the UAW and a major figure in the NAACP; Charles Chiakulas, president of a UAW local; and myself as the effective core. Chiakulas, who was to be a very close friend for the next twenty years — until he was killed in an auto accident — was a remarkable person. Tall, handsome, buoyant, Charlie could (and did) smash his fist through a glass window to pull a driver, intent on crossing a picket line, from the cab of his truck. He often told how he had become head of his local by beating up a bully who was urging people to stay out of the UAW. But Charlie also had a remarkably fast brain, and though his education was limited he read books voraciously — and retained what he read better than anyone I can remember. He often quoted verbatim passages from one or another of my own books that I had long forgotten. I called him an "uncultured pearl," but in the course of the next two decades as he became a UAW international rep, and then the head of the regional organizing staff for the CIO industrial union department, his "culture" improved perceptibly.

The strategy we adopted to win Hickman's release was two-tiered. The first was legal. We hired two additional lawyers, Leon Despres — a labor attorney who would soon become alderman of the fifth ward and for more than twenty years act as a gadfly to Mayor Richard Daley in the city council — and William Temple — a black attorney who had represented heavyweight champion Joe Louis. The team concluded that Hickman's only legal defense was temporary insanity, and that was the strategy we all concurred on. We hired two prominent psychologists to examine Hickman and testify to the validity of our claim of temporary insanity. In point of fact this was no synthetic argument. When Hickman took the stand months later to explain "how God instructed me to kill that man" everyone in the courtroom was struck by his intense sincerity. There was no snickering, you could hear a pin drop in that august chamber, and few people listening to the accused man would doubt that in the great crisis of his life, the death of his beloved children, he had lost touch with reality.

The only friction between the lawyers and the rest of us on the Hickman committee was over how much of the social problem — housing shortages, landlord greed, discrimination against blacks — should be introduced into evidence. We finally arrived at a modus vivendi, agreeing that the primary objective of the lawyers must be to secure Hickman's freedom, but within that context they must strive to paint for the jury as much of the social issues as possible.

The second tier of our activity, I believe, was the more important. Fried toured the country setting up Hickman Defense Committees, and in between did the day-to-day work in Chicago as well. He was an extremely effective organizer, a talent he displayed to great advantage when he became Chicago's leading folk music impressario many years later. Eleanor Roosevelt, the late president's wife, lent her name to the cause and that gave us a big boost in raising the funds we needed for legal and other expenses.

In Chicago itself we enrolled a number of luminaries such as Ralph Helstein, president of the CIO packinghouse workers; Henry McGee, president of the Chicago NAACP; Richard Rober, star of the play *Call Me Mister;* and Willard Motley, who was then enjoying great acclaim coast to coast for his novel *Knock on Any Door.* I took Motley, whom I had known while he was writing his opus, to see Marshall Field, owner of the Chicago *Sun-Times.* It was an important step for us since we were certain to have the hostility of the leading newspaper in town, the blatantly conservative Chicago *Tribune.* Field, though immensely wealthy, was a liberal of the old school and obviously taken with Motley; he promised to give our side of the story full play — and did. Motley also wrote an article on the case, which appeared in papers coast to coast.

Another coup was the involvement of the famous stage and screen star Tallulah Bankhead. I was leaving my office on Dearborn Street one evening when I noticed her name on the marquis half a block away. She was starring in a new play. On the spur of the moment I went to the stage door and asked for her. To my surprise she knew about Hickman and was immensely sympathetic. When I asked her, however, to speak at the rally we planned at the Metropolitan Community Church, she shuddered as if I had hit her with a blast of arctic air. "Why, Mr. Lens, how can I make a speech?" It took a little while to figure out that what she meant was that while she was capable of reciting other people's lines, she was incapable of constructing a speech of her own. I agreed therefore to write a speech for her, and a couple of days later she advised that "I read it to my secretary and made her cry. I'll be happy to deliver it." At the rally itself she drew tears from the whole audience, a couple of thousand people. I followed her with a collection speech that also brought out tears, and even better, much needed dollars.

Our meetings and the scores of thousands of leaflets we distributed created a favorable climate for Hickman, especially in the black community. The gist of our appeal, as expressed in a leaflet I wrote for the defense committee, was that Hickman was one of the "millions of common people who are victims of the scandalous housing shortage and of landlords' greed." We conceded that his "action was not an answer to the problem but it was an expression of the frustration and resentment of the underprivileged against those responsible for their misery. The real criminals are real estate interests who put profit above the welfare of the people. The real criminals are those who foster racial segregation and condemn millions to the congested, vermin-infested fire-traps of the black ghetto. The real criminals are the public officials who permit landlords to violate all safety regulations and refuse to launch a public housing program to relieve the shortage."

The trial, which took place toward the end of the year, was a dramatic affair that attracted considerable attention. Charlie Chiakulas, who was sitting in the audience as the jury was being picked, whispered in my ear: "Holy Christ that's one of my best shop stewards they just put on." We had a sure vote for acquittal. Unbeknownst to us until later, the prosecution also had a sure vote on the jury — the mistress of one of their police witnesses. What a thin thread a human life hangs on under our judicial system!

The state, in the person of an assistant state's attorney named Samuel Friedman, put on a simple case, identifying the victim, the murder weapon, and so on. Our case was much more complex. In addition to Hickman's testimony — which Friedman was unable to batter down — that God had told him to exact retribution, there were the psychologists, and a number of people who testified about Hickman's plight and the social conditions of the building. In the end the jury was hung — seven, sparked by Charlie's shop steward, for acquittal; five for conviction. Afterward I approached Friedman, with whom I had developed cordial relations, and asked whether he intended to go ahead with a second trial or was willing to work out some arrangement. Here, I think the general popular sympathy we had generated affected the state's attorney's office. In due course, our lawyers and Friedman worked out a deal for Hickman to plead guilty in return for a sentence of two years probation. We thought it was a great victory, quite the reverse of what usually happens to blacks in Chicago's courts. After the sentence, Hickman, his wife, the three lawyers, Abner, Chiakulas, Bartell, and I posed for a picture on the steps of the county courthouse — but I never saw Hickman or his wife again.

Viewed against the traditional life I had become accustomed to in the RWL, the Hickman campaign offered a new type of experience. It may have added a few members to the Trotskyites, but for Abner, Chiakulas, and me the only reward was that we had secured the release of a man who would otherwise have been jailed or executed.

With Chiakulas as my frequent sidekick I became involved in similar activities as the occasions presented themselves. Around the same time as the Hickman case we formed the Council for Job Equality on State Street, whose purpose, as stated in its bylaws, was "to seek the employment of qualified sales clerks and other employees in the retail stores of State Street without discrimination because of race, religion, or national origin, and specifically for the immediate hiring of Negro sales clerks." The idea wasn't very popular with many of the employees we were trying to unionize, but it was morally justified, so we pursued it. Along with Homer Jack, a Unitarian minister who was to play a role in the peace movement for many years, my union associate Martin Heckmann, a local black alderman Archibald Carey, and others, we put picket lines in front of the two department stores at opposite ends of the Loop, Marshall Field's and Goldblatt's, then met with management to discuss the issue. Both Field's and Goldblatt's insisted they had no prejudice in their hearts, but would make no commitment for a specific program to hire blacks. It wasn't until a decade later when Martin Luther King began marching in the South that the barriers began to fall. During that period too Chiakulas and I put picket lines in front of State Street stores, the target this time being the Woolworth chain which had incurred the wrath of the civil rights movement nationally.

VI

Until my life found a new focus in the antiwar movement a decade later, I became a sort of political fireman. Wherever there was a crisis of some sort I became involved. Thus, when the Trotskyites contacted me in 1949 about one of their comrades, James Kutcher, a World War II veteran who had lost both his legs in the battle of San Pietro and had subsequently been fired from his job as a clerk in the Newark Veterans Administration office for being a "subversive," my union's former attorney Francis Heisler and I formed a committee in Chicago to publicize the issue. This was a particularly reprehensible manifestation of the McCarthyist mood then beginning to sweep the country, since there were obviously no secrets in the Veterans Administration that Kutcher could peddle to the Russians. But a great nation, unsure of its new-found power, succumbed to a host of delusions, one of them being that communists were ten-foot-tall conspirators who could accomplish almost any deviltry unless exposed. Our committee held a few public meetings and prevailed on many people to protest the discharge of Kutcher, but we were unable to build a big movement on behalf of this poor man. It was eight years before the nation recovered enough of a sense of tolerance to reinstate Kutcher.

The country was moving perceptibly to the right and drawing the liberals along with it. The Americans for Democratic Action, formed on the initiative of refugee socialists such as James Loeb, future ambassador to Peru, began by damning both Soviet imperialism and British imperialism, but in the end yielded to the Cold War thesis that the main enemy was the Soviet Union. Labor leaders grumbled against the Taft-Hartley Act, which required them to sign affidavits that they were not communists or advocates of overthrowing the government, but in the end they all signed — except for beetle-browed John L. Lewis of the miners. Since unions whose leaders refused to sign could not petition the NLRB for an election, many communist unionists circumvented the law by formally resigning from the Party, but otherwise maintained their allegiance. In the shops and mills, however, the mood against "commies" was turning bitter, even violent. It was not surprising, therefore, that the Kutcher case did not ignite a big campaign by labor leaders. Most of the former socialists, such as the Reuthers, were trying to establish their credentials as "good Americans" who scorned the communists.

On the other side of the equation it must be admitted that the communists made it difficult for anyone but a communist or an innocent to work with them. When the Progressive Party was formed in 1948 Chiakulas and I discussed for hours whether we should join it. (I had been opposed to a labor party in the 1930s but had changed my mind in the 1940s.) We concluded that it would be useless. The communists, who dominated the Progressive Party, would never allow anyone to play a role without controlling them, and neither Charlie nor I would submit to being manipulated like puppets. There was also the matter of the Progressive Party's image; it had acquired by osmosis, so to speak, the same image as the Communist Party, that of being an unquestioning parrot for the foreign policy of the Soviet Union. I agreed with some planks in that foreign policy. Accepting *every* plank, as the American communists did, simply tainted one as an agent of a foreign power. I'm sure that was a major reason for Henry Wallace's poor showing — 1,157,326 votes as against 1,176,125 for Dixiecrat J. Strom Thurmond — and 24 million for Truman. A man who had once been vice president of the United States should have fared better, even on a third party ticket. In 1924, Senator Robert La Follette, also running on a third party ticket, had garnered almost 5 million votes — against 16 million for the winner, Coolidge.

One of the subtle changes in my behavior in those years after I left the organized left was a tendency to work closer with certain liberals who were not caught up in the McCarthyist hysteria. Elmer Gertz, the well-known Chicago lawyer (he represented Jack Ruby after Ruby murdered Lee Harvey Oswald), recruited me to the Public Housing Association. Some years later I was added to the executive board of the Chicago Council on Foreign Relations. I joined with Homer Jack and Jack Bollens, then peace secretary of the American Friends Service Committee (AFSC) in Chicago, to form a chapter of SANE (Committee for a Sane Nuclear Policy) in our city. And I found myself appearing on lecture platforms of such organizations as the City Club of Chicago ("Are Labor Unions Monopolies?") or debating at Commerce and Industry luncheons on whether "Labor and Capital" can "Get Together." Somewhere along the way — it must have been in the mid-1950s — Chiakulas and I became involved with Bill Abner in a fight to take the leadership of the NAACP from a group that was an alter ego for the Democratic Party machine. Though we had the vast majority of the active members on our side, the machine outmaneuvered us by buying hundreds of memberships for its black precinct captains a day or two before the balloting (at $2 apiece). But while Abner lost the presidency of the Chicago area NAACP, I organized a branch in the Hyde Park–Kenwood area and served as its president for a number of years until the branch was dissolved. We scored a number of successes, most notably in forcing a local hospital to desegregate its facilities (one of the patients, it turned out, was the mother of a black alderman who joined our campaign and gave it considerable weight).

Unbeknownst to my conscious self my scattershot activities were in fact the beginnings of a subliminal reformulation of political philosophy. I had believed for a decade or more that the central necessity for revolutionary change was a revolutionary party like that of the Bolsheviks in Russia; I was moving toward the conclusion that an American revolution would be led by a movement more like the American Populists of the 1890s — a decentralized *coalition* of movements. Even more subtly, I was moving to the concept that an American revolution would not necessarily come about like November 7, 1917, in Russia or 1789 in France, but could take place in stages — like the bourgeois Danish revolution of the eighteenth and nineteenth centuries.

But all of this, as I say, was a subliminal change, not yet within my intellectual grasp or thought out in detail. Before I could make the transition consciously I would have to do much probing, studying the issues — and writing about them — in greater depth than I had been accustomed to in my previous incarnation.

I resumed my writing career, albeit in different form, combining it with lecturing and teaching. After the RWL folded, a few friends and I published a little magazine, *Left Wing,* in the hopes it would galvanize a small force of leftists willing to relate to each other on a less formal basis. It didn't catch on, unfortunately. Concurrently I began working on a book to explain some of the anomalies of the American Labor movement. How, for instance, was it possible for out and out gangsters to burrow into a movement born out of idealistic concern for the underprivileged? Why did the communists — Stalinists — alternate from working within to working outside the established labor structure? And though labor and capital were mortal enemies by the circumstance that each fought for a bigger share of the same dollar, was there any way in which the development of capitalism shaped the contours of labor? It took about a year to write the book (which I originally titled *Trojan Horses in the House of Labor*), and another year to peddle it, have it edited and published. Re-reading it now, it is still a solid dissertation on how the trade union movement became what it is. I showed how prosperity had eroded the idealism of the socialists (e.g., Sam Gompers and Peter McGuire) who originally organized the AFL, converting them within two decades into "business unionists"; how racketeers could muscle into unions with the support of employers and politicians; how John L. Lewis and Sidney Hillman had formed the CIO in order to contain the communists and other radicals who were the true organizers of the upsurge of the 1930s.

Publishing a book was an exciting experience — certainly the first one. The publisher, Henry Regnery, was a wealthy man, scion of a conservative family in Hinsdale, Illinois, that had supported America First in the prewar period. Henry would again turn severely to the right a year or two later, when he published books by Freda Utley and William Buckley, but at the moment his politics were in a state of flux. He was flirting with Morris Rubin, editor of the old La Follette magazine the *Progressive* — presumably because of the *Progressive*'s anti-militarist position — and he had an exceedingly level-headed editor, Paul Scheffer, who was smitten by my opus. Scheffer turned out to be the best editor I've ever had, a man with both keen insight and a decent sense of humor ("All writers are crazy," he would say, "except you, of course, Mr. Lens"). Making literally hundreds of suggestions he brought out the best in my book, prodding me to correct many inconsistencies I would have passed by. Scheffer and I remained friends until he retired and left Chicago. He was no radical — "I'm a bourgeois liberal," he would say — but he understood the left better than most "experts."

The book, retitled by Scheffer *Left, Right and Center, Conflicting Forces in American Labor,* came off the presses in May 1949 and caused a greater than normal stir. It was reviewed in scores of papers and magazines, ranging from the New York *Times* to the *Annals of the American Academy* — almost all were very favorable. Regnery financed an autograph party at Roosevelt University, where a few hundred people listened to verbal reviews by three labor writers — Joel Seidman, Jack Barbash, and the vice president of the ladies' garment workers' union, Rose Pesotta. Particularly pleasing to me were the blurbs written for the jacket by A. J. Muste with whom I had recently re-established contact, and Kermit Eby, former research director of the CIO and just then a social science professor at the University of Chicago. Each review that appeared in the press was nectar to my ego — especially those in the local Chicago press, and in the *Times Literary Supplement* in far-off London. Regnery's public relations people put out a four-page folder to promote the book, with blurbs from a business magazine, *The Executive,* calling it "one of the best commentaries for the understanding of the labor movement," and from the UAW publication, *Ammunition,* calling it "a very good book."

As pleasing as was the appearance of the book in print were some of the spinoffs. The liberal *Daily Compass* in New York published a written debate with Senator Wayne Morse of Oregon on the topic "Should Labor Have Its Own Political Party?" with Morse taking the negative and I the positive.

The industrial relations center at the University of Chicago, headed by Fred Harbison, began to take a special interest in me. Two members of its staff, Art Carstens and A. A. (Sandy) Liveright (with whom I remained lifelong friends), recruited me for lectures and courses on labor problems, out of which I distilled an article entitled "The Meaning of the Grievance Machinery." Harbison placed the piece with the prestigious *Harvard Business Review.* Harbison, a middle-of-the-road figure who liked to cultivate spry leftists, offered me a Ph.D. if I would write another book and attend the university full-time for one year. It was a flattering proposition for a man totally without academic credits, but I saw no value to a Ph.D. unless I intended to shift from the labor movement to academia, and I didn't.

By the end of the 1940s, then, I was drifting with a new tide I didn't fully understand, and functioning in unaccustomed diversity. On a given day I might get up at 6 A.M. to do a little writing, meet at 9 with a chap named Cooper, a Trotskyite who had gained control of a company union at the Weiboldt department stores and was trying to swing them into our Building Service International (we ultimately succeeded), shout myself hoarse over the phone a little later arguing a grievance with a personnel director, have lunch with Chiakulas and ruminate about the state of the world, participate in a contract negotiations session after lunch, attend a meeting of an organization on which I was a board member, and teach a class either at my own office or at a university. It was an interesting daily fare, though without the kind of determined direction that punctuated life in the 1930s and the first half of the 1940s.

In the 1950s I would come closer to the new direction — teasing it out of the unconscious.

Chapter 7
The Cold War Through
Two Prisms

I

There is this story of the two cloak and suiters who meet on the avenue. "How're things going?" one salesman asks. "Terrible," the other replies. "I haven't sold a suit in three days." "So what," says the first man. "With me things are even worse. On Monday I sold one suit. On Tuesday, none. Then on Wednesday the fellow who bought the suit on Monday brought it back."

That's how many of us felt in the late 1940s and early 1950s: not only had the expected turn to the left failed to materialize, but we were experiencing a shift to the right such as the nation had seldom witnessed before. It was a depressing period filled with tension and anxiety — for leftists as well as for the nation per se. The American establishment had won a sensational victory; its rule of the planet was almost unchallenged. But somehow it didn't feel secure; and in that insecurity it was lashing out at dangers that didn't exist and searching out enemies that didn't threaten it. McCarthyism — a word that would soon be on millions of lips — was an excrescence of this mood; the mood itself, however, was more pervasive, saturating a society imbued with the fear that its great victory might be stolen from it.

One of the first manifestations of this insecurity was the Atomic Energy Act of 1946, which imposed the death penalty for disseminating atomic "secrets" — even in peacetime — a law more stringent than the Espionage Act in force during the war itself. As of 1949, the Atomic Energy Commission (AEC) held 308,000 reports in its file, 90 percent of them marked "secret." Three months after the energy law, President Truman issued Executive Order 9835, calling for investigation of the "loyalty" of every person employed by the government. His attorney general, Francis Biddle, prepared a list of organizations he considered to be "totalitarian, fascist, communist, or subversive . . . " and anyone who appeared to be linked to one of these 200 groups was ferreted out. When the Dies Committee — House Committee on Un-American Activities (HUAC) — made that list public it became a bible for blacklisting and firing workers in private corporations. For most employers it didn't matter whether the person had severed his or her membership or whether the organization still existed, the safe thing to do was to fire the suspected worker.

Later the "loyalty" program was replaced, under Congressman Richard Nixon's prodding, by a "security risk" program, which meant that employees had to prove their loyalty; the government no longer had to prove disloyalty. Still later, Eisenhower's famous Executive Order 10501 gave government agencies the right to classify documents secret, top secret, and so on, and withhold them from public perusal. By the time Jimmy Carter became president in 1977, 70 to 100 million records were being concealed through classification, according to the General Accounting Office. The public's right to know — so that it might restrain its government if it wanted to — was converted into a relationship where the government restrained its electorate through secrecy.

A second effect of the growing psychosis over security was the establishment of what in effect was a dual government, superimposed on the old one. The National Security Act of 1947 created a number of boards to orchestrate military procurement and military research, as well as the octopuslike Central Intelligence Agency (CIA) which, according to its first director, Allen Dulles, was empowered to intervene in "the *internal conflicts* within the countries of Europe, Asia and South America" (emphasis mine). This of course violated the United Nations Charter, which the United States had signed just a few years before, and scores of treaties with individual nations; but legalism and legality got lost in the "war against communism." Equally ominous, the act provided for a National Security Council composed of four statutory members — the president, vice president, and the secretaries of State and Defense — plus others designated by the president. The council was charged with coordinating "domestic, foreign, and military policies," a formula under which it effectively formulated long-term programs, supervised the CIA, and, according to a report by Senator Frank Church's committee in 1976, sanctioned literally thousands of covert undertakings around the world — a coup d'etat in Brazil, the financing of friendly political parties in Italy, the disruption of a union movement in France, and so on. The National Security Council, almost unknown to most citizens, became the fulcrum of the national security state, a lean, covert, secretive, institution at the center of American power, but far removed from popular checks and balances.

Reflecting the national insecurity, anti-communism attained the fervor of a religion. Soviet losses in the war included 15 to 20 million dead; 15 large cities, 1,710 towns, 70,000 villages partly or wholly destroyed; 6 million buildings demolished; and 10,000 power stations ruined. No one could seriously believe that in that state of disarray Moscow was preparing new military adventures. As late as March 1949, John Foster Dulles conceded in a national magazine interview that the Soviet government "does not contemplate the use of war as an instrument of its national policy. I do not know any responsible official, military or civilian, in this government or any government, who believes that the Soviet government now plans conquest by open military aggression." As for the U.S. Communist Party, it was a shell of its former self. Yet Congress, the Justice Department, and all kinds of self-appointed political vigilantes pursued alleged communists — many of whom were so designated because they belonged to the NAACP or the American Civil Liberties Union (ACLU) — with intemperate fury.

In 1949, eleven Communist Party leaders were put through the ordeal of a nine-month trial (a twelfth, William Z. Foster, was severed because of poor health), and convicted on charges of a conspiracy to teach and advocate the overthrow of the government by force and violence, and membership in an organization that advocated that policy. The trial was a clear repudiation of the established legal principle that advocacy — of anything — in itself was not a crime; only acts, not thoughts, were prosecutable. Yet for days on end the prosecution read into the record Marxist classics such as Lenin's *State and Revolution* or the *Communist Manifesto* by Marx and Engels, as if the books themselves could unsettle a society that had just come out almost unscathed from the bloodiest war in history.

Peggy Dennis, wife of the Party's national secretary, Eugene Dennis, tells a heart-rending story in her autobiography of the effect of her husband's incarceration on her young son. The seven-year-old not only was suddenly deprived of a father in a formative period of his life, but had to contend with such mean tricks as red rubber rats placed on the apartment doorknob, constant surveillance by the FBI wherever he and his mother went, threatening notes, and obscene phone calls. Theirs was not the only tragedy. Families were disrupted, hundreds of communists went underground fully expecting that their party would soon be outlawed. (Senator Hubert Humphrey, the liberal Democrat, did in fact introduce such legislation at one point, presumably to prove that liberals were as good anti-communists as conservatives.) One of the convicted communists, Gil Green, became a good friend of mine in the 1960s after he was released from jail. Whatever the crimes of Stalin in Russia, or the shortsightedness of the Party in the United States, Green was a decent person, completely trustworthy in his relationship with other people – and he was certainly no automaton who believed what he was told to believe. He opposed the Soviet invasions of Hungary and Czechoslovakia, and disagreed with the Party on other issues as well. Nonetheless the government put him in jail simply for believing in socialism.

The new decade – the 1950s – was to see this hysteria reach a crescendo. It began in late January 1950 with the conviction of former high State Department official Alger Hiss on perjury charges that he had lied at a HUAC hearing in 1948 when he denied he had given secret documents to self-proclaimed communist agent Whittaker Chambers. Half a year later Julius and Ethel Rosenberg, along with others, were arrested and convicted on the charge of having passed "secrets" of the atom bomb to the Russians – stolen for them by Julius's brother-in-law David Greenglass. What was distressing about both these cases was not whether the defendants were guilty (my personal opinion was that passing information to a wartime ally was no terrible misfeasance anyway), but the injudicious spirit with which the U.S. government pursued all three. Hiss, it should be noted, was not convicted for espionage but for perjury – at a hearing dominated by young Congressman Richard Nixon who himself had been elected by brazenly lying about his opponent, Jerry Voorhis. The Rosenbergs were executed in 1953, leaving two young children behind, whereas Klaus Fuchs, a British scientist who had worked on the Manhattan Project – and therefore knew far more than the Rosenbergs or Greenglass about The Bomb – admitted he had spied for the Russians but was sentenced to only fourteen years by a British court. The American establishment, is seems, was not noted for tolerance.

Between the Hiss conviction and the Rosenberg arrests, an obscure Republican Senator from Wisconsin, oddly enough elected with the support of the Communist Party, made history of sorts with a bizarre speech early in February 1950 at Wheeling, West Virginia. Joseph McCarthy, holding his hand aloft, told an audience in that city: "I have in my hand a list of 205 . . . a list of names that were made known to the Secretary of State as being members of the Communist Party and who nevertheless are still working and shaping policy in the State Department." McCarthy never produced that list, or any list for that matter, and never proved a single major allegation, but such was the insane fear of communism that the nation was mesmerized by such charges. It never bothered to question whether the government had a right to discharge a person simply because of political views — especially from a nonsensitive position — or whether private industry had such a right. The idea spread, instead, that communists had to be uprooted wherever they were, because just a handful of them in the right places, even one or two, could do untold damage. Many people even believed that a few traitors in the State Department had turned over China to Mao's communists. The charges fed on each other like a tapeworm, each one more lurid than the previous one, so wild in fact that when McCarthy accused America's wartime chief of staff, General George Marshall, of being part of the communist conspiracy, "whose every important act for years has contributed to the prosperity of the enemy," the Wisconsin senator's popularity, instead of vanishing, shot up.

There were actually millions, tens of millions of people who believed such nonsense, so much so that before long some "patriotic" workers were harassing suspected "reds"; Hollywood writers were being fired by the movie moguls for tainted associations; politicians and generals were cowering before the McCarthy assault. "Dangerous" people were denied passports and had to fight in the courts to force the government to reverse itself. Many just dropped the matter lest they draw attention to themselves by seeking judicial review. I knew one such woman in Chicago — former secretary to Jay Lovestone in the Communist Party, later a member of the Trotskyites, but in the 1950s totally inactive — who let the matter lie because she was afraid that notoriety would cause her to lose a job as school clerk. Unlike Nazi Germany, no one was killed or put into concentration camps, but the mentality for doing such things was in the germination stage, as evidenced by the law passed under the sponsorship of Senator Pat McCarran early in the Korean War, which among other things set up detention camps to imprison "subversives" during an emergency. I can't say I consider it much of an honor, but I learned from FBI records turned over to me and other plaintiffs during a lawsuit in 1978 that I was included in this "security index," scheduled for incarceration.

My personal experience with McCarthyism was far less harrowing than that of communist leaders, but I did not come out unscathed either. In accord with the mood of the time a disgruntled rank-and-file member of my union would occasionally berate me as "a communist" or post a newspaper item about me on his shop bulletin board with a derogatory comment. But the fifty to sixty members of Local 329's executive board stood solidly in my corner, as did the people on the staff, Socki, Deans, Bob Swanson (a college man whom I hired around this time), and others. Part of my immunity was due to the fact that I constantly declaimed against the "red scare" at union meetings, and explained how it adversely affected labor's bargaining power — and pay scales. I also poked at it in print. In a 1952 column for the union paper, I wrote that "nobody has been yelling more about the horrors of socialism than that bigoted idiot from Wisconsin, Senator Joe McCarthy. Recently Joe himself got sick, he needed an operation. And where do you think this hater of Socialism went to be operated on? . . . To the GOVERNMENT-OWNED Bethesda Naval Hospital where he got an operation free of charge. It seems that Joe is opposed to free 'socialized medicine' for you and me, but it's OK for him." Another reason the communist issue didn't hurt me within Local 329 was that the general political level of the membership, especially the executive board, was higher than in most unions. We conducted regular classes and seminars on international affairs, and we published a monthly paper, including a column I wrote and another by Socki which often dealt with politics.

But if McCarthyism didn't undermine my position in the union, it affected me adversely in other ways. In the summer of 1951, Dr. Clyde Kluckhohn, head of the Russian research center at Harvard, tried to get me a grant to study trade unions in Europe and Asia. I had published two pamphlets for the prestigious Foreign Policy Association in New York entitled "Labor Unions and Politics in Britain and France" and "Social Democracy and Labor in Germany" as well as articles in the *Nation* and the *Progressive* on related subjects. Kluckhohn felt I had both the practical and literary qualifications to shed some light on a neglected subject. After I had written up the proposal, he took me to see John Gardner, vice president of the Carnegie Corporation (later Secretary of Health, Education and Welfare in Lyndon Johnson's cabinet, and still later chief officer of Common Cause) to arrange for a $15,000 grant. Neither of us anticipated any difficulty, since Kluckhohn was receiving large sums for his Harvard center and he made it clear my work would be an excellent supplement to his own research. Gardner too seemed favorable; he asked me to find two academic sponsors and work out an arrangement with a university (whose role would be confined to accepting a 10-percent administrative fee).

Unfortunately we reckoned without the spirit of the times. Fred Harbison and Bert Hoselitz, two professors at the University of Chicago, were happy to act as sponsors and to associate me with their school. But in due course I got a letter from Gardner that "although your project struck us as interesting, we could not give it a high enough priority among the many projects before us." Hoselitz told me what really happened. The foundations, he said, were so fearful of financing controversial studies (and controversial people) that they cleared those projects with the State Department. They sent formal letters to the State Department asking whether a program submitted by such and such a person to do such and such a study would be "in the best interests of the United States." In my case, Hoselitz said, the State

Department was less than enthusiastic. Any study by Sid Lens, they told the Carnegie people, according to Hoselitz, could not be in America's interest. Carnegie, thereupon, dropped the matter.

Later that same year, the State Department refused to renew my passport. According to A. J. Nicholas of the passport division with whom I met in Washington, the department was using its "discretionary powers" to deny foreign travel to a man it considered a security risk. After a long talk he hinted at what he might consider proof of my loyalty. "Have you ever been interviewed by a government agency," he asked me, "about the groups you were in?" When I said I hadn't, he came to the point: "Would you give such an agency information about those groups if you were called in?" This of course would be the first step to becoming a spy. I said I might be willing to discuss well-known political ideas, but would never give information about individuals. It took months to change the State Department's mind, and then only after I had enlisted the help of Muste; Norman Thomas, many times Socialist candidate for president; Max Kampelman, an assistant to Senator Hubert Humphrey; Senator Paul Douglas; Clarence Pickett of the American Friends Service Committee; and others. Under that kind of pressure the passport agency finally yielded.

It was only a temporary victory, however, because next time around I had to go through the same ordeal. In 1955, the State Department again denied me travel privileges, this time on the ground that I had made "disparaging remarks" about the United States on a previous trip. I had told a group of trade unionists in Beirut, it seems, that "America, like Lebanon, had employers who exploit labor." For this criminal idea I was being refused a passport. When I asked the State Department official if there was any way I could appeal his decision, he said "No, only communists have the right under the law to appear before a special board. Since you're not a communist, you don't qualify." I took the matter to the ACLU, and it was only when it filed a suit on my behalf (and three others) that the State

Department relented. On the day the ACLU went to court, my passport was issued.

Four other encounters with the McCarthy syndrome occurred both before and after the senator from Wisconsin passed from the scene. One involved Shirley. We had hardly unpacked our bags from a trip to Latin America in late summer 1955, when Sara and Bob Pickus came by to discuss "an urgent matter." They were friends of ours; we had attended their wedding and we remained on close terms for some time, until Bob was smitten with the anti-communist virus. Sara had served on Walter Reuther's staff in Detroit and was now working as a substitute teacher in the Chicago school system, for which Shirley also worked as a tenured full-timer. The urgent matter had to do with a recently passed law, generally known as the Broyles bill, which required all teachers to sign an oath that they were not members "of nor affiliated with the Communist Party or any organization which advocates overthrow of the U.S. or Illinois government." Since the bill had been introduced as an amendment to a finance act, the penalty for not signing was nonpayment of salary rather than discharge. Sara was determined not to sign when school opened a couple of days later, but wanted allies, especially from teachers with tenure. Shirley agreed immediately; as it turned out she was the only tenured teacher who didn't sign the oath. Albert Soglin, another substitute teacher at the time (father of Paul Soglin, who would eventually become mayor of Madison, Wisconsin) also joined Sara and Shirley.

As planned, when school resumed the day after Labor Day the three dissidents refused to sign while the ACLU went to court to seek an injunction against the Board of Education. The case made headlines for months, but was lost in both the lower courts and the state supreme court. Shirley went sixteen months without pay, but when the ACLU decided not to take the issue to the federal supreme court (their lawyers felt if they lost in the U.S. Supreme Court, other states might institute a loyalty oath) Shirley signed the oath because, as she put it, "I have an investment of over ten years in the teaching profession and I do not wish to give it up. It must be obvious to everyone by now that the test oath does not uncover communists or subversives or do anything to make America more secure. On the contrary, it makes America weaker because it strengthens conformity, and inhibits dissent." It is instructive that out of 17,000 or more teachers only three were willing to challenge this oppressive bill. Throughout the sixteen months that the issue was being tested there were fist fights between Shirley's mentally handicapped kids and other students, the former defending their teacher, the latter calling her "a dirty communist." But as one of the students with an IQ of 60 put it: "Mrs. Lens you couldn't be a communist, because if you was you would have signed this thing."

In September 1962, when I was running for Congress along with thirty-two other peace candidates around the country, I was put through the McCarthy buzz saw of a Chicago *American* columnist named Jack Mabley. He dredged up my record in the RWL, the fact that I had changed my name, and similar tidbits.

Ironically, one decade later, on October 29, 1972, Mabley wrote a full column apologizing to me. Referring to me as "one of the nation's most prominent peace activists," he confessed that "one of the meanest, and in retrospect, most unfair columns I ever wrote was in 1962, attacking Lens for his radicalism." He praised me for having been right about the Vietnam War, about the Soviet people's desire for peace, and "about the insanity of the [antiwar] arrests, as he [Lens] marched the streets, his only outlet a placard on a stick."

In the late 1950s or early 1960s the American Security Council — again in the best McCarthyist tradition — published a four-page fact sheet on me, complete with photograph, warning the world about my subversive record. A few months later, while on a speaking tour for the American Friends Service Committee, a listener read part of the brochure over the air. It became a problem for the AFSC when a few of its supporters asked that my tour be cancelled; to AFSC's credit, it refused. It would be untrue to say that such harassment didn't affect me; it made me feel like a pariah, and wonder on occasion whether I wasn't really a misfit. In time, fortunately, I learned to parry questions about my leftist politics adroitly — and even enjoyed the confrontation. I would say to a heckler: "Yes, everything said about me is true. In addition I've just murdered my father-in-law and pilfered the gold at Fort Knox. But I hereby make the statement that two and two are four. Is that correct?" The idea came across to anyone who was not prejudiced beyond redemption that whatever a person's record, good or bad, each statement must be judged on its own merit. The American Security Council brochure and the Mabley column cost me the friendship of the president of a subsidiary to a big oil company and his wife who were sympathetic to the peace movement and often visited us, as well as contributed to Women for Peace, the organization Shirley chaired.

Finally there was my appearance before the internal security subcommittee, chaired by Senator Eastland, in October 1963. A. J. Muste suggested that I refuse to appear or refuse to answer questions if I did appear, on the grounds that the committee was unconstitutional, but I rejected that advice — perhaps wrongly — because I didn't want to spend months in court as well as time raising money to pay for a court challenge. There were other tests of the legality of these "un-American" committees under way; it wasn't necessary, I told A.J., to add another one. I betook myself to Washington, hired Joe Rauh, the well-known liberal and labor attorney to represent me (for the minimal sum of $100), then appeared before Eastland and the subcommittee's counsel, J. G. Sourwine. Ostensibly they were there to investigate "Castro's secret network in the United States" but they asked me few questions about Castro or the Fair Play for Cuba Committee of which I was a national founder. Instead they ranged over a wide spectrum wanting to know about the pamphlet I wrote (with an introduction by Norman Thomas) defending the Mine, Mill and Smelter Workers Union against government harassment; about a couple of dozen causes to which I had appended my name, including some I didn't remember; and of course my association with the RWL. I didn't have any trouble answering Sourwine's questions, all but those about the RWL. I took the Fifth Amendment on those because it would have required me to name scores of former comrades. Carleton Kent, writing in the Chicago *Sun-Times* after the transcript of my testimony was released, referred to the "rather spotty results of [the subcommittee's] effort to portray Sidney Lens . . . as a villain in what it calls Castro's network in the United States." Kent was amused by my response to one question in particular — whether I had signed a letter demanding free and open trials for Polish workers who had rioted in Poznan in 1956. "I assumed the committee would be very much in sympathy with that," I replied. By 1963 the McCarthy bite had lost its sting, and though anti-communism still remains part of the American mystique to this day, it does not evoke anywhere near the hysteria it did in the early 1950s. It would take the emergence of a civil rights movement, a new left, and an antiwar movement, however, to defang it.

II

It was stretching a point to equate McCarthyism — as horrible as it was — with fascism, but it was not difficult to visualize one blending into the other. To begin with, McCarthyism was a byproduct of the militarization of America — the need to exact conformity in an era of continuous confrontation — and the militarization of America was now a permanent feature of American life. The United States, which had foreign bases only in Guam, Hawaii, the Philippines and a few spots in Latin America before the war, now was ensconced in 434 major and a couple of thousand minor installations around the world from which to mount campaigns against any possible adversary. It had a navy second to none, a large stockpile of nuclear weapons, a few million men under arms, and a Central Intelligence Agency that was intervening in the internal affairs of foreign nations daily. The nation in fact was in a constant war stance — a Cold War, as it was called — and as Woodrow Wilson once pointed out, war demands conformity. "So soon as you have a military class," he told a Kansas City audience in 1919, "it does not make any difference what your form of government is: if you are determined to be armed to the teeth, you must obey the orders and directions of the only men who can control the great machinery of war. Elections are of minor importance." McCarthyism was an extreme method of imposing obedience to the state, but it meshed with the militarization of the nation, and it was not difficult to visualize it taking the next step — forming hooligan squads of black shirts or brown shirts or green shirts to enforce conformity through extra-legal methods. Working against this possibility was the fact that the nation was so prosperous, and there was no example as yet of a society that went fascist in a period of economic upswing. Still, one could never tell.

A second factor that catered to the fear that fascism might not be a long way off, was the thin resistance — for the most part, the lack of resistance — by liberals. Hubert Humphrey, as already noted, tried to out red-bait the red-baiters. The CIO expelled eleven unions charged with being communist-dominated. Few liberals were speaking out openly against McCarthyism. In an article for the *Progressive*, "Sewer Liberalism" (October 1956), I compared the bulk of liberals to socialists of another era who were "willing to forget the goal of social ownership in favor of mundane and immediate gains such as sewers." Liberalism, I said, had embraced virtually the same social security, minimum wage, and foreign policy programs as the Eisenhower Republicans. "In the field of internal security most liberals are still far behind the conservative former Senator Harry Cain. Except for one or two Senators . . . none has had the courage to vote against an appropriation for Senator McCarthy's infamous committee, or against putting Senator Eastland into the chairmanship of the committee dealing with civil rights." No liberal was asking for a "vote on war," most, including the famed theologian Reinhold Niebuhr, were as intoxicated with atomic bombs as the brasshats. In printed rejoinders after my article, liberal Senator Richard L. Newberger (D.-Ore.) and former socialist Gus Tyler of the International Ladies' Garment Workers' Union (ILGWU) took me to task for "unfairness" and "clumsy slander," but looking back at that article a quarter of a century later it still seems sound to me. The liberals might have placed serious obstacles to the national security state and its political cretinism, but they didn't; the bill would come due later in a runaway arms race, the Vietnam War, and the crises of the 1970s.

In any case, the conservative state of national affairs as the new decade began demanded a reconciliation with reality. It was folly to consider socialism in the United States as a subject for the immediate agenda; socialism in America was on a distant horizon, not imminent. It was necessary, I felt, to reassess the old leftism. Somewhere along the way we had gone wrong: we had expected revolution in the advanced states after the war, instead there was stability, growing prosperity, and in the United States, reaction; we had expected economic collapse, instead there was unprecedented growth. The more I thought of it the more it became apparent that we had applied Marxism and Leninism schematically. Instead of using them as *methods* for analysis, we had used them as *texts* to justify positions we had taken a priori. We had been too prone to believe that the past would repeat itself almost in the same form everywhere: soviets (workers councils), red guards, dual power, collapse of the old order in one heap, a centralized political party guiding the masses to victory. We had also smugly disregarded the capacity on the other side to develop strategies for survival such as Keynesianism. We had been loath to study non-Leninist ideologies, such as Gandhianism; we knew practically nothing of the American revolution, the Danish revolution, the Meiji Restoration, and other events that did not conform exactly to a predigested formula; and we had an unprofessional feel for other nations, especially for former colonies which still staggered under the load of feudal and tribal carryovers.

Just as I had joined the Trotskyite movement a decade and a half earlier on the basis of an open-minded comparison of

Trotskyism and Stalinism, so I decided after the publication of my first book, *Left, Right, and Center,* that I needed to broaden my political horizons by a closer study of ideas (both establishment-oriented and lower-class-oriented) that I once scorned, and by traveling to countries I had never been to to see for myself how, for instance, Swedish and British social-democracy worked, what Titoism and Stalinism looked like in the bare flesh.

Early in 1949, on a trip to New York, I reacquainted myself with A. J. Muste whom I knew slightly from the days when I was a member and he the head of the Workers Party. Since the mid-1930s A.J. had gone back to the church and had served as secretary of the Fellowship of Reconciliation, an old pacifist organization also headed at one time by Norman Thomas. That meeting was to be a fateful event in my life. At the end of our talk he gave me a copy of one of his books, *Non-Violence in an Aggressive World,* and we began a brief correspondence on the subject. I never became a thoroughgoing Gandhian like Muste, nor religious, but Muste and I became close friends from that time until he died in 1967. He stimulated my thinking and influenced my activities more than any other single individual.

"Your theme," I wrote A.J. in August 1949, "is that it takes education to teach workers the essence of Leninism-Marxism; the same outlay of energy and education could bring our working class around to a program of non-violence." There were two weaknesses to this thesis I claimed, first that Lenin never hoped to educate the masses to Marxism, for that an elite political force, a party, was necessary; he expected workers to mobilize for revolution not because they read Marx but because they galvanized around such slogans as "peace, bread, land." Secondly, I didn't think you could train workers for a program of absolute nonviolence; "In my opinion," I concluded, "nothing in this world is either good or bad — in itself; neither socialism nor violence, nor anything else. Socialism is a good thing theoretically but very poor in Russia. Violence is a bad thing theoretically but very good when defending one's self against a thief. We must stress fundamental principles — social change, peace, etc. — rather than strategical or tactical considerations."

I'm sure I didn't realize it at the time but this last sentence was a plea for a broadly based radical movement in which differences over tactics and strategy would not be allowed to create the schisms they had in the old Stalinist and Trotskyite movements.

Muste's reply was that pacifism, like Marxism, depended on "a trained and intellectual cadre," which proceeds "partly by methods of education, but mainly by example and in other ways to carry the masses along. I still do not see why if the inner group were as thoroughly committed to the Gandhian approach, for example, as leftists have traditionally been to the Marxist, they would not have as good a chance of winning the masses in the latter case. In addition, those who are genuinely opposed to both physical and psychological violence would refrain from the kind of conscienceless manipulation of the masses in which the Communists have so frequently engaged. The result of that manipulation is to de-educate the masses, to make them mechanical robots and material for Fascism or otherwise for Stalinist totalitarianism."

Through the ensuing eighteen years I had many discussions with Muste about nonviolence and religion. I particularly chided him in 1960 concerning Fidel Castro's *violent* revolution, which he supported. "You're inconsistent," I said. "The least you should do is write an article explaining your inconsistency to the many people who believe in you." But for Muste, as for other left-wing pacifists — Dave Dellinger for instance — the emphasis was on resistance and revolution. Though, like Gandhi, they would have preferred all revolutions to be nonviolent, they were not about to turn their backs on social change because it did not follow their pre-scribed course. A.J. always referred to Gandhi's famous dictum: that while he, himself, would never use violence, it was better to resist evil violently than not to resist at all. A.J. was also loose on the matter of religion. "Do you really believe," I asked him, "there is a supreme being that determines each of our activities?" He was nebulous in his answers, at least as I saw it, because he really equated God with the humanist spirit. "Why, then," I would argue, "are you a Christian instead of a Buddhist or a Moslem?" He parried that by claiming to belong to *all* religions, but practicing Christianity because it was the religion in which he was reared. "You know," Muste chided me back on a number of occasions, "in my understanding of the term you're the most religious person I know."

Muste caused me to set radical theory in a different frame. We on the left had tended to think of it in absolute terms: there was one truth, which we imbibed by digesting Marx, Lenin, and either Stalin or Trotsky. Everything else was a perversion of it. We defined our own views as Marxism or Marxism-Leninism; we designated others as "reformists" or "centrists," both outside the pale of decent society. But Muste made me realize how tendentious was this kind of nomenclature. There was a world outside the narrow borders we had set that had to be met and addressed. Radicals could not isolate themselves from good, decent people by a barrier of labels — "reformist," "centrist," "revisionist" — for whatever a person was, there was a core of decency in him that could be aroused against social injustice if you didn't isolate yourself from him with derogatory labels. I had always felt that socialism needed an input from the science of psychology, that socialism needed to remake not only society but the individual human being. Oehler used to take me to task for this "dereliction," hinting it would inevitably lead me to "revisionism." But A.J. opened my eyes to the fact that the true revisionism consisted in disregarding the human element. I never fully accepted Muste's concept of *physical* nonviolence; I still don't see how the people of South Africa can be liberated through Gandhian techniques. But I believe totally in the principal of *psychological* nonviolence, and while I have never had the full self-confidence needed to practice it coherently, I have *tried* to live by it and have always insisted that any movement I was associated with live by it. I have never, for instance, engaged in a fight in my union or in the peace movement without telling the person or persons whom I opposed beforehand why I was doing it and when I would initiate the campaign. Immediately after such a fight, whether I won or lost, I always sat down with the other side to discuss the possibility of collaborating. This may seem like small potatoes — to use one of John L. Lewis's terms — but it is in fact a very essential aspect of true radicalism, for if we cannot love human beings we cannot change society — in fact we have no reason to.

Muste's help in political reassessment and the stultified state of affairs at home whetted my appetite to see the rest of the world, to gauge for myself how the Cold War looked from the other side of the planet. Except for hitchhiking to Canada as a teen-ager and a trip to Mexico in our second-hand Packard in 1947, I had never been abroad. The situation in my union was stable; we were adding one or two new shops a year to the roster, negotiating moderately good contracts; Frank Socki could handle matters in my absence without difficulty. And the executive board of the local, far from being distressed that I was going away for an extended period, gained vicarious pleasure from my trip.

III

From 1950 to 1970, Shirley and I visited ninety-four countries, some four or five times, but none of the trips was as exciting as the first one in 1950, which lasted almost seven months and took us 20,000 miles through Europe. It was a great adventure confronting new languages and cultures, like acquiring a multiple personality. I knew a little French from high school days, and every night in Paris I would sit at a table, dictionary in hand, translating a newspaper article to myself, heedless of grammar and other niceties, simply trying to develop a vocabulary. In time I absorbed enough to be able to conduct an intelligent conversation on political matters. I did the same thing in Germany, using my mother's Yiddish as the foundation for a crash course in German. By the time we got to Italy and Spain my brain was too exhausted to digest any more; I merely memorized the hundred or so words needed to hold a rudimentary conversation.

Making our money match our travel appetites was also a challenge. Our total savings was $3,800, of which we budgeted $700 for passage both ways (third class on a ship going, low-cost chartered plane coming back), $800 for a Renault to be picked up in Paris, and the other $2,300 for twenty-eight weeks of "high living." It worked out moderately well; life was less austere than we had expected. On the *Queen Mary* headed for Le Havre and Dover we learned how to sneak into first-class quarters, watch the movies there, and drink at the bar. I even entered the first-class Ping-Pong tournament, and would have won it except that I disappeared after the semifinals for fear that I might have to reveal my third-class room number.

In Europe we worked out a routine for economizing. Having a car allowed us to shop around for the cheapest quarters. Food costs could be kept low by staying away from restaurants. Each morning Shirley would boil water for tea on a little foldaway stove that operated with meta tablets (a solidified alcohol), while I shopped for bread and cheese. Lunch, eaten in the car while driving around, was cheese sandwiches, with tomatoes and fresh fruit. Only for dinner did we splurge at a third-class restaurant, a place like Lyons in London, or one of those tiny eateries behind the rue Tronchet in Paris. Actually we over-economized, because the money I earned writing for the *Christian Science Monitor,* the *Progressive,* the Chicago *Sun-Times,* the *Reporter,* and other publications repadded our bankroll and put Shirley and me a leg-up for our next trip.

On the light side, we enjoyed browsing in the great book stores and going to theaters in London; listening to the musical sounds in French, Italian, Spanish cities; visiting the Louvre in Paris, the Fountain of Trevi in Rome, floating on a gondola in Venice, driving in our little Renault from one end of the continent to the other. Then, of course, there were the people. An American radical was considerably more welcome in the House of Commons than in the U.S. Congress,

and in the trade union offices of Europe than in the AFL or
CIO headquarters in Washington. We met and dined with a
variety of prominent people. Fenner Brockway, a member of
parliament who had been leader of the Independent Labor
Party — an organization not far removed from Trotskyism —
before it dissolved into the official British Labor Party,
introduced me to all kinds of political figures. Fenner, as the
head of a worldwide anti-colonialist movement, knew hosts
of leftists in Asia, Africa, as well as on the continent, and I
subsequently got to meet many of them. When he visited the
United States, Fenner usually stayed with us in Chicago, and
I often wish I had a tape-recording of him and Shirley arguing
as she cut his long, silky white hair — whether to trim here or
slice there.

We met a number of people in London who were destined
to become cabinet members — Richard Crossman, Michael
Foot, Denis Healey; and trade union leaders of the stature of
Dave Beck and George Meany, such as Jack Tanner and
Arthur Deakin. In Paris there were friends I had corre-
sponded with when I was national secretary of the RWL such
as Jose Rebull (leader of the left wing of the POUM during
the Spanish Civil War) and W. Solanno (secretary of the
POUMist youth). There were leftist Catholics like the philosopher Paul Vignaux, and independent socialists like author
Daniel Guerin (close to the Trotskyites and a friend of the
Algerian Ahmed Ben Bella); young Michel Crozier (who
would become an internationally known sociologist); Claude
Bourdet, a tall, handsome former guerrilla who wrote for the
Nation; and Jean Rous and Charles Ronsac, editors of a
leftist paper called *Franc Tireur.* In Italy there was the
renowned novelist Ignazio Silone and his red-headed British
wife, and a host of leaders in Nenni's socialist movement. In
Germany I visited with Ernst Reuter, mayor of Berlin; in
Belgium, the brilliant Trotskyite theoretician, Ernest Mandel;
and in Holland, the novelist Jef Last. Most of all, however,
we met people at union meetings, in the streets, in villages.
"Travelling abroad is really an eye-opener," I wrote Scotty
Deans in April 1950. We met people of different nationalities

and cultures, each with specific problems, and soon realized how difficult it was to translate the abstractions of Marxism — valid as they might be — into concrete strategies for dealing with those problems.

Western Europe, it became apparent fairly soon, was not geared to the Cold War; it had to be dragged into it. Five years after the end of hostilities, the physical evidence of the hot war was enough to make anyone eschew another conflict. The debris had been cleared away in London and Coventry, but there were grave reminders of the bombings in the empty lots where buildings once stood, or in burned-out churches such as the one off Fleet Street. In Hamburg the rubble was still there. One section at least a mile square was physical evidence of the firestorm in which so many thousands had died from lack of oxygen. It was still impassable; as a matter of fact the Germans eventually developed a machine that ground up the rubble, bricks, stone, steel and all, spitting it out as red sand. War was a vivid reality for the Europeans; unlike Americans they had bled and died and lost many more loved ones. On a trolley car going around the Ring in Vienna one day a little woman sitting next to me remarked as the car paused to let a parade go by, "There they go again." It was not really a military parade, but every parade reminded her of the son she had lost. There were millions like her.

Viewing Dachau was a more biting reminder of what Europe had suffered. The man who took us through this former German concentration camp was a Pole who said that of the 575 political prisoners who had been brought here with him only two were still alive. There were the usual barracks, barbed wire fences and moats, but also two crematoria and a gas chamber. The smaller crematorium, in use since 1933 we were told, had two openings, accommodating one body each, and two ash exits, one for coal and one for human ashes. It took about ten minutes to burn a body, the Polish guide said. The other crematorium was next to a gas chamber. Before entering this large room marked *Brussbad* — "showerbath" — prisoners took off their clothes and were given soap and towel. Inside there were spigots on the ceiling, catering to the illusion that the victims were really going to have a shower. Within seconds, however, gas would seep in from the floor and within fifteen minutes all would be dead. Their bodies, after being divested of such things as gold teeth, would be burned in the crematorium, which had four big stoves manned by prisoners (who themselves would be liquidated after a short time). Some 250,000 people of thirty-two different nationalities had perished here.

Even the tragedies that had happy endings were grim reminders of how torturous life must have been for many people. I came across many tales whose humor was only retrospective. Jef Last's daughter had spent most of the war in jail because she was reading a novel while walking home, and forgot to look up to see whether there was a plant on the windowsill — the family signal that their home was being raided by the Gestapo. Jef Last was one of the best-known writers in Holland, an important figure whose family was in the Dutch underground, and an active anti-colonialist who helped his friends Mohammed Hatta and Achmed Sukarno win independence for Indonesia. The arrest of his daughter was the only mishap he experienced during the hostilities.

Susanna Leonhard's lot was more torturous. About fifty-five when I met her, she had been in the socialist and communist movements of Germany before World War I and had been jailed under Kaiser Wilhelm. She had left the Communist Party in 1925, but returned when Hitler came to power in 1933 to work in the underground. In 1935 she escaped to Sweden with her son Wolfgang, just hours before the Nazis were primed to arrest her. Unfortunately she took the advice of the Soviet ambassador Alexandra Kollontai to take a teaching job in the Soviet Union. She was arrested by Stalin's secret police in 1936, at the time that Zinoviev and others were on trial, spent ten years in the Vorkuta prison camp, and was able to return to Germany in 1948 only because her son had befriended Walter Ulbricht while in the Soviet Union and went back with him to East Germany after VE day. Ulbricht, soon to become head of the government, arranged for Mrs. Leonhard's emigration from the Soviet Union.

Among Fenner Brockway's list of a dozen Germans who had been active in the Socialist Workers Party (SAP), a group of former communists and former socialists dissatisfied with both parties, were two who became good friends of ours for the next ten or fifteen years. Each had had more than his share of adventure. Ulrich Hecht, a Hamburg doctor about forty years old, had joined the communist youth group while a student but had left it for the SAP around the time Hitler came to power. He was active in the underground from 1934 to 1942. As a medical man with an automobile, he transported many Jews and others to the frontier so they might make their escape from Germany. After being drafted into the military early in the war he was put in charge of a medical team that had ten ambulances at its disposal. Ully, an easy-going man with a boisterous laugh, related how every ambulance in due course became the hiding place for a doctor's mistress, the lead ambulance housing his own Belgian girl friend — who later became his wife — Jo.

When it became evident that Hitler had lost, Ully led his team in a wild escape over hundreds of miles to avoid the ragtail remnants of the German army, and more important, the Russians. He finally made it to the West, wearied and broke, but joyous. Here he confronted two immediate problems. When he and Jo had begun living together following the conquest of Belgium, Ully had had to hide her because the Nazis prohibited intermingling with "inferior" peoples. Now the British prohibited her from marrying him and deported her to Belgium. (Fortunately she made her way back by circuitous means and the story ended happily.) The other problem Ully faced was that he didn't have any money or clothes. He shared a pair of shoes with an old comrade who worked nights. He found himself an office — but had absolutely no equipment. One day an American soldier came to see him seeking heroin. Ully, who spoke English well, politely refused to sell drugs but assured the young man he would not report him to the American officers. For this kindness the soldier left him a $10 bill which, in the state of chaos that Germany was in at the time, was enough to outfit a doctor's office with rudimentary medical equipment.

Herbert Tulatz, of the trade union school at Oberursel, near Frankfurt, had also been in the SAP and the underground. He was arrested by the Gestapo after another comrade had broken under torture and revealed his identity. Herbert, soft-spoken but quite astute, had spent a couple of years in a concentration camp, then had been drafted for Division 999, made up of prisoners Hitler literally intended to use as cannon fodder — the first lines of an attack column sure to be killed by the enemy or by German troops behind them if they dared turn back. By some miracle Tulatz evaded this fate; he was captured by American troops in Africa before he had fired a single shot, and sent to a prison camp in the States for the duration. In the ensuing years I spent quite a bit of time with him on visits to Germany, Holland, or Belgium where he was on the staff of the International Confederation of Free Trade Unions as well as in Chicago where he stayed with us whenever he came through. He died prematurely, in his late forties or early fifties, in part I'm sure because of the ordeal he had endured.

Compared to the horror of the war itself, the trillion dollars in destroyed property, and the 50 million lives lost, individual trauma seemed almost irrelevant. But each person carried those scars, and, whereas Americans could contemplate future wars with a thin sense of reality, the desire of the ordinary European for peace was an almost religious phenomenon.

Two incidents point out the difference between European anxieties and what the late Margaret Mead called America's "fraudulent masculinity." One occurred early in the Korean War while American forces were being pushed back by the Chinese. In answer to a question at a press conference, President Truman stated that the United States would "take whatever steps are necessary to meet the military situation." Did that "include the atomic bomb?" he was asked. Yes, it included "every weapon that we have." Has "active consideration" been given to its use, the reporters egged him on, and he replied with words that sent shivers down millions of spines in Europe, "There has always been active consideration of its use." Coming on the heels of a call by Secretary of the Navy Francis P. Matthews for a preventative war, and a boast by General Orville Anderson, commandant of the Air War College, that the Air Force was ready and waiting to drop The Bomb on Moscow, the people of Europe were justly disturbed that America might be writing the scenario for Doomsday. Prime Minister Clement Attlee of Great Britain, reflecting these anxieties, hastened to Washington to express his shock.

Another incident a few years later underscored Washington's recognition that the Europeans were not as lyrical about nuclear bombs as American policymakers were. In December 1953, President Dwight Eisenhower was scheduled to give a talk before the United Nations. In his memoirs the late president recorded that in "draft after draft" of his intended speech "the exposition left the listener with only a new terror, not a new hope." The world, and Europe in particular, had been shocked by America's detonation of a hydrogen bomb in October 1952 and a similar explosion by the Soviets in August 1953. No ordinary citizen on either side of the Cold War had been aware that development of a weapon of such magnitude was underway; sudden knowledge of a nuclear device a thousand times more powerful than the atom bomb caused a pervasive alarm in Europe. Eisenhower, catering to those fears, finally hit on the idea of giving a speech on "atoms for *peace.*" This proposal, writes Steven J. Baker of Cornell's Center for International Studies, "helped to render politically acceptable" the U.S. "decision to go ahead with the H-bomb." It did not, however, allay the anxieties of the old world.

It was obvious that the leaders of Europe had become enmeshed in an alliance with the United States and with the Cold War because they had no other way out of staying in power or preventing the disintegration of their system.

Theoretically, the United States and Europe were partners, but it was the partnership of the lion and the lamb. As a London businessman named Sam Gilby put it: "Britain faces the choice of being the tail to a lion or the head of a lamb." The American military directly controlled West Germany and a part of Austria, shaping those nations to its own design. Britain had greater leeway, but it too had to accept the role of supine mendicant when it came to matters that Washington thought decisive. For instance, the British wanted to nationalize the Ruhr factories, heart of the German economy, in accordance with wartime pledges to "eliminate or control all German industry that could be used for military production . . ." Even the conservative weekly, the London *Economist,* counseled that conditions in the Ruhr "make far-reaching socialist experiments a necessity . . . " But the United States vetoed the idea, even though the Ruhr was in the British zone of occupation, and the British did not dare act out their own wishes.

There was a more subtle condition that European workers resented, namely the American expectations that Europe would adopt its own philosophy of free enterprise and "trickle-down." The day-to-day supervision of the Marshall Plan from Washington and the Hotel Talleyrand in Paris steered the European economy toward a productivity program in which labor paid the cost but management reaped the reward. Time after time workers in French factories told me how new American machinery had increased productivity monumentally, but their own wages had remained at previous levels. In some cases, in fact, the "reward" for higher productivity was a lay-off of workers. One day in Paris I bumped into Harold Gibbons of the teamsters and Leonard Woodcock of the auto workers (later its president after Walter Reuther died, and still later ambassador to China) who were there on behalf of the U.S. government to study labor conditions under the Marshall Plan. They took issue with me when I pointed out that the plan was tilted toward the corporations. But after I steered Gibbons to a few factories and union halls, he wrote a report with two other unionists in which he listed instance after instance of workers getting no benefits from productivity improvements. A factory near Paris, for example, had hiked productivity 500 percent by the use of new Marshall Plan equipment. But it paid the same wages as a neighboring firm that had made no changes. When Gibbons asked another French employer why he didn't tell his workers that the machinery being installed in his plant was obtained through the Marshall Plan, the reply was: "If I tell them that the Marshall Plan is responsible for this new machinery, I must also tell them it is responsible for the lay-offs that go with its installation."

Not only was Europe remade to fit American concepts of free enterprise but its political mold was also recast, sometimes subtly sometimes with a sledge-hammer. Just before the Marshall Plan was proclaimed, for instance, the Ramadier government in Paris was prevailed on to dismiss communists — who had been part of a coalition since the end of the war — from the cabinet. Prime Minister Alcide de Gasperi did the same in Italy some months later. He had told the American ambassador that "without your help we have only a few weeks to last," and when the ambassador, according to columnists Joseph and Stewart Alsop, informed him that it would be hard to provide such help "as long as the Italian Government included Togliatti and his communists," de Gasperi took the hint.

The status of Europe — hence of the whole world — would have been very much different without American pressures of this type. The first surge of sentiment at war's end, I learned, had been to the left. There were no revolutions such as during and after World War I, but in many places socialists and independent radicals set up their own governments and arrested Nazis before the British or the Russians dispossessed them. Trade unions were re-established in countries like Italy — and later Germany — that hadn't had them for decades. The Tories were replaced by the Labor Party in Britain, coalition governments including the socialists and communists sprang to life throughout the Continent. And despite the postwar economic crisis quite a few social reforms were implemented — national health insurance in Britain, works councils in France, "co-determination" (inclusion of workers on corporate boards of directors) in Germany. There was no McCarthyism in Europe; on the contrary, communists functioned openly and no one would think of firing a person for political views.

One of the first articles I wrote for the *Reporter* magazine was about Arthur Horner, a communist who was general secretary of the British miners' union, an organization overwhelmingly noncommunist. Horner, a jovial and friendly person, became a split personality during national elections. As the National Union of Mine Workers leader he sounded off for the Labor Party; as a communist, he made a wide detour of the coal fields, where he would be forced to campaign for the hated Attlee crowd, and confined his activity instead to other constituencies where he could talk as an individual communist. I attended perhaps half a dozen union meetings where a communist president presided over an organization of nonbelievers. At the famous Hyde Park in London one could hear speakers of all shades, from fundamentalist religionists to communists and Trotskyites, something that had become impossible in the States. Even after the communists were expelled from coalition governments and socialists prevented from taking power in Germany, as they almost certainly would have in a united country, communists and socialists continued to exercise considerable power through their control of the labor movements and the sizable votes they mustered at the ballot box.

IV

In Berlin, for the first time in my life, I had an opportunity to see what life was like in a communist country. I had written about communism, spoken about it, but had never viewed it in the flesh. Shirley and I could hardly wait. After depositing our bags in a fifth-floor apartment where we were lucky enough to get a room (hotel space was impossible), we made our way to the dividing point between West and East.

There was nothing to see of course except the usual devastation, but the place held a certain fascination, if only because it was in a sense *terra incognita*. Before crossing over I had an interesting conversation with a short middle-aged man walking in front of us, wearing a faded gray suit. He was picking up cigarette butts in the gutter. The man was embarrassed to see us watching him, but after a while he told us something of himself. In the heyday of Nazism he had been vice president of one of Berlin's largest banks. He never thought anything could disturb his place in the sun. "When Hitler said the Third Reich would last a thousand years," he recalled ruefully, "I believed him." The Third Reich actually lasted twelve, leaving behind human casualties like our ex-banker. Empires, it occurred to me, are not as enduring as their citizens think they are, including the American empire.

The sign welcoming a visitor to East Berlin bespoke the differences between the two worlds. It read, as you entered, BEGINNING OF THE DEMOCRATIC SECTOR OF BERLIN, and on the other side, as you exited, END OF THE DEMOCRATIC SECTOR OF BERLIN. There was no democracy, of course, in the sense of free speech or free press, but whereas the capitalist West viewed the problems of the world in material terms — "recovery" — the communist East emphasized ideals and visions. In material terms there was no comparison of East and West. The West Berlin stores carried butter, sausages, fruits; the improvised kiosks in East Berlin displayed candles, household hardware, magazines, but little or no food. At the state chain store, Handelsorganization (HAO), a watery ice cream sandwich, selling for one and a half marks, was far inferior to what one could buy on the other side for twenty pfennig, one-seventh as much. One of the reasons for the disparity of course was that the Soviet Union — unable to wangle recovery loans from the United States (Truman had abruptly ended aid shortly after he became president) — had taken advantage of the terms of the Potsdam agreement to ship 4,000 East German factories back home. The Russians, badly strapped for cash and equipment, were placing as much of the burden of recovery on the East

Europeans as they could. The result inevitably was dissent and resistance on the one hand and purges and executions of East European communist leaders, who evidently spoke up against such policies, on the other — Laslo Rajk, foreign minister and minister of interior in Hungary (hanged in October 1949); Wladyzlaw Gomulka, Poland's number one communist (expelled from the Party and jailed for treason); Traicho Kostov, once secretary general of the Bulgarian Communist Party (hanged in December 1949); Vilem Novy in Czechoslovakia; Lucretiu Patrascanu in Rumania; and countless others also liquidated.

Yet with all that — the material hardship and the repression — the communists had a better appreciation of how to appeal to human idealism than the leaders of the West. On every newsstand was a pamphlet "USA, in Words and Pictures," depicting the horrors of capitalism — an emaciated black child, an old furrow-faced Navajo Indian woman, two chain-gang blacks with chains and striped suits. By contrast, the communists said, "We are building for the future." In East Berlin, a young man named Zadick in the East German information ministry told me, "Ninety percent of the lawyers, sixty or seventy percent in the West German government offices are old Nazis . . . . The West had done nothing but regroup the old German powers." What he said was at least partially true.

My friend Herbert Tulatz had told me of instance after instance where Nazi leaders escaped the de-Nazification courts unscathed. Herbert in fact had resigned from one such court because it was pointless. Zadick, a thin chap who spoke perfect English, also had a ready explanation for the poverty in his zone. "Very likely many in the East have worse conditions than people in the West, but we started without Marshall Plans which bind us politically . . . . We still have no bananas or oranges in our shops, and our shops are not quite as full as in the West, but we have factories, our own factories, to produce for us." The communists, he said, had granted land to 250,000 farmers who were landless before, had introduced machinery-lending stations everywhere, had completely wiped out unemployment (whereas there were 2 million jobless in the West), had entirely assimilated refugees (again by contrast with the West), had introduced excellent social legislation and given scholarships to 60 percent of the youth in colleges. Above all, said Zadick, there were no capitalists in East Germany.

Zadick shaved the truth here and there, but it is noteworthy that while the publicists in the West stressed something materialistic — recovery — those in the East catered to the dream of a beautiful tomorrow. On the one hand they gave the people something to hate — imperialism, landlordism, racial discrimination; on the other they held forth a vision of a better day coming. Many of course hated the regime, but not a few were willing to bet on the future, and even more were ready to resolve gnawing doubts in favor of the East. I met one such man — a former magazine editor who had lived in New York before returning home in 1946. For four years Kantorowicz (I have forgotten his first name) had held off joining the Socialist Unity Party (SED), but three months before I met him he had taken the step. "I felt I must now make a choice. I could no longer stay out without being a traitor." He admitted without hesitation that "yes, we do have elements of a police state here. But how can we help ourselves? One of your American generals has openly bragged that an army of hundreds of thousands was being built up to sabotage the East Zone. Hundreds of barns have been burned by saboteurs, industrial machinery has been deliberately broken. We need a strong police to stop all this." He opposed a police state, and he hoped to fight against its extension within the SED, but in the meantime he felt there was no choice. I asked him why the Party couldn't explain its problems to the masses and enlist their cooperation to fight American saboteurs. His answer was startlingly frank: "The people are not yet on our side. They don't understand the significance of what is going on." But, he continued, "there are many types of freedom. I myself used to think that only the western type of free speech, free assembly, and the rest was a valid form of freedom. But I know now I was wrong.

What good is the right of free assembly when so many people live at substandard levels, when Negroes are lynched with impunity, when the rich control everything? Here in [East] Germany we are eliminating all that. There are no rich. There is no Jim Crow or anti-Semitism. We are building a future . . ." The East German regime might be imperfect, "but I have no other alternative than to be a communist. I cannot support the West."

That was a position I heard expressed by many people. They were not happy with existing Communism but they saw a future in it; they did not see any future in capitalism. According to Hugo Buschmann, a socialist who had been close to Otto Grotewohl and had served the East German government for a short period after the war, this was the rationale of Grotewohl for merging his Social Democratic Party with the much smaller Communist Party in the Russian zone — it was better to be with the communists than the capitalists. Grotewohl pointed out in fact that if the two working-class parties had united in 1932 Hitler would not have come to power. Similar reasoning caused a number of former Trotskyites and SED members to accept posts with the East German regime.

V

I tried to go on from Berlin to Moscow, hoping to see something of four or five other communist countries in our little Renault, but a phone call to the Foreign Office in Moscow indicated it would take months to process a visa and get a trip ticket for the car. Yet the contrast between East and West, apparent even in a brief visit to Berlin, indicated why Western capitalism was on the defensive. Communism, with all the repression and poverty in its own zone, nonetheless remained visionary particularly in the politics it projected for the rest of the world. Irving Brown (the AFL representative in Europe), the State Department, and the CIA might stress ceaselessly to the people of Egypt, Greece, Algeria, or China that there was no democracy in the Soviet sphere of influence. But these peoples hadn't tasted democracy for centuries, if at all. What attracted them was the dream of national independence, social equality, and economic abundance. The communists held forth that dream; the capitalist world, bent on preserving Western dominance over the underdeveloped countries, couldn't and didn't.

It couldn't and didn't, alas, even though it was already apparent that the Cold War would pivot around national and social revolution. Peoples everywhere were seeking — and achieving — liberation. India had won it in 1947, China in 1949. Dozens of others were already free of colonialism or about to become free — Madagascar, Egypt, the Gold Coast, Kenya, Indonesia, Burma, Ceylon, Morocco, Tunisia, Algeria, and so on. The Soviets tied their tail to that revolutionary kite, with material and moral support — if for no other reason than the fact that secession from the American orbit was inevitably a gain for the Soviet Union. The enemy of my enemy is my friend, goes an old political adage. The United States, leader of the "free world," was not capable of joining the revolution of rising expectations, or capable of the utopian imagery I had heard in East Berlin. Even Irving Brown's rhetoric was primarily negative. He was against communism, as practiced by the Stalinists, but what was he for? The only answer he and others could make was "democracy," "free speech," something which was far lower on the scale of priorities for a peasant in China or Algeria or India than a piece of land, a clinic, a school, all of which were encompassed by the word *revolution.*

In New York and Chicago the image of communism was one of fear and terror, immune to change or modification. But in fact if one were not quite as bigoted as the average American politician one could see the fissures in the communist world, in their incipiency in 1950, but well advanced by the mid-1950s. I had an opportunity for a second look at communism in 1950 in a country that had seceded from the main body, Yugoslavia. Superficially the disparity between Titoism and Stalinism seemed insignificant. People were almost as afraid to talk with you in Zagreb or Belgrade as in East Berlin. A one-legged man who engaged us in conversation on the main street of Belgrade suddenly realized he had been with us fifteen minutes. He turned on his heel with a parting sentence that took me aback: "I must be going now because I shall be questioned about this conversation as it is." Near the center of town there were people working on a building under police guard, indicating that there was more forced labor than the regime was willing to admit. And the stores along the main street were a disaster, with so little to buy that when a rack of dresses was put up for sale, women fell over each other to buy the first garment they could grab — regardless of size and color. A few minutes later Shirley and I would see them bartering their wares around the corner, hoping to exchange what they had for a better fit. We also saw a mob of peasants descend on a store to purchase four-drawer filing cabinets suddenly put up for sale; the peasants obviously had no papers to file, but money was burning in their pockets from the marketing of grain and there was no place to spend it. They bought literally anything they could lay their hands on.

In future visits to Yugoslavia through the next two decades I found an amazing turnaround from a centralist to a de-centralist form of communism. But in 1950, just two years after Tito's break with Moscow, this was still a typically Stalinist economy such as had prevailed in Russia for better than two decades — rapid industrialization and emphasis on heavy industry such as steel, de-emphasis of consumer goods. The government never seemed to have the money to build new homes or apartments; what one saw therefore was five families crowded into a six-room flat because there weren't enough units to house them individually. The government never seemed to have the money for new trolley cars. And since there were always shortages — particularly after the war and in times of Western trade embargoes — the state centralized planning to the point where it decided every price, every wage, and exactly how much should be produced. The inevitable result was that factory managers concentrated solely on meeting their *quantitative* quotas, disregarding the matter of quality.

The Yugoslavia I saw in 1950 bore all these markings — and all the hostilities that accompanied an economy of scarcity. Even though Tito was a genuine hero because of his conduct in the guerrilla war against the Nazis, his popularity had waned measurably during the years he ran his country on the Stalinist model. But Tito had not been imposed on Yugoslavia as were the regimes of Poland, Bulgaria, Hungary, Albania, East Germany; he had led his own revolution and maintained a sense of independence into the postwar period. Almost inevitably, that put him at odds with Stalin. The Titoists complained of the number and the behavior of Soviet secret police on their soil. They resisted Stalin's request that they remain a raw-material-producing country, dependent on the Soviets for their manufactures. And they tried in 1947 to form a customs union with Bulgaria (and hopefully, later, with other Balkan states) which evoked fury in Moscow. The result was the schism that plummeted Yugoslavia on a perilous path; it lost 51 percent of its foreign trade overnight and was truly headed for collapse.

In this state of affairs Tito had to develop another type of socialist economy, as different from Stalinism as Greek capitalism is different from British capitalism. To sell Yugoslav goods on the world market he had to compete effectively with Austria, Italy, and other much more advanced capitalist states. To compete he had to promote efficiency and innovation; and to do that he had to call on the initiative of millions of people, not only managers and technicians but rank-and-file workers. The dimensions of these changes were not yet apparent in 1950, but in talks I had with Mosha Pijade, the number-three man in the regime, and Djuro Salai, head of the trade union federation, it was apparent that broad and breathtaking mutations were in the making. We have learned, the Titoists were already saying, that the mere seizure of power does not ensure the victory of democratic socialism. It is possible in fact for a communist government to move in one of two directions: toward workers' democracy, self-determination for minorities, and the slow liquidation of the prerogatives of the state; or conversely, toward the bureaucratic centralism practiced by Stalin — machine power, abrogation of the right of minorities, vastly enlarged prerogatives for the state. Titoism, they said, was moving in the first direction.

To give meaning to this thesis, the Yugoslav communists thereafter granted increasing amounts of autonomy to the various republics — Slovenia, Croatia, Macedonia, Bosnia, Montenegro, Serbia. Workers in industry were given veto power over acts of management, by virtue of a June 1950 law that established elected workers' councils as the final authority in each factory. The government put a halt to collectivization in the rural areas, correctly noting that since Yugoslavia did not have enough machinery, chemicals, fertilizer, or consumer goods for the peasantry, collectivization could only be implemented by force. The hated "buy-up," by which peasants were required to deliver a certain amount of grain or vegetables to the state at fixed (usually low) prices, was also terminated. Special stores and privileges for the bureaucracy, which existed in all communist countries, were abolished.

In the ensuing years (I visited Yugoslavia again in 1953, and on other occasions), Yugoslavian communism took on a character of its own, pivoting around a principle called "self-management." In industry and trade, management rights are vested in a "collective" of the workers of a given enterprise or group of small enterprises. Each collective elects a workers' council which sets policy, hires and fires managers; and each council selects a subcommittee which meets every few days with the plant director and is consulted on various details. Each department similarly functions as a collective, sharing assignments, choosing the foreman, establishing rules, and generally policing itself. The profits of the enterprise are divided, part going to the state for new investment, part remaining with the collective to be used for machinery, housing, and of course higher earnings.

Unlike the Stalinist system, Titoism is de-centralized. State planning is called indicator planning: the state determines how much more steel it would like to produce, for instance, then tries to guide the enterprises into doing so by a system of inducements (such as lower taxes for basic steel production, as against higher taxes for a factory that makes bobby pins). The government tries to function as a guiding force, not as the direct administrator of the economy. It will determine, for instance, that a new factory should be built, but the actual building will be assigned to one of the republics, which in turn will vest the job with a particular locality or an existing enterprise. Most important, unlike the Soviet Union, the state does not set either prices or wages: they are determined by supply and demand in the one instance, and by collective bargaining in the other. And in the realm of civil liberties the Yugoslav people enjoy more freedom than ever in their history; not as much perhaps as some would like but more than they have ever known. Political arrests are infrequent. Travel abroad is almost totally unhindered. There is a single party system, but at least two candidates are nominated for each office; party candidates are beaten as often as not — especially in elections to the workers' councils.

Yugoslavian communism, especially as it evolved after 1950, was most impressive to me. Even Milovan Djilas, Tito's close associate who went to jail for condemning the lack of democracy in Yugoslavia, considered Titoism an essentially democratic form of socialism. I visited with Djilas on a number of occasions in subsequent trips — he and his wife lived in a small apartment not far from the center of Belgrade — and each time his endorsement of self-management was stronger. There were still things about the system that he deplored, but not its economic pattern.

I'm convinced that the communist societies will eventually adopt self-management as their modus operandi. I didn't come to this conclusion in 1950, but it was strengthened with each succeeding trip to the communist world. The Hungarians have adopted a large part of the Titoist model; the Czechs tried it in 1968; the Chinese are currently considering it. I'm sure it will become the standard form of communism, when Russia finally decides — as it must — that it can make no further economic progress unless it calls on the initiative of its people to introduce innovation and improve productivity. At that point it will have to jettison the rigid centralism that has alienated so many people, and adopt what it fought in Czechoslovakia, "socialism with a human face."

Chapter 8
A Time of Reversal

I

When I returned from Europe in 1950, the political atmosphere was as bleak and humorless as when I had left. Particularly distressing was the fact that the war in Korea, which had begun a few months earlier and would ultimately take 54,246 American lives and leave 103,824 wounded, failed to spark an antiwar movement. There were no demonstrations in the streets, no move by members of Congress to cut off funds for the war effort, and as far as I can remember only one prominent book — *The Hidden History of the Korean War* by I. F. Stone — that took sharp issue with the government's position that it was defending South Korea against North Korean aggression. Instead, the war fed rightist sentiments, sustaining and enhancing the movement around Joe McCarthy.

There was plenty of room for controversy on this war, certainly as much as on World War I, but it never asserted itself. Americans, almost unanimously, held the view that South Korea was the innocent victim of a surprise attack by 70,000 troops and 70 tanks from North Korea. But this may or may not have been true — Stone offers evidence that a high official on General Douglas MacArthur's staff put it precisely the opposite way to author John Gunther a few hours after the conflict began. "A big story has just broken," the official said, "the *South Koreans* have attacked North Korea" (emphasis mine). But whether the message received by Gunther's informant was garbled — as was later contended — it was well known to everyone that there had been repeated forays all along that border for months. Moreover, South Korea's aged dictator Syngman Rhee desperately needed the war to stay in power. Less than a month earlier he had suffered a humiliating defeat at the ballot box, winning a scant 47 seats in a national assembly of 210 members; war was his only means of political survival since it offered him the opportunity of proclaiming dictatorial powers. War also meshed with the strategies of MacArthur and Formosa's Chiang Kai-shek, who saw the engagement in broad geopolitical terms as a means of reconquering the mainland of China from the communists. In any case, though Rhee had been boasting for two years how simple it would be for his army to conquer North Korea and his minister of defense had stated in Tokyo (October 31, 1949) that "we are strong enough to march up and take Pyongyang [the Northern capital] within a few days," it turned out just the other way around. North Korean forces cut through the South like a knife through butter, confining Rhee's troops — despite U.S. air, naval, and some ground aid — to a small perimeter around the port city of Pusan.

Chauvinism nonetheless asserted itself in the United States, where few people sought to explain why the American client state, South Korea, with 21 million people was being manhandled by the North, with only 9 million. Instead, as in the Chinese debacle a year earlier, when Mao Tse-tung did the same thing to Chiang Kai-shek, rightists sought and found scapegoats for what were deemed to be "American losses." It wasn't that our policy was wrong in supporting unpopular dictators, they said; no, it was that a small band of secret communist agents and fellow travelers in high places such as Alger Hiss and John Carter Vincent were betraying our allies. They never presented an explanation, alas, as to why dictators on our side — such as Rhee, later Diem and Thieu — were unable to fight their own battles without calling on

American troops, whereas Soviet allies such as North Korea and North Vietnam could give a good account of themselves without foreign forces.

One of the men who had been making this point consistently was a much-maligned expert on Asian affairs, Owen Lattimore, with whom I appeared on a number of occasions on the lecture circuit for the American Friends Service Committee. On one of those occasions he gave me a copy of a book he published in 1949, *The Situation in Asia*, in which he predicted with remarkable accuracy what would happen. The South Korean army, he wrote, "cannot be trusted to fight; the people do not trust the government . . . If there is to be a civil war, South Korea would not be able to subdue North Korea . . . [whereas] North Korea would be able to overrun South Korea without Russian help, unless stopped by American combat troops." Events proved Lattimore right, a circumstance which unfortunately brought down on him charges of being soft on communism.

For a year, the Korean War proceeded indecisively, the North Koreans driving the Southerners to Pusan; the Americans, under MacArthur, landing at Seoul and pushing the Northerners north; China joining the fray and throwing MacArthur back; then a military stalemate and two years of negotiations for an armistice. After that first year, the level of fighting was sufficiently subdued so that the war dropped ever lower on the American public's list of concerns. Americans were not ripe for social protest, being imbued with a sense of impregnability they had acquired in World War II, and thriving economically.

In the absence of social protest the American left continued to shrink. Compounding its difficulties was the appearance of a spate of books, articles, and interviews by former communists, some in leading positions, which told of gross deceptions and outright dishonesty by the Communist Party or of spying for the Soviets. Among those making the accusations were Benjamin Gitlow, a founder of the Party; Louis Budenz, once associated with Muste and then managing editor of the Party's organ, the *Daily Worker;* Hede Massing, another self-confessed agent who had been the wife of a Communist International official. The stigma cast by these people was against Stalin and Stalinism, but the effect rubbed off on everyone else on the left. If this were the way socialism was practiced, who needed it? Another group of equally harmful exposés was contained in books by ex-inmates of forced labor camps in the Soviet Union. People like Eleanor Lipper, who spent eleven years in one such camp, told stories of imprisonments without trials (except sometimes a secret administrative trial) and gruesome conditions causing mal-nourishment, disease, death. Hundreds of thousands, perhaps millions, had gone through this slave labor experience; vast numbers had died or disappeared.

One of the people I befriended in this period was a Pole by the name of Jerzy Gliksman, who worked for the Jewish Labor Committee, which had an office in the same building as my union. Jerzy, a left-wing socialist lawyer, was the half-brother of Victor Alter, the well-known leader (with Henryk Erlich) of the Jewish socialist Bund. Though he was not a communist he represented members of the illegal party in court more often, he told me, than any other lawyer, and was consequently on excellent terms with the Party. On one occasion, he went to the Soviet Union with a group of law-yers and in the course of their tour was shown a "labor camp." Jerzy told me its conditions were exemplary by Western standards (to his dismay he would soon learn from personal experience that this one show camp was far from the norm).

When Hitler overran Poland at the outset of the war, Jerzy headed eastward, expecting to cross into Soviet-held territory where he was sure his record would win him sanc-tuary. As he walked with a few communist friends, he said, "I could see their attitude toward me slowly changing, and when I got to the town where Victor Alter and Henryk Erlich were being held by the Soviet army they simply dropped me." Gliksman sought out the Russian authorities to plead for the release of his half-brother, citing his own work on behalf of the Polish Communist Party as a recommendation for their good will. To his surprise they gruffly threw him down the stairs, and within a few weeks arrested and sent him to a forced labor camp in Siberia. Here he endured all the horrors that were revealed by Eleanor Lipper, and later Alexander Solzhenitsyn and many others. He lost all his teeth from a deficient diet, suffered a heart attack, wasted away to a near-skeleton, until finally — under an agreement made by the Soviets with the Polish government-in-exile — was released along with other Poles. Later he made his way to America and wrote a moving book called *Tell the West.* Jerzy's experience was to me a constant reminder of that callousness of certain radicals who dismissed such an ordeal as an "unfortunate aberration" or "one of the many sacrifices made for the revolution." I never have been able to accept this notion, for if a radical immunizes himself to the pain of a simple, single human being he immunizes himself to radicalism; he will not build a brave new world, but an abortive one with as many vices as the old one.

In any case, the mixture of war, McCarthyism, and the disclosures of Stalinist slave camps and spying, on the one hand, and the relative affluence of the nation on the other was not conducive to radical activity in the early 1950s. Even if I had been affiliated with some leftist group, there were few opportunities for proselytizing. A case in point were the members of my union staff; all of them were radicals in the broad sense and they agreed generally with my socialist views, but none would have joined a leftist party at that time even if I had asked them. In the elections they invariably voted for liberal Democrats because they felt that voting for a minority party was a withdrawal from the real world, a gesture of protest that no one would hear. That was also true of my friend Charlie Chiakulas, who was assigned by his UAW to the congressional campaign of Roman Pucinski, a Chicago Democrat. At lunchtime Charlie would discuss with me high points of socialist theory; after lunch he would return to the campaign office of a semiliberal Democrat. Even for the best of people radicalism seemed devoid of realism; it was a good set of principles to *believe* in, but practicing it was another matter.

One of the terms that became current in the 1950s was *third camp socialist* — a socialist who disagreed with the foreign policy of both the American State Department and the Soviet Foreign Office. In retrospect the term was not meticulously scientific, since it implied *equal* hostility to both foreign policies; but it was accurate enough to indicate where people like Muste, Dellinger, Irving Howe, and I stood, and was one of the reasons we could not become — as did the socialists who had formed the Americans for Democratic Action — advocates of either American capitalism or the Russian Soviet system. It was inconceivable for a third camp socialist to join either the Democratic Party or the Communist Party.

My own position, then, was that of an unfulfilled, abbreviated man without a political home. I couldn't affiliate with the Communist Party or return to the Trotskyites. I might have joined the Socialist Party or the Independent Socialist League (Shachtmanites), but the former was small and dominated by its right wing and the latter suffered from all the vices of the official Trotskyites and there was something about the wiseacre attitude of Max Shachtman personally (though that is not a good reason) that alienated me.

The lot of an independent thirty-eight-year-old radical in the early 1950s would have been excruciatingly frustrating and lonely if not for my union work, writing, and travel. Half of the mornings I would be up at a factory gate before 7 A.M. together with Socki, Swanson, Deans, or rank-and-file workers distributing leaflets. The leaflets with an application card attached urged employees to join the union: "Your Ticket to More Dough." Each such morning was an experience; you didn't know whether the look you got from a passing worker indicated hostility, agreement, indifference, or what. A certain percentage always refused the leaflet (you were tempted to yell after them, "Can't you read?"), others took them and ostentatiously tore them up. Always, however, there was a smiling face and one or two people who wished you luck. After a while you were able to strike up a conversation with some of them or meet them in a nearby tavern. The idea was to form a nucleus of five or ten people, call them to a meeting—always kept secret in the initial stages lest the employer discharge the ringleaders—and let them do the recruiting from the inside. Invariably a few application cards would be mailed into the union office after each distribution, and we would visit each such worker at home during the next day or two, or at least telephone. When television became the opiate of the masses, we found workers were offended if we interrupted the Milton Berle or Bob Hope show. We tried to catch them during the lunch period, at a bar after work, or at home before dinner.

The rest of the day usually was taken up with servicing, which included negotiating contracts, taking up grievances, counseling workers on personal problems, teaching classes, and attending various types of meetings. It was not a drab existence, but it was filled with tension. In negotiating a new contract there was the meeting of an "action committee," ordinarily one representative for every ten workers, which proposed the demands, chose the negotiations committee, monitored the progress of the talks, and made the ultimate recommendation to the membership on whether to accept an agreement the committee and I had negotiated, or strike. Here the problem was always to hold in rein wild and irrelevant demands. It made no sense, for instance, to ask for a 60-cent-an-hour raise when the rest of the industry had settled for 7½ cents; or to ask for unrealistic improvements such as a washroom attendant in a factory with sixty-five workers. The package had to appear reasonable even though in the final analysis the issue was settled by power—whether the union had the muscle to close down the operation and keep it closed, or whether the company could take a long strike without pain. If we were going to strike, however, we wanted to show the public that we had been fair-minded.

The negotiations themselves were invariably high-pitched, with each side accusing the other of being unreasonable, one-sided, lacking in compassion. The union — with either Socki or me as spokesperson — presented its demands and explained why they were justified: for instance, because workers elsewhere in similar jobs earned more or had better conditions, or that we had to keep up with the rise in prices, or that the company had earned a large profit (if it did) and ought to share it with us. Next came what I called the "tears flow like water" phase. Management always had a good reason for rejecting our demands — its competitors were underselling it, competition was too stiff, the market was soft, or what have you. The first session would end with the company promising to "take your proposals and study them — but don't expect too much." Our practice at Local 329 was to put out a leaflet after every session or two to inform the members what was happening and prepare them for a strike "if necessary." After eight or ten bargaining sessions, we usually came to terms; contrary to the image of militant union leaders as smarting for a "strike," officials like me spiked behavior with realism. I always assessed beforehand whether we could win, and if I didn't think so I would urge the action committee to settle — and fight again another day. Even if you were dedicated to socialism, losing was not the way to inspire your members with the need for stepped up social activism. Moreover, as I often reminded employers who accused me of being a socialist, "I am, but I don't believe in building socialism in one factory."

When we were strong enough to get a good settlement without a strike, I often agonized over whether we might have squeezed an extra 2 cents if I had held out longer. In time I developed what I think was a sixth sense for recognizing when the company was ready to settle and at approximately what terms, and a seventh sense for recognizing what would be an acceptable deal for our membership. In the more than three decades that I negotiated union agreements, the vote of our members for acceptance was always more than 90 percent, except on only two occasions: once when the membership of a factory instructed us to go back and renegotiate one relatively minor item; another time when we dropped a cost-of-living clause in favor of a substantially higher raise at a plant called Handy Button. The vote was about 60 to 40 for acceptance, but it came after a hard sell by two other union officials and myself. I regretted it almost before the secret ballots were counted, and even more when it turned out that my calculations vis-à-vis the expected rise in the cost of living were considerably lower than they turned out to be. With those two exceptions, however, there was always a warm reaction at the membership meeting that voted acceptance, testifying to the fact that we had correctly gauged the workers' desires.

Once or twice a year we did have a strike at one of our units, and then I had to draw on an extra fund of adrenalin. Would we be able to keep all the workers out? Would we be able to prevent trucks from going through our lines? How long could the strikers hold out? Sometimes the ranks were so solid there was nothing to worry about – except the normal logistics of a strike, arranging for a headquarters, having coffee and food delivered, selecting picket captains. In 1952, we had a stoppage at the South Center Department Store on Chicago's South Side. The 100 black workers were thoroughly united, there was not a chance in the world any would defect. I was absolutely sure this was a winner, even though the store was only a small part of the owner's holdings – a man named Harry Engelstein. Early in the strike Engelstein announced he was closing down operations "forever" and called in reporters to say he was open to bids. I countered his gambit by announcing that the workers were ready to buy and operate the place, which also got good press. Then one day Engelstein started yelling at me on the picket line – and pushed. I pushed him back, into the display window. He called the police to have me arrested; I swore out a warrant for his arrest. The police drove us off in the same paddy wagon, put us in the same cell . . . where we both cooled off and negotiated an agreement giving the workers exactly what they had asked for, a dime-an-hour raise and the reinstatement of their chief steward whose discharge had started the strike.

Another strike that I took in stride was a slow-down at the candy factory owned by Hillman's, also involving 100 or 150 workers. We were negotiating for three units of this company — the factory, a chain of restaurants, and a chain of food supermarkets — but making little progress. The thought occurred to Socki and me that our strength in the candy factory was so solid we could use it as leverage to prod management into a settlement. I called together the stewards and told them to instruct everyone to work harder than ever before — but just move the candy from one place to another, without producing very much. Here again I wasn't worried that anyone would break ranks or even tell management what was going on. After a few hours the company attorney called: "There's a strike in the factory, you better get down there and stop it." I offered to tour the place with him, and as we went from station to station I could honestly point out that the workers were working as hard as anyone could expect. They just weren't putting out any production — but of course I didn't admit that. No one was fooled on either side, but the company didn't want to ignite a strike of its whole operation just then, and we were able to settle matters in the next week or two.

But if all this sounds idyllic, most strikes were wearing on the nerves and often ended indecisively or in defeat. One of the most disheartening was against the same Hillman company in 1953; it was called off after two weeks with such meager gains it can only be classed as a defeat. The trouble was not with our ranks but with the butchers union, which demanded that we pay their members full salary for the time they were out of work as a price for respecting our picket line. Otherwise they not only would go through our lines and sell meat but also handle some of the work traditionally done by our members. This was certainly not in the accepted tradition of labor solidarity, but the head of the butchers union was still hostile because we hadn't affiliated our organization with his local. I took up the matter with my international president, Bill McFetridge, who surely had enough power to change the other official's mind, but, since he wasn't enthusiastic about the strike himself, he simply shrugged his shoulders.

I learned the hard way those two weeks that being aligned with the AFL was no sure guarantee of an AFL union's support. Each day I had to appeal to McFetridge to buoy the butchers union and the teamsters, who also sulked because a dozen of their members employed at Hillman's lost pay while respecting our picket lines. Finally the pressure became intense. The butchers union advised it would break ranks and return to work the following week. One day McFetridge called me to his office — "come alone," he said — to tell me that the company would make a "fair settlement" if I resigned from the union. I asked McFetridge what he thought I should do; he parried the question, saying he would get me a job elsewhere. When I told Socki about the conversation he hit the ceiling: "We're not letting either the company or McFetridge pick our leaders for us." I stayed on with the union, but we lost that strike. All we gained for two weeks' lost pay was a better cost-of-living clause. I told the members we were going back with morale still high, and we had prevented the company from breaking the union, both of which were true, but such facts did not make the pill any less bitter to swallow.

Another total defeat was suffered at a lamp factory called Popeil, where we kept a picket line going for six weeks in an effort to win reinstatement of workers fired in an organizing drive. We never were able to shut down operations; many of the employees who crossed the line shouted words of encouragement to the pickets — then went to work. Inevitably there was a certain amount of pushing and shoving and a few arrests, including that of myself and another member of the staff. But management was able to continue production, and to sneak out enough shipments on rented trucks Sundays and after midnight to keep going.

The most depressing feature of being a union organizer in Chicago, I think, was the business union mentality of the labor leadership. I had friends, like Charlie Chiakulas, Herman Rebhan (now general secretary of the international metal workers federation in Geneva), Carl Shier, Al Verri, Seymour Kahan, and others in the UAW, who were socialists of one stripe or another, but the run of the mill union official in the city, from McFetridge and Bill Lee (president of the Chicago Federation of Labor) down was a business unionist. You never could depend on such people for support of any progressive cause, or even support of an organizing drive.

To illustrate the point, in 1954 I ran into a hail of back-door contracts. That happened to be a bad year for me personally; my mother in New York had sarcoma and had been operated on four times. She died in November after eleven months of illness. Every second weekend, and later, when her condition grew worse, every weekend, I would fly to New York to sit by her hospital bed. It was an enervating experience emotionally, not only because I was constantly trying — without success — to get my mother to try unorthodox methods for a cancer that orthodox doctors declared hopeless, but because the hospital culture was so depressing in itself. There was the woman in the next bed, a nurse, who died while I was trying to reassure her husband in the visitors' room that she might pull through. There was the old woman who was operated on in a bed near my mother's because they couldn't move her to the operating room. Everything reminded me of the fragile character of human life. Then on Mondays I would be back in Chicago giving out leaflets in the morning to workers at Michael Reese Hospital or at one of a half dozen factories we were unionizing. All-told that year we unionized perhaps 2,000 men and women, but were unable to win bargaining rights for more than a dozen due to back-door agreements.

The most traumatic for me was the experience with a factory of 300 workers, all black and all smarting from a sell-out by another AFL union. We signed virtually every one to a union card, and at the first meeting I promised by everything I held holy that we would stick by them no matter what. Next day I phoned the corporation president to discuss union recognition; he said his attorney would contact me. In a few minutes I got a phone call from Sidney Korshak, a lawyer whom Seymour Hersh of the New York *Times* describes as a middleman for employers and unsavory unions, that went like this: "Sid Lens! I've been wanting to meet you for years." After a few pleasantries he asked me what the problem was and I told him. "No sweat," he said, "I'll call you back in an hour and we'll work it out." He called me back three or four hours later with a saccharine apology, "Gee, Sid, in looking through my files I find that we have a signed contract with the teamsters union." None of the workers, I told him, had ever heard of this contract or paid any dues to the teamsters union. He admitted that was true: "We haven't gotten around to telling the workers about it," a strange comment from a lawyer who must have known that the law gives workers the right to *choose* their own representatives. Law or no law, however, the back-door contract — which may have been signed and predated the same afternoon Korshak was contacting me — held up. I asked McFetridge for strike sanction; he refused to grant it on the grounds that "we need the teamsters more than they need us." In desperation I took all 300 signed application cards and the three or four leaders of the group to Henry Anderson of the CIO Retail, Wholesale, and Department Store Union. He agreed to file a petition on their behalf with the NLRB — and did; but the board ruled that the "existing" contract was a bar to an election, without probing as to whether the "existing" contract really represented the wishes of the workers.

II

My second book, *The Counterfeit Revolution,* was published by Beacon Press in 1952. It had been scheduled for publication by my first publisher, Henry Regnery, and in fact had been listed in his firm's catalogue that year under the title, *Why Moscow Is Winning.* But Regnery wanted me to take out a few paragraphs criticizing the Catholic Church, and I refused. Though it was not central to my theme, I resented the heavy prodding for what amounted to censorship. Beacon was happy to have the book though we had an amusing disagreement over the title. I wanted to call it *The*

Bastard Revolution, to indicate that the West was losing the Cold War to a Soviet revolution that had been corrupted. Ed Darling of Beacon objected to the word *bastard* on the grounds that it would offend the public as well as the Unitarians with whom the publishing house was associated. I agreed to change the word to *counterfeit,* but a few days later he called to ask if I wouldn't consider substituting another word for *revolution,* which might conjure barricades and bombs. To my ever-lasting self-esteem, I held the fort: giving up one half the title to popular prejudice was enough. Today, of course, no one would raise an eyebrow over either word; even our soapflakes are now revolutionary, and bastard is almost mild enough for prime-time television.

The Counterfeit Revolution sought to explain that Stalinism, despite its derelictions, attracted many millions of people in the noncommunist world. "The Stalinist world, we say," I wrote in the introduction, "is one of slave labor camps, tyranny, economic inequality, imperialism, and dictatorial suppression of all rights . . . . But then how do we explain the simple fact that millions of people this side of the Iron Curtain pay homage to the dictatorship, join its movement, work for it with religious fervor? How do we explain the allegiance to Stalinist causes of great scientists like Joliot-Curie, writers like Dashiell Hammett, singers like Paul Robeson, men of religion like the Dean of Canterbury, and innumerable others?"

In the context of the times I was trying to show that if the purpose of American policy was to "defeat communism" it was going about it in the wrong way, that Stalin communism — despite its corrupted character — was bound to win by default because the West was so linked to the status quo that it could not excite idealism. The world was in the most extensive revolution in history, but the United States was aligned with the other side. I detailed, among other things, what I had learned during my 1950 trip and ended with a call for a worldwide "crusade against poverty and Stalinism."

Rereading the book, communism may appear to be more harshly treated than if such a work were to be published today. But that was in a period when the world was first learning of the extent of Stalinist terror and slave camps; it was a few years before Khrushchev's revelations about the so-called cult of personality, and before communism mellowed to the point where dissidents were either ignored or jailed instead of executed. I note — again in rereading — that the tone is that of an advocate, but all my writing has that characteristic. I write in the hopes of educating, converting, and I'm convinced that those who claim to be "objective" writers are merely hidden supporters of the status quo. In any case, *The Counterfeit Revolution* shed light on the national revolution then in progress. I am especially happy with the interviews I reported with the leather-faced Neo-Destour leader Habib Bourguiba, who is now president of Tunisia, and with a half dozen Vietnamese socialists who told me in detail why they had no place to go but with Ho Chi Minh and the communists. They described how France refused to introduce a land reform program in Indochina or grant self-determination. Instead it was using American military aid to establish "order," which meant, a Vietnamese socialist named M. Ly Vinh Khuon told me, "the burning of villages, tortures, and executions." Summarizing what I learned from Khuon and the others I wrote that "The French continue to pour men and money into Indochina . . . . but it is hopeless . . . .The equivalent of more than three-quarters of the monies France received from the Marshall Plan annually was being used in a fruitless war from which she very likely will retire the loser. And, as for the socialists and other anti-Stalinists, there no longer is any choice. Hope of American help is completely gone; there remains only the unfavorable alliance with the Stalinists and a prayer that perhaps a more democratic form of Titoism may come to Asiatic Communism and transform it into a more tractable ally."

Of the many favorable reviews of this book the one I treasured most was by Justice William O. Douglas, which expressed the hope that "every person in government would read it." Douglas's comment gave me an opportunity to exchange letters and visit with him in Washington, but more than the friendship it offered me with a supreme court justice, I gained an insight into the thinking of a certain type of liberal that was to be useful in building the antiwar movement a decade later.

Douglas did not refer to himself as a socialist, but his analysis of the ills of capitalism, particularly of its imperial role overseas, was not much different from mine. (By contrast, another type of liberal, Arthur Schlesinger, Jr., chided me for not understanding "the concrete difficulties . . . of conducting an ambitious and comprehensive foreign policy under the guns of a hostile and economy-obsessed Congress," and for not discussing "the problems of U.S. foreign policy with men like Harriman, Bohlen, or Kennan . . . " Presumably all that was wrong with American policy was that Congress was economy-minded, and, if I talked with such good people as Harriman, Bohlen, or Kennan, they would straighten me out on this point.) Justice Douglas, as a member of the judiciary, could not involve himself in the antiwar movement of the 1960s, but I'm sure his heart was with it. Other liberals of that genre, with less restrictions on their behavior, did cross the threshold both to activism and radicalism — the most notable case I can think of being Dr. Benjamin Spock with whom I became good friends in the 1960s. Undergirded by a basic humanism, liberals of the Spock and Douglas type could be depended on at the very least to defend the civil liberties of leftists; and some, as already noted, went further. This may seem like an insignificant detail, but it was very important in the evolution of both the civil rights and antiwar movements of the 1950s and 1960s. Had there been no rapport between the Douglas-type liberals and radicals neither of these movements could have achieved the size and influence they did, and their leaders would have been isolated and subject to the same kind of repression that befell the communists in the 1940s and 1950s.

I repeated this theme — of the need to maintain sound relations with the liberals — in editorials for *Liberation* magazine during the time we were building the movement against the Vietnam War, and I'm sure that this approach was the prime reason the U.S. government, which had been so "successful" in hounding communists during the late 1940s and early 1950s was so unsuccessful in prosecuting antiwar activists during the 1960s.

Not long after the publication of my new book, Shirley and I took another trip overseas, this time spanning the world west to east for almost a year. Again we met many interesting people. We ate at the home of Aneurin Bevan, former minister of health who introduced socialized medicine in Britain, and his wife, Jennie Lee, herself a left-wing member of parliament. (On my return to the United States a CIA agent queried me about that luncheon; I dispensed with niceties and threw her out of the office.) Bevan did not sound as fiercely radical as the American press pictured him, and he was not well informed, I thought, on American affairs; he considered Walter Reuther, for instance, a "left wing socialist."

In Egypt I interviewed the head of government, Mohammed Naguib, who with Gamal Abdel Nasser had overthrown British puppet King Farouk in 1952. In Lebanon I was the guest of one of the most decent people I've ever known, a Druse feudal lord, Kamal Jumblatt, who was also the leader of the socialist party. Tall, thin, soft-spoken he was worshiped by the people around his ancestral estate at El Moukhtara. A few years later, as a member of the government he led a revolt against the right-wing forces of Camille Chamoun, which led to U.S. intervention; and twenty years later, while conducting a similar campaign, was assassinated. Jumblatt was not a pacifist but his socialism contained a strong element of the Gandhian philosophy, a fact that endeared him to A. J. Muste — and myself — when he visited with us in the United States.

In Iran, I had a long talk with Prime Minister Mohammed Mossadegh in the bedroom of his home where he was propped up next to an end table with a bank of telephones. The world was then being fed — mostly by a wire service reporter — all kinds of mischievous copy picturing Mossadegh as a weeping weakling, given to fainting spells. In fact he had an ear defect that required spending considerable time stretched out. But he was a very intelligent man, and his explanation for nationalizing the British-owned Anglo-Iranian Oil Company was impressive. Four out of five Iranians, Mossadegh told me, lived on the land, almost all at mere subsistence. Fifty per-cent of the people suffered from trachoma and other diseases, three of every ten children died at birth. In his view, there-fore, there could be no progress without land reform, and no true land reform unless there was money for seed, credits, roads, cooperatives, electrification, dams. The only place such money was available was in oil, and Mossadegh, a fervid nationalist and (noncommunist) socialist, simply followed his instincts to nationalize the British concessions — promising full compensation in due course. To his consternation he was confronted at U.S. instigation with a world boycott against Iranian petroleum; Mossadegh could find neither tankers to transport his oil nor customers to buy it. In 1953, the United States, taking the lead in protecting the Western world's prize possession, sent in the CIA, under the direction of Teddy Roosevelt's grandson, Kermit Roosevelt, to over-throw Mossadegh. The thirty-three-year-old shah, who had fled to Iraq, was brought back to complete the coup d'etat — the same shah who was forced into exile again twenty-six years later by one of the most surprising revolutions in all history under Ayatollah Khomeini.

Another very interesting personality was Jayaprakash Narayan, who next to Nehru was probably the most popular man in India when Nehru was prime minister, and who many years later would drive from power Nehru's daughter, Indira Gandhi. Jayaprakash, though a socialist, did not opt for political power; instead he spent his time at the grass-roots level, mobilizing for Vinoba Bhave's voluntary land contribu-tion movement. Bhave and Narayan believed they could convince landlords to yield their acreage to landless peasants or tenants, and in fact they succeeded to an extent, but the land given up was almost always marginal and next to useless without credits for development. Since the government's program was also equivocal, the net result was a national revolution that bypassed its main problem, land reform. The results were evident in an incredible rural poverty. (In parliament, a socialist leader, Ramonohar Lohia, charged that a majority of people in the country lived on about six cents a day; Nehru angrily countercharged that it was a "damn lie," the true figure was fifteen cents a day.)

In Burma, as in Iran, Shirley and I were given a wonderful reception. The heads of the government, Ba Swe and Kyaw Nyein, held a state dinner in our honor, perhaps to punctuate the fact that they considered two fellow American socialists as important as the Democrat they had feted shortly before, Adlai Stevenson.

During this year-long trip, we found kindred souls in the socialist, left-Catholic, and pacifist movements who shared their wisdom and time. I wrote pieces for a number of publications — *Progressive,* the *New Leader,* the *Foreign Policy Bulletin,* the *Toronto Star, Frankfurter Hefte,* and the *Antioch Review.* And on my return I did another book, *A World in Revolution,* published in 1956. Stringfellow Barr, author of a pamphlet that made such an impact in the 1950s, "Let's Join the Human Race," gave me a big send-off with his review of this third work. He related that two years previously, while on a trip from India to the Mediterranean, he had run into Asians "who asked me if I knew Sidney Lens. The way they asked made me want to meet Mr. Lens. Now, after reading this book, I know why they asked it that way." Barr expressed the hope that "John Foster Dulles would read this book. I wish that even Adlai Stevenson would read it. For the sad fact is that neither Republicans nor Democrats have shown more than a hazy understanding of the world revolution this book analyzes."

An unsigned review in another magazine gave the gist of my theme succinctly: "The author bases the discussion on his view that there are three, not two, major social systems existing in the world today: capitalism, communism, and feudalism. It is among the people, not the governments, of the feudal world (bearing a veneer of capitalism, but feudal and antiquated nonetheless) that this century's major decisions will be made, he states, and as has been shown by guerrilla movements in Yugoslavia, Indochina and elsewhere, no military organization is capable of permanently subduing the inexperienced, uneducated, and poorly-equipped masses who believe in their goals. Because Western foreign intervention in recent years, including such programs as Point Four, has checked reform and entrenched the old corrupt classes instead of hastening social change, the author contends, America and thus the West is no longer trusted by the people." A quarter of a century later — with the events in Indochina, Angola, Mozambique, Cuba, Ethiopia, and Iran — that thesis stands up quite well.

Travel and reporting became a routine part of my life. Every year or two we would betake ourselves to distant lands, usually for a three-month period, sometimes longer. Our next tour after the 1952–53 trip was to Latin America in 1955. I did not write a new book about it this time, but I did publish many articles — again indicating the twin revolution that was in history's womb. Among the interesting people I met were Rafael Caldera, then a left-wing Catholic associated with the trade union movement in Venezuela who used to keep a packed suitcase next to the door to take with him to jail on his frequent arrests. He later metamorphosed into a middle-of-the-road Catholic and became president of his country. Despite that, he was a pleasant man and — I think — honest. When we had lunch with him after he had become president, he boasted most about introducing civil liberties and freeing communist political prisoners. Another man we visited was Salvador Allende in Chile who would ultimately become the first socialist president of his country and then be overthrown and killed by rightist generals secretly encouraged by the United States. Allende, a doctor, impressed me as both humanistic and doctrinaire, but quite tough — as he demonstrated in office and in death. There was a delightful twinkle in his eye as he punctuated a point. Though he has been criticized by Trotskyites and others for not removing the leaders of the old military establishment, I think he knew what he was doing, and had he had the time would have fashioned an army of an entirely different kind. He took a long gamble, but I believe it was preferable to waiting another five or ten years. Allende, in any case, was a man of stature, a martyr to socialism; it was an honor to know him.

III

By the middle of the 1950s there were tangible indications that the long winter might be coming to an end. Joe McCarthy's charge in 1954 that Secretary of the Army Robert T. Stevens had concealed evidence of espionage led to dramatic hearings in which McCarthy himself was counteraccused by Stevens's attorney Joseph N. Welch. Public sentiment changed from pro-McCarthyism to ambiguity as McCarthy was censured by the Senate in December 1954 (he died in 1957), and Eisenhower finally took courage and spoke out against him.

Other signs of reversal were the birth of two independent left-wing publications (in both of which I played some part), the emergence of the so-called beatnik, and most of all the evolution of a civil rights movement led by blacks and centered in the South rather than the North.

Irving Howe and A. J. Muste were the spark plugs of the magazine projects, Howe of *Dissent* and Muste of *Liberation*. It took some courage at the time McCarthyism was still formidable, for Howe, Stanley Plastrik, and Lewis Coser to initiate a quarterly publication dedicated to revival of the socialist movement. Howe, a young professor who had been active in leftist groups, had written a book entitled *The U.A.W. and Walter Reuther* with B. J. (Jack) Widick, but was nowhere near as well known as he would become later after publication of *World of Our Fathers*, a large tome on "the journey of the East European Jews to America and the life they found and made." Six editors functioned as the board of *Dissent* — Howe, Plastrik, Coser, plus Travers Clement, Harold Orlans, and Meyer Schapiro — and seven others were recruited as contributing editors — Muste, myself,

Erich Fromm (who would soon publish his magnum opus, *The Sane Society*), Norman Mailer (author of the postwar best-seller, *The Naked and the Dead*), Bert Hoselitz (a professor at the University of Chicago), Frank Marquart (of the UAW), and George Woodcock.

Dissent was a lively magazine, exceptionally well written and edited, as it was bound to be under Howe's tutelage, but I never became part of its inner-circle; first, because I lived in Chicago and the others were clustered on the East Coast and, second, because my political bent was closer to that of Muste and *Liberation*. But I did write more than my share of articles for *Dissent* and formed a socialist study group in Chicago which, at Howe's request, we associated with the magazine. Through the years, however, I developed misgivings about the publication's tendency to read the communists out of the radical movement, to label them in fact as reactionaries. Much as I disagreed with the Stalinists I found this distasteful — and inimical to any hopes of building an antiwar movement. I wrote an article critical of the editors on this score. My piece was a few thousand words, but I received friendly letters and memoranda from various editors totalling more than 10,000 words, explaining why my piece should not be published. I suggested that the article and the critiques both be printed since this was, by everyone's admission, an important issue. The editors disagreed. I stopped writing for *Dissent*, our relationship became cooler and in the end Howe asked me to remove myself as a contributing editor. Muste, showing solidarity for my position, resigned.

Liberation magazine, published monthly and ultimately attaining a circulation of 11,000 or 12,000, was oriented toward the radical pacifist, but it included among its editors and contributors men like myself who were radicals but not committed to the Gandhian philosophy. Muste had assembled a prestigious lot to give the publication a wide audience. He was of course the key figure, though Dave Dellinger in fact assigned most of the articles, did the editing, and actual printing at his shop across the river in New Jersey. Another editor was Bayard Rustin, a charismatic man who had worked for Muste in the Fellowship of Reconciliation and had served on a North Carolina chain gang in 1946 for refusing to sit in the back of the bus. Though Bayard parted company with us in 1964 when he took over the A. Philip Randolph Foundation, an institution subsidized by the AFL-CIO, and decided to support Lyndon Johnson for president, he still is remembered for his sizable contribution to the civil rights movement. Bayard was close to Martin Luther King, Jr., and during the Montgomery bus boycott trained King's followers in nonviolence, then helped form the Southern Christian Leadership Conference (SCLC), and was the prime organizer of the largest civil rights demonstration in American history — the one in Washington in the summer of 1963 that drew 150,000 people. In fact it was at the joint headquarters of *Liberation* and the War Resisters League that the first meeting to work out details for this demonstration was held (I happened to be in New York at the time and sat in on it).

The other two editors, Roy Finch and Charles Walker, left after some time, and I was added to the list. As Dellinger recalls it "we wanted to break out of the pacifist mold and Sid was the kind of person who had ties to a broader milieu, including the unions." Among the associate editors and contributors were such well-known figures as Lewis Mumford, Norman Mailer, the legendary Catholic pacifist Dorothy Day, Mulford Sibley of the University of Minnesota, Michael Harrington (whose book *The Other America* would soon make a great impression), Paul Jacobs, Milton Mayer, Waldo Frank, Pitrim Sorokin, Kenneth Rexroth, Bill Hesseltine, and others. *Liberation* didn't try to be as scholarly as *Dissent;* it stuck closer to mundane problems. A few months after it was born, for instance, it joined with the Committee for Justice to Puerto Ricans to send me to San Juan. I had a long talk there with the first elected governor, Luis Marin Munoz, a socialist with close ties to American socialists such as Clarence Senior. After discussing Operation Bootstrap (the economic plan by which Munoz hoped to lift Puerto Rico above its poverty), the independence movement, and similar matters, I came to my real purpose for coming to Puerto Rico, namely to secure an interview with nationalist leader Pedro Albizu Campos, in jail for his activities on behalf of independence. I pleaded with the governor for permission, but while he was generally gracious, he was absolutely fierce when it came to Albizu Campos. He would not let me see him or send questions in to him, and he himself — Munoz — would give me no information about the aging nationalist — was he alive, sick, or what have you. The title of the article I did, "The New Colonialism," gave my opinion about Washington's relationship to the small island.

The second issue of *Liberation,* in April 1956, carried a major piece by a Baptist minister, Martin Luther King, Jr., who was just beginning to capture public attention for his leadership of the Montgomery bus boycott, plus a commentary on the dynamics of the new South by me, and a "Montgomery Diary" by Rustin, who had spent a few weeks with King. There was a close affinity between the civil rights fighters, who were about to break out of their isolation, and the pacifists and socialists at *Liberation* who would wait another decade to become the fulcrum of the largest antiwar movement in American history.

The incident that led to the Montgomery bus boycott was one of those events that normally passes unnoticed, but on this occasion altered history. On December 1, 1955, a black woman, Mrs. Rosa Parks, took a seat on the Cleveland Avenue bus and refused the bus driver's demand that she give it up to a white man. Mrs. Parks, long active in the NAACP, was arrested, starting a chain of events as consequential as William Lloyd Garrison's decision to publish the *Liberator* in 1831. Within twenty-four hours the black leaders of the city proclaimed a boycott of the local buses. Seventeen thousand black people organized car pools or walked back and forth to work, in rain or shine, for 381 days, rather than accept second-class status. Among those who launched this movement and soon would lead it was the twenty-six-year-old minister of the Dexter Avenue Baptist Church, Martin Luther King, Jr.

Until then his life had been unexceptional. Born in Atlanta of religious parents — his father and maternal grandfather were also ministers — he had attended a seminary in Chester, Pennsylvania, had been ordained, and served from 1947 to 1954 in his father's church until assigned to the one in Montgomery. Studious, well-read, King formed a social and political action committee within his church, and urged its members to join the NAACP and register to vote.

Leadership in the Montgomery bus boycott, which ended in victory and desegregated buses more than a year later, not only made King world famous but spawned a great civil rights movement with — for the first time — black leadership. King's home was bombed, and he and others were arrested many times, but their nonviolence and willingness to sacrifice for a cause won them a massive constituency. The boycott was followed by "freedom rides" of blacks and whites in Southern buses, demonstrations in dozens of cities for jobs, voter registration rights, equal use of city facilities. Hardly a day passed from 1960 on without some civil rights headline. Police brutality against demonstrators in Selma, Alabama, shocked the nation to the point where President Lyndon Johnson introduced a far-reaching new voting law. Like other revolts, the black revolt buried many martyrs — including Medgar Evers of the NAACP, three young people shot in Neshoba, Mississippi, in 1965, a white minister killed in Selma. In the course of the revolt there emerged a plethora of groups ranging from King's Southern Christian Leadership Conference (SCLC) — added to the older Urban League and NAACP — to the Student Nonviolent Coordinating Committee (SNCC), which gave the movement momentum. The leaders of SNCC — young men such as Robert Moses, John Lewis, James Foreman, and later Stokely Carmichael (author of the slogan "black power") — were a remarkable group of zealots. They guided a staff of two hundred people in their teens and early twenties operating throughout the

South — usually at salaries of $10 to $20 a week. Though not professing an explicit ideology, SNCC was certainly leftist in mood, most of its leaders, especially Moses and Carmichael, seeing a clear relationship between the campaign for civil rights and those against poverty and war.

I was not at the center of this civil rights revolution, though many people I knew were — Jim Peck, a courageous man from a wealthy white family who was arrested on innumerable occasions riding the bus with blacks; Staughton Lynd, a professor of history at Yale whose parents had written that famous book of the 1930s *Middletown;* Glenn Smiley and James Farmer, two of Muste's associates at the Fellowship of Reconciliation; Rustin; and so on. But I was active on the local front in Chicago.

In addition to the civil rights movement another phenomenon, little understood at the time, portended the birth of a left-wing force of white youth a few years later. The beatnik was the subject of much derision, but in fact reflected the disenchantment of sections of America's youth who were only waiting for a cause to latch onto. The beatniks were disillusioned young men and women in their late teens or early twenties who in effect resigned from the hypocritical society of their middle-class parents. Their parents' generation, they said, spoke of peace but spent billions on nuclear bombs, chemical weapons, and military bases; spoke of brotherhood but were unwilling to grant equality to blacks; spoke of democracy but ruled out freedom of speech for unpopular minorities like the communists. The beatnik (and later the hippie) internalized what the New Left would soon externalize. They wore old clothes, frequented jazz haunts and lost themselves in hedonistic pleasures that seemed to be telling the older generation: "There's no use trying to change your world; it's hopeless. The only thing left is to have fun, smoke pot, and enjoy music."

It was a confusing era among white youth. Many were deserting an old culture to form a new counterculture; but some were beginning to demonstrate against the HUAC, were joining freedom riders and picket lines against Woolworth and Kresge stores, staging rallies for free speech. Unwilling to embrace the Old Left — the Socialist Party because it was small and was consumed by a residual anti-communism; and the Communist Party because it was a disciplined apologist for forced labor camps, purge trials, and authoritarian practices in the Soviet Union — the new radicals gravitated toward small pragmatic actions and ad hoc committees. In this sense they resembled the radicals of the early nineteenth century — before Marx. They were opposed to "the system" and to "the establishment" that operated it, but they had no coherent set of ideas to explain what was fundamentally wrong or how to deprive the upper classes of their power. To many of the older generation they appeared to be youthful pranksters who would, in due course, outgrow their foibles.

To my friends and me, however, they confirmed that a new radicalism in America would develop an organizational structure that allowed for diversity — what the Chinese had subsumed under the slogan "let all flowers bloom" — and was oriented toward pragmatic goals. It also confirmed that the old technique of forming a political party by recruiting around the accredited ideology of a great thinker (Marx, Lenin, Rosa Luxemburg, Trotsky, Gandhi) was not going to work in post–World War II America — at least not yet. A New Left would result, instead, from the coalescing of many movements — antiwar, feminist, civil rights, civil liberties, trade union — much like the People's Party that had been formed at the end of the nineteenth century. The important thing therefore was to concentrate at the grass roots, and let nature itself bring together all the forces working in various fields. These were, I must confess, subliminal thoughts originally, but they became conscious and overt in the late 1950s, and my activities synchronized with that conviction. I concentrated on issues rather than party-building, which among other things made it easier to be tolerant of political rivals.

Ironically, 1955 was the year when the AFL and CIO merged to form the hyphenated AFL-CIO, but I did not consider a united labor movement the vehicle for a New Left. On the contrary, as I wrote in the *Nation,* for whom I covered the merger convention, it was a recognition that the CIO "had not reduced the AFL to impotency, as John L. Lewis had once thought it would. Instead the AFL accepted part of the industrial union approach and rolled with the punch. On the other hand, AFL business unionism had never engulfed the CIO; yet by a process of osmosis CIO had introduced a goodly share of conservative unionism into its bloodstream. The two strategies and the two philosophies had blended toward each other . . ." I debated a management consultant who asserted that the united federation would spawn a labor party that would capture political footholds in the smallest villages. In my view, that was as realistic as predicting that George Meany would join the Communist Party. The unification was a confirmation of weakness, not an expression of strength, and in any case it would not promote radicalism — old or new — in any way.

IV

One day in 1955, A. J. Muste sat me down on a chair in his small New York apartment near Riverside Drive to bounce some ideas off my head. He had been talking with some of the secondary leaders of the Communist Party and had come to the conclusion that major changes impended in world communism. "They're much less dogmatic," A. J. said, "than I've ever known them before, ready to concede mistakes not only by themselves but by the Russians. I get the impression also that the same soul-searching is going on in the communist movement overseas. If they really open up it may be possible one day soon to re-unify the revolutionary movement." Muste wanted my view on this possibility and what we could do to help bring it about. Considering that this was a year before Khrushchev's speech at the 20th Congress of the Soviet Communist Party, which finally admitted some of Stalin's more flagrant crimes, and before the popular uprisings in Poland and Hungary, Muste's speculation was almost oracular. He was wrong in expecting more than what actually happened, but he did perceive what most other noncommunist leftists did not, namely that the post-Stalinist movement was due for severe shake-ups. The only advice I could give A. J. that day was to widen our contacts with Communist Party members and continue the discussion to see where it led.

Muste decided to go somewhat further. Before Christmas that year he drew up a petition to President Eisenhower calling on him to "grant an amnesty of the sixteen [communist] men and women now in prison under the Smith Act . . . and to use your influence to secure the postponement of the trials in the 180 cases presently awaiting Trial Court or Appeals Court decisions under the Act." It was signed by fifty-three people in addition to Muste and myself, including Eleanor Roosevelt; Norman Thomas; John Bennett, dean of the Union Theological Seminary faculty; Lewis Mumford; historian Henry Steele Commager; playright Elmer Rice; and *New Republic* publisher Michael Straight. John Gates, editor of the *Daily Worker*, who was in jail at the time, told me later he could hardly believe it when the news came through that a noncommunist like Muste would take an interest in him or other communists. "I wouldn't have done the same for him," Gates admitted. The wives of Gil Green, Claude Lightfoot, and one other communist leader came to my office to thank me for signing the petition and circulating one locally. Green had been convicted but was in hiding (he would give himself up in 1956 and serve six years), the other two were subsequently saved from imprisonment when the law was declared unconstitutional. But as we exchanged pleasantries, I thought how ironic it was that the same communists who had applauded loudly when the Trotskyites were sent to jail under the Smith Act during the war were now victims of a similar frame-up under the same law. Muste also must have had such thoughts when he conceived the letter for amnesty, but he was truly the least vindictive person I've ever known, and I'm sure he was also thinking of the long-term need to strengthen relations with the communists by showing good faith in deed rather than rhetoric.

After the petition, Muste organized a series of public meetings in which communists were offered a platform for the first time in years. Such was the hysteria of the period that landlords refused communists a meeting hall or canceled when they learned the identity of the sponsors. Even a good clergyman like Muste had trouble, but it was more difficult to turn him down, particularly since the symposium format he worked out included on the podium a communist and another person close to the communists on the one side, and Muste and either one or two third camp socialists on the other. Five meetings were held in all, one each in Philadelphia, Detroit, and Chicago, and two in New York, one of them at Carnegie Hall drawing 2,500 people to hear Muste, Norman Thomas, W. E. B. Du Bois, Communist Party national secretary Eugene Dennis, and as moderator Roger Baldwin, founder of the American Civil Liberties Union. The same format was followed elsewhere, except that in Detroit and Chicago I substituted for Thomas, and in Chicago we added Bert Cochran of the American Socialist.

Nineteen fifty-six was a critical year in the annals of communism. Late in February party secretary Nikita Khrushchev delivered a six-hour talk to a closed session of the 20th Congress of the Soviet Communist Party in which he reviled Stalin as a "criminal murderer," a "slanderer," a purveyor of "moral and physical annihilation," who had arrested and shot 98 of the 139 members of the Central Committee elected at the 17th Congress in 1934, and had imprisoned more than half the delegates to that convention, 1,108 of 1,966. He denigrated Stalin's military "genius," giving one example from his own experience in which the late dictator's refusal to order a retreat of an encircled force led to the loss of "hundreds of thousands of our soldiers." Khrushchev alluded to one crime after another, ascribing them in totality not to any fault in the Party or its policy but to the "cult of the individual" that Stalin had created. The speech was not published in the Soviet Union, but the U.S. State Department secured a text (from Polish sources) and released it in June 1956. The effect was traumatic. For decades the rank-and-file Party member in the United States (and elsewhere) had brushed aside such charges as "capitalist propaganda" or "red-baiting." Now the words of authenticity came from the highest source in the world communist movement. Eugene Dennis, secretary of the Communist Party of the United States published a heretical article in the *Daily Worker* speculating about whether Khrushchev and other Soviet leaders had not been accomplices in Stalin's crimes. Innumerable Party members who had been silent about their doubts began expressing them, writing letters to the editor of the *Daily Worker*, rebuking their leaders for hiding Stalin's sins and for undemocratic and sectarian practices. Open debate was heard for the first time in a quarter of a century. John Gates, editor of the *Daily Worker*, poured fuel on the flames by publishing the text of Khrushchev's speech.

While the Soviet leader's revelations were still reverberating, two events of historic magnitude added further to the malaise. Even before the famous speech, young students in Poland were talking, half-openly, of Soviet imperialism. Polish writers began to write a little more irreverently. In June 1956, there were strikes and riots in Poznan. (A year later a Polish social-democrat rode around with me showing me where the strikes and riots had taken place, and he and I were both arrested as I took pictures of the secret police building. Fortunately I had had dinner with a high official in Warsaw the night before — a former American professor named Oskar Lange — and the magic name plus the fact that there was an international fair in Poznan just then with thousands of foreign visitors led to our release. Evidently, even in the course of "liberalization" the habits of the past die hard.) Four months after the events in Poznan, demonstrations by students brought Wladyslaw Gomulka, a communist moderate who had been jailed in the Stalin era, back to power. The Poles called these events their October Revolution, and indeed it had many characteristics of a social revolution — strikes, demonstrations, the arming of factory workers. At the peak of the crisis, while the Polish party's central committee was meeting to confirm Gomulka, Khrushchev and a few associates arrived from Moscow to thwart the plan. Tanks and soldiers, under command of a Russian general who had been born in Poland, Marshall

Konstantin Rokossovsky, stood in readiness near Warsaw. In the factories, simultaneously, workers were given guns and told to remain at their benches ready to fight back. When the troops began to move, Gomulka threatened to speak to the people over the radio to mobilize them for defense. Khrushchev backed down, and a much altered Poland emerged.

Soon after the Polish October Revolution, similar events occurred in Hungary, but with less fortunate results. Led by students and by intellectuals of the Petofi Circle, masses of people demonstrated in front of the statue of Joseph Bem and at the radio station; secret police fired on the crowds and thereby initiated a period of turmoil that became known as the Hungarian Revolution. For a few weeks the socialist and liberal parties, long underground or defunct, operated openly, held meetings, and published newspapers. The regime of Erno Gero, which had only recently taken the helm from the oppressive administration of Matyas Rakosi was replaced by a liberal communist government under Imre Nagy. This time, however, events went farther than the Russians were willing to tolerate. When Nagy threatened to withdraw Hungary from the Warsaw Pact and pursue a neutralist course, Russian troops and tanks struck at the population in a bloodletting that shocked not only foes of communism but many party members. Estimates in Budapest put the number of civilians killed at 47,000. At a time when many thought Stalinism was buried for good, the Hungarian events caused deep consternation. The National Committee of the American Communist Party, expressing that consternation, condemned Soviet-imposed premier Janos Kadar and the Russians for suppressing popular aspirations: "Instead of meeting the legitimate grievances of the Hungarian working class and people, they again resorted to repression." Gates in the *Daily Worker* was even sharper: "The action of the Soviet troops in Hungary does not advance but retards the development of socialism because socialism cannot be imposed on a country by force."

In the wake of this turmoil within the communist movement, Muste called a "private" conference of sixty people for
early December 1956, about half of whom attended. The
invitees did not include any present members of the Communist Party, though there were some who had been and
some who were close to the Party. Indicative of the spectrum
A. J. wanted to influence was the invitees list: at the core,
his own close associates — Dave Dellinger, Bayard Rustin,
Mulford Sibley, Charles Walker, and myself; a sprinkling of
unionists — Louis Goldblatt of the West Coast longshoremen,
Ernie De Maio of the independent electrical workers, Ben
MacLaurin of the sleeping car porters, Robert Travis of the
UAW; a number of Trotskyites and Trotsky split-offs —
Max Shachtman, Cochran, Mike Harrington, Irving Howe,
Hal Draper, Ernie Mazey; some prominent left-wing indi-
viduals — I. F. Stone, Carey McWilliams (editor of the
Nation), authors Robert and Helen Lynd, Lewis Mumford,
Meyer Schapiro, Vincent Hallinan, Paul Sweezey and Harry
Magdoff of *Monthly Review*. The purpose of the session, as
A. J. explained it, was to promote "the process of dis-
cussion of the problems of socialism in the U.S. and the way
in which a democratic socialist movement might eventually
be built . . ." A month later he followed with a call to form a
Socialist Education Association (the name actually chosen
was the American Forum for Socialist Education), and this
time he invited a number of communists "who have moved
to a significant degree away from Stalinism."

In May we met formally to launch the American Forum,
with A. J. as chairman, myself as national secretary, five vice
presidents, and a national committee of about twenty-five.
Our biggest disappointment was that Shachtman and his
people, whom we considered third camp socialists, didn't
come along, but the time seemed to be ripe for socialist
discussion and everyone, most especially Muste and I, wanted
to see the process go further. We formed branches in various
cities, held forums and did a small amount of recruiting, even
though we were only a "discussion" group. In Chicago a

number of communists left the Party at about this time to become active with the American Forum.

American Forum got a fair amount of publicity (in fact, one piece in the New York *Times* cost me a number of lucrative writing assignments, canceled while Shirley and I were on a trip to Europe), but it didn't catch fire as Muste and I and our associates hoped it would. In retrospect I think there were two reasons for it, first that we didn't give ourselves anything to *do* — there was a limit to how much you could discuss before the attention span and the allegiances of your discussants began to flag. We should have organized some activities together — demonstrations, picket lines, vigils on social issues. Here, I think, Muste's patience stretched a little too long. Our second deficiency was that it wasn't clear what the next step would be. Implicit in what we were doing was the formation of a new political movement, but we shied away from proclaiming that. One day when I was in Muste's office in New York, only a block or so from the headquarters of the Communist Party, John Gates burst into the room, red-faced angry. He was coming from a meeting of the Party's political bureau (or whatever it was called then) and he was furious about a dispute he had had with some of its conservative members. "Do you think," he asked A. J., "I ought to form my people into a faction?"

At the time there were four tendencies in the Party, three of which were born from the disenchantment brought on by Khrushchev's exposé of Stalin, and of these three Gates commanded the largest contituency — the one in New York. The issues on which they disagreed with the old conformists around William Z. Foster were also significant: Was war and fascism inevitable, as the Party had been saying for some years? Was the idea of a vanguard and centralist party valid or would the American revolution be made by a *grouping* of radical parties? And, finally, should the Party become an "indigenous" movement, free of Soviet domination? All of this was the kind of organizational perspective Muste, I, and our associates in the American Forum had. But A. J. refused to give Gates any advice as to whether he ought to consolidate his forces into a formal internal faction to seek control of the Party. I'm sure that if A. J. had uttered the magic word, Gates would have gone ahead. After he left I had a small argument with Muste over his advice.

Today, in retrospect, I think that was the moment when American Forum lost whatever viability it possessed. Had Gates formed his faction we could have put meat on the bone of the "discussion" group, and moved one step further toward the amalgamated grouping we were aspiring to. As it was, the forces around Gates, Eugene Dennis, and a smaller faction dissipated; within two years a large number, perhaps most of them, had simply left the Party — but found no other home. By that time the American Forum for Socialist Education had also folded its tent. We had published two small works, one a mimeographed six-page article by me on "What Is Socialism," which argued that the mere seizure of power and the nationalization of industry did not guarantee *humanistic* socialism (what the Czechs would later call "Socialism with a Human Face"), the other a printed pamphlet — also by me, with commentaries by six people, and an introduction by Muste — called "Questions for the Left." The seven questions I posed were in fact a reformulation of my political philosophy. "According to some," I wrote, "socialism is the nationalization of industry and planning. But if that is so, socialism is hardly the dream and source of inspiration that it was intended to be . . . . The Russian experience teaches clearly that so long as there are no means of influencing the decision of the state, conditions are bound to deteriorate." Socialism, I said, "must offer a new and better life than that of capitalism or Soviet communism if it is to have any appeal or meaning." And the socialist movement, I argued, must look at the state and at economics from different eyes than those of Lenin, who lived in an entirely different milieu. The state is, as Lenin claimed, an instrument of the ruling class, but "it is also the arena where opposing classes can make their weight felt," and we ought therefore to take advantage of evolutionary possibilities toward the revolution. As to economics, it seemed to me that the left had given no coherent explanation for Keynesianism, and why it had been so effective in saving capitalism. I didn't offer the answer to that one either, but it was a question to which I addressed myself extensively in ensuing years; the answer, of course, was that Keynes's "compensatory spending," designed for peacetime as a means of fighting depressions, had in fact only worked during the war and Cold War when the nation was living on a prosperity based on the "compensatory spending" of 2 trillion dollars on the military. In the 1930s it had only partially allayed the national misery, reducing unemployment from a quarter to a fifth of the working class. Only the expenditure on arms and soldiers put the American worker back at his work bench — and though that prosperity lasted more than most Marxists anticipated, it tapered off in the 1970s.

"Questions for the Left" was to have been the opening gambit in a publications program, but American Forum for Socialist Education expired before we proceeded much further. We held many useful discussion meetings throughout the country, one of the most successful being one in Chicago of 1,000 unionists who heard Harry Bridges, Ernie Mazey of the UAW (brother of its secretary-treasurer Emil), and Sam Pollock of the meat cutters. But the American Forum didn't jell. Muste went back to nurturing *Liberation* magazine and traditional Gandhian activities.

In the next few years he organized such protests as the Omaha action — a dozen pacifists, including himself, climbing over the fence at the Strategic Arms Command base and getting themselves arrested; the San Francisco to Moscow Walk, again a small band walking clear across America and Europe (except for a boat trip) giving out leaflets and holding meetings to protest the arms race on both sides of the Cold War. Muste also took a small crew to Northern Rhodesia (now called Zambia) to demonstrate in favor of independence and black rule under Kenneth Kaunda. He joined the national committee of SANE, which was formed by one of his followers, Bob Gilmore, as a vehicle for bringing liberals into the peace movement.

Since my own time was mostly taken up with union work and writing for the *Progressive,* the *Nation, Labor's Daily,* and a book every few years (*A World in Revolution* in 1956, *The Crisis of American Labor* in 1959, *Working Men* in 1960), I did not join Muste in his pacifist actions. I thought at the time that work in the trade unions was more urgent, and to some extent I was right. I was able to mobilize labor people for the peace movement in the 1960s because I had developed a base in previous years. But what Muste did was of greater significance because it worked on the American conscience and consolidated the forces of Gandhianism that would later constitute the core of the peace movement.

Chapter 9
Outreach

I

On January 1, 1959, Fidel Castro's July 26th Movement entered Havana and Fulgencio Batista, the former army sergeant who had installed himself in power for a second time in 1952 (with U.S. help) was forced to flee. Castro's odyssey was amongst the most dramatic events of this century. A handsome young lawyer of revolutionary (but not yet Communist Party) persuasion, he had been jailed in 1953 for leading an assault on the Moncada barracks in Oriente and was fortunate enough to be freed in a grant of amnesty by Batista — to fight again another day. After a period of training in Mexico he and eighty-two men aboard an overcrowded fifty-eight-foot yacht landed on Cuban soil in December 1956, but were decimated to a mere dozen by the time they reached Sierra Maestra — the best known of those remaining being Fidel's brother Raul and the colorful doctor from Argentina, Che Guevara.

It was certainly not military superiority that propelled them to victory. Ray Brennan, a reporter for the Chicago *Sun-Times* who visited with Castro while he was in the hills, told me of an incident that illustrates how the Fidelistas won. "See those Batistianos down there," Castro told Brennan,

"I'm going to try and win them to our side." With a micro-phone and a booming voice Fidel then sent a stream of Spanish toward the Batista soldiers below, and sure enough, after half an hour or so, a small group came over with their American-made weapons. With a fighting force that never numbered more than 1,200 the Fidelistas defeated the American-trained Batistiano army of 43,000.

More properly, the dictatorship collapsed under the weight of its own corruption. Hundreds of millions of dollars had been embezzled by Batista and his associates — the word in Havana was that of every dollar invested in public works 33 cents went surreptitiously to the bureaucracy. At the other end of the social scale, one third of the Cuban working force was unemployed — 700,000 people; three quarters of the sugar workers labored only three or four months a year, during the *zafra* (harvest) season; more than a third of the population was totally illiterate, another third partially so. In the farm sections, 90 percent of the people suffered from worm diseases such as dysentery, or from anemia. Only 9 percent of the rural homes had electricity, and 3 percent indoor toilets. Cuba, however, was a fertile garden for almost a billion dollars of American investment. North American firms owned 40 percent of the sugar industry; with the Dutch-British firm Shell they owned the whole petroleum industry, 90 percent of the electric and telephone industries, mines, and cattle ranches, and 25 percent of banking facilities. Profits from the large sugar companies ran to 23 percent of capital annually, and almost always was repatriated to the U.S. rather than reinvested in Cuba.

The Cuban Revolution was a blood transfusion for the American left, offering a new pole of attraction, and a reaffirmation that socialism was still viable. Soon many people were making the pilgrimage to Cuba, to cut sugar cane, talk with its citizens, listen to Castro. The American government, which had tried as late as the night before Fidel came to power to forestall his victory by imposing a typical Latin-American military junta on the island was of course displeased with the turn of events. It knew, as deputy CIA director C. P. Cabell told a Senate committee, that Castro was not a Communist Party member or even a fellow traveler. But it instinctively understood that he was determined to make a true revolution — and that boded ill not only for the billion in direct U.S. investments, but for Washington's domination of the hemisphere. The administration made little effort to come to terms with Castro.

In April 1959, when Castro came to New York for a U.N. meeting, President Eisenhower avoided him, and Vice President Nixon, who did hold a private conversation with the Cuban leader, recommended immediately afterward that the United States organize a force of Cuban exiles to invade Cuba and topple Castro. The word went out that Castro was a "secret Communist," the formula that has been repeatedly used since World War II as an excuse for American intervention. American leaders, riding high and mighty as the rulers of what was euphemistically called the free world, didn't realize it at the time, but Cuba marked the beginning of a series of devastating defeats for Pax Americana — to be followed by Vietnam, Cambodia, Ethiopia, Angola, Iran, Nicaragua, and others. Roy Finch, in a lead editorial for *Liberation* magazine the month that Castro took power, hit the nail on the head: "The Cuban people," he noted, "have administered a lesson not only to Batista but to the United States. The Cuban revolution of 1959, the most important in this hemisphere since the Mexican revolution of 1917, calls for a new look in American foreign policy. It is our own State Department which now needs the revolution."

It took a little while for leftist support in the United States to galvanize around the Cuban revolution, perhaps because few people thought Washington would revert to its ancient policy of gunboat diplomacy. My own involvement was delayed by a three-month trip to Africa in 1959, and half a dozen other projects. In March 1960, however, I received a long letter from Carleton Beals, the foremost radical writer on Latin American affairs in the 1930s, asking me to join the newly formed Fair Play for Cuba Committee and append my name to an advertisement scheduled to run in the New York

Times. Nominal chairman of the Committee was Waldo Frank, another long-time expert on Latin America, but the key figure was Robert Taber, a courageous CBS news reporter who had smuggled television equipment to the highest mountain in Cuba to interview Fidel in April 1957 and had lived with the ragged band of rebels, suffering their trials and tribulations for some time. He admired Castro personally, but his decision to "combat the massive propaganda campaign . . . against the Cuban people, their leaders, and the new nation that they are building" was truly based on a commitment to "fair play." Taber was no ideologue, and from what I could see, had no roots in the leftist movement — indeed the ad he put together carried barely twenty-eight signatures, including those of Beals, Frank, Taber, myself, and three foreigners (Jean-Paul Sartre, Simone de Beauvoir, and Kenneth Tynan). The best-known Americans on the list were novelists Truman Capote, Norman Mailer, and James Baldwin. It was obvious from Taber's correspondence and telephone conversations that he didn't know many independent liberals, radicals, or trade union leaders. He formed the Fair Play for Cuba Committee exactly for the reason stated in the name, and nothing else.

The storm that swirled around Taber and the others who joined his committee, however, was reminiscent of the days of McCarthyism. Along with a friend of mine John Rossen I formed a Chicago Fair Play for Cuba Committee, whose activities consisted of nothing more dire than holding meetings, appearing on television, distributing tracts and leaflets. But we were castigated from here to Moscow for defending a "new Hitler," apologizing for communism, and similar malfeasances. It was impossible to get a rational discussion going on the subject. When I appeared with Pedro Lanz Diaz, a former Fidelista turned anti-Castro, on the widely heard *At Random* show, hosted by columnist Irv Kupcinet, the calls, about 900 and most of them hostile, rang the phone off the hook. The argument between Lanz Diaz and myself in front of the cameras was equally bitter. A debate with Roberta Montero before 500 students at the University of Chicago, on "Is the Cuban revolution serving the needs of the Cuban people?" was interrupted constantly by partisans of each side. The propaganda machine mobilized against Castro, fueled by lurid firsthand "reports" of middle-class exiles, worked remarkably well.

Taber kept asking me to visit Cuba to see for myself, but for one reason or another — including a trip to the Soviet Union in the interim with a group of trade unionists — I didn't get there until the end of 1960. Taber happened to be around at the same time and he introduced me to Castro for a brief talk. I also had a chance to meet with Guevara, Regino Boti, minister of economics whom I had met in Chile some years before, plus a number of others. Mostly, however, Shirley and I traipsed around speaking with union leaders, intellectuals, and ordinary workers. It was impossible not to be impressed with what was going on, if you were willing to put the situation in perspective.

Castro, I learned, had informed the Americans that he intended to introduce land reform, which obviously would affect land owned by U.S. investors. He offered a form of compensation for those investors similar to that Mexico had granted Standard Oil when Cardenas nationalized the Mexican oil industry, but the State Department was adamant. It wanted full compensation and it wanted it in a period so short that it would have been impossible for a nation with so small a gross national product to meet. The only thing Washington was generous about was its willingness to give military aid and military training to the old army. Castro was therefore put to the test almost immediately: since he would not yield to Washington's attempt to bring back the past (a Batista system without Batista), no grants or loans would be forthcoming from the colossus to the north (not even a picayune one for $1 million), and in that case the only way to secure capital for land reform, clinics, schools, industrialization would be to "squeeze" the middle and upper classes. The situation became particularly dire when the United States cut off the purchase of 3 million tons of sugar (sugar constituted 82 percent of Cuba's exports), and when American oil companies refused to refine oil bought from the Soviet Union. In this circumstance Castro decided to place the burden for development on the wealthier classes, rather than the workers and peasants, causing hundreds of thousands to leave the country (just as Tories had left the United States for Canada during the American Revolution).

The middle classes, admittedly, suffered, but the lower classes — and in particular the farm population — gained immeasurably. Everywhere homes were being built, new schools and clinics constructed. Jim Crow was abolished with one sweep of the pen, and though it lingered in human hearts, it was totally dismembered juridically. For a couple of weeks I tried to track down the charges I had heard of scrip being used instead of money, shortages of goods, labor conscription, Soviet missiles, universal hostility to the regime, and so on, but most were easily discredited and the overall sentiment was so strongly for the revolution it left you breathless. I had never seen such a high pitch of popular sentiment, not even in the days in Detroit during the sit-down strikes. "I have visited sixty-six countries in the last decade," I wrote for *Fellowship* magazine, "Nowhere, except perhaps in an Israeli kibbutz, have I seen the kind of idealistic enthusiasm that prevails in Cuba today. Young people hardly out of their teens are working around the clock for what they consider to be a Cause. They are so immersed and so dedicated that few have time even to contemplate the Revolution's weaknesses — and that of course is unfortunate. One can hardly believe, however, that such dedication could be generated unless there were a deep humanistic strain within the Revolution itself."

Back in the States early in 1961 I wrote a report for the Fellowship of Reconciliation, which its officers transmitted to the Cuban desk in the State Department and then discussed face to face. I didn't know at the time of the elaborate preparations underway to invade Cuba, but I theorized that there were just three alternatives for the United States. The first one, I wrote, was a direct invasion by U.S. troops. They would subdue the big cities, I stated, but would then face endless guerrilla warfare in the villages and hills because the population was overwhelmingly Fidelista. A second alternative was to send in a force of exiles but that was doomed to an even more ignominious failure, for the same reason, namely that there was no chance that the counter-revolution would gain popular support. The third alternative, of course, was to come to an understanding with the Cuban government.

State Department officials were polite with the pacifists, but patently smug. We have more information than Mr. Lens has, they said. We have hundreds of people weighing the issues, and we're sure his estimate of things is completely wrong. They didn't say of course that they had already opted for the second alternative, an invasion by exiles, but it was obvious they had little relish for an accommodation with Castro. History would soon prove that the State Department, with all its vaunted resources, was off track; that the predictions of a single observer were more reliable than that of hundreds of U.S. spies and analysts who understood little of the mechanism of revolution. The counter-revolutionary forces collapsed during the Bay of Pigs invasion before they could gain a foothold.

I had another encounter with the obstinance and myopia of the U.S. government as a result of this stay. Regino Boti, minister of economics in Castro's regime, suggested a formula for mending diplomatic relations with the United States and asked me to pass it on to the new administration. The proposal was approved by Castro and his cabinet, so that I wasn't on a fishing expedition but acting as an intermediary between two governments. Boti asked me specifically to wait until John F. Kennedy was installed because it didn't make much sense to approach an outgoing administration that had less than a month in office. The proposal was simple: if the United States would resume normal diplomatic relations and refine oil bought from the Soviet Union, Cuba would agree to indemnification of American property owners, the money coming from the bonus that the United States had been paying for foreign sugar (then fluctuating at around 2½ cents a pound). I thought it was excellent for both sides: the United States would be reimbursed for the seized property of its capitalists; Cuba, which desperately needed American technicians and machinery, would continue functioning with the least disruption to its economy. Back in Chicago I called Adlai Stevenson, the former governor of Illinois and twice-defeated candidate for president who was about to be installed as the U.S. ambassador to the United Nations, and transmitted the plan. Stevenson took copious notes (he evidently didn't know much about Cuba because his secretary called me two hours later to ask how to spell Guevara), but he was disappointingly noncommittal. He refused to say whether it was a viable plan or whether he would recommend it; I got the impression he wasn't sure of his way in the Kennedy administration thicket. (A couple of years later, after another trip to Cuba and another offer by the Cuban government along the same lines, I submitted the proposal to Senator Paul Douglas of Illinois. Unlike Stevenson he was lyrical about the plan, but alas he too was given short shrift when he took it up with the administration.) Perhaps Stevenson knew that the Bay of Pigs adventure was in the works, although there is some doubt that Kennedy took him into his confidence; perhaps he was wary for other reasons. In any event he phoned from Washington a few days later to say that Kennedy wasn't interested. By April 17, it was obvious why: Kennedy's solution to the Cuban problem was the Bay of Pigs.

Historical experience dictated that the United States was bound to intervene, but emotionally I entertained the residual hope that this time the American government would be intelligent enough — and moral enough — not to grab for the sword. It was a vain hope. On the day that the counter-revolutionaries landed at the Bay of Pigs a group of us were meeting at the Fellowship of Reconciliation office in Nyack, New York. Among us was the famed sociologist C. Wright Mills, author of *The Power Elite* and *White Collar,* whose paperback on Cuba, *Listen Yankee,* had been published the year before; A. J. Muste; Al Hassler, then secretary of the

Fellowship; and a few others. Mills and I wrote an ad for publication in the New York *Times,* calling on the United States to end the invasion, and a telegram to Secretary of State Dean Rusk with the same message spelled out a bit differently. Muste got on the long distance line to solicit signatures. Soon he had added the names of Erich Fromm, Stewart Meacham of the American Friends Service Committee, Norman Thomas, critic Maxwell Geismar, Bob Gilmore, and John Nevin Sayre, but he ran into a shoal with another world-famous sociologist who urged that we be prudent, wait and see how things developed. Mills, who had a bad heart (he died not long afterward), exploded in anger such as I had seldom seen before. What annoyed him — and me too — was that this same man had been preaching to all and sundry that war was in the offing and that the human species might only have a few years to end the arms race or perish, yet when an actual war was under way he found all kinds of reasons not to be "hasty" to express opposition. The so-called objectivity of some intellectuals was often — to put it simply — a pain in the neck.

After the fiasco at the Bay of Pigs, Americans looked for scapegoats rather than flaws in national policy. Many blamed Kennedy for not sending American pilots into the fray when the Cuban counter-revolutionary effort foundered. Very few were willing to concede that intervention per se was becoming an unviable alternative; it was inconceivable that America couldn't work its will wherever it pleased. A couple of days after the exiles were routed I had lunch with Basil (Stuffy) Walters, editor of the Chicago *Daily News.* Stuffy and I used to get together periodically so that he could pick the brain of a radical and I could try to influence his paper's policies; I also did some writing for the *News* during trips abroad. Ordinarily Walters was on the light-hearted side, but this time he was more depressed than I had ever seen him. "What caused this defeat, Sid?" he asked, and almost fell apart when I responded, "You." I wasn't kidding. A friend of mine, a reporter on Stuffy's staff had gone to an office of the Cuban exiles in Chicago some weeks before and been given fairly detailed plans of the pending invasion. The *News,* however, just like the New York *Times,* which also knew of the impending invasion, suppressed the story. "It's still on your spike, Stuffy," I told him. "If you and others had publicized what was going on secretly, the American people would not have let it take place." Walters, a conservative who disagreed with me on almost all matters, nevertheless had enough of a sense of decency to admit that I was probably right. Irv Kupcinet, on whose TV show I had defended the Cuban Revolution a number of times, noted in his *Sun-Times* column a few days after the Bay of Pigs that "Labor leader Sidney Lens is a 'prophet without honor' in his home town. He was roundly criticized and rebuked for his report on Cuba, which, incidentally, he had turned over to the State Department. Now it develops he was essentially correct."

The Cuban revolution and the Fair Play for Cuba Committee impinged on my life — in a circuitous fashion — when President Kennedy was assassinated. I was on a speaking tour for the American Friends Service Committee at the time, being driven to Amherst College in Massachusetts, when the man in the toll booth told us Kennedy had been shot. We thought he was kidding until we arrived at the school and found the campus in a state of shock. Since my meeting was canceled, there was nothing to do but go home; so back we went, the young driver and myself, to Hartford where I made a reservation for the next plane to Chicago, four hours later. Sitting next to me as I dawdled over a cup of coffee were two truck drivers pointedly cursing Lee Harvey Oswald and the "communists" for "murdering our president." The radio by now was revealing that Oswald had once been a member of the Fair Play for Cuba Committee, and when I phoned Shirley she said that news media had been calling in droves to find out if I knew Oswald — *Life, Newsweek,* the New York *Times,* local papers, TV stations, and so on. Actually I had never heard of him (though that wouldn't have been unusual), but I'm convinced even now that Oswald's flirtation with Fair Play was a gambit for a more sinister purpose. A man who had the telephone number of a top local FBI

agent in his pocket and had been cleared for re-entry into the
United States so quickly despite having defected to the
Soviet Union, could not have been a left-winger. I don't pre-
tend to know what his game was or who his true associates
were, but he certainly wasn't one of us. Nonetheless, it
occurred to me as I talked with Shirley and listened to those
two truck drivers calling for the extermination of all communists, that I might be in danger of arrest that night. Would
the new administration order the incarceration of thousands
of radicals under the provisions of the McCarran Act, which
gave it the right to do so in a national emergency? I weighed
the alternative of returning home against that of hiding out
for a few days, perhaps in New York, but finally decided
that making myself scarce, even for a day or two, would confirm for many that the committee in fact had been part of
Oswald's conspiracy. That the hysteria would not have been
hard to fan is evidenced from an anonymous letter I received
four days after the assassination: "Well! You murderer! How
does it feel to contribute to the assassination of President
Kennedy? Oswald was a communist and a member of the
Fair Play for Cuba Committee. I recall a year and a half ago
how you were praising that madman, Castro, and telling how
wonderful he was. Frankly I think Castro hired Oswald to
murder Mr. Kennedy, and I wouldn't be surprised if you and
the other Commies were in on it." Fortunately the new
president, Lyndon Johnson, decided against a round up. He
let the situation cool off.

II

Gratifying as was the reaction of younger folk to the Cuban
Revolution, it nonetheless illustrated that there were limits
to left-wing outreach. That was a word we would hear
throughout the sixties and seventies — *outreach.* Why was the
leftist movement unable to involve unionists? Why didn't
it enroll blacks and Latinos? Why couldn't it win friends in
office or penetrate the electoral process? The answer of
course was that it did . . . within limits, but that in the
absence of an economic crisis only a small percentage of the

American public could be involved in maverick politics of any kind.

I had a chance to test this thesis on a number of fronts from 1959 to 1962. The climate had changed sufficiently so that there were now two card-carrying peaceniks in Congress; labor officials as high up as the secretary-treasurer of the UAW were beginning to speak out against militarism; and solid bourgeois papers like the Chicago *Daily News,* the Detroit *Free Press,* and the New York *Post* were willing to publish articles by a known leftist. One had the feeling of a new movement inching forward — but not yet ready to gallop.

The two peaceniks in Congress — they lasted a single term — hadn't won because of their espousal of an antiwar position; there were special circumstances accounting for victory in each case. But Byron Johnson of Colorado and William (Bill) Meyer of Vermont had brought the issue to the forefront in their districts and had been given a favorable reception by their constituents. Byron was an economics professor, active in the Fellowship of Reconciliation (his wife, Kay, was even more active), and Bill was a forestry expert, a long-time reader of the *Progressive,* with a philosophy that blended populism and socialism. His son Karl, whom I knew well, was a member of Dorothy Day's Catholic Worker movement in Chicago, who later spent more than a year in jail for refusing to pay income taxes on the grounds they sustained militarism.

By way of a small digression, I should record that non-payment of income and telephone taxes as a means of protesting armament expenditures was a pacifist tactic during the 1960s. I withheld both taxes — income and telephone — for a number of years; the Internal Revenue Service developed a routine, calling my office for the money then seizing my checking account. Muste went further than most protestors did, he not only refused to pay, he refused to file a return and he arranged his finances in such a way that there was nothing the government could seize. The IRS was loath to prosecute an old man whom *Time* had called "the

Christer." It tried therefore to work out a compromise. One of the agents it sent to see A. J. had been a Musteite in the 1930s; he was willing to settle the whole matter if the aging pacifist would write on a blank piece of paper that he owed the government such and such an amount of money. Muste wouldn't. He gave his old follower, instead, a long lecture on why he too should refuse to pay taxes. Ultimately the government sued and won a judgment, but it never collected a nickel.

Back to our peacenik members of Congress, Johnson and Meyer. I hadn't known either of them previously, but I sought them out and in short order we became fairly good friends. Both knew of me and had read many of my articles in the *Progressive,* the *Nation,* and *Fellowship.* One day I suggested that the two of them call a conference of a dozen members of Congress at which some of us could give briefings on the military issue. It was my hope that we might consolidate a small peace bloc which would introduce a variety of anti-militarist bills around which activists outside the halls of Congress could mount a campaign. Ten years back I would have frowned on such tactics as a waste of time, and working with Democrats — even like Johnson and Meyer — a transgression of principle. But I had come to the conclusion in due course that to overlook the schisms on the other side not only divided us from the few legislators who could serve our cause but deprived us of a useful technique for proselytizing around specific legislation. It didn't work out too well on this occasion, but I still think it was a sound principle.

Bill Meyer's letter to thirty-eight representatives brought eleven members of Congress to a conference held on May 23, 1959, at the Hotel Congressional where John Swomley of the Fellowship of Reconciliation, Dr. David Hill, a nuclear physicist, and I discussed the misconceptions of the arms race. Everyone listened attentively and agreed — generally — with what was said, but they were loath in the end to form themselves, as I wrote to Meyer in an evaluation of the affair, into a "small but dedicated nucleus . . . 100 percent against the militaristic foreign policy." I had urged the group to introduce legislation to eliminate military spending over a three-year period and to divest the military immediately of public relations funds, "turning the job over exclusively to civilians." Such bills had no chance of passage of course but they could be rallying points for mass action, just as the Lundeen bills had galvanized mass support for unemployment compensation during the 1930s. Fear of isolation, I think, caused the participants to shy away from such a course — isolation not only from their fellows in Congress but from their constituencies. Had they decided to act as a bloc against militarism they would have had to conduct a sustained educational campaign in their home districts, and run the gauntlet of a military-minded press. It was more than they were willing to do at the time.

A project that turned out better was the formation of an antiwar nucleus within the house of labor. The 1950s, it may be recalled, was the decade of three major military innovations — the hydrogen bomb, the nuclear submarine, and the space satellite (forerunner of the intercontinental ballistic missile). John Foster Dulles, exuding a sense of power that came from these technological breakthroughs, was threatening "massive retaliation" with nuclear weapons if the Soviet Union crossed into what Washington considered the free world.

On the other side of the equation Bertrand Russell was conducting peace marches in Britain, and Muste more modest actions in the United States. Where, however, was labor? With the help of our friends in the American Friends Service Committee (we needed their letterhead for "respectability") Charlie Chiakulas and I called together a conference on Labor and World War III in February 1959 at the University of Chicago. About one hundred unionists attended, from whose ranks we formed a "labor advisory committee." The Quaker — AFSC — umbrella was a useful shield against our national union presidents who might otherwise accuse us of forming a "dual" union.

The labor advisory committee functioned for a number of years, issuing statements and holding conferences. For the most part it was a regional affair, centered in Chicago, but I'm sure it stimulated other forces to speak out, especially union officials who had been close to the Old Left in the 1930.

Another step, again with the help of the Quakers, was to organize the Peace, Jobs, and Freedom conference in April 1961. This time Chiakulas and I drew in as sponsors six nationally known union leaders: Frank Rosenblum, secretary-treasurer of the Amalgamated Clothing Workers; Emil Mazey, who held the same post with the UAW — second in command to Walter Reuther; James B. Carey, president of the International Union of Electrical, Radio and Machine Workers; A. Philip Randolph, president of the Brotherhood of Sleeping Car Porters; Pat Gorman, top official of the Amalgamated Meat Cutters; and Arnold Zander, then president of the American Federation of State, County and Municipal Employees. The conference was attended by 300 unionists from fourteen states and Canada, featuring Rosenblum — who called for universal disarmament "as essential for national security" — and Mazey, as the lead speakers.

Early in 1963 we had a chance to test labor sentiment on the war-peace issue in a relatively conservative community. Out of the blue I received an invitation from a man I had never known before, Al Bilik, president of the Cincinnati central labor body, to speak on "Our No-Win Foreign Policy; Are We Depending Too Much on Missiles" at his organization's annual educational conference. Bilik, a medium-sized man with a booming voice, had once been a Yipsel (an abbreviation for Young People's Socialist League), and after college in New York had found a job as an organizer for the American Federation of State, County and Municipal Employees. In six years he enlarged the AFSCME local in Cincinnati from 500 to 5,000 members, and was elected chief of the city's central labor body as well. McCarthyism was on the wane by this time, but the militarist spirit was not; it took courage for Bilik to pivot his educational conference around the arms race issue — and to invite a known radical as its keynote speaker. Al, however, had been reading articles and books of mine for years; and since I carried the label "union official" he thought my ideas might be palatable to other union officials — even in a city like Cincinnati, which was much less liberal than, say, New York, San Francisco, or for that matter Chicago. I suggested to Bilik that we might hedge our bet a little by inviting a union leader of higher standing, Emil Mazey. I had known Emil as a young non-Stalinist radical in Detroit during the 1930s when he was a leader of the unemployed and then of Local 212 — and Chiakulas and I had already involved him in other labor conferences. When I phoned Emil, he told me that though he had spoken on the issue before, he was not secure in his knowledge of the subject: "give me time for a crash course over the weekend and I'll call you back Monday." On Monday he agreed and though his speech was peppered with more anti-communist comments than I liked, the combined effect of our two talks was far better than I had expected.

Not much later, Chiakulas and I organized our largest meeting in Chicago, attended by about 700 unionists, most of them from the UAW, who came to hear their secretary-treasurer. We never were able to involve Walter Reuther or other top UAW leaders, but we did include in these and future efforts many important labor luminaries.

The result of our efforts was that discussion of the military issue became somewhat more acceptable in the house of labor, and some secondary leaders and a few rank-and-filers walked in our semiannual peace marches. Though we failed to pierce the barrier between unionists who had matriculated in the 1930s and the younger generation of leaders, Chiakulas and I took comfort that we had accomplished something: we had seeded the soil.

Ultimately, at the peak of the Vietnam War, Murray Finley (now president of the Amalgamated Clothing Workers), Rosenblum, Gibbons, Bridges, and others formed the Labor Leadership Assembly for Peace. By that time Chiakulas was dead and I was self-relegated to a job as part-time consultant for Local 329. I sat in occasionally with Finley on planning sessions for certain meetings, but, while our personal relations were good, we didn't see eye to eye on basic matters. Murray didn't involve rank-and-file unionists, concentrating instead on their leaders: he was lukewarm toward the movement's traditional demonstrations and rallies and he tried too hard, I thought, not to offend the labor establishment. Yet, with all that, I must say he performed a valuable service to the movement through the assemblages he organized — one at which Eugene McCarthy spoke, another at McCormick Place in Chicago (where Muste was put on the program at the last minute), and a third in St. Louis where Harold Gibbons and his teamsters were host. The Labor Leadership Assembly for Peace did not play as big a role in the peace movement as it might have, but here and there (in New York and San Francisco especially) it did turn out thousands of people for the protest marches. Additionally I was able to pick up a thousand dollars every now and then from Rosenblum or Gorman for our National Mobilization Committee to End the War in Vietnam.

Another attempt at outreach by antiwar elements in the early 1960s was the formation of the Committees of Correspondence at a meeting in Bear Mountain, New York, to promote "unilateral steps towards disarmament." The name of course was plagiarized from the committees that functioned during the American Revolution, and was deliberately chosen for that purpose. The twenty-four participants, assembled on the initiative of Robert Gilmore of the American Friends Service Committee, included Harvard sociologist David Riesman; Erich Fromm; H. Stuart Hughes, also of Harvard and a grandson of the Supreme Court Justice who ran for president against Woodrow Wilson; Muste; Mark Raskin, a founder of the Institute for Policy Studies; psychologist Jerome Frank; physicist William Davidon; AFSC's Stewart Meacham and similar luminaries. Riesman, who believed that there was only a short time to prevent nuclear holocaust, was the guiding intellectual figure. Under his aegis and young people he selected to run the organization, committees were formed in a few cities, a bulletin was published sporadically and fifty or one hundred additional people were enrolled as supporters (including the present conservative senator from California S. I. Hayakawa). But the Committees of Correspondence failed to evolve into a mass movement. For one thing it confined itself too much to intellectual discussion rather than action; for another it appealed to much the same audience as SANE. After a couple of years the Committees of Correspondence folded their tent; Riesman, so far as I know, played no further role in the antiwar movement. Erich Fromm, with whom I had corresponded for many months about publishing a theoretical socialist magazine in English and Spanish (another effort that expired, this time because we couldn't raise the money), joined the Socialist Party and tried with might and main to convince Muste, Meacham, and myself to follow him.

A group that showed much more promise for outreach was SANE. Organized in 1957 by Bob Gilmore, a left-wing pacifist at the time and a follower of Muste's, it was conceived as a vehicle for liberals. (For radicals there was the Committee for Nonviolent Action.) And, in fact, it did attract a considerable number of liberals, 15,000 or 20,000. In Chicago, Homer Jack formed a branch of SANE together with Jack Bollens of the American Friends Service Committee, myself, and a few others. Nationally, Norman Cousins, editor of *Saturday Review*, became the guiding figure. He was a good choice, erudite, linked to many liberal milieus, and sufficiently well known and respected to give SANE both status and prestige. Cousins, however, could not escape the anticommunist virus of his times. At a critical juncture he yielded to it, causing a disarray in SANE's ranks from which it never fully recovered.

Early in 1960, as its biggest project to date, SANE scheduled a rally at Madison Square Garden for May 19 at which Walter Reuther, Eleanor Roosevelt, and Alfred Landon (the 1936 Republican candidate for president) were to speak. In charge of promotion for the rally was Henry Abrams, who had been active in Henry Wallace's Progressive Party campaign of 1948, and was charged — cardinal sin — with having also been a communist. A couple of weeks before the rally Senator Thomas Dodd, vice-chairman of the Senate Subcommittee on Internal Security, threatened to blow the whistle on Abrams and other alleged communists unless they were removed. Cousins, a neighbor of Dodd's and friendly with him personally, prevailed on the senator to hold off his attack until after the rally. In return, however, he questioned Abrams about his affiliations and when he was told that, as a matter of principle, Abrams would not answer the famous question, "are you now or have you ever been. . . ," fired the rally director. The affair went off as scheduled, but the tumult within the organization could be heard far and wide. Linus Pauling and Bob Gilmore resigned from its board; Muste wrote an article for *Liberation* criticizing Cousins and also resigned; a number of SANE groups, most notably in New York, disaffiliated to form federations of their own; and most of all SANE lost its foothold with youth.

III

Two trips abroad — a three-month journey to black Africa in 1959 and a three-week visit to the Soviet Union in 1960 — bisected a growing burden of activities. They were useful, however, not only because they changed the pace of daily existence but because the world was being altered so rapidly that, unless you saw a little of it for yourself, it was difficult to grasp what was going on even in your own country. From 1944 on there had been a string of national revolutions throughout Asia, and from 1952 on, when Gamal Abdel Nasser and Mohammed Naguib had liberated Egypt from British domination, a string of similar upheavals occurred in Africa. Winston Churchill may have been cavalier about the Atlantic Charter promise to allow the people in the colonies to "choose the form of government under which they will live," and Harry Truman may have blithely disregarded the Roosevelt-Churchill pledge made in August 1941, but the people in Africa and Asia took it seriously.

In December 1947, a few months after Kwame Nkhrumah returned to what was then called the Gold Coast, black war veterans demonstrating in front of the Government House were met with a hail of bullets in which two were killed. As might have been expected the event triggered outbreaks throughout the capital, Accra. In three days 29 people were killed, 237 wounded, and Nkhrumah was on the telegraph wiring London that the "people demand self-government immediately." They didn't get it immediately, but in 1951, after a general strike, they were granted partial self-rule, and in 1957 total independence — and a new name, Ghana. The revolutionary pace, however, was slow. As of 1958 there were only eight nominally free nations (excluding apartheidist South Africa) amongst the forty-seven countries in Africa. Two of them had been "free" for a long time: Ethiopia and Liberia; Egypt had been free in name since before World War II, but in actuality only since 1952; then there was Libya which had gained its independence in 1951, and Morocco, Tunisia, the Sudan, all freed in 1956; and Ghana. But this was obviously only the beginning, a great explosion was on history's agenda for Africa, and I wanted to see how it was developing.

Four incidents stand out in my mind from this trip, two that happened in Ethiopia, one in the Belgian Congo (now Zaire), and one in South Africa. I didn't know a single person in Ethiopia, nor did I have an introduction to anyone. In my usual visit to the American Embassy to get economic, political, and labor briefings, therefore, I asked for a list of political leaders, for and against Emperor Haile Selassie. The political officer laughed: "You won't find any revolutionaries in this country. The closest thing to an opposition is a wild-talking chap named Seyoum Sebhat, but he has no party or group." Unfortunately for the embassy's sources of information, there were opposition groups in existence and through Seyoum I was able to contact some of them. In fact before I left I sat in on a meeting of a dozen opponents of the regime and listened to them make plans to overthrow the government, a plan they put into operation a year later — unsuccessfully, alas — in December 1960.

The myopia of the embassy officials in Ethiopia was punctuated in another way. Since there were few American writers coming through Addis Ababa they gave a party for Shirley and me "so you can talk with our people and learn what is going on." I suspect they also wanted to learn from me what I had learned on my own from native Ethiopians, but I of course kept that to myself — especially the plans for a revolution. One of those who insisted on explaining how to improve relations with Ethiopia was a naval officer. "What we have to do," he said, "is give the emperor a destroyer or two. That's what these people go for." But what do they need destroyers for, I asked him. To defend against the communists. What communists? Where? He wasn't very clear, but he knew the emperor would enjoy having a battleship.

The American government was woefully out of touch with the revolution in Africa. That was brought home to me pointedly in Leopoldville (Kinshasa), capital of the Belgian Congo (Zaire). I had met a Belgian in Hamburg in 1957 who guaranteed me that the Congo would remain Belgian "for at least a thousand years," but the riots in Leopoldville in January 1959 made it certain that the period would be considerably foreshortened; in fact independence was wrung out of Belgium the following year. Yet American Embassy officials told me they hadn't met a single one of the leaders who would soon be ruling the country — not even Joseph Kasavubu or Patrice Lumumba. They gave me a list of the sixty native parties that had recently mushroomed and asked me to come back for a chat after I had talked with some of their people — obviously to pump me for information they themselves didn't have. I didn't find the request hard to disregard, but it is significant that in a nation close to revolution the American Embassy knew so little about the revolutionaries. (The same thing would be true during the Iranian revolution of 1978-79: the embassy and the CIA had limited their contacts to the shah and his cronies, eschewing the opposition.)

The fourth incident was in Johannesburg, South Africa. We were having dinner with a former cabinet member, an Afrikaner, who was telling us how much his servants loved him. "Every night we pray together," he said, "and they always give me their money to save for them." That patronizing attitude made me seethe inside, so much so that I asked the most irreverent question of all: "What are you going to do when the black people in South Africa rebel?" The ex-cabinet member, a leader of the church, smiled condescendingly. "These kaffirs will never take up arms." "But what if they do?" "Well," he said, "we shall suppress them. We shall suppress them even if we have to use atom bombs on Soweto." In 1959 that sounded like nonsense — atom bombs on Soweto. Today it no longer seems that way, since it is widely believed that South Africa either already has atom bombs or can readily make them.

"The African revolution, like Africa itself," I wrote for the January 1960 issue of *Liberation,* "is removed from the streams of both the West and East." It doesn't subsist, I pointed out, on Marxist doctrines, but on "a more elementary fare, around such slogans as 'One-Man, One-Vote,' 'Africa for the Africans,' 'Independence in 1960.' . . . One of the reasons for the special character of the African revolution is the role played by race. The racial struggle is for all practical purposes the class struggle. The European [white] is the upper class; the Negroes or the Arabs form the worker or peasant classes; and the Indians, where they exist, the middle class. For a century, racism has been the bulwark of Western rule; a rigid, frightening racism, such as prevailed nowhere else. The focus of revolution therefore is racial equality. In that one concept is tied all the elements of freedom and social change which other revolutions have formulated in such slogans as 'Peace, Bread, Land' or 'Liberty, Fraternity, Equality.'" I wrote a more popular series of articles, emphasizing the same points, for the Chicago *Daily News* and the seventy-odd papers which subscribed to its foreign service.

The trip to the Soviet Union was arranged by Jack Spiegel of the shoe union, who was asked by Soviet officials in Washington to assemble a labor delegation to visit their country. The Cold War was now more than a decade old, but there were still no signs of a relaxation of tensions. The CIO had long ago broken with the World Federation of Trade Unionists (WFTU) and become part of the rival International Confederation of Free Trade Unions (ICFTU). The Russians had no hopes of healing this breach in the near future, but I'm sure they felt that trade union visits would, at least to a limited extent, act as a brake on the Cold War. Joseph Curran, president of the National Maritime Union, had already accepted an invitation to travel on his own and was rewarded with an interview with Khrushchev. Our delegation was to be made up of secondary figures, except for Harold Gibbons whom I recruited for the trip. (Spiegel told me that the Russians were not overjoyed about inviting me, but had become enthusiastic when I bagged Gibbons for the visit.) Gibbons, unfortunately, backed out at the last minute, asking us to substitute for him an official of the textile union, who turned out to be a square peg in a round hole.

Since the death of Stalin in March 1953 and particularly since the Polish October Revolution in 1956, I had been anxious to see the "workers fatherland" for myself. Obviously there had been significant changes. The arrest of secret police chief Lavrenti Beria in June 1953 and his execution on Christmas eve — the last time, incidentally, a leading opponent was shot for political differences — signaled the downgrading of the secret police and the return of a semblance of legality. Leaders who subsequently fell out of favor, including Molotov, Malenkov, and Khrushchev were removed from office but not imprisoned or executed. Average citizens, too, found it possible to take up a grievance at the factory or to press the case for a new apartment without looking over their shoulders to see if the NKVD (the Soviet secret police) was watching. This, added to the fact that the new leadership had freed hundreds of thousands of people from the forced labor camps and had formally abolished the camps as an institution operated by the hated GULAG (The Main Camp Administration), was a great improvement over the past, even if it didn't constitute what we Westerners would call freedom. There were still cases of dissenting writers and intellectuals jailed for their views, or thrown into mental institutions. On the whole, however, average citizens had lost their fear of capricious imprisonment or exile to the labor camps.

Within the Party, too, there was a loosening of monolithicism, at least insofar as the higher bodies were concerned. Members of the Presidium and Central Committee, who in Stalin's day voted exactly and invariably in accordance with the dictator's wishes, now expressed their convictions more freely. In June 1957, for instance, the Presidium voted to remove Khrushchev from office by a vote of eight to three, but were overruled by a hastily assembled Central Committee which voted the other way. There were also sharp differences on such issues as the accession of Gomulka to power in Poland, the Hungarian Revolution of 1956, and dealings with China. Moreover, for a while under Georgi Malenkov "liberalization" promised to go much further. Malenkov promulgated a "new course" under which there was to be a sharp rise in consumer goods, abolition of the compulsory buy-up from collective farms, an increase in farm income by 2 billion rubles, and a pledge of lower prices and higher wages for the worker. Malenkov unfortunately was removed to make way for Khrushchev, who tightened the reins appreciably. Yet the Russia of 1960 was very much different from what it had been seven years before.

Unfortunately our delegation of eleven people ran into problems that made an assessment of the Soviet situation more difficult. Our Soviet hosts wanted us merely to visit factories and union offices; I insisted we have talks with economists and social scientists as well. The Russians grudgingly gave in on this point, but even so our contacts were limited. Then we had bitter quarrels amongst ourselves. Four or five of our people were lyrical every time they saw a Soviet housing project or a new machine. A minority, including Shirley and me, pointed out that better apartments were being built in Sweden and that capitalism also used modern machinery — even more modern. We were not downgrading Soviet progress but we hoped that the report we wrote would be realistic enough to have an impact on American people, rather than be a useless puff job. Ernie Mazey, an important secondary leader in the UAW and later of the American Civil Liberties Union, was chair of the delegation and an excellent peacemaker. So too Sam Pollock, an old Musteite of the 1930s era who now headed a large butcher workmen's local in Cleveland. On the other side the fellow from the textile union, Charles Sobel, derogated whatever anyone said, subtly insulted the Russians, and added to the tensions immeasurably.

The Russians too were not much help. They denied, for instance, that there was any breach between themselves and the Chinese, when the entire world knew there was. In Leningrad they took us to the museum in what was once the Winter Palace — the place where Lenin and Trotsky directed the uprising of November 7, 1917. We were shown a movie of the great event, which was like no other movie I've ever seen. Periodically a figure in the front lines of a parade or making a speech would appear on the screen with his head cut out. We knew of course that this was Trotsky, but the museum guide responded to our queries with the bizarre comment that it was an unimportant person. Then, too, there were the stilted and rudimentary answers to our economic questions — a sharp contrast to the kind of responses we had received during our three-day stay in Poland.

With all that, however, we did learn something and our comments at the press conference when we returned did do a small amount of good in mitigating the harshness with which most people viewed the Soviet Union. I wrote a series of articles for the New York *Post,* the Detroit *Free Press,* the Chicago *Sun-Times* and other newspapers that stressed the point that "within the context of communism, the Khrushchev form is substantially different from that of Stalin." The series in the Detroit *Free Press* was headlined

STALINIST TERROR IS GONE, and pointed out that while Russians for the most part still talk only of trivialities with foreigners, they do talk more freely. In that regard I recalled a strange incident in Tashkent. We had just checked into a hotel overlooking a small park. Shirley stayed in the room to unpack; I took a walk. When she looked out the window and saw me surrounded by hundreds of people, she ran down to rescue me from what she thought might be a sullen mob. It was not sullen at all. What had happened was that I began an innocent conversation with a man in German, who translated it into Russian to someone else who translated it into Uzbeki. The questions and answers were about mundane things: what do you do for a living, how many cars do you own, how many rooms do you live in, how much money do you earn. But the whole park was a babble of voices as each person translated to the one behind him, and then relayed questions to me. The thing became even more complicated when an American schoolteacher came by. Now there were four languages involved. She spoke to me in English, I translated into German, a German-speaking fellow translated into Russian, and someone else into Uzbeki. It was a great day for international relations.

IV

On the home scene, the 1960s, one of the most portentous decades in American history, began with an extended presidential campaign in which, as historian Samuel Eliot Morison notes, "both candidates promised about the same things — peace through strength, continuation of welfare, streamlining the federal government, etc." Senator John F. Kennedy and Eisenhower's vice president Richard Nixon were both committed to "getting tough" with Fidel Castro. Nixon — still trying to overcome the Tricky Dick sobriquet — was in the embarrassing situation, however, that he knew an invasion on Cuba was in preparation, but had to damn Kennedy for being reckless, as a cover to hide plans that the invasion in fact was pending. Kennedy was handsome, charming, charismatic, but his liberalism was skin deep, a compound of colorful phrases written for him by master craftsmen such as historian Arthur Schlesinger, Jr., and Theodore Sorensen, a midwest Unitarian who had once had a flirtation with the peace movement. Kennedy's choice of conservative Senator Lyndon B. Johnson of Texas may have helped him carry that crucial state, but it almost lost him liberals like Walter Reuther (for a while) and it proved that in a pinch Kennedy could forget avowed principles as well as the next politician. He was also not averse to a little demagogy when it helped his cause, as for instance when he asserted there was a "missile gap" — the Soviets were superior in missiles because the Eisenhower administration had been laggard. (Once elected, Kennedy had to acknowledge there was no such gap, just as there had been no "bomber gap" the previous decade, both gaps being either the product of overactive imaginations or the Pentagon's propaganda for a bigger war budget.)

Nixon raised hackles in many quarters for his vicious red-baiting and obvious opportunism, but even so it took a small miracle to put Kennedy in the White House. If the economic recession that had been predicted but disregarded by the Eisenhower administration had not reached its nadir in late October, and if Nixon somehow had been able to swing just 4,500 more votes in Illinois and 28,000 more in Texas, Kennedy would have been denied the prize. It was an interesting campaign, what with the debates and the football atmosphere that campaigns now exuded, but as Michael Harrington observed in *Liberation*, "The victor in the 1960 elections can now be predicted with scientific accuracy. It will be the Ruling Party in a walk. . . . Heads they win, tails you lose."

The image of Camelot gathered around Kennedy, and history added considerable luster to it because of his assassination in 1963, but in fact, as Rutgers historian William L. O'Neill points out, his domestic program suffered one defeat after another and is best labelled "dismal rather than disastrous," whereas "his foreign policy was both." He speeded up the arms race, adding $7 billion to the military budget in the first year of his presidency, and $10 billion over the next two years. Kennedy, I said in an interview with *Newsweek,* "has compromised between disarmament and an accelerated arms race. The stable deterrent is a fantastic illusion which has added $10 billion to the arms budget while disarmament has been given a mere whiff . . . There is activity, but sometimes I feel we'd be better off with Eisenhower reading cowboy stories and doing nothing, rather than doing the wrong thing." When a delegation of Quakers visited Kennedy to press their plea for disarmament, he told them that if they built a public opinion in favor of it he would lead their crusade; otherwise he would do what he was doing.

Kennedy was deft with the verbiage of peace — "mankind must put an end to war — or war will put an end to mankind," "the risks inherent in disarmament pale in comparison to the risks inherent in an unlimited arms race" — but under him the Cold War grew colder, and the arms race more frenzied.

With all that, however, and with all the trauma that came with the Bay of Pigs adventure and later the more threatening October 1962 missile crisis, a peace movement of substance was finally emerging, and we in *Liberation* (now minus editor Roy Finch who resigned over differences on Cuba) were the heart of it. Within two years it reached a peak of sorts when thirty-three candidates throughout the country ran for Congress, either on old party tickets or, as in my case, independents on a peace program.

In the prelude to this development, a host of new groups and new activities blossomed. The most important of these new groups (or a renovation of an old one, if you will) was the Students for a Democratic Society (SDS), which became the cornerstone for what C. Wright Mills labelled the New Left. Youth of the Students League for Industrial Democracy, a nearly defunct Socialist organization, decided to change the name of their organization to Students for a Democratic Society. More than a change in name was involved, however, for SDS captured the mood of the times as did no other young people's group of the 1960s. Somewhat later a University of Michigan student named Tom Hayden prepared a document for an SDS convention in Port Huron, Michigan, which was to become one of the ideological foundations for the New Left.

"We are the people of this generation," began the Port Huron statement, "bred in at least modest comfort, housed now in universities, looking uncomfortably to the world we inherit." When "we were kids," it continued, "we were influenced by American values such as freedom and equality for each individual, government of, by and for the people. . . . As we grew, however, our comfort was penetrated by events too troubling to dismiss. . . . The declaration 'all men are created equal . . .' rang hollow before the facts of Negro life in the South and the big cities of the North. The proclaimed peaceful intentions of the United States contradicted its economic and military investments in the cold war status quo."

I was invited to speak at the Port Huron conference (I don't really know why, except that someone may have been impressed by a term I used in my first book *Left, Right, and Center, participative democracy,* which was almost identical with the term the SDS was now popularizing, participat*ory* democracy). At any rate, I turned down the invitation because I felt that any offshoot of the League for Industrial Democracy was bound to be too moderate to matter. I couldn't have been more wrong. The Port Huron statement was refreshing new language that spoke to the American condition, not a foreign situation. It criticized both the rigid anti-communism of American politics and the communist movement itself. It dissociated itself from the Cold War, came out four square for the revolution in Asia, Africa, and Latin America, catalogued the failures of the liberal and labor movements, and proposed wide-ranging reforms that would lead to "participatory," rather than "manipulative," democracy. It was not exclusively oriented toward the working class, but toward society as a whole. The students felt called upon — in alliance with others — to radically transform the American way of life.

Though I was not immediately involved in SDS affairs, I was engaged in more activities in the first three years of the new decade than in almost any other period I can remember. Some of them were one-day events such as running a banquet honoring Muste on his seventy-fifth birthday, or a Debs Day dinner in October 1961 at which Norman Thomas and I were the guest speakers, or the dozens of occasions I appeared on the *At Random* show, the *Marty Faye Show*, a TV talk show, and many similar debate or interview formats on radio. Some were ongoing affairs which did not demand anything more than attending an occasional meeting, such as my induction onto the board of the Chicago Council on Foreign Relations, or the advisory council of the Student Peace Union. Others involved a greater commitment in both time and political concern. One of those was sponsorship of another small magazine, *New Politics*, whose leading spirit was Jules Jacobson of New York. *New Politics* considered itself to the left of *Dissent*, but it included as contributing editors many of those who had aligned themselves with *Dissent* as well as others generally considered in the same milieu, such as Mike Harrington, Muste, novelist Saul Bellow, columnist Murray Kempton, cartoonist Jules Feiffer, writer Nat Hentoff (who later wrote a biography of Muste entitled *Peace Agitator*), Erich Fromm, novelist Harvey Swados, Hal Draper, and myself. *New Politics* was like *Dissent* at the time, a quarterly, and while I didn't write for every issue I did do pieces at least a couple of times a year.

Then there were the usual speaking engagements and meetings, some of which were most rewarding. A speech I gave at the University of Illinois on The Cuban Situation in May 1961, for instance, was reprinted by the university paper and helped the local peace group burgeon in both size and influence. In November 1962, just before the elections, I debated William Buckley at Purdue University in Indiana before thousands of people. That was one of the most gratifying evenings I can remember. The issue was the feasibility of the arms race, but Buckley kept poking fun at me personally for "sleeping with a picture of Bertrand Russell" under my pillow and being "too cowardly" to die. He had used that tactic against Norman Mailer in a debate in Chicago a few months before, impugning Mailer's sex life, and it had gotten Mailer so angry he lost the thread of his argument. In my case, I simply said, "Yes, I'm guilty of everything Buckley said. I'm also a member of the polit-bureau of the Communist Party and I murdered my father-in-law just before I came here. But I state that there can be no winner in a total war, and that military power no longer serves any political purpose, that in fact it is counter-productive. Now answer those points." Buckley responded with more witticisms, but after a while the students began to shout "answer the questions" and though the crowd was overwhelmingly on his side, a few began to boo him. The next day, the university sheet criticized Buckley for talking down to the audience, and while disagreeing with my politi-cal point of view congratulated me for treating the audience maturely. Buckley, I'm sure, realized he had made a mistake because he reneged on an agreement we had both made beforehand to release the tapes of the debate to school audiences that wanted to play them. Next time I debated him — in Arizona (and once when we appeared on TV together) — there were no jokes; Buckley confined himself to the subject. In the course of that decade I debated many right-wingers — Russell Kirk, Fulton Lewis III, M. Stanton Evans, and others — perhaps more than anyone else in the antiwar movement.

Two of the subjects on which I lectured frequently at the time, in addition to the arms race and labor, were revolution and mass man, the latter a dissertation on how the average American eschewed controversy and creativeness in favor of being a homogenized social climber. One lecture trip I particularly enjoyed was the two weeks I spoke on the Latin American revolution for the American Friends Service Com-mittee in Mexico. Twice or three times a day I appeared at college — or occasionally high school — campuses (as well as on radio and TV) to discuss the need for a Latin revolution that would free Mexico from North American domination. The presentation was marred because my English had to be interpreted by Heberto Sein, an internationally known interpreter who was also a pacifist. But invariably, the response was enthusiastic; often there was a standing ovation.

Only the American Embassy was unhappy with the tour; a member of the embassy staff whom I knew from the labor movement told me about its discomfiture, though he himself — a former socialist — was delighted.

Three pieces of writing also gave me an especially good feeling of accomplishment in the early 1960s. One was a pamphlet I wrote at the request of the independent Mine, Mill and Smelter Workers Union, called "The Mine-Mill Conspiracy Case," for which I also persuaded Norman Thomas to write a brief introduction. Nine present or past leaders of Mine-Mill, it seems, were convicted of "conspiracy to defraud the government" by falsely signing Taft-Hartley affidavits that they were not communists. They were subject to prison terms of eighteen months to three years, but worse than that was the stigma of communism that attached to the union itself as a result of the case and severely hindered its organizational efforts and negotiations. Whether the leaders of Mine-Mill were communists was not the issue, I wrote; the issue was the government's vendetta against a legitimate union. Tens of thousands of copies of this pamphlet were distributed throughout the labor movement, paid for by a number of AFL-CIO unions like Pat Gorman's Amalgamated Meat Cutters. The epilogue to this story, after I received the thanks of Mine-Mill officials and a telegram in March 1962 that the appeals court had reversed the convictions, was a subpoena in 1963 to appear before a Senate subcommittee on internal security to answer for my own leftist derelictions.

Another pamphlet I wrote that had a fairly wide impact was for the AFSC Beyond Deterrence series called "Revolution and Cold War." It condensed in sixty pages what I had written on this subject in many articles, and in my 1956 book, *A World in Revolution.* The third long piece that stands out in my mind from this period was an article on "The Case Against Civil Defense," which took up the whole issue of the *Progressive* in February 1962. Kennedy, it will be recalled, was urging the nation to build fallout shelters, and a number of pieces had already appeared in liberal publications decrying this folly. Mine was the last and longest of the series, coming out a month or two after the mania was beginning to die down. To do the piece I spent a couple of weeks in Washington interviewing scientists, atomic energy officials, and critics. I was particularly pleased with the encouragement I got from Arthur Schlesinger, then on the White House staff as a Kennedy speechwriter, who thought the whole plan was ridiculous but couldn't say so publicly. The most distressing talk I had was with Secretary of Defense McNamara's deputy, Adam Yarmolinsky. He conceded that civil defense was not likely to save many lives, "but it will force the Russians to spend money to counter our actions and thereby weaken their economy," he said. "What's wrong with that?" I could think of a hundred things.

Also from 1960 through 1962 I published innumerable articles, including one for *The Rotarian* on "My Wife's Retarded Children," a string of anecdotes about the educable mentally handicapped children my wife, Shirley, was teaching, which won me an award of some sort, and two books for young people, both of which received an excellent response, *Working Men* (a history of labor), and *Africa — Awakening Giant*. All in all I was getting a considerable amount of exposure, so much so in fact that *Who's Who in America* added me to its "firmament of fame," as one writer put it, in March 1962.

The two activities, of course, that took up most of my time were still my own local union and the peace movement. Nothing extraordinary was happening in the union — except that I slid off the curb and broke my toe while directing a picket line in the strike of a union at Marshall Field's department store just a few minutes before the strike was settled. Antiwar activity was much less routinized, always subject to exciting innovation, but certain days of protest by now were becoming standard — Easter, tax day (April 15), Hiroshima Day (August 6), and, for Women Strike for Peace, usually Mother's Day. The marches that had been attracting a few hundred previously, were passing the thousand and multi-thousand mark — even in Chicago, where the level of leftist politics was notches behind New York, Boston, or San Francisco. The Easter march in 1962, for instance, organized by AFSC, SANE, and Women for Peace culminated in an indoor rally at Chicago's Orchestra Hall with 1,200 in attendance, probably two-thirds the number of those who marched. I had no particular post in any of the organizations, but as a charter member of the movement dating to the 1950s and as a trade unionist and writer, I was included in the committee of preparations and was almost always on the program as a speaker. I also began traveling to other cities for rallies — Minneapolis, St. Louis, Detroit.

In 1961–62 it occurred to some of us that we ought to try and turn protest action in the streets into electoral dividends; use one, so to speak, to supplement the other. I outlined the plan over lunch to Lucy Montgomery, wife of a wealthy lawyer, who knew of me because of the *Progressive* article on civil defense, and she agreed to donate $15,000 for an antiwar electoral campaign in the Chicago area. That kind of money was more than I was accustomed to at the time and really more than we needed to get started; I accepted $5,000 initially with the promise (or threat) that I would draw on the rest if we needed it. Then Henry Wineberg, Irving Birnbaum, and I called together a few dozen people to form a new organization which we christened Voters for Peace. Henry's career as a dissident went back to 1938 when, as a writer for the Chicago *Herald-Examiner* he became embroiled in the Newspaper Guild strike that went down to defeat after a year and a half. A meticulous organizer, always armed with a bundle of three-by-five file cards, each with a memo of something to be done, Henry and I worked together in many projects. Birnbaum enjoyed a flourishing legal practice, until — as he correctly says — he met up with me. As a leading figure in the American Veterans Committee, he invited me to speak at one of his meetings and thereafter turned into a full-fledged activist for the peace movement. For a number of years, he was the only lawyer the Chicago antiwar forces could depend on to represent them free of charge. He represented the SDS when it moved its headquarters to Chicago, and was the attorney of record for the Chicago 7 conspiracy trial in 1969. Irving always joined whatever project Henry and I were working on, including a Peacenik Poker Party we formed for monthly relaxation.

Voters for Peace fielded three peace candidates for Congress as part of a loose coalition of thirty-three around the country, thirty-two for the House of Representatives and one, H. Stuart Hughes, grandson of the late Supreme Court Justice, for the Senate in Massachusetts, running against Ted Kennedy and Henry Cabot Lodge. We held a meeting of most of these candidates in Chicago in mid-summer, but we didn't form any kind of national coordinating machinery. A few were Democrats or Republicans, and some — like George Brown in California — won. For the most part, however, we were running to put our antiwar message across, and we either didn't try to get major party support (as in my case) or couldn't.

Our local team in the Chicago area consisted of Alva Tompkins, a pacifist minister running in the inner-city 9th District, Robert C. Cosbey, a professor at Roosevelt University running in the suburban 13th District, and myself in the 2nd District, centered around the University of Chicago in Hyde Park. My two young campaign managers (serving without pay of course), Pete Allen and Allan Kaplan (today a national vice president of the American Federation of Government Employees), went through the traditional routine of printing petitions, enrolling precinct workers, and soliciting signatures to put my name on the official ballot. The number we needed was astronomical, many times what would be needed if we were to run in the Democratic primary, but we succeeded in getting more than enough. Unfortunately the Daley-controlled elections committee used one technicality after another (like the failure to spell out the word *Street*) to rule our petitions invalid. Since our purpose was to get our political views across, not win court cases, we went ahead with a write-in campaign. Surprisingly, we did very well.

Barratt O'Hara, the long-time incumbent in the 2nd District, was a fine human being personally and certainly one of the more liberal members of Congress. When it was evident that I intended to run he phoned from Washington to dissuade me; he talked to me, in fact, for two hours, but wouldn't — or couldn't — agree to the two requests I made, namely that he come out in favor of an immediate end to nuclear testing and for a progressive reduction of the military budget. He feared that to do so would cause his defeat, since more than half the district was outside the influence of the liberal Hyde Park community. I think he genuinely feared that I would drain off enough liberal and radical votes that the Republican might squeak in. "Will you be better off with Bixler [the Republican]?" he asked me. That alas is the question we have had to contend with for decades, whether to support a lesser evil to avoid a greater evil. In this instance both candidates were for a strong defense, but O'Hara could argue — correctly — that on domestic issues he was much better. The trouble with the lesser evil argument is that you never wind up with a candidate who supports the program you want; worse still you don't create the climate of public opinion — the educational underpinning — for disarmament; you even downgrade the disarmament issue in the mind of the public. If a peacenik can vote for a candidate who favors an *increase* in armaments, the issue of disarmament can't be all that important. In any case I've always been against the lesser evil theory — I refused to vote for Truman against Dewey, Stevenson against Eisenhower, Kennedy against Nixon, Johnson against Goldwater, Humphrey against Nixon, Carter against Ford. In every instance, I voted for a minority party ticket, whatever one was on the ballot, and I'm convinced that was the only way not to waste my vote. I might have voted for McGovern against Nixon because of the overwhelming importance of peace in Vietnam and the general conviction that McGovern would get us out quickly, but by election time his chances were so infinitesimal I decided to stick with one of the socialist third parties.

Allen and Kaplan put on a vigorous campaign. Each night I spoke to at least two parlor groups, sometimes three. We opened a storefront office, recruited 140 people as precinct captains to canvass their neighborhoods and bring out the vote; we distributed 100,000 pieces of literature; raised a few thousand dollars; and got a considerable amount of publicity in the daily press, radio, and TV. Best of all, I got the endorsement of the University of Chicago's student newspaper, the Chicago *Maroon.* Ordinarily, it said in an editorial of November 2, 1962, "we would endorse Barratt O'Hara . . . had not Sid Lens run as an independent peace write-in candidate. . . . Members of the UC community have an obligation to vote 'for peace' this year. Votes for Lens will be not 'wasted,' even though they won't aid a winning candidate. Rather, votes for Lens will help form a needed 'peace constituency,' a bloc of people who feel strongly enough about the destruction the arms race threatens to bring to civilization to withhold support from one of the nation's more liberal Congressmen just because he has not done all he could to end this race."

To say I was delighted with this endorsement is to understate the matter. In a letter to the editor, I praised "the independent position of the *Maroon* in endorsing an amateur politician . . . and endorsing him because he stands for de-escalation of the arms race indicates to me that this generation of youth will not remain satisfied with predigested cliches and conventional wisdoms."

The low point of the campaign came at the end of September when a Chicago *American* columnist Jack Mabley wrote his column about my "strange past." The column hurt me with some people, but we distributed a letter I wrote to the editor in which I restated my position on war and peace; insisted that I should be judged on that rather than on anything else; and ended with what I think is a good counterargument to the McCarthyist frame of mind: "It is always easier to demolish a man than discuss his ideas. This is one of the unfortunate characteristics of our era — that conformist writers and politicians, who are afraid to discuss ideological subjects, reject an idea by attaching labels to the man. This fear of ideas and of democratic discussion is one of the most potent enemies we have in the United States today, and Mabley's scare column is an unfortunate contribution to that danger."

The high point, however, of the campaign was the windup rally at McCormick Place where we had a packed hall — 1,800 people — to hear speeches by Norman Thomas; Dr. Benjamin Spock, who was just becoming active in the anti-war movement; and the three candidates, Cosbey, Tompkins, and me. Henry Wineberg had put the affair together on behalf of Voters for Peace and it turned out to be an inspiring success — particularly so because it came just a few days after the harrowing October missile crisis. All the peace candidates throughout the nation were forced on the defensive by that crisis, as the world waited with bated breath wondering if seventeen years after Hiroshima the two superpowers were about to blow each other — and a good part of the rest of the planet — to smithereens.

The root of this crisis lay, in large measure, in the Bay of Pigs fiasco. The taste of defeat remained strong and sour with both the citizenry and the official family. Many regarded it only as a temporary setback and waited for the next act in the drama. Richard Nixon urged Kennedy to "find a proper legal cover and . . . go in" anew. Senator Kenneth Keating of New York proposed a naval blockade and a trade embargo to "isolate Cuba and reduce Castro's military machine, his iron grip on the Cuban population — to impotence." Kennedy seemed to follow this course. Cuba had already been driven out of the Organization of American States under U.S. prodding (even though six nations with two thirds of Latin America's population either voted against this resolution or abstained). Step by step thereafter, with Washington again wielding the pressure, the governments of the Hemisphere suspended diplomatic and commercial relations with Cuba. The U.S. embargo on shipments to the Caribbean island included everything but food and drugs, badly crippling an economy that had been overwhelmingly dependent on its northern neighbor. Meanwhile Washington continued a $2.4-million-a-year subsidy to the Cuban Revolutionary

Council, tolerated air drops to anti-Castro guerrillas, sabotage, infiltration, and boat raids which either originated in Florida or were directed from there. As late as September 1962 a group of exiles known as Alpha 66 attacked three ships along the Cuban coast, and the following month conducted another foray, which allegedly resulted in the killing of twenty Cubans and Russians.

Both in Havana and in Moscow all this was viewed as preliminary to a second invasion. To add fuel to the fires Kennedy's Secretary of Defense Robert McNamara had unsheathed a counter-force doctrine in a speech early that year — the threat of a surprise attack against Soviet missile silos. The Soviets and Cubans responded to both dangers by placing Russian nuclear missiles on the island — as a *deterrent* according to Castro. "Six months before these missiles were installed in Cuba," Castro told French newspaperman Jean Daniel, "we had received an accumulation of information warning us that a new invasion of the island was being prepared under the sponsorship of the Central Intelligence Agency." Castro doubted at first that Kennedy would approve another such venture, but in a meeting between the president and Khrushchev's son-in-law, Alexei Adzhubei, these doubts were dispelled. Kennedy supposedly told Adzhubei that the situation in Cuba was "intolerable" and reminded him that the United States hadn't interfered when the Soviet Union intervened in Hungary in 1956, an unsubtle suggestion that the Soviet Union return the favor if the United States were to do the same thing in Cuba. After the Adzhubei interview the Soviets and Cuba decided on the missiles; and it was the discovery by American intelligence sources that missile sites were being prepared that triggered the hair-raising confrontation between the world's two nuclear powers.

During the last week of October 1962, the world came as close to an all-out nuclear holocaust as it has ever been before or since. Crews of 144 intercontinental ballistic missiles were put on a special alert in the United States, and 183 naval ships with 110,000 men, including 8 aircraft car-

riers, were deployed around Cuba, with hundreds of thousands of men poised for attack elsewhere. It should be noted
that, though scores of millions of lives were in jeopardy,
Kennedy didn't see fit to ask Congress for a vote on war (as
provided for in Article 1, Section 8, of the Constitution),
nor did he offer the American people a referendum as to
whether they wanted to live or were ready to die. Anxiety
was so rampant that a number of active members of my
campaign packed their belongings and betook their families
to sparsely inhabited places in Wisconsin and Michigan. They
were evidently justified because Kennedy later observed that
had war broken out, no matter who had pressed the button
first, the two nations would have suffered "150 million
casualties in the first 18 hours," and after a few days many
more. Everything the United States had worked to build in
300 years, he said, would have been destroyed in less than a
day. "Even the fruits of victory," he said, "would be ashes in
our mouths." Finally, Khrushchev backed down on October
28, agreeing to withdraw the missiles in return for a secret
pledge — later confirmed by President Nixon in 1970 — that
the United States would not invade Cuba or permit hostile
actions against it to originate from North American soil.

Meanwhile, however, a spasm of chauvinism shook the
United States. The Cubans were trying "to sneak something
over on us"; they and the Russians were preparing to attack
us. All defense of the Cuban revolution and all our calls for
disarmament were viewed by many people as nothing short
of treason. Even so, the peace candidates continued to stand
their ground, though a few watered down their position a bit,
or evaded the Cuban question. No doubt we lost many supporters in those few hysterical days. To add to my own woes,
the election clerks refused to even tally write-in votes in
scores of precincts; where they did make the tally I received a
total of slightly less than 2,000, according to the unofficial
results sent in by my captains. I ran for state representative —
also under the Voters for Peace standard — a few years later,
but that ultimately was the end of my incursion into electoral
politics.

Chapter 10
Give Peace a Chance

I

John F. Kennedy, the youthful and handsome thirty-fourth president, a man of charisma and literacy, was a master of the double-edged sentence: "If a free society cannot help the many who are poor, it cannot save the few who are rich"; "Ask not what your country can do for you, ask what you can do for your country." JFK catered to the disaffection of a generation now finding itself — but never unstintingly and never by embracing its radical implications. His administration was prepared to ameliorate the pain of blacks, but not to lead the civil rights "revolution"; it talked of putting an end to war, but increased the military budget by a hefty sum. The result was that the swirl of protest gained momentum throughout Kennedy's abbreviated 1000 days in office, as young black leaders like Robert Moses, Martin Luther King, Jr., John Lewis, Julian Bond, Stokely Carmichael, James Foreman, James Farmer, and Bayard Rustin concluded that the fate of their people lay in direct action, not petitions to the White House.

Almost a year before the administration changed hands, four black college freshmen asked for a cup of coffee at a Woolworth store in Greensboro, North Carolina, but were turned down. Influenced by a comic book about nonviolence, distributed by the Fellowship of Reconciliation, the four young men sat where they were. Within two weeks there were similar sit-ins in fifteen other southern cities, involving 50,000 people both as participants and demonstrators, and 3,600 had been arrested. A couple of months after Kennedy was inaugurated, James Farmer assembled two busloads of freedom riders, made up half of young blacks and half of white pacifists, to journey from Washington into the deep South. On May 14, one of the buses was set on fire in Anniston, Alabama; riders on the other bus were severely beaten as they went through Birmingham and Montgomery, including one of President Kennedy's own representatives who was riding with them. The first freedom rides were followed by others, each leading to more violence and more arrests. The rides forced the Interstate Commerce Commission to order desegregation of bus and train stations, but an effort by black and white activists to test the new regulation in Albany, Georgia, led to 700 jailings, including that of Martin Luther King, Jr. A year and a half later black protest reached a peak of sorts in Birmingham, where a sadistic police chief called Bull Connor had his men savagely beat 1,000 black youngsters as they walked downtown from a Baptist Church. In the wake of these events the home of King's brother was bombed, as was a motel in the black area. During the next ten weeks there were 750 riots in 186 cities and towns throughout the nation. The mood created by these events undoubtedly contributed to the massive outpouring for the March on Washington, organized — as already noted — by Bayard Rustin, that summer.

The domestic scene was clearly unstable during the Kennedy years, and would grow even more so after his death. Few people, however, could see any serious fissures in the fabric of America's *foreign* policy. America's imperial position overseas appeared to be safe and sound for the indefinite future. True, the Bay of Pigs fiasco had tarnished Kennedy's image, but the Soviet retreat during the 1962 missile crisis had repaired the damage. Washington's hold on the free world seemed to be as firm as in the past.

I had an opportunity to gauge America's power first hand a few months before Kennedy was assassinated. That summer I was again on a tour, this time of Latin America, concentrating on the Caribbean and the northern part of South America. In the Dominican Republic I spent a few hours with Juan Bosch, the first democratically elected president of that small country since the United States imposed dictator Rafael Trujillo on its unfortunate people thirty-two years before. Bosch, a novelist with iron-gray hair, was a democratic socialist and humanist who believed, as I wrote in the Chicago *Daily News,* "that communism can only be set back if the state builds a true democracy and fulfills its promises of a better life." Unfortunately that approach did not sit well with the American military attachés and the Dominican generals who constantly pressured the new president to act "against the communists." Bosch, however, refused to outlaw either the traditional left or the Fidelistas. "If I suppress the left," he told me, "I must lean on the right. In that case there is no chance for my reform program." Bosch contemplated distributing land to 70,000 of the 98,000 families who were landless or had inadequate holdings. His program also called for a $150 million project at Puerto Plata in the north that would have supplied jobs for 40,000 workers and resulted in the building of 1,000 schools, additional electrification, and irrigation. In a country with a midget gross national product of $800 million, this was progress indeed.

But Bosch was never given a chance to implement his program. He was overthrown by the military and its friends — who had an eye on the land holdings of former dictator Trujillo — with the connivance of the U.S. labor attaché and U.S. military advisors (though not U.S. ambassador John Bartlow Martin, who opposed the coup). He had lasted barely a half year. Bosch should have been an ideal leader for the United States to support: intelligent, noncommunist, yet progressive and vigorous. But America was consumed by a negative foreign policy that equated every liberal or socialist with communism, and communism with every evil since the dawn of civilization.

The following year, 1964, I published a book on the subject: *The Futile Crusade: Anti-Communism as American Credo* (with an introduction by Nobel laureate Linus Pauling), in which I argued that American policy was reaching its watershed. "The United States," I wrote, "sidetracked and repressed by a negative anti-Communism is rapidly approaching the most critical moment in its history. It is being called on to respond to the most dire challenge it has ever faced. It can follow the principles of the past, towards futility and eclipse, or it can chart a new, positive course that will renew its vigor." I think that estimate stands up well in the light of what has happened since.

The next time I saw Bosch was at his home on the outskirts of Santo Domingo a few years later, after Lieutenant Colonel Francisco Caamano Deno and other "Constitutionalist" officers conducted a revolution to restore Bosch to the presidency. Unfortunately a week later President Lyndon Johnson sent in the marines, ostensibly to protect Americans in Santo Domingo, but in fact to prevent Bosch's return. A year after the defeat of the revolution, elections were scheduled, and the Fellowship of Reconciliation sent a delegation composed of Glenn Smiley, Ron Young, and myself to report on conditions and pave the way for American groups to monitor the elections. This time Bosch was solemn and depressed. He knew he was going to lose because he couldn't campaign; he was a virtual prisoner in his home, sure of being assassinated if he strayed too far or too often. He did lose and disappeared from the political scene.

Another head of state suffering the lash of American power was Cheddi Jagan, prime minister of British Guiana, whom I also met on the 1963 trip. Jagan's wife, Janet Rosenberg, was glad to meet visitors from her home town, Chicago. Both of them knew, I felt, that their chances of remaining in power as their country neared independence were diminishing. There was the usual uproar about him being a Marxist (which he was) and a secret Fidelista (which he wasn't), and the usual efforts to prevent a radical from gaining another foothold on the western hemisphere. A general strike financed almost entirely by the AFL-CIO and the CIA to topple Jagan — in protest, oddly, against a Jagan labor relations law modeled on the Wagner Act — ended after eighty days with Cheddi still in power. But his rival, Forbes Burnham, leader of the blacks as Jagan was of the Indians, ultimately took the scepter — with British and American connivance.

All of Latin America was a cauldron of human misery — shanty towns everywhere (worse than our Hoovervilles during the Great Depression), rampant disease, hunger, and polluted water. Rebellion was never more than a foot below the surface, being contained only by the modern guns and military training given rightist armies by the United States. If there was any "stability" in the area it was only because of the pervasive, though camouflaged, American military presence. I saw much evidence of frustration in Latin America, young people in a dozen countries resisting the alliance of their tyrants with North American capital. In Colombia tens of thousands had died in *La Violencia;* I met some of the guerrilla leaders in Bogota and visited a town in the interior whose inhabitants were openly aligned to the resistance movement. The odds, however, were next to hopeless — at least for the time being, until the Colossus of the North weakened. I also met guerrilla leaders in Peru, Venezuela, and Bolivia.

One night at 3 A.M. in Guatemala City, Shirley woke me: "Sid, there's a revolution going on." "How can you tell there's a revolution?" I demanded, not a little distressed about the loss of sleep. Sure enough, in the morning I learned from a judge I was interviewing that a revolution was indeed in progress. Shirley heard airplanes flying overhead and since she had been told that Guatemalan planes did not fly after dark except in emergencies, she deduced that there was a revolution. Nothing of course came of the revolt though the president of Guatemala called me in the next day to chastise me for sending out the story. While reporters from half a dozen American newspapers were at the cable office trying to send out a dispatch — in vain — I picked up the telephone, called Jimmy Wechsler, then editor of the New York *Post,* and dictated a story.

Something similar happened to me on a visit to Port-au-Prince, Haiti, that summer. Shooting broke out some miles away between the troops of President François Duvalier, an unbridled tyrant, and followers of rebel leader Clement Bardot. I didn't see the fighting or hear the machine guns and mortars, but it was common knowledge around town, confirmed by the U.S. embassy and a Haitian civilian I knew who was close to Bardot. I telephoned Chicago and dictated a story to the *Daily News;* since I was the only non-Haitian writer on the scene, the dispatch was reprinted all over the world. The *News* boasted that I was an "old hand in trouble spots," but it frightened me that a single writer's words summarizing events he heard about but didn't actually see could become fact for millions of readers. The Bardot rebellion of course disintegrated, not because Duvalier had popular support — far from it — but because he had American guns and American military training.

Few North Americans were concerned about this state of affairs, and even fewer realized that the horrendous condition of the people South of the Rio Grande was due, in part at least, to their own lack of concern. In any case, the American government as of 1961–63 felt perfectly secure; it was training the armies of four or five dozen states, it had secret "contingency" agreements with countries such as Spain, Iran, Jordan, Congo Republic, Ethiopia, Tunisia, and so on, to de-defend their regimes against popular revolt. It seemed like a foolproof system — as it had shown itself to be in the Dominican Republic and throughout Latin America. So determined were the Kennedy people to guarantee continued American invincibility that when they took office they jettisoned John Foster Dulles's inflexible strategy of massive retaliation, in favor of what they called "graduated response," leaving themselves the option of fighting anything from a counterinsurgency war — such as Vietnam — to a full-scale nuclear war. They also added $6 billion to the Pentagon's budget that year, and proclaimed in their inner circles that they were prepared to fight two and a half wars simultaneously — two big ones in Europe and Asia and a small one in Latin America. Therefore, when Kennedy stationed 23,000 American troops in Vietnam — euphemistically called advisors — no one in high office thought it posed a threat to American imperial ambitions, or that it would drastically change American history itself. I had a brief ringside seat at this drama too.

Less than a year after Kennedy's assassination we made another trip around the world — while Lyndon Johnson and Barry Goldwater were dousing each other with the usual campaign rhetoric. We visited India and Burma again, Indonesia for the first time, and Iran once more. My articles reporting the killing of 2,000 unarmed demonstrators in Teheran the year before evidently infuriated the shah because everywhere they appeared, a high diplomatic official in the Iranian embassy in Washington wrote letters to the editor disclaiming the story. But the strongest memories I have of that tour were a talk with Indira Gandhi in India (she then held a cabinet post but was not yet prime minister) and, most of all, what I learned in Vietnam.

What stands out in my talk with Indira Gandhi — to whom I gave regards from A. J. Muste — was her comparison of conditions in India and China. Nehru's daughter, who would become prime minister herself some years later, had not yet shown any of the dictatorial traits that she manifested when in office. Dressed in an impeccable sari she was a beautiful woman, with shiny thin features that looked as if they had been carved, and she spoke in calm, measured tones that belied the fire beneath. "The Chinese revolution," she said, "has done far more for its people than the Indian revolution." She agreed there were more hardships and fewer democratic rights, but Indians too knew hardship, and democratic rights were of little value to parents whose children were expiring from malnutrition. Before the two countries were liberated, Gandhi said, the Chinese standard of living was much lower than the Indian; now the situation was reversed.

Obviously she was trying to position herself to the left of her Congress Party, but what she said was attested to by most of the intellectuals in India who had visited China, namely that the Chinese revolution, with all its faults, had done far better for the ordinary citizen than the Indian.

Vietnam was a revelation — in the sense that things that I knew but had subliminal doubts about became forcefully real. Presidents Kennedy and Johnson had been insisting that American "advisors" were there to train Vietnamese troops, airmen, and civilian technicians, but though all of us in the peace movement shrugged that claim aside I wondered as we arrived in Saigon whether perhaps we weren't exaggerating. Just a few words with the correspondents on the scene, most especially an editor of *U.S. News & World Report,* disabused me of my doubts. Americans were not waiting to be shot at before returning fire, as Kennedy and Johnson claimed, they were shooting first and, as the saying goes, asking questions later. The American military command arranged for me to fly a helicopter headed for Can Tho. Only minutes after we had cleared the trees and were in open country, the two gunners on either side were shooting like wild at targets that were barely visible and certainly could not be identified. Someone did shoot at and hit our helicopter but that was long after the two Americans had initiated the shooting. Clearly U.S. "advisors" were not waiting for the enemy to fire first, and they weren't on the sidelines just giving advice.

Most of the territory we passed was flat land. I wondered where the Viet Cong, so called, were hiding, and I asked John Masters, the young captain who had been sent along by the U.S. military as our guide. "The guerrillas," he said, "don't hide. The villagers know where they are — but they do not report them to the authorities." That meshed with what we believed — the Viet Cong and North Vietnamese had the support of the people. Masters's explanation — the one we heard constantly from officials — was that the villagers didn't turn in the "murderers, bandits, and criminals" because they feared they would have their throats cut. Yet an hour later, when we landed at Can Tho, the same guide contradicted this theme: "The Vietnamese people," he said, "lack a sense of urgency. They have no feeling of loyalty to their government." This hardly jibed with the propaganda at home that we were in Vietnam to defend democracy.

Another talk I had that contradicted the party line back home was with a colonel at MacV — Military Assistance Command, Vietnam. I asked him where the Viet Cong got their weapons. "From us," he said to my surprise, "and from some home manufacture. They capture weapons every time they launch an attack, or they get traitors to give or sell to them." Are they getting weapons from the outside, China or the Soviet Union, I asked. "No," he said. "They don't really need foreign military supplies yet." While Johnson was picturing the war as a North Vietnamese invasion inspired by Russia and China, an innocent colonel on the scene was telling me quite the opposite.

Finally, as a vivid memory of Vietnam, I recall a long talk with a man in his late forties, a Trotskyite who had been jailed for many years. He told me an interesting tale, almost unknown in the West, of an internal conflict early in the postwar period. It seems that Ho Chi Minh's strength was concentrated in the North, in a coalition of communists, socialists, and nationalists. But a rival coalition had formed in the South — with the Trotskyites playing the key role — and held power for a time. The Southerners disagreed with Ho's policy of trying to come to terms with the French; instead they counseled resistance even while Ho was concluding an agreement for a sterile independence. This all became academic of course when the French attacked Haiphong in November 1946, killing at least 6,000 people and sparking the war that followed. But there had been violent confrontations between the two groups of Vietnamese before that, and some jailings of anti-Stalinists, including the Trotskyite who gave me the information.

In 1946, few people had ever heard of Vietnam and probably no one realized what an effect it would have on Western civilization. Eight years later, in 1954, the French were completely surrounded at Dienbienphu and forced to eat crow. Still, even then, no one believed that this was more than a peripheral defeat for the West, especially since the French were considered inferior warriors. John Foster Dulles and Admiral Arthur Radford, chairman of the Joint Chiefs of Staff, proposed a joint U.S.-British-French offensive that would include airstrikes by 200 U.S. planes and, according to French Foreign Minister Georges Bidault, the possible "use of . . . one or more nuclear weapons [supplied by the U.S.] near the Chinese border" and two against the Vietminh at Dienbienphu. Eisenhower vetoed the plan only because Britain refused to participate and because leading figures in Congress, among them Lyndon Johnson, gave it a cool reception. After the French defeat and the signing of the Geneva Accords in 1954, the U.S. threw itself into the fray through a series of puppets, beginning with Ngo Dinh Diem.

Just as in Cuba, the American leadership was grossly overconfident, and just as in Cuba, but with worse consequences, it was destined to be humiliated. Johnson had not yet sent in the new divisions, but it was evident to me while in Vietnam — as I wrote in a letter to Senator Wayne Morse — that "the war . . . is already lost. . . . We have lost this war because we reversed a simple principle learned in the Philippines and above all in Burma, that we must 'win the people FIRST, then win the war.'" There was already talk of bombing and invading North Vietnam, just as there had been talk of invading Cuba a few years before. But even American officials on the scene understood that this was no panacea. "A high member of the Embassy," I advised Morse, "told me that most military men do not believe that attacking North Vietnam would make any difference. One leading American officer, he said, had told him personally that 'if we built a 50-foot wall around this country it wouldn't change things.' Bombing the North would only be an act of vengeance, serving neither a military nor political purpose. It would kill people uselessly and immorally. An army captain who escorted me to Can Tho told me 'we're darn lucky we're not doing the fighting here ourselves because we'd be slaughtered. ALL of the people would be against us.'"

Americans were not thinking in this vein when we returned home a couple of months before the presidential elections. Most people were sure Lyndon Johnson would win, and that Johnson was dedicated to *containing* the Vietnam War. Barry Goldwater, the handsome but very limited conservative from Arizona, had a capacity for scaring people half to death with such programmatic planks as granting control over nuclear weapons to commanders in the field, and expanding the war in Vietnam. The image he projected was of a gung-ho militarist ready to wage war — nuclear or otherwise — at the drop of a hat. Johnson, by contrast, seemed to most people to be the peace candidate. "I have had advice," he said, "to load our planes with bombs and to drop them on certain areas that I think would enlarge the war, and result in our committing a good many American boys to fighting a war I think ought to be fought by the boys of Asia to help protect their own land. And for that reason, I haven't chosen to enlarge the war." This was pure poppycock because the plans for a full-scale invasion of Vietnam had already been made and were merely waiting for Johnson's election and inauguration. Disclaimers of intended escalations, however, continued. A few weeks before the polls opened LBJ stated unequivocally: "We are not about to send American boys 9,000 or 10,000 miles away from home to do what Asian boys ought to be doing for themselves. . . . Losing 190 American lives in the period that we have been out there is bad, but it is not like 190,000 that we might lose the first month, if we escalated the war."

A considerable majority of people in the peace movement were advocating a vote for Johnson, though some expressed their malaise over supporting a man of such conservative mien by wearing buttons put out by SDS, stating they were only "part of the way with LBJ." The peace secretary of the American Friends Service Committee in Chicago took me aside to urge that I lend my name to the Johnson campaign. When I demurred he said, "How can you refuse? Johnson has the same position on war that you have." In retrospect I'm sure my friend at the AFSC does not consider this his most incisive political evaluation. But he had plenty of company. At *Liberation* magazine three of the four members of the editorial board, Muste, Dellinger, and I, took the traditional position of supporting neither major party candidate. But Bayard Rustin came out four-square for Johnson and soon resigned both from our board and his post as executive secretary of the War Resisters League

Vietnam clearly was the catalyst for many things. Fear of further involvement drew many people into the Johnson camp, because, unlike Goldwater, he was committed to containing hostilities; on the other hand Johnson's deceptions and lies, coupled with a stubborn war that wouldn't go away, gave wings to the radical spirit and sired a new leftist movement unlike anything in this century. In August 1964, the administration caused a stir with its announcement that two American destroyers had been "attacked" in the Tonkin Gulf by North Vietnamese PT boats — though neither was hit. In the heat of national outrage Congress voted Johnson power to "take all necessary measures to repel any armed attack against the forces of the United States and to prevent further aggression." The vote in the House was 466 to nothing, in Senate 88 to 2 (only two courageous senators, Wayne Morse of Oregon and Ernest Gruening of Alaska had the courage to oppose Johnson). Administration official Nicholas de B. Katzenbach called the resolution the "functional equivalent" of a declaration of war, thus clearing Johnson's skirts — presumably — of violating Article I, Section 8, of the Constitution, which gives Congress the right to declare war. In due course it became known through a senatorial investigation that the whole business had been grossly misrepresented. The two U.S. destroyers were not innocent bystanders, they were in the gulf acting as cover for South Vietnamese ships that were attacking two North Vietnamese islands. There is also some doubt as to whether the American destroyers were really shot at. As someone once said, "The first casualty of war is truth."

But if jingoism could sway events for a time, it also had the countereffect of putting the antiwar forces into the field — especially as each lie was exposed and as U.S. troop strength in Vietnam expanded from 23,000 in 1964 to 185,000 in 1965, 385,000 in 1966, 485,000 in 1967, and a peak of 542,000 in 1968. Antiwar demonstrations and civil disobedience grew apace.

II

One day, as we marched in one of those demonstrations, Stewart Meacham, national peace secretary of the American Friends Service Committee and like me a co-chair of the New Mobilization Committee to End the War in Vietnam, looked back at the crowd with obvious elation. Stewart, a round-faced ex-minister with a southern drawl, had been a socialist in the 1930s, and had served on the staff of the Amalgamated Clothing Workers under Frank Rosenblum. "I never thought," he said, "we'd ever see things like this again, a real movement just like the one in the 1930s. For the first time in decades I think we can build a big socialist force again."

It was a real movement all right, involving millions of people, but it was very different from what we witnessed in the 1930s. The radicalism of the Depression era was centralized, coordinated through the parties of the left. If you picked up the *Daily Worker,* the *Militant,* and the *Call* you had a fair idea of what was happening in the leftist milieu. It was a movement that had live heroes like Earl Browder and Norman Thomas, and dead ones like Eugene Debs and Big Bill Haywood. It had a tradition, a history, a mystique, and systematized links to other milieus, particularly the labor unions.

The movement of the 1960s was decentralized, discordant, cacophonic. It was not subordinate to any party (except to the extent that the Trotskyites founded and controlled one of the major antiwar blocs, the National Peace Action Coalition, after 1970). It promulgated no line, published no books or newspapers, owned no bookstores of its own under any central leadership. It was so seemingly unfocused that many people didn't consider it radical at all. A radical or leftist in the popular stereotype was a Marxist and a member of a political party that had a blueprint for each step in the overthrow of capitalism. The movement of the 1960s did not match this stereotype. Nonetheless it was radical in the sense that it opted out of the system, worked outside its parameters, and considered the establishment and the system its enemy. Its radicalism was implicit, destined to grow with political crisis, not preordained or explicit.

The movement of the 1960s was composed of hundreds of groups and grouplets in hundreds of communities, loosely tied together by a vague leftism that was neither Marxist nor anti-Marxist, that never bothered to spell out an ideology. Whatever political parties were involved — the Communist Party, Socialist Workers Party, Progressive Labor Party, and so on — they were not the leaders of the movement, but adjuncts to it, who took their seats at conferences just like delegates from Women Strike for Peace or the War Resisters League. So decentralized was the movement in fact that its two major segments — the one fighting for civil rights and the other for peace — had only tenuous ties. Antiwar activists often marched in civil rights demonstrations, but black civil rights workers were less noticeable in antiwar actions until later in the decade. Of course, the leaders of the two segments knew each other, but they consulted only spasmodically and were not close personally. In any case, by the time the antiwar segment of the movement took wings, Martin Luther King's crusade had lost much of its momentum.

The movement of the 1960s had few definable and revered leaders. A mystique surrounded Martin Luther King of course, and to a slight extent A. J. Muste, but it did not attach to others. It was a movement that was porous, with people moving in and out constantly. Unlike the 1930s, the movement of the 1960s drew sparingly from the working classes (only from a dozen or so unions); its base was with millions of students, liberal faculty, older men and women, and the marijuana-rock-music counterculture, whose adherents had only a vague concept of politics, but were dissidents of the deed, available for demonstrations, teach-ins, occupation of school administration buildings, and similar activities. It was a movement without a sense of history — except for the radical parties and the few thousand politically minded — and without the kind of tradition that had inspired socialists, Wobblies, and communists of another day. It was a dispersed and amorphous movement, its quarrels out in the open, but usually achieving consensus. A dispute in the 1930s could be resolved behind the scenes, often by a directive from the Communist Party, but a dispute in the 1960s talked itself into the wee hours until some formula to which all could agree was suggested.

The movement grew more spontaneously than any leftist force I have ever known, perhaps more so than any in American history. Not even the Populists, whose origins go back to the founding of the Grange in 1867, had such a severe turnover of groups and grouplets. Sometimes the impulse came from a single location and spread out nationally, as for instance when the Women Strike for Peace was organized in 1961. Dagmar Wilson, a children's book illustrator, and a few of her friends sent out letters and made phone calls to women around the country, calling on them to conduct a "women strike for peace" on November 1, 1961. My wife Shirley got one of those letters, went to a meeting of one of the old-time peace groups, the Women's International League for Peace and Freedom, and recruited the first pickets to demonstrate at the Fifth Army headquarters in Chicago. The idea of striking captured the feminine imagination in scores of communities. Women, often with babies in their arms, carried signs reading END THE ARMS RACE — SAVE THE HUMAN RACE, BAN ALL ATOMIC WEAPONS TESTING, TURN OVER THE MONEY USED FOR WAR PREPARATIONS TO BUILD SCHOOLS, HOSPITALS, MENTAL CLINICS, LOW-COST HOUSING, TAKE STEPS TOWARD WORLD-WIDE DISARMAMENT, SUPPORT THE UNITED NA-TIONS. Ultimately the group in Chicago coalesced to become Women for Peace (they left out the word *strike* in the Windy City), those in the suburbs formed a group of their own. Women Strike for Peace prided itself on the fact that it was not an organization in the traditional sense; it had no membership lists, charged no initiation fees or dues, subsisting entirely on contributions, and its decisions were made by consensus rather than a pro and con vote. Women for Peace, unlike most women's groups, including women peace groups of the past, was oriented toward *action* — a common denominator for most antiwar groups of the 1960s. Every month it conducted a demonstration, vigil, or picket line somewhere. After Johnson escalated the war it held a weekly vigil, rain or shine, in subfreezing weather and blistering heat, every Saturday from 11 A.M. to 1 P.M. on State and Madison streets, the dead center of Chicago, for eight long years.

Typical of how antiwar groups were formed during this period is the story of CADRE — born out of the opposition to the draft.

Early in 1966, General Lewis B. Hershey announced that draft boards would soon induct college students — previously immune — into the services. Male college students, however, would be ranked based on their scholastic abilities, as determined by an examination. SDS, then at the peak of its influence, conducted a campaign against the Selective Service, which included the issuance of Freedom Draft Cards and half a million copies of a counterexam, about the war in Vietnam. At the University of Chicago, students abetted by faculty members Dick Flacks and Jessie Lemisch formed an ad hoc committee, Students Against the Rank (SAR), and seized the university's administration building on May 11, 1966. For the next few days there were rallies and meetings — comedian Dick Gregory was one of the speakers, so was I. But when the school term ended, SAR disappeared.

Next year the resistance became more focused. A small band of liberals formed an organization called We Won't Go, to emphasize their determination not to be drafted under any circumstance. After We Won't Go had been in existence for a while two itinerant organizers from Palo Alto came through town, urging that students turn back their draft cards to the government — an act of civil disobedience punishable by a jail sentence. The organizers also asked them to attend the scheduled action in New York, where young men, led by Gary Rader, a former Green Beret, would burn their draft cards. After the events in New York (there were other activities besides the draft card burning), Rader, a tall, blond, charismatic young fellow, and a group of students and nonstudents met at the home of a University of Chicago history professor to form CADRE (Chicago Area Draft Resisters).

CADRE never numbered more than a few dozen determined young people like Rick Boardman (a draft counselor at the American Friends Service Committee), Bob Freeston (a former Vista or Peace Corps worker, I don't remember which), and Rader (who left town after a while), but its impact was far greater than its size. Its adherents were highly motivated; they often lived in communes, both to save money and to act more effectively. CADRE distributed circulars at draft boards urging young people to refuse to be drafted; it held demonstrations at induction centers, where its members were often arrested. I recall Freeston being at our apartment often those days, either planning with Shirley for Women for Peace to join CADRE's demonstrations — which they did often — or to collect a weekly $50 that Women for Peace contributed to its operations.

CADRE survived a few years, then vanished — like most of the groups that came into being during this period. What distinguished them was their ad hoc character and their emphasis on action. The byword of the movement of the 1960s was not ideology, but action — action, moreover, which frequently risked imprisonment.

III

A radical movement, we learned in the 1960s, builds like a fire — the more fuel the bigger the blaze. In the 1930s, it was a basic defect in the system (economic collapse), compounded by the mistakes and callousness of the Hoover presidency, which kindled dissidence. And though the fuel was of a different type in the 1960s, it was the same combination of fundamental weakness in the system, compounded by errors and miscalculations that stoked the fires of the later-day radicalism.

It was not all Lyndon Johnson's doing; he inherited a foreign affairs strategy, which despite its arrogance had been effective. American power had fashioned a free world alliance indispensable for domestic prosperity — and held it together through economic and military pressures. American leaders often talked of the revolution of rising expectations, but in fact they wanted no disturbance of the social status quo. Washington was willing for India or Kenya to win independence from Britain, but it resisted efforts by third-world countries to move beyond the *national* to the *social* revolution. Thus the CIA was used to overthrow the Arbenz government in Guatemala, the Mossadegh regime in Iran, the Goulart administration in Brazil, and the Bosch state rule in the Dominican Republic. Vietnam, in other words, was not unique. Only luck prevented Vietnams from flaring elsewhere, say, in Brazil in 1965, where a group of colonels, headed by Humberto Castelo Branco, drove an elected neutralist, Joao Goulart from power.

It was inconceivable to American leaders, therefore, that a band of guerrillas in a backward country could inflict a defeat on a U.S. ally, armed with American weapons and trained by American advisors. By 1962, when there were already thousands of U.S. advisors on the scene and the Ngo Dinh Diem regime was deploying many divisions against the guerrillas, Defense Secretary Robert S. McNamara said he was "tremendously encouraged" by developments on the fighting front and pledged that there was "no plan for introducing combat forces into South Vietnam." McNamara's subsequent prophecies were equally myopic. "The corner has been definitely turned toward victory," he said in May 1963. That was the month government troops fired on Buddhists in the old imperial capital, Hue, killing nine and unleashing riots and demonstrations in many other places. As the turmoil continued a number of monks burned themselves alive, dramatizing for a shocked world the terrible state of affairs in Vietnam. Still, neither Diem nor his family in Saigon, nor Kennedy and McNamara in Washington were ready to admit that the situation was hopeless. Diem's sister-in-law, Mme. Ngo Dinh Nhu, came to the United States for a speaking tour in the fall of 1963 and callously referred to the immolation of monks as a "barbecue." She was met by small, jeering crowds of students wherever she went — one of the first manifestations of national opposition to the war.

Washington, however, continued to exude synthetic optimism, particularly from the lips of Defense Secretary McNamara: "The major part of the U.S. military task can be completed by the end of 1965" (October 1963); "We have every reason to believe that plans will be successful in 1964" (December 1963); "The U.S. hopes to withdraw most of its troops from South Vietnam before the end of 1965" (February 1964). And in November 1965, after all these trumpets of near victory, he blandly announced that "we have stopped losing the war." Diem had already fallen on November 1, 1963, in a coup executed by three generals, which apparently was sponsored or at least cleared with Ambassador Henry Cabot Lodge, and both he and his brother were murdered. In the next nineteen months there was an endless train of coups and changes in government — four under military leaders, three under civilians. The situation deteriorated to the point — despite McNamara's grotesque public optimism — that General Maxwell Taylor, on returning from Vietnam in September 1964, portrayed the situation to a cabinet meeting in such dire terms that his appearance at a press conference had to be canceled lest, as McNamara told Johnson, he leave "the impression the situation is going to hell."

Unwilling to let the puppet regime in Saigon collapse (General Taylor reported that it controlled at most 30 percent of the country), and unwilling to negotiate with the NLF (National Liberation Front) except on subtly put terms for surrender, Johnson took the only other path possible. He made it an American war. Using the Tonkin Gulf resolution as cover, he ordered the bombing of North Vietnam and later dispatched American troops to the South. Since North

Vietnam had virutally no defense against aerial bombardment, it was felt she would soon be brought to her knees, leaving the local guerrillas in the South — still doing almost all of the fighting, according to American officers who briefed me in Saigon — isolated and subject to quick decimation.

The first of many marches on Washington to protest the war was called on the initiative of the SDS. Until the week of Christmas 1964 SDS, though opposed to the war, had been applying its talents elsewhere, in community organizing efforts under its Economic Research and Action Project (ERAP), and in preparing for civil disobedience against banks that loaned money to South Africa. But a speech by journalist I. F. Stone to SDS's national council meeting that holiday week made a strong impact and led to a decision for a march on Washington (actually a demonstration) on April 17, 1965. At the time it was expected that perhaps a few thousand young people would assemble for the event, but in the interim between planning and execution a number of developments boosted interest. The first was President Johnson's sensational announcement on February 7, 1965, that the U.S. henceforth would bomb North Vietnam as well as send American ground forces to the scene in South Vietnam — in direct contradiction of his campaign pledges. A second development, suggested by an anthropology professor as a counter to a planned student strike, was a new type of meeting called a teach-in, which spread like wildfire after its debut at the University of Michigan on March 24. The teach-in was a long-lasting meeting — sometimes around the clock — in which speakers from all points of view were heard, questions were posed and answered, unstructured and sometimes impromptu debates took place. Literally hundreds of such teach-ins took place throughout the country. The one at the University of California in Berkeley drew 35,000 people during a thirty-six-hour session on May 21–22. A National Teach-In, involving professors on both sides of the issue, was held in Washington and piped to 122 campuses by radio and television for twelve hours. (Of the many teach-ins I participated in, the largest one was in Colorado Springs on July 7, 1965, where Professor Hans Morgenthau and I debated two government officials. It was an uneven contest, so much so that the State Department and Pentagon refused every subsequent request to debate with me — and perhaps also with Morgenthau, I'm not sure.)

The demonstration in Washington — a tribute to the organizing skills of Clark Kissinger, a mathematics major at the University of Chicago; Paul Booth of Swarthmore; and a handful of others — was an inspiring affair, as symbolized by the speech of SDS president Paul Potter: "What kind of system is it that justifies the United States or any country seizing the destinies of the Vietnamese people and using them callously for our own purposes? What kind of system is it that disenfranchises people in the South, leaves millions upon millions impoverished and excluded from the mainstream and promise of American society . . . that consistently puts material values before human values — and still persists in calling itself free and still persists in finding itself fit to police the world." The crowd of 20,000 was five or six times more than had been originally expected.

Unfortunately after this great success SDS removed itself as chief organizer of national antiwar marches. Its leaders argued that an antiwar movement could not halt present hostilities; it might be able, they said, to stop "the seventh Vietnam from now," but not this one. The 1965 event was noteworthy, however, as the transition from the old to the new peace movement. Clark Kissinger and his friends injected two new ideas into the political equation — nonexclusion and immediate withdrawal — and while neither was fully accepted at the time, they both became the unyielding principles of the new movement. Nonexclusion meant that no one — specifically communists and other Marxists — would be excluded from planning or participating in antiwar activities. This was an important digression from the past when SANE insisted on political purity, and it was opposed by many of the old leaders in SANE, Turn Towards Peace, and similar groups. When Muste, who had been at the planning meeting for the April event, reported to the editors of *Liberation* about the discussion that had taken place on nonexclusion we unanimously agreed to the principle, but our original reactions ranged from firm and unqualified on the part of Staughton Lynd to an expression of concern by myself that while we had to adopt the principle it would cost the movement adherents. I couldn't have been more wrong, it gave us an impetus that moderate groups such as SANE or Turn Towards Peace could never have achieved.

The slogan "immediate withdrawal," though not yet fully accepted, was indispensable for the expansion of antiwar activity. There was no justification for American intervention, hence the United States had no right in Vietnam except to get out. Again the moderates thought radicals were making a mistake, that the movement ought merely to call for negotiations between the U.S. and North Vietnam. I (and others) spent many hours arguing that point with men like Bob Pickus or Alfred Hassler of the Fellowship of Reconciliation, whose concern was that American withdrawal without certain guarantees would simply leave the door open for the communists. In the next few years, there would be many peaceniks who took the opposite view, that the antiwar movement should endorse a Viet Cong victory. But the main body adhered to the position that it was up to the Vietnamese to decide, by whatever means they saw fit, who would rule them, not we Americans. We were committed to getting U.S. armed forces out of Vietnam, not imposing a government on the people there — whether the left-wing Buddhist regime that Hassler wanted or the right-wing Ky and Thieu regimes that Johnson and later Nixon wanted.

The succession of protests, teach-ins, and vigils, and the organizations that conducted them, after April 1965, is impossible to chronicle. There were just too many, and their scale of importance depended on the eyes of the beholder. In my own mental schema, the next important event in the saga was the Speak-Out at the Pentagon on June 16, 1965. Though it only involved two hundred people — associated with Muste and the Committee for Nonviolent Action — it was an act of conscience typifying the pacifist elan, and it was the first link in the chain toward establishing a very loose but *national* antiwar leadershop. Muste conceived of the action as a nonviolent invasion of the linchpin of American militarism; we would give out leaflets in the Pentagon, then hold meetings inside and outside regardless of legal niceties, fully expecting to be arrested — in fact hoping for it. Two days before the event A. J. informed me over the phone that the Defense Department had decided to take no steps to stop us; Secretary McNamara who had once belonged to the American Civil Liberties Union was going to show the world he respected the right of free speech. On the appointed day all went almost as scheduled. Some of the officers who took our leaflets (very few refused) were good-natured about it, most were sullen but had been instructed by their superiors not to interfere with our rights. McNamara had issued an order as well that no one was to be arrested without the specific authorization of him or his deputy.

After the leafletting we held open meetings on the lower floor of the Pentagon just as if we were at Hyde Park, London — again with no interference by the police or anyone else; and during these meetings six of us — Muste, Staughton Lynd, former Congressman Bill Meyer, I and two others — disengaged for a thirty-minute chat with McNamara. It was an interesting experience, with military punctiliousness. McNamara walked into the room exactly at the prescribed second, and left exactly thirty minutes later. Except for a shouting match with Meyer he listened politely and answered politely, but there was no getting through to him. When my turn came, I pointed out that the Pentagon itself had commissioned a study that concluded it would take ten to fifteen regular troops to contain one guerrilla. "Since you say that there are 240,000 Viet Cong," I said, "that would mean you need two and a half to three million troops to hold them in check. Apart from the fact that the war is immoral, where will you get the three million soldiers to win it?" McNamara, still polite — he had just finished yelling at Bill Meyer — gave the standard bureaucratic answer: "Mr. Lens, I can't discuss that with you. We know things that you don't." No doubt he did, but they must have been the wrong things because his predictions of impending American victory somehow never came to pass.

After a couple of hours, the police found a way to force us out of the building without arresting us: they formed a phalanx of hundreds of police and security officers, moving in one motion to push us toward the exit a few feet at a time. Arthur Waskow, a normally pleasant fellow who had once been a Congressional assistant and was now a senior fellow with the Institute for Policy Studies, was pushed back and forth like a volley ball; each time the police shoved against him I shoved him back. But they made no arrests; McNamara, in a sense, had carried the day.

The sequel to the Speak-Out at the Pentagon was the convening a few weeks later of the ad hoc Assembly of Unrepresented People, which held a number of workshops, then started marching toward the Capitol. It was considerably larger than the earlier action (1,500 to 2,000 people) but led by most of the same people, virtually all from the pacifist wing of the movement—Muste, Lynd, Dellinger (who had missed the Speak-Out), SNCC leader Robert (Moses) Parris, Eric Weinberger of the CNVA. More than 300 were arrested as police stopped the marchers within the shadow of the Capitol. Members of a right-wing group indelicately tossed red paint at Dellinger and Lynd, walking arm in arm, making them the subjects of a photo published on the cover of *Life* magazine and hundreds of newspapers. In the full flush of national attention the Assembly gave birth to a National Coordinating Committee to End the War in Vietnam (NCC), headquartered in Madison, Wisconsin (because the communist-controlled Du Bois Clubs and University of Wisconsin students outmaneuvered other leftist forces, including the Student Peace Union and the Trotskyist Young Socialist Alliance), and coordinated by Frank Emspak, a twenty-two-year-old graduate student and son of the late secretary-treasurer of the United Electrical Workers, Julius Emspak.

An inhabitant of a remote planet, viewing the antiwar

movement at this point, would see a bedlam of animosities and fiefdoms. Within the NCC there were the rivalries of communists, Trotskyites, the May Second Movement (M-2-M, a satellite of the Maoist Progressive Labor Party), pacifists, and innumerable splinters — each force arguing as if the fate of the human race depended on a certain tactical decision, especially who should speak at a particular rally. In addition there were what might be called the independents, groups such as the Women Strike for Peace, and the old-time peace organizations, such as the American Friends Service Committee or the War Resisters League, as well as individuals who represented paper organizations, those with imposing letterheads but no followers. Happily I seldom chaired the steering committees and coordinating committees that evolved, and when I did I had to use all the acumen gained in a lifetime in the labor movement to keep the discord manageable. Very little of that discord was venal; it did exist, however, and grew progressively worse as the pacifist segment of the movement was outweighed by the politicos.

Muste understood this problem better than anyone, I think, because he always tried to have somebody like Dellinger or me with him at such conferences to inject a plea for forbearance and help mold a consensus. At about this time he began pressing me to move to New York — "You can be far more useful there." I thought about that suggestion for a long time; there was no doubt I could do more in the peace movement of the eastern metropolis than in Chicago. A peace movement could certainly grow faster in a city with a radical or strong liberal tradition, such as San Francisco or New York; and it was obvious as well that New York would inevitably become the movement's center, despite its temporary lodgment in Madison.

There were too many things preventing me, however, from making the transfer Muste wanted. I didn't want to leave my union work, even though I had been working only part-time since 1963. I still handled the major negotiations of Local 329, published its monthly paper, taught its classes, and processed many grievances and arbitrations. Even as a part-time official, I felt I had access to labor leaders and labor organizations that I would not have had otherwise. I could, for instance, join a Committee for Miners, in defense of an Appalachian miner named Berman Gibson who was being framed for murder and give some authenticity to the committee by including my union affiliation. I wanted to remain involved in that type of activity, and I feared I couldn't if I severed entirely from the labor movement.

Another deterrent to moving to New York was that I knew so many people in Chicago, and many more knew me from my appearances on TV talkshows and radio, and from many articles in the daily press. If we had to set up a citizens committee to investigate police brutality or a writers committee against the war or a group of prominent sponsors for a rally, I could pick up the phone and gain ready access to people in a dozen different milieus.

There was also my writing to consider. At the time Muste made his first pitch for me to move to New York, I had just published a long piece in the *Nation,* "Lovestone Diplomacy" – which, in the words of the editor, lifted "the curtain of secrecy and silence which has long obscured the role of Jay Lovestone in what *Business Week* calls 'labor's own version of the Central Intelligence Agency.'" It was the first such exposé by an American and was translated and republished in many countries. The previous year I had published two books – *The Futile Crusade: Anti-Communism as American Credo* and *A Country Is Born,* the story of the American Revolution written for high school students; and I was finishing a history of the left from colonial times to the present, which appeared the following year under the title *Radicalism in America.* Every morning in town I was at the typewriter two or three hours (more when I came close to deadline) pounding out an article or book. If I moved to New York, I was sure Muste would immerse me not only in expanded peace work but in *Liberation;* my writing would continue but be curtailed. (I was also worried about relations with Dave Dellinger; they were friendly enough at the moment but I wasn't sure how they would remain if both of us were serving as A. J.'s subalterns.)

Finally there was the matter of loose ends, all the things big and little that I had a finger in — as well as the things Shirley was involved in — that I would have to give up if I moved. In 1964, I had been nominated on a third slate for the state legislature, and Birnbaum, Wineberg and I were still working on independent political action (in 1965 we had founded the Chicago Peace Council). In January 1966 we were able, with the help of such figures as University of Chicago professor Robert Havighurst; nationally known comedian Dick Gregory; and SDS leaders Paul Booth, Lee Webb, Richard Rothstein, and Rennie Davis to bring together 800 people to form the Committee for Independent Political Action. SDS had just moved its headquarters to Chicago, and I enjoyed working with its young people, especially Richard Rothstein and Clark Kissinger. Rothstein and Rennie Davis headed an organization called JOIN (Jobs or Income Now) on the North Side. Once the police raided the JOIN offices, ostensibly looking for marijuana, but in fact to smash the mimeograph machine and other equipment, and arrest a few of its leaders. Fifteen or twenty of them came to my apartment on the South Side that night to hammer out a strategy for dealing with the bust. It was a delight to listen as the young people talked themselves — after five hours — into a consensus.

My response to Muste was negative; I couldn't make the move to another city at my age (fifty-three) and with my roots in Chicago, anymore than I think Muste or Dellinger could have cut themselves adrift from New York. I stayed on in the Windy City functioning as strategist and national representative of its peace movement, almost always serving as the chairperson or a speaker at its rallies.

During the hectic years from 1965 to 1972 it was often said in our antiwar circles that we didn't really need organizations or leaders, all we needed was someone to proclaim a date. That wasn't entirely true — committees were needed to decide on slogans, to select speakers, to train marshalls in nonviolence, to handle the press, to issue leaflets and get publicity, to provide for medical care and for bail if someone was arrested. But it was true in the sense that there was a big constituency out there ready to respond to a call. The National Coordinating Committee to End the War in Vietnam was neither effective nor very visible, but its call for "international days of protest," October 15–16, 1965, was heeded in ninety-three cities and drew more than 100,000 participants. In Chicago, we held a march and rally involving perhaps 1,000 people, but in New York 13,000 turned out and in Berkeley, 15,000 on the first day and 5,000 on the second.

These were not large numbers (except by comparison with the past), but a new mood of resistance was already in evidence, very much different from previous years. (The intensity of feelings reminded me of an incident in the 1930s when the principal of a Brooklyn High School locked the doors to prevent students from attending an antimilitarist rally I was conducting outside the building. The young people were so outraged, hundreds of them slid down drainage pipes or crawled out of windows to attend.) Two months before the "international days" small groups of young people in California, sometimes a few hundred, often less, held demonstrations in front of moving troop trains, trying to stop or slow them to get a message across to the GIs. In New York a twenty-two-year-old pacifist named David J. Miller burned his draft card at the October 15 rally – a criminal offense for which he was arrested three days later and sentenced to five years. On April 18, 1967, 178 young men burned their draft cards in Central Park, New York, and on October 16 a thousand turned in their draft cards at the Oakland induction center. Induction centers in New York, Oakland, Chicago, and many other places were under siege from draft resisters; and in January 1968 William Sloane Coffin, Dr. Spock, Mitch Goodman, Mark Raskin, and Mike Ferber were indicted in Boston for conspiracy to "counsel, aid, and abet" draft resistance. (After they were convicted I got a call from an FBI agent asking to interrogate me, since I was slated as a defendent in the second draft resistance case. He was distressed when I told him that I would forego the pleasure. Fortunately the decision in the first case was reversed and the Justice Department decided to drop its pursuit of others.)

Soon too there were soldiers in or out of uniform marching in the front rows of our parades along with Vets for Peace who had served in other wars. In November 1965, Lieutenant Henry Howe, Jr., was sentenced to two years for marching, on his free time and in civilian clothes, with a handful of antiwar protestors at Texas Western College near El Paso. The following year three soldiers, James Johnson, David Samas, and Dennis Mora, a member of the Du Bois Clubs, informed the army at a press conference in New York's Community Church that they considered the war "immoral, illegal, and unjust," and while they would report as ordered to the Oakland Army Terminal, they would "under no circumstances . . . board ship for Vietnam." The three were court-martialed and spent two years in prison, but the Fort Hood Three (as it became known) case developed a life of its own, sparking petitions and rallies calling for their freedom. In time the antiwar protest within the GI community took violent form as officers were "fragged" (beaten or killed) by subordinates, and in the opinion of former GI David Cortright, who published his story under the title *Soldiers in Revolt*, "the Defense Establishment was busy contending with rebellion from within its own ranks." GIs by the thousands visited coffee houses opened by antiwar activists like Fred Gardner, where they could speak freely and plan a protest. Eventually too there were antiwar papers being published at military camps both here and abroad — at least 259, according to a tabulation made by Cortright.

There was an interesting interplay between the civilian part of the movement and soldiers or would-be soldiers. When draft refusal became a public phenomenon, for instance, Muste circulated a "Declaration of Conscience," in which post–draft age people expressed their solidarity with the youth who "refuse to serve in the armed forces" and stated their determination to encourage acts of civil disobedience "to stop the flow of American soldiers and munitions to Vietnam and other countries" (a reference to the Dominican Republic). The declaration, sponsored by about fifty people including the Catholic priests Phil and Dan Berrigan, Dorothy Day, Julian Bond, Ping Ferry, Paul Jacobs, Phil Randolph, and all of us on the staff of the War Resisters League and *Liberation* magazine, was signed by many thousands of people around the country. Another such interplay was the demonstrations we held at military bases on Veterans Day, such as the ones organized annually by Vets for Peace at Fort Sheridan near Chicago. Most of the soldiers were indifferent, but there were quite a few who talked with us — and some who organized an antiwar group at the camp as a result of our contact.

The profusion of groups in every conceivable milieu (150 affiliated to the Fifth Avenue Peace Parade Committee in New York, 30 to the Chicago Peace Council) was the direct result, I think, of the national actions. They cast a beam on the issue as nothing else did, generated publicity, and inspired youthful imaginations to find ever more daring means of protest. They also buoyed the commitment and erased the doubts of hundreds of thousands whose original attachment to the crusade was tenuous. I remember a woman throwing her arms around my wife after Shirley had finished speaking to a women's group on the South Side of Chicago, and bursting into tears. "All I have in life," she said, "is my one son. My husband is dead and the boy is now sixteen. In a year or two they'll draft him and my life will be empty." Until she had seen the demonstrations and heard speakers like Shirley, she had doubted her patriotism. "Am I the only one," she asked herself, "who wants to keep her son out of the army?" When she realized that her anxieties were shared by large numbers of others she began to feel comfortable both with her thoughts and with the idea of working in the antiwar movement. "Setting the date," as innocent a task as it might seem, then, was in fact pivotal to the burgeoning of what Norman Mailer would call "armies of the night."

Between the first "international days of protest" and the second one in March 1966, SANE held its largest — and last — March on Washington for Peace in Vietnam. It drew 35,000 people, the largest antiwar assemblage thus far. Sanford (Sandy) Gottlieb, its coordinator (he used to be managing editor of *Labor's Daily* when I wrote for it), had expressed the hope that "Communists would not participate" and Seymour Melman went around giving people tiny American flags to carry so no one would accuse them of being leftists, but in fact radicals came in considerable number, and carried signs calling for immediate withdrawal, which the march organizers were helpless to remove. As a concession to the left, Carl Oglesby, president of SDS, was called to the rostrum as the last speaker. He made an eloquent plea in the name of America's "dead revolutionaries" who must be wondering "why their country was fighting against what appeared to be a revolution," to concentrate on the war against poverty at home rather than against "communism or revolutionaries" abroad.

The second "international days of protest" in late March 1966 was the last meaningful act of NCC; its leadership was too weak and its base of operation in Madison too far off the beaten path to keep it viable. Despite that, the second "international days of protest" came off remarkably well. There were demonstrations this time in more than 120 U.S. cities, as well as in 30 foreign countries — in Europe, Japan, the Philippines, Africa, New Zealand, Australia, and Latin America. In New York 50,000 people paraded and in Chicago we mobilized 8,000 marchers and 5,000 to an indoor rally, the biggest antiwar demonstration we had ever had up to that time — even though two of the four speakers and SANE withdrew from the planning sessions. Father G. G. Grant of Loyola University and Pat Gorman, secretary-treasurer of the Amalgamated Meat Cutters union, made headlines when they accused our coalition of thirty-odd organizations and seventy-five prominent individuals of being tainted with "Hanoi flavor" — because we allowed such organizations as the Young Socialist Alliance and the M-2-Movement to participate. My relations with Father Grant and Gorman improved considerably in the ensuing years, but I never could understand this last gasp of exclusionism on their part. They were willing to march with people who had supported the candidacy of Lyndon Johnson, the man in charge of the criminal action in Vietnam, but they couldn't bear walking with a young Trotskyite or Maoist. In any case the Chicago Coliseum was packed to the rafters when I introduced the remaining two speakers, Staughton Lynd and Julian Bond, the Georgia state legislator who had been unseated by the Dixiecrats because of his opposition to the war.

V

Rennie Davis coined the phrase *creative discord* to describe how the movement was forcing the general population to come to grips with the war. Average citizens, living in pleasant prosperity, wanted no incursion on their way of life, nothing to disturb things as they were. The movement, however, impinged itself on their conscience by marching, parading, going to jail. It forced people to think, to react. Sometimes their reactions were confusing: they hated the war, but they also were furious at the people who actively opposed it. But "creative discord" brought them into the national dialogue.

One of the means of fomenting "creative discord" was contact with the "enemy" — so that he appeared not as a rampaging vulture but as an ordinary human being seeking nothing more than to till his land, raise his family. In July 1965, ten American representatives of Women Strike for Peace, including my wife Shirley, met with ten Vietnamese women in Jakarta, Indonesia. Heading the delegation from South and North Vietnam was Mme. Nguyen Thi Binh, who would eventually become foreign minister of Vietnam. They showed the Americans pictures of bombed homes and hospitals, dead civilians; and they talked for five days of husbands, children, shopping, literature. Back home the American women issued a widely circulated statement calling for U.S. withdrawal. "As women," it said, "we cannot rest until Vietnamese children, American children, all children, are free to grow up in peace and security."

The next meeting with Vietnamese, beginning in December 1965, was even more dramatic. Herbert Aptheker, an American communist scholar and author of many books on various subjects, arranged a trip to *North* Vietnam for Staughton Lynd, then a history professor at Yale, and Tom Hayden (both Lynd and Hayden were associate editors of *Liberation* magazine). The outcry around the country was deafening; this was "treason," visiting the "enemy" during wartime. There was an insistent demand among the alumni at Yale that Lynd be fired. In time, many people would make this trek — Muste, Cora and Peter Weiss, Dave Dellinger, Dan Berrigan, a women's delegation, even Harrison Salisbury of the New York *Times* to name only a few. I was also scheduled for a trip to North Vietnam in 1970 but had to cancel for personal reasons. No one paid much attention to such things by that time, but back in 1965–66 it raised hackles everywhere.

A few months after the Lynd-Hayden-Aptheker visit to North Vietnam, Muste took a delegation of six to Saigon to hold demonstrations on the scene. Their press conference was disrupted, their lives threatened, their leaflets confiscated, and they were unceremoniously deported. But they made their point, that South Vietnam was hardly the democratic mecca that the Johnson administration claimed it was.

To force a dialogue on the issues in Vietnam — creative discord — the antiwar movement had to prove and reprove constantly that what was afoot in Vietnam was a civil war in which the United States had no business intervening, rather than an invasion by North Vietnam against another country, South Vietnam. Contact with the Vietnamese people, North and South, civil disobedience such as burning of draft cards, and local activities were part of that process, and were all going well in the early part of 1966. What we needed, however, was a stronger leadership than the one that had assembled under the NCC umbrella. It was forged in the latter half of 1966 on the initiative of the Inter-University

Committee for Debate on Foreign Policy, an outgrowth of the organization that had sponsored the national teach-in a year earlier, but that until then confined itself to educational and electoral activities. The leading figures in the Inter-University Committee were Doug Dowd, its president, an economics professor at Cornell; Sidney Peck, a sociology professor at Western Reserve in Cleveland, a former left-wing trade unionist and amateur prize fighter; and Bob Greenblatt, an assistant professor of mathematics at Cornell — three solid citizens, independent radicals. After a couple of preliminary meetings they called a National Leadership Conference in September 1966, at which they installed Muste as chairperson. After the usual bickering on three dozen proposals for action and organizational structure, the 140 delegates proclaimed the November 5–8 Mobilization Committee. Those were the dates antiwar groups were asked to take whatever action fitted their local situation to dramatize the Vietnam issue for election time. The leading committee, as suggested in the organization report I made to the conference, was to be loose and temporary — only until the action was completed and the next conference called to order. Everybody trusted Muste, who was designated chairperson, yet concern that an established bureaucracy would evolve in the peace movement was the reason why few people on the left were willing to delegate power for more than six months or a year at a time.

The November mobilizations were modest affairs, judging by some in the past, and diverse in character — demonstrations, vigils, leafletting of army bases and political meetings, art fairs, doorbell ringing to meet one-on-one with people. In New York, 20,000 citizens turned out to still another demonstration, and in Cleveland, Detroit and elsewhere smaller numbers. But there were signs aplenty that a growing defeatism was eating into the body politic and that the most severe polarization of this century was gripping the United States. Americans were learning that their government was using napalm, a jellylike substance that caused horrible burns and deaths; they saw American troops on television setting fire to Vietnamese villages; and they learned of "strategic hamlets" where peasants were placed in barbed-wire encampments away from their land and villages, which were in fact concentration camps. Most of all they realized that the United States, despite the soporific statements of its president ("a communist take-over . . . is impossible"), its secretary of state ("we are in a much stronger position than two years ago"), its former vice president ("the defeat of the communist forces in South Vietnam is inevitable"), that victory was growing less likely by the day. A referendum in Dearborn, Michigan, asking whether citizens wanted a cease-fire and withdrawal of U.S. troops "so the Vietnamese people can settle their own affairs," lost by the margin of 40 percent to only 60 percent — an amazing sentiment in wartime. Johnson found it almost impossible to go anywhere except a military base without confronting hecklers and pickets.

On the other side, the hawks were expressing their rage over the elusiveness of victory by demanding ever more brutal action. "Bomb them into the stone age," was a demand one heard frequently. I recall a big meeting at a university in Kentucky where Sandy Gottlieb and I were speaking. A heckler in the balcony kept yelling "bomb Hanoi." "And what do you do for an encore," I yelled back, "after you finish bombing Hanoi? Are you ready to bomb Moscow?" "Sure," he shot back, "bomb Moscow, bomb them all until they surrender."

Another sign of the times was the increase in death threats to antiwar leaders. I'm sure the number I received was far from the record (Rennie Davis once told me how many he was getting and the figure — which I no longer remember — was astounding), but approximately once a month someone would call and say, "You have been tried by such and such a group and found guilty of treason. You will be executed on such and such a date." Or I would be told a bomb was under my car. Or I would get a letter with a single sentence: "The day might come when you will be guilty of treason."

VI

A. J. Muste died suddenly on February 11, 1967, just as anti-war activity was about to take a new leap forward. He had recently come back from a trip to Hanoi with a group of clergymen — a trip I had pleaded with him not to make because it was bound to be too exhausting for a man eighty-two years old. He was not exactly frail, his walk was firm and well-paced, but he had a quiver in his hands when he held a cup of coffee and I'm sure he had other maladies of old age. But Muste intended to die in the saddle — and he did. Shirley met me at the door of our apartment with the news as I came home from a speaking date in Kansas, and I found it hard to believe that Muste, like everyone else, was mortal. There was a service for him at a Quaker meeting hall in New York, where anyone who wanted to spoke; Dellinger and I sat together and listened with a trace of bitterness as Bayard Rustin (who had broken totally with A. J.'s politics) made the longest talk of the day. Dave said a few words, but I couldn't. Later in the year we published an eighty-page issue of *Liberation* in tribute to the man who had been our mentor.

Muste's death left Mobilization with a leadership problem, but between Dellinger (who acted as chairperson) and Sidney Peck (the leading organizer for the next three years), abetted by a dozen others, the gap was filled. I drew closer to Peck than to Dellinger in the next period (we tended to see eye to eye on "Mobe" tactics), but they were both exceptionally talented people. Dave, brought up in Massachusetts, graduated Phi Beta Kappa from Yale in 1936, *magna cum laude,* and all the rest. During World War II he was jailed twice, for refusing to serve in the military forces, though he could have had a deferment since he was going to school at Union Theological Seminary. Dellinger's mind was keen and on fundamentals he was solid. Peck's background was with the Old Left and the Minnesota Farmer-Labor Party until he joined academia as a sociology professor. He was also strong on basic issues, and he had a feel for strategy and tactics that was superb.

Nineteen sixty-seven turned out to be a bedlam of projects for us. The November 5–8 Mobilization Committee metamorphosed into the Spring Mobilization Committee, with the major action as proposed by Peck scheduled for April 15 simultaneously in New York and San Francisco. Preliminary to that we in Chicago held still another parade and rally on Saturday March 25, featuring Martin Luther King, Jr. He walked in the first row of the parade with his friend Ralph Abernathy and Al Raby, leader of the civil rights movement in Chicago, drawing great media attention. When I introduced him to a full house at the old Coliseum on South Wabash Avenue, it was the first time he had appeared at a public meeting against the war. I sat behind him as he read from a prepared text wondering what was the source of his magnetism. He didn't gesticulate wildly as some orators do, and his phrases, though colorful, were not more so than those of many other speakers. But his diction and his method of presentation, distant yet empathetic, were so overpowering they riveted audiences to their seats, when they were not yelling or applauding.

Less than a month later, King was the main speaker at the national mobilization in New York — this time to a crowd somewhere between 200,000 and 400,000. On the podium with him, symbolizing the broadening nature of the antiwar movement, were Floyd McKissick of CORE, Stokely Carmichael of SNCC, Jim Bevel, a black minister and SCLC staff person who was project director of the mobilization, and Dellinger. The civil rights and the antiwar movements that day were closer than ever before. The action itself was in the traditional mold — large crowds gathering at Central Park (where draft card burning took place beforehand), a long parade with a mammoth picture of A. J. Muste at its lead, heading toward a four-block area between 43rd and 47th streets on First Avenue near the United Nations, and then, of course, the speeches. In San Francisco, 75,000 participated, the bulk of them students — as in New York — but with an especially sizable group of unionists, most of them from Harry Bridges's longshoremen.

The Spring Mobilization was by all odds a great success — even though Secretary of State Dean Rusk pointed out uncharitably that the crowd represented only a minute part of "a population of almost 200 million." But success, instead of mitigating dissension, exacerbated it. At the end of August, a few weeks after the traditional Hiroshima commemorations, the National Conference for New Politics (NCNP) convened at the Palmer House in Chicago, hopefully to capitalize on recent gains of the movement. NCNP was just a couple of years old, a composite of groups that had been working in the electoral field, like CIPA in Chicago.

The purpose of the five-day session was to plan electoral strategy, the choice being among three positions — immediate formation of a permanent third party, selection of a presidential ticket for 1968 (Martin Luther King, Jr., for president, Benjamin Spock for vice president, being the most likely choices), or continued concentration on grass-roots community organizing. Before the sessions began, unfortunately, 350 dissatisfied blacks left to hold a convention of their own in another part of the city. The remaining blacks formed a Black Caucus, adopted a thirteen-point program (including a condemnation of Zionism, which was bound to raise hackles) and demanded that they receive a bloc vote equal to that of the rest of the delegates. In effect this gave them control of the conference since they needed only one out of 28,000 white votes for a majority. (Two Chicago police spies, whom I exposed in the Chicago press a few months later, sat in on the Black Caucus and egged its members on not "to give in to Whitey." They also stole two typewriters, money, and files.) I was part of a vocal minority that opposed giving blacks control of the convention on the grounds that it was "reverse racism," but younger people, doing what I felt was a mea culpa for centuries of black suppression, prevailed. On the substantive issues the third party idea was jettisoned early, leaving a choice between a King-Spock ticket and something nebulous called "community organizing" (which would have taken place anyway). The vote alas was 13,519 for the latter — community organizing — and 13,517 for the independent ticket. Attempts to reconsider failed, and when the smoke cleared all that was left of this promising effort was a compromise resolution leaving it to each state to decide for itself what to do — in effect a decision to let things stand where they were previously. I was greatly disappointed with the results, not only because it was a personal defeat — I had been spokesperson for the King-Spock position — but because I felt we could have made a strong impact on the American people in 1968. "If we are to avoid the tragedy of 1964 when a majority of liberals and radicals voted for Lyndon Johnson on the misguided theory he was a 'peace' candidate," I wrote in *New Politics News*, "it is necessary to assess both the purpose and limits of electoral politics. The New Politics convention is . . . a beacon against the darkness of Vietnam, the arms race, resurgent colonialist attitudes, continued racism, and the hoax of antipoverty." The controversy over the black issue, alas, reduced our deliberations to ludicrousness and shredded what remained of our hopes.

Fortunately the NCNP fiasco was not the rule. That summer I attended an international conference in Stockholm of 435 people from sixty-six nations, including the U.S. and Vietnam, to approve an Appeal to the World for Vietnam. It was the usual international conference with speeches by leading figures from many nations (Ben Spock spoke for the United States), workshops, and a final declaration meant to impact on world opinion. I was chosen chairperson of the thirty-five-member U.S. delegation, representing the range of the American antiwar movement. At the end of the affair, the chairman called to the podium two spokespersons for the Democratic Republic of Vietnam and three for the National Liberation Front. Everyone stood and applauded. A moment later the thirty-five Americans were called to join the Vietnamese, again to a standing ovation. Nguyen Minh Vy of North Vietnam, a short man with an excellent sense of humor, made a brief talk about the common interests of the Vietnamese and American people, and I, for the American delegation, stated that "We Americans don't want to fight the Vietnamese, we want to go to their country as tourists."

After the conference had adjourned Vy and an associate, Do Xuan Canh, called me aside for a private meeting. The war, they said, was going well as far as they were concerned. "We are ready for anything, even a full scale U.S. invasion" of the North. They also gave me some figures disputing American claims of losses ("we have shot down 2,050 U.S. planes, not 600 as the Pentagon says"), and then came to the point. They wanted me to carry a peace proposal to the White House. President Johnson had been saying that he was "ready to go anywhere at any time, and meet with anyone" to negotiate an end to the war. When he had launched the bombing of North Vietnam in February 1965 he stated, as paraphrased by the New York *Times,* that he did it to "extract from North Vietnam an indication that it is ready to negotiate a truce." (He always pretended incidentally that the NLF was irrelevant.) The Vy-Canh proposal met that condition and was at least as good as the agreement Nixon and Kissinger were forced to accept five years – and many thousands of lives – later. Both sides had been talking "points" – four points, five points, fourteen points. The plan Vy and Canh wanted me to carry back was a single point – if the United States would stop the bombing of North Vietnam and issue a simple eight-word statement to that effect "We have stopped the bombing of North Vietnam" negotiations could begin, and Vy assured me "good things can follow."

It was unmistakable that the end of bombing could lead quickly to a cease fire, and talks between the Hanoi and Saigon governments for a final resolution. That was all the United States finally got in 1972, and it wouldn't have had to make promises of billions of dollars in aid (which it didn't keep, incidentally). When I got back I went to see my cousin Arthur Okun, who was chairman of the Council of Economic Advisors at the White House, and asked him to transmit the proposal to the national security council and Johnson. I also contacted Senator Charles Percy of my state and asked him to do the same. I then held a press conference to give the story to the media. Nothing came of this peace initiative, however, for what Johnson understood by the term "unconditional discussions" was in fact "unconditional surrender." He wanted and expected, as he made clear at Manila in October 1966, that the North Vietnamese troops *and* the Viet Cong would withdraw from the South to the North, while American forces remained long enough to make sure an American puppet was firmly ensconced. The White House responded to the new offer by saying it contained nothing new.

VII

In the wake of escalating hostility to the war and increased numbers at antiwar demonstrations, there was talk of an escalation in numbers of protesters. Bettina Aptheker, daughter of Herbert Aptheker and a top leader of the communist-controlled Du Bois Clubs, had been calling on the student movement to "bring a million people" to Washington. The Trotskyites picked up the idea and were promoting it vigorously in the preliminary meetings of the Spring Mobilization Committee — soon to be called National Mobilization Committee. The Trotskyites were by no means the dominant force in Mobilization, but they were vocal, disciplined, and they had outmaneuvered the communists and pacifists to assert a dominant position in the Student Mobilization Committee. I must say that practically all of us in the leadership of the Mobilization Committee found it easier to work with the communists, not only because their caucus discipline was more lax and they stopped trying to manipulate people, but because their caucus leaders Arnold Johnson and later Gil Green were flexible. The Trotskyites were harder to live with because they operated in almost military fashion and their caucus leaders were less prone to compromise. On the other hand, the Trotskyites boasted a younger and more vigorous membership, and their contribution to the movement was serious and sizable. Fred Halsted, a tall, heavy man who almost always was the co-chief marshal — along with Chicago pacifist Brad Lyttle — was an important figure in our ranks and considerably less rigid than some of the people with whom he was associated. In any case a fall event, proposed at a conference in Washington, seemed to be focusing on October 21, 1967, as the date, and on an escalation of numbers — to bring out a million people — as the target.

On the plane to the meeting where a final decision was to be made — I think it was in New York — Jack Spiegel and I, representing the Chicago Peace Council, worried about the unrealism of that target. I suggested that what we needed was not an increase in quantity but an improvement in quality. At the meeting, therefore, I proposed on behalf of both of us that the rally scheduled for October 21 in Washington emphasize a turn "from protest to resistance" to "confront the warmakers" at the Pentagon. I could tell as I spoke that the proposal caught most people's imagination, and it carried with almost no opposition. That was to be the theme, then, of one of the most unique confrontations in American history. The orignial National Mobilization Committee press release talked of an action "which will shut down the Pentagon," and Yippie Abbie Hoffman, a psychology major with a wonderful sense of humor, predicted "we're going to raise the Pentagon three hundred feet in the air." But while some of the Mobe's leaders may have been carried away in talking with the press the vast majority understood that this was essentially a symbolic action. Most people would participate in the traditional peaceful type of demonstration and march, at the end of which a few hundred would try to enter the Pentagon and be arrested. The call made it clear that those who did not want to or could not afford to be jailed would not have to engage in "resistance." The two events would be separate.

A new element was being injected into the movement — or at least one that I hadn't been sufficiently aware of until that time — the Yippie. Many weeks before the demonstration Dave Dellinger and Jerry Rubin came through Chicago, staying in our apartment for a few days. Rubin was to be the project director for the impending Washington event, serving under Dellinger and Mobe's national coordinator, Bob

Greenblatt. He was a strange person, given, I thought, to extremes. One day, for instance, he told me he was opposed to "personal property." "You mean 'private property,'" I said, "don't you?" No, he said, all kinds of property, even the suit on your back. "Do you mean to say, Jerry," I asked, "that you have a right to steal my silverware or my ties?" "Sure," he replied. Needless to say he didn't steal silverware or ties, but he loved to shock people. Prior to the demonstrations during the 1968 Democratic Party convention, he and Abbie Hoffman (who was an even better actor and comedian) brought a pig to the Civic Center in Chicago and announced they were running him for president. But when I visited him in Cook County jail a year or so later, he told me "confidentially" — contrary to what he was saying publicly — "our only hope is for the Democrats to win." Rubin and Hoffman viewed life as theater and they made a significant contribution to the new counterculture with their shock therapy ("kill your parents," "steal this book") and their general behavior (drugs, music, devil-may-care attitudes).

Nonetheless, the Yippies made little impact on the events that October, though Rubin was the project director. There was little room for levity, let alone guerrilla theater. The day prior to the mobilization, William Sloane Coffin, Ben Spock, Mark Raskin, Mitchell Goodman, and Arthur Waskow delivered a thousand draft cards to the Department of Justice as an act of defiance, while a few thousand people outside listened to speeches, including a brief one by Jane Spock and another by myself. There had also been an indoor meeting at which novelist Norman Mailer spoke. Late in the evening Dellinger called fifteen or twenty people to his room for an "emergency meeting." The authorities, it seemed, had grudgingly agreed to issue a permit for an assembly at Lincoln Memorial, a march across the Arlington Memorial Bridge, and a rally in one of the Pentagon's parking lots on the north end. As part of the agreement the General Services Administration had promised to repair one of the streets where two wide ditches were being dug, but had failed to make good on their word. Mobe leaders were worried that as the front lines narrowed and the parade slowed down police might attack; the meeting in Dellinger's room was to consider whether to call off the whole affair on the grounds that the government hadn't kept its word. Strange as it may seem, we argued on this point far past midnight, with a majority for cancellation originally, and only SNCC leader John Wilson, attorney Arthur Kinoy, and myself speaking against the idea. "We'll look silly to the whole world," I argued, "after making all the claims about taking over the Pentagon, then announcing we won't go through with it because the government that we criticize so bitterly didn't repair a street." The idea of cancellation died at about 1 A.M. by unanimous agreement. Probably that was the only way a movement so diverse could function; but it also proved, as I see it, that even though the wildest ideas were often put forward, sanity usually prevailed.

A few hours before the parade, Dwight Macdonald, a writer for *Esquire* and a former Trotskyite, poet Robert Lowell, and Norman Mailer approached me with the suggestion they would like to be the first people arrested. I talked to Dellinger, then arranged for the three of them, Father Charles Rice of Pittsburgh, a few others, and myself to occupy the first row, offering ourselves to the police or troops, whichever, as the first sacrifices of the confrontation with the Pentagon. As luck would have it, however, when we reached the section of the road with the two big ditches it became necessary to contract the lines, and in the resulting confusion Macdonald, Lowell, myself, and Father Rice found ourselves two or three dozen rows back. Mailer, however, stuck tenaciously to his goal and was the first to climb the steps of the Pentagon and be jailed. (The jacket of Mailer's book about the Pentagon confrontation, *Armies of the Night,* carries a picture of a half dozen of us locked arm in arm at the front of the parade. The book described me flatteringly as a "tough" trade unionist, but that is about the last word I would have applied to myself.)

Confront the Warmakers was an inspiring affair in many ways. A hundred thousand people rallied near Lincoln

Memorial, heard the usual speakers introduced by Dellinger, then crossed into Virginia over the Arlington Memorial Bridge. The agreement with the government called for entering the north Pentagon parking lot at a certain gate, but within a few minutes the fence was breached in three or four places and what was to have been a single march became a confused welter of Indian lines. Dellinger told me he had made an agreement to begin civil disobedience at a certain time, but by then Mailer and many others had been hauled away. Dave assembled some of the more prominent people, including Spock, Noam Chomsky, Dick Gregory, myself, and a dozen others to march arm in arm toward the soldiers — to curry arrest. However, while they were assembling, Gregory and I went looking for a way to climb into the Pentagon through a window; we thought we had seen a spot where it was possible, but it proved unbreachable.

On our way back to Dellinger's line, I got caught in a melee near the top of the Pentagon steps and was tear-gassed; by then Dave and a few others who had massed with him were under arrest. Instead of a few hundred people on the steps of the Pentagon there were thousands, and perhaps 25,000 in the nearby mall. As darkness fell there were dozens of meetings, smoke-ins, and what have you. Periodically the police or troops would attack and haul away a few prisoners. On the steps a phalanx of troops confronted us ominously, but few demonstrators were disposed to leave. I took a bull-horn and addressed the troops for about an hour; I would make a one- or two-minute speech about how we are working in their — the troops' — interests as well as that of humanity in general, then the crowd behind me would chant "join us, join us, join us." We were told later that a couple of soldiers did desert ranks. Apart from that the confrontation had resulted in no great defections and no occupation of the military headquarters, though on one or two occasions our people came close to entering. Almost a thousand people were arrested, making the confrontation the main item of news that day. Most Americans, I'm sure, were disturbed by this action; only a minority sympathized with what we were doing. Yet it contributed to "creative discord"; it forced the nation and people overseas to think about the war, to discuss it, and in the end to damn it.

VIII

"Let none disparage, henceforth, the power of protest!" I wrote in the April 1968 issue of *Liberation*. "The removal of [General William] Westmoreland from the scene of his folly, the unilateral — though limited — bombing pause, and the sensational self-dumping of Lyndon Johnson are testament, above all, to the might of shoe leather. None of these events would have happened without the walks, marches, parades, confrontations, and draft resistance which escalated in cadence with the escalation of the war. This is attested to by no less an authority than the President himself . . . Mr. Johnson has removed himself from the race, he says, because he is fearful of the expanding 'divisiveness' in the country. . . . This was, I feel, the greatest victory we peaceniks have won since the late A. J. Muste began to form the modern peace movement thirteen years ago."

Nineteen sixty-eight was one of those years of historical benchmarks, the Tet offensive in Vietnam, the assassination of Martin Luther King, Jr., early in the year and Robert Kennedy later, the ghetto riots, Johnson's surprise announcement he would not run, the removal of General Westmoreland as commander of U.S. forces in Vietnam, the nationwide demonstrations in April, the surprising showing of Eugene McCarthy in the Democratic Party primaries, the nomination of Hubert Humphrey by the Democrats and Richard Nixon by the Republicans, and finally the Chicago police riots in April and again in August.

"We begin '68," said an American embassy publicist at a Saigon press conference on January 24, 1968, "in a better position than we have ever been before . . ." A week later nineteen NLF commandos shot their way into the American embassy compound, killing two military police. It took the surprised American forces six hours to regain control of the embassy area. That same morning 84,000 NLF troops hit at every major U.S. base, five of the six biggest cities in South Vietnam, thirty-six of the forty provincial capitals, and five dozen district capitals. Parts of eleven NLF battalions drove into Saigon, and elements of their forces actually moved into the grounds of the presidential palace, seized a government radio station, and battered into the Tan Son Nhut air base to blow up a number of planes. This was the Tet (Vietnamese New Year) offensive. The NLF had penetrated behind the American and Saigon lines, had smuggled weapons and ammunition to key spots in the big cities, had placed troops where they would be needed. American leaders had always said that the NLF was afraid to fight in the open, that it was unwilling to join in battle except in the hinterlands; yet here it upset both calculations. It fought remarkably well, and though the offensive did not achieve the ultimate goal of victory, the U.S. lost property and men on an unparalleled scale. An American officer, in explaining why his troops had to level the town of Ben Tre, made the classic comment that would soon be on millions of lips: "We had to destroy it in order to save it."

After three weeks the American command placed the civilian toll at 165,000 and the figure for new refugees at two million. That did not include the toll in Hue which the NLF seized and held until late February. Ambassador Ellsworth Bunker put on a strange show of synthetic optimism in a CBS interview, when he said that the Saigon leaders had "demonstrated their ability" to ward off communist attacks and had "gained confidence in themselves." The Saigon government, Bunker also said, "has probably a wider support today than it had before the Tet offensive." But despite those saccharine phrases it was recognized far and wide that the United States had suffered a major defeat. All kinds of people in the establishment began calling on Johnson to end hostilities, and public opinion polls showed that confidence in the way he was handling the war had dropped to 35 percent. By contrast, Gene McCarthy's campaign for the Democratic nomination, coordinated by young people like

Sam Brown, David Hawk, and Marge Sklencar (who would later lead the Moratorium action in 1969), took wings.

In April, hundreds of thousands of college and high school students went "on strike" against the Vietnam war. The New York *Times* estimated the number in New York alone at 200,000. At Columbia University students seized a number of buildings in protest against treatment of blacks both at the school and in the neighborhoods, as well as war research conducted under the aegis of the university. In addition there were the normal spring demonstrations in scores of cities, drawing 200,000 to Central Park's Sheep Meadow, 30,000 in San Francisco, and 7,000 in Chicago. The Chicago event that spring was an augury of things to come in the summer. Police charged the demonstrators as they left the Civic Center, arresting eighty people and beating considerably more with impunity. My wife Shirley was in charge of the van that carried the picket signs; she pushed a dozen kids into the back to save them from police fury. Later Jay Miller, director of the American Civil Liberties Union, and I contacted a dozen prominent religious and civic figures, headed by retired president of Roosevelt University Edward J. Sparling to form a Commission to Investigate the Peace March of April 27. It was truly a blue-ribbon commission, consisting of a vice president of Inland Steel, a former alderman, three or four of the most prominent clergy, a professor, a leading surgeon. Its report, issued only a few weeks before the better known "police riot" that summer, asserted that "the police badly mishandled their task.... Yet to place primary blame on the police would, in our view, be inappropriate. The April 27 stage had been prepared by the Mayor's designated officials weeks before. Administration actions ... were designed by City officials to communicate that 'these people have no right to demonstrate or express their views.'"

I've never fully understood why Mayor Daley reacted so viciously to protests that year. Our *local* peace groups had seldom had trouble. But Daley lost perspective when spontaneous rioting broke out in the black ghettos after Dr. King was killed, ordering police to "shoot to kill" looters. And he may have reacted to distorted information he was getting from his police spies. In the summer of 1967, the offices of the Chicago Peace Council, Women for Peace, and Fellowship of Reconciliation — all headquartered at a building on Ashland and Madison owned by my friend John Rossen — were burglarized. In addition to money, typewriters, a mimeograph machine, and mailing lists were taken. Something similar happened to the Latin American Defense Organization. A few weeks later around midnight Shirley and I got a phone call telling us (in a voice disguised to sound like a black man) that our typewriters and mimeo were in a certain hallway two blocks from our own apartment. We jumped into our cars, and sure enough the equipment was there — but no files, no money. A few weeks later two people from within the police department contacted me, first by phone, then in person. They gave me the names of the burglars (three undercover policemen who had been assigned to infiltrate the peace movement and one civilian spy), and related exactly how the burglaries had been committed. One of those two sources met with me every few months and fed me information about police spying for a number of years; based on that information I exposed four spies to the press in December 1967.

One of the things I learned in the course of my meetings with the police-informant was that one of the spies had given the Red Squad a report in the summer of 1967 describing exact details of the demonstration the National Mobilization Committee intended for August 1968 — a year later. It was a neat trick, especially since Mobe didn't hold its first planning session for that action until a half year later. The "report" listed alleged routes we were going to take on our way to the Amphitheater where the Democratic Party convention was to be held, and pinpointed spots where Dick Gregory was going to provoke riots in the black community. It was all fiction, of course, but exactly the kind of nonsense a police spy might invent to ingratiate himself with superiors. If that report reached Daley, as it probably did, it may explain the hysteria with which he reacted.

The Democratic Party convention was the major target for the National Mobilization Committee to End the War in Vietnam in 1968. We expected Johnson to run for another four-year term, and in that case we were confident of a massive turnout since it had become axiomatic that the president could go almost nowhere without encountering blistering hostility. The problem we ran into when a couple of dozen of us met early in the year in a Manhattan apartment was what kind of a protest to organize. With the Pentagon affair behind us there were some who felt that the slogan "from protest to resistance" meant we ought to physically disrupt the convention, prevent it from going on. One Chicago peacenik had an idea for buying or renting a grocery store near the Amphitheater, which could be used as a base for various unpleasant functions such as, I assume, throwing stink bombs. The Chicagoan was vehemently disabused, but there were some words in the draft proposal put forth by Rennie Davis and Tom Hayden, "An Election Year Offensive," which were ambiguous on the question of nonviolence. Stewart Meacham and I made it clear to Rennie that the ambiguity was not only wrong in principle but aberrant nonsense. "Unless you think we're on the verge of revolution," I told Rennie, "they can kill every one of us if we choose to make it a contest of violence." The offending phrases were changed but there was still no clarity on exactly what we were going to do in Chicago. What if Gene McCarthy, who had all but sunk Lyndon Johnson in the New Hampshire primary, had a chance for the nomination? Most peaceniks would support his candidacy and would resent it if National Mobe hindered his chances with a "confront the warmakers" type of demonstration.

Another possibility was to hold a counter convention, with delegates, speakers, votes, and nominations of peaceniks — seeking to capture a little publicity. A third possibility was the one put forth by Jerry Rubin and the Yippies for a big celebration, a sort of funfest making light of the Democrats.

Jerry's scenario, as described by Fred Halsted in his book *Out Now,* read in part: "Chicago is in panic. The American youth festival has brought 500,000 people to Chicago to camp out, smoke pot, dance to wild music, burn draft cards and roar like wild bands through the streets, forcing the President to bring troops from Vietnam to keep order in the city, while he is nominated under the protection of tear gas and bayonets." Another possibility was for McCarthy to hold a big rally at Soldiers Field, of perhaps 50,000 or 75,000. That was a viable possibility at one point until McCarthy himself appealed to supporters not to come to Chicago — unless they were delegates.

All options became more or less academic when Johnson withdrew as a candidate. In the same speech in which he made that surprise statement he also declared a halt to the bombing above the 20th parallel, and made an offer to begin peace talks with the other side. The peace talks were hampered and stretched out over such picayune matters as the shape of the negotiations table and where the NLF representative should sit, yet in many American minds the war was winding down. I concluded early in the spring, and so did others, that any demonstration in Chicago would be small and probably uneventful.

Shirley and I decided to take a trip to North Africa and Eastern Europe that summer. A young woman in the Women for Peace stayed in our cooperative apartment, and as the summer wore on gave shelter to half the leadership of National Mobe — Sid Peck, Tom Hayden, Dick Fernandez (a founder of Clergy and Laymen Concerned), Dellinger, and others. Meanwhile the two of us were wending our way through two lightly traveled but socially important sections of the world. My impressions of that trip are vivid, but not particularly incisive except for what we saw in Czechoslovakia. We met opposition leader Mehdi Ben Barka in Morocco — a short, stocky, likable man who would be assassinated in France a year or two later. Tunisia, whose president, Habib Bourguiba, I had met in Paris back in 1950, had made only minimal social progress from what I could see, and

Algeria, where a much deeper revolution had taken place, seemed unable, under Houari Boumedienne, to build a popular mass party. Yugoslavia was most interesting: I thought that self-management was providing its people with more freedom and a better life than in any other socialist country. Hungary too was a pleasant surprise; despite the Soviet incursion of 1956 and a few bitter years afterward Janos Kadar had proved to be self-effacing, had improved the lot of his people appreciably, and was incorporating many of the Yugoslav self-management ideas into his society. Budapest had the look of a modern city and its restaurants were excellent, by contrast with the shabbiness in other cities of the communist world.

The most heartening part of the trip, of course, was a visit to Prague. "Socialism with a human face" had taken the tiller in Czechoslovakia and it was a delight to see: open-air meetings at Myslbek Square, free press, vital unions, beginnings of a new economic plan. I spent hours talking with Antonin Liehm and other dissident writers, with the new youth leaders, economists, and the "man on the street" at open-air meetings near the center of town. What emerged was a bifocal image of developments. Prior to 1968, intellectuals like Liehm and Ludvik Vaculik who had been demanding democracy for years were often fired from their jobs and only allowed to publish under pseudonyms. The new impulse, as I described in an article for the *National Catholic Reporter*, was "the most hopeful development within the Communist world in decades . . . an attempt to wed socialism with humanism."

The other impulse, however, was perhaps more important. Czechoslovakia was in a blind alley economically. Most of the economic advance in communist countries through the years had resulted in part from improved technology and in part because of additions to the labor force from amongst the underemployed in the villages. The economies were so backward in places like Bulgaria or Rumania that there was plenty of such labor available and no place to go but up. But in Czechoslovakia, which had been one of the ten leading manufacturing nations before World War II, the supply of labor from the villages had long been exhausted. The country, as economists like Ota Sik saw it, was stagnating — and falsifying its statistics to cover up the stagnation. The only way out of this dilemma was to import more modern machinery and computers from the West, but that required better quality of products and lower costs for the goods Czechoslovakia hoped to export to the West to pay for imports. The only way to achieve that, according to Sik, was to introduce a system like the one in Yugoslovia — with decentralized, indicator planning, worker participation in decision making, free speech, and assembly. This was the underlying rationale for what became known as "socialism with a human face." Unfortunately the Russian reaction was that the Czechs were moving too fast, that there was a danger the change would be *uncontrolled* and that Czechoslovakia might secede from the Soviet orbit and go neutralist. On August 20, 1968, Soviet and East European troops invaded the country, removed liberal communist Alexander Dubček and installed a regime more in compliance with the Soviet model. Just five hours before the invasion, Shirley and I had left for Warsaw. When we arrived there and learned of the Russian action we canceled the rest of our East European trip and took the next plane home for Chicago.

At the first Mobe steering committee meeting I attended after returning to Chicago, reports by Tom Hayden, Jerry Rubin and others indicated that not more than 3,000 people were in town for the demonstrations. On this occasion, at least, it was apparent that merely "setting a date" was not enough to trigger mass protest. There had to be a target, both personal and political, on which to focus attention, and with Johnson's decision not to run and the promise of negotiations, the targets were not so clear.

We decided at that August steering committee, therefore, that the only way to pad the ranks was from local sources. I wrote a leaflet, and we printed 100,000 copies for distribution in parts of the city where there was an antiwar constituency. The result was a turnout of 12,000 people at the largest meeting, on Wednesday, August 28. Had Daley issued a permit for a march to the Amphitheater, the march and rally would have taken place in orderly and nonviolent fashion, would have drawn a few negligible paragraphs in the press, and been forgotten.

But Mayor Daley turned what would otherwise have been a movement fiasco into a worldwide media sensation. Every attempt by Rennie Davis, coordinator of the action, to get permits had been denied or deflected. The city rejected out of hand Davis's request that demonstrators be allowed to sleep in the parks (100,000 people were expected, he told authorities, and the Chicago Peace Council could find only 30,000 sleeping units—both figures, as it turned out, were grossly wrong). Permits to march on State Street to the Grant Park bandshell for one rally, and on Halsted Street to the Amphitheater, were similarly denied. Use of Soldier's Field on the lakefront was refused on the spurious ground it was being held for a celebration of Lyndon Johnson's birthday. Quite obviously Daley was playing hardball with the dissidents.

The week of the convention, therefore, was sheer tension throughout. Unbelievable as it sounds, Daley mobilized 6,000 regular army troops and 6,000 Illinois Guardsmen—all in full gear—plus his own 12,000 Chicago policemen to contain an unarmed group of men, women, and children who never grew to more than 12,000. The police in particular were imbued from the first with a spirit of petty meanness and brutality—as evidenced by the fact that sixty newsmen, of a contingent of three hundred who covered the parks and streets that week, "were involved," as the Walker Report later noted, "in incidents resulting in injury to themselves, damage to their equipment, or their arrest."

On August 25, the day before the convention was to begin, a number of workshops and protest activities were held, the largest one being the Festival of Life, held by the Yippies at Lincoln Park about three miles north of the center of Chicago. At 11 P.M., police ordered the participants to leave, using tear gas, clubs, and unbridled brutality to enforce their edict. Many innocent people blocks away were beaten by cops gone wild, including not a few who didn't even know a demonstration was underway.

During the next couple of days, there were various marches, one of them by pacifists walking on the sidewalks toward the Amphitheater. I joined this march, which included Staughton Lynd, but left it after a few miles to take over my duties running the National Mobe office. Neither these marchers nor any others got near the Amphitheater, which was ringed off by police and fences for miles around. That night again there was police violence in and around the parks. The denouement, however, came on Wednesday, the day the Democrats were set to nominate their candidates. Some 10,000 peaceniks were gathered at the Grant Park bandshell to listen to speeches and music. My wife, Shirley, was sitting at the front near a flag pole, with another Woman for Peace and an eighty-two-year-old woman who had been through the radical mill. Suddenly, looking up, Shirley spied two young people who looked suspicious, pulling down the American flag. She threw her arms around the pole in a futile effort to prevent the two from raising a red shirt and pleaded with the men to go away. The shirt unfortunately drew attention from police who started beating people with careless abandon, including Rennie Davis, who had come to see what was happening. Rennie's head was battered, requiring medical attention.

Meanwhile on the stage, Tom Hayden grabbed the microphone, and Sidney Peck, fearing he was going to call on the participants to resist the police physically, grabbed it away from him and told the audience to remain as calm as possible. Shirley, who had the $4,000 collection from the rally in her possession, barely made it to her friend's car with the eighty-two-year-old woman, soft-speaking Guardsmen and police about the need to get the aged lady back to a nursing home. They were among the small number to escape police fury that afternoon. A few thousand people lined up on the sidewalk, at Dellinger's suggestion, prepared to walk peacefully to the Amphitheater and if need be accept arrest; the rest were asked to move north and disperse. As the 3,000 marchers, hemmed in on the south by guardsmen and troops, reached Columbus and Balboa drives, their way was blocked. Attempts by Sidney Peck to negotiate for a peaceful parade might have been successful but in the meantime the crowd dispersed. Ultimately a few thousand demonstrators made their way to the Conrad Hilton Hotel, one of the main convention hotels. Here in front of scores of newspeople — and grinding cameras — police shouting "kill, kill, kill" drove into the crowd with swinging clubs, battering hundreds of people, many of whom had nothing to do with the demonstration. A thousand people were hurt, some as they fled into the hotel lobby, some as they were shoved through plate glass windows. Sidney Peck, pleading with deputy police superintendent James Rochford to stop the carnage, was himself severely beaten and arrested. Six hundred and sixty others, including Jerry Rubin, were hauled off in paddy wagons that night. Later that evening 2,000 people, including 25 delegates and some correspondents, marched southward with Dick Gregory, but were accorded the same treatment — tear gas, violence, and about six dozen arrests, including that of the future editor of the *Progressive* magazine, Erwin Knoll, and the future managing editor of the Chicago *Sun-Times*, Stuart Loory.

At the National Mobe headquarters, meanwhile, I was on the phone with Daley officials four or five times still trying to get approval for a parade; and after the police violence began, arranging with the Medical Committee on Human Rights for treatment of our victims and with others for bail money to spring those arrested. The McCarthy delegates at the Conrad Hilton were most generous; so was the public generally. I was on radio — by telephone — dozens of times that night, urging people to wire money to the Chicago Peace Council headquarters where Sylvia Kushner stood by to convert checks and wired funds to cash to bail out our people. One Chicagoan on business on the West Coast wired $5,000, which I applied to bail out Jerry Rubin and a woman who had been pushed through a window at the Hilton.

During all this excitement the fire alarm went off at the building where Mobe was headquartered — someone had set fire to a trash can. It was a half hour before we could get back to work.

The reaction of the public to the police riot — as the Walker Report called it — was ambivalent. The liberal community was shocked by what had happened, but conservatives, influenced by Daley's charge that his police were only retaliating against extreme provocation, felt the police had been justified in what they did. In answer to Daley's claim, I issued a long statement to the press, charging that "all the violence that emerged from the events was police instigated. . . . More than 90 percent of those injured or gassed were injured or gassed when police charged from positions that were never under attack by the demonstrators. It was a deliberate attack under orders by superiors." Regardless of who won the battle of words after the battle on the streets, there is little doubt that Daley's police riot lost the election for Hubert Humphrey; it siphoned off considerably more than the half million votes by which he lost to Richard Nixon.

A month after the August horror, University of Chicago professor Bob Levin and a few friends organized another parade and rally to commemorate the one that had been aborted. On September 18, 35,000 Chicagoans marched and rallied without interference — on the same State Street we had been denied previously. As the lead speaker at that event I asserted that this time the authorities had put no obstacle in our way "not because they wanted to but because their image was so bad throughout the world they had to."

Chapter 11
Stumbling Goliath

I

How does an empire die? Sometimes it is swept away in a great deluge — the Russian empire in 1917, for instance. Sometimes it withers away, like the British Empire in the two decades after World War II. The American empire began to wither away sometime between 1968 and 1970 when, with all its military and economic might, it was unable to subdue what its leaders called a "fourth-class nation."

Most people in the United States saw no correlation between the Vietnam venture and American power. They viewed the war either as an unfortunate tactical error or as a necessity in a world where you had to "fight fire with fire." Russians were doing the same thing in Hungary, Czechoslovakia, Cuba. During a debate between Fulton Lewis III and myself at a convention of the right-wing Young Americans for Freedom (YAF) in Chicago, a delegate asked a question he thought painted me into a corner: "How come you supported the Russian invasion of Czechoslovakia but refuse to support your own country when it invades Vietnam?" Even in this hostile audience I got a ripple of applause when I replied that Richard Barnet and I had engaged in vehement argument with Yuri Zhukov, a central committee member of the Soviet Communist Party and a *Pravda* columnist, when we were in Moscow as part of an eleven-person peace delegation in late 1968 on exactly that question, the Soviet takeover of Prague. (The Soviets refused to let me travel to Minsk, where my parents were brought up, and I was unable to collect a few thousand dollars in royalties due me for a book that had been translated and published in Moscow without my permission, *The Crisis of American Labor.*) The attitude of the young questioner, however — that if *they* can do it, why can't we? — was widespread amongst the American people.

Unfortunately neither of these approaches to the war in Indochina was particularly incisive. The war was much more than a tactical mistake, and whether it was justified because "the Russians do the same thing" was beside the point. The war was a watershed for a militarist policy that led to all kinds of economic difficulties — balance of trade and balance of payments deficits, devaluation of the dollar, divorce of the dollar from gold, and all the corollary consequences. In the eight years after 1971, the dollar, in terms of the yellow metal, fell by more than 1000 percent — from one thirty-fifth of an ounce to one four-hundredth. The war ushered in a decade of economic chaos, inflation, unemployment, uncertainty, reduced living standards, and other vices. It also decisively, and probably permanently, altered America's geopolitical position. The defeat of the United States in Vietnam was certainly a major factor in OPEC's 1974 decision to quadruple the price of oil, in Washington's loss of standing in Africa, the defeat of the shah in Iran, and other American setbacks.

The vision of America's leaders unfortunately did not encompass the pitfalls ahead. The war was viewed as part of a chess game with the Soviet Union and China, little more. "Are you telling me," Henry Kissinger said to his national security staff, "that [Vietnam] is the first country in history with no breaking point?" During the midterm election campaign of 1966 Richard Nixon stated that "this is a war that has to be fought to prevent World War III." By 1968 however, he realized that a new mood pervaded the nation; the American people wanted the war ended. Nixon tuned his band to this wavelength. He had a plan, he said, "to end the war," though he would not say what it was lest it jeopardize the four-sided Paris negotiations for peace. The only hint he gave of the "secret plan" was in a private meeting with Southern delegates at the Miami Republican convention: "We need a massive training program so that the South Vietnamese can be trained to take over the fighting, that they can be phased in while we phase out." This was in essence the future "Vietnamization" program, to withdraw U.S. troops while increasing the fighting role of the Saigon regime.

But Nixon's "secret plan," we learned long afterward, was more comprehensive than substituting Saigon soldiers for American. "He was absolutely convinced," writes his former chief aide, H. R. Haldeman in *The Ends of Power,* "he would end it in his first year. . . . 'I'm the one man in this country who can do it, Bob.'" As Nixon explained it to Haldeman: "I call it the Madman Theory, Bob. I want the North Vietnamese to believe I've reached the point where I might do *anything* to stop the war. We'll just slip the word to them that, 'for God's sake, you know Nixon is obsessed about communism. We can't restrain him when he's angry — and he has his hand on the nuclear button . . . '" The president-elect, writes Haldeman, "saw a parallel in the action President Eisenhower had taken to end another war. When Eisenhower arrived in the White House, the Korean War was stalemated. Eisenhower ended the impasse in a hurry. He secretly got word to the Chinese that he would drop nuclear bombs on North Korea unless a truce was signed immediately. In a few weeks, the Chinese called for a truce and the Korean War ended."

This was Nixon's "secret plan" — to brandish the nuclear stick, to emulate his one-time mentor, Eisenhower. "I decided," he writes in his own memoirs, "to 'go for broke' in the sense that I would attempt to end the war one way or the other — either by negotiated agreement or by an increased use of force. . . . I decided to set November 1, 1969 — the first anniversary of Johnson's bombing halt — as the dead-line for what would in effect be an ultimatum to North Vietnam." From information supplied by one of Kissinger's former assistants to Daniel Ellsberg, it is clear that the nuclear plans were worked out in elaborate detail. Ellsberg reports that the assistant, Roger Morris, saw at least two nuclear targeting folders that were part of the contingency plan for what was called the November option. One called for dropping two nuclear bombs at the border between Vietnam and Laos, another for a low yield air burst at a transshipment center a mile and a half from the Chinese border. A third nuclear bomb, reported by other sources, was to have been directed at a mountain pass. National security director Henry Kissinger, according to Haldeman, did deliver the threats to Russia and China but it didn't work. The Vietnamese refused to budge. Morris was assigned to write a speech for Nixon, to be delivered November 3, 1969, announcing a major escalation of the war.

If Nixon's willingness to resort to limited nuclear war seems bizarre, it was really not out of character with the approach of his predecessors. Eisenhower, as Haldeman noted, threatened to use nuclear weapons in 1953 against China and North Korea "if there was not going to be an armistice." The following year, when French forces were surrounded by the Vietminh at Dienbienphu, John Foster Dulles offered French foreign minister George Bidault three atom bombs, one to be dropped on Chinese territory near the Indochina border and two against the Vietminh at Dienbienphu. Four years later, when there was doubt that Chiang Kai-shek's Nationalists could hold on to two islands, Quemoy and Matsu, near the Chinese mainland, the American Joint Chiefs considered using nuclear bombs to defend them; otherwise, said the Chiefs, they would fall.

A few years later, during the Laotian crisis of 1961 the Joint Chiefs again recommended using nuclear bombs — against Laos in the first instance, and if necessary North Vietnam and China. That same year, according to Arthur Schlesinger, Jr., everyone in the highest echelons of government "agreed that we might eventually have to go on to nuclear war" to allay the Berlin crisis. There was disagreement over timing and intensity, but no one was "foreclosing the option" of using atomic weapons. In 1962, of course, there was the October missile crisis, in which the danger of total nuclear war was made explicit by the Kennedy administration. Then, in 1968, when the Marine base at Khe Sanh was surrounded by the North Vietnamese and the National Liberation Front, President Johnson queried the chairman of the Joint Chiefs of Staff, General Earle Wheeler, on whether he would have to use nuclear weapons to hold that base; and General William Westmoreland, as stated in his memoirs, formed "a small secret group" in Saigon to study the contingency of "nuclear defense of Khe Sanh." He reasoned that "if Washington officials were so intent on 'sending a message to Hanoi,' surely small tactical weapons would be a way to tell Hanoi something, just as two atomic bombs had spoken convincingly to Japanese officials during World War II."

Nixon's secret plan obviously was in accord with plans made by his predecessors in similar situations: they considered The Bomb as the weapon of last resort. Nixon himself alludes to the urgency of speed in getting the war ended — either through negotiations or "an increased use of force." "One reason for making this decision," he writes, "was my feeling that unless I could build some momentum behind our peace efforts over the next several weeks [after the end of June], they might be doomed to failure by the calendar. Once the summer was over and Congress and the colleges returned from vacation in September, a massive new antiwar tide would sweep the country during the fall and winter." Nixon, however, backed off. The November 3 speech that was to have announced the escalation was scrapped in favor of one appealing to "the silent majority" for support. The plan was placed in limbo, as another White House assistant at the time, Jeb Stuart Magruder, reports because the president was alarmed over the immense nationwide Moratorium demonstrations on October 15 and the New

Mobe Washington march and rally scheduled for November 15, which also was expected to be massive. This was one demonstrable instance where the antiwar movement impeded an expansion of hostilities that would have taken many thousands of lives.

But if Nixon did not go all-out to nuclear attack he refused to let the war be "lost"; the minimum he would settle for was a Korean-type stalemate in which the North Vietnamese and National Liberation Front forces withdrew north, and Vietnam was divided into two permanently separate nations. A "peace proposal" made on May 14, 1969, illustrates this point. The president offered to withdraw U.S. troops over a 12-month period simultaneous with North Vietnamese withdrawal. The popular impression was that Nixon meant *all* U.S. troops. What he actually proposed, however, was to bring home "*the major portions*" of the American military contingent. At the end of twelve months "*the remaining*" soldiers "would move into designated base areas and would not engage in combat operations." In other words, 300,000 to 350,000 American men would be sent home, but 200,000 or 250,000 would be holed up in Vietnamese enclaves — perhaps for decades, as in Korea. The inevitable result of proposals such as these — unacceptable on their face — was that the fighting continued, and grew bloodier. Nixon withdrew troops regularly after mid-1969 — 60,000 by December 15 — yet American casualties were substantial, 15,000 dead in the first three years of his administration, and Saigon's troop and civilian losses even greater than in the previous three-year period. In two years and a few months after Nixon took office, the tonnage of bombs dropped on Indochina exceeded the tonnage used by the U.S. in the European and Pacific theaters during World War II. Clearly the war was not winding down: the incremental withdrawal of American troops was more than compensated for by an accelerated air war. After a brief honeymoon, then, millions of Americans who had given Nixon the benefit of the doubt originally were once again disenchanted. They were grist for the biggest antiwar demonstrations in American history.

II

None of us in the National Mobilization Committee of course were privy to Nixon's nuclear plan, but we were certain he would continue the war into the foreseeable future. What divided us was how soon the American public would see through the Nixon charade. Dave Dellinger and Rennie Davis took the optimistic view; they proposed a Counter-inaugural to challenge Nixon immediately, confident that large numbers would respond. Sidney Peck and I were more negative — or realistic, if you will. The public, I said, would give Nixon a period of grace to put his "peace plan" into effect. "If we try to bring people to the streets for the January inaugural," I argued, "they will be lost in the crowd, and attract little attention. There will even be a certain resentment against us for interfering with what is considered a hallowed American ritual. But in six, eight, or ten months many people will have lost faith in Nixon and we will be able to bring hundreds of thousands into the streets."

Peck and I were outvoted and the Counterinaugural proceeded as planned. On Saturday, January 18, 1969, educational workshops were conducted in Washington on a panoply of subjects; on Sunday, January 19, there was a small parade on Pennsylvania Avenue and a Counterinaugural Ball in the evening featuring rock music and entertainment. On Monday, the pivotal day when the new president was sworn in, movement people spread out on the sidewalks along the line of the inaugural parade, chanting slogans and hoisting antiwar signs aloft. The number of participants was small, perhaps 10,000 or 12,000. Worse still, in that state of affairs some substituted adventurism for numbers. A few of the smaller radical forces, including a dissident group of Yippies called Crazies and elements in the SDS (which was being taken over by ultraleftists and Maoists) planned a confrontation to disrupt the inaugural *physically.*

National Mobe disavowed that strategy, sticking to the usual pledge of nonviolence, but the groups committed to havoc were not to be dissuaded. They interrupted speakers at the Mobe rally (demanding "action"), they seized the

Mobe headquarters during the Counterinaugural Ball (only Dellinger's patience in negotiating with them prevented a riot), and under the guidance of a group called Coalition for an Anti-Imperialist Movement (Co-Aim) they tried to crash the presidential motorcade itself. When that degenerated into meaningless shoving and pushing (there were large numbers of troops with rifles and bayonets, not to mention large numbers of police, ready to quash anything more serious) they dispersed through downtown Washington turning over garbage cans and breaking windows. Had our numbers been substantially larger these childish games would have gone almost unnoticed; as it was they stood out. A few weeks after the demonstration I asked Stewart Meacham of the American Friends Service Committee to call together a caucus of pacifists (and semipacifists like myself) so that we might strengthen the nonviolent contingent in Mobe and act on our own occasionally. The caucus, which adopted the uninspired name National Action Group (NAG), projected thirty Easter demonstrations for 1969.

For the rest of that year, it was a game of cat and mouse between the antiwar elements and Richard Nixon. The administration pretended we were irrelevant; "under no circumstances," said Nixon, would he be influenced by what the movement did. But constant efforts were made to disrupt our functions. At the end of March the Department of Justice in Chicago secured indictments under the Civil Rights Act of 1968 against Dave Dellinger, Mobe's chairperson, Rennie Davis, Tom Hayden, Jerry Rubin, Abbie Hoffman, Bobby Seale of the Black Panther Party, and John Froines and Lee Weiner. They were charged with "travelling in interstate commerce to incite a riot," subject to sentences of five years in jail on each of two counts. The indictment was, to say the least, bizarre. To begin with, why these eight? Froines and Weiner had played no role in the leadership of Mobe — in fact I had never heard their names until that time. Neither had Bobby Seale, his only involvement so far as I know being a speech he made during convention week in 1968. Dellinger was the last person in the world to incite violence; Davis had had his own head cracked open by police; Hayden was — and is — a strategist, not a riot leader; and Hoffman and Rubin were actors and mischiefmakers (in court Hoffman gave as his place of residence the "Woodstock Nation," and when asked where it was, replied that it was "a state of mind") but not warriors.

The flimsiness of the government's case was underscored by a conversation I had in my home with a police spy named Erwin Bock. We knew Bock, an infiltrator into Veterans for Peace and the Chicago Peace Council, was a spy, but we were waiting for definitive evidence to expose him publicly. "Erwin," I said, "the government says that we trained our marshalls to use violence at the Democratic convention. You were one of the people trained. Did anyone give you instructions to provoke violence?" "No," he said, "definitely not, on the contrary we were taught to prevent violence." I had Bock go down to a movement lawyer, Irving Birnbaum, and swear an affidavit. I'm sure that what he said to me privately was entirely true, but on the witness stand during the conspiracy trial he disavowed what he told me, claiming he was forced to give this affidavit in order to not blow his cover.

The trial, which began in late September 1969 (Judge Julius Hoffman, a prejudiced tyrant if I ever saw one, refused to postpone it even though Seale's attorney, Charles Garry, was scheduled for a gall bladder operation), consumed the energies of two of the antiwar movement's key people, Dellinger and Davis. More than that, however, it was meant as a warning to all of us that organizing a peace demonstration could be dangerous to one's health and security; it would lead to indictments, trials, and perhaps convictions for nothing more than engaging in a constitutionally guaranteed protest. Nixon and his attorney general John Mitchell both knew that nothing more was involved, but they operated on the thesis that repression and disruption would immobilize us. (After the conspiracy indictment the government tried many other ploys. For instance, in August 1969 Mobe received a letter from a so-called Black United Front of Washington, demanding $25,000 as part payment for allowing an antiwar demonstration in "our" city. The letter provoked an argument between Dellinger and Davis, on one side, who wanted to pay the group something, and Peck and myself, who were adamant against it. Two years later a former FBI agent, Robert Wall, exposed the fact that the letter was composed by the FBI and that those who presented it to us were FBI plants. Fortunately, a black politician and Mobe supporter, Julius Hobson, set our committee straight on the Black United Front and the idea of paying tribute was finally rejected.)

The conspiracy case ended in conviction of five of the defendants on one count, but even that was overturned by the appeals court; Bobby Seale was first gagged and chained in the courtroom for insisting on his own lawyer, then was severed and freed in a separate trial; the vast majority of the contempt of court citations by Judge Hoffman were overturned after an appeal, and even those that were upheld did not result in jail sentences. The whole case was so raw that the judicial system would have been tainted beyond measure if it had sustained Hoffman's decisions.

The spring demonstrations in 1969 were fired up and large, as many as 100,000 in New York, 40,000 in San Francisco, 15,000 or 20,000 in Chicago, even 4,000 in Atlanta and 1,200 in Austin, Texas. Our National Action Group affairs, too, were better attended than expected, and what gave all the rallies a special flavor was the participation of active GIs, members of the armed forces openly flaunting their officers by showing their aversion to the war they were being asked to fight. All of this, however, was prelude to the big events of that year. We didn't know that Nixon had set himself a November 1 deadline to win a negotiated settlement or implement the Madman Theory. But we sensed that fall would be a critical time.

On July 4 and 5, therefore, National Mobe held its national conference at Case Western Reserve University, where Sid Peck was teaching, to make final preparations for the fall demonstrations. The antiwar forces by now were so sizable that delegates attended by invitation only, rather than in response to a general call. The evening before, a twenty-four-member steering committee met to discuss agenda, action recommendations, and so on, and as happened so often in our ranks the coalition almost sundered. Dave Dellinger and Rennie Davis had brought to the meeting Mark Rudd and Kathy Boudin of SDS, who informed us they planned a national protest in Chicago concurrent with the opening of the Chicago conspiracy trial, and regional activities in November. There was also a Trotskyite proposal for a mass demonstration in Washington that would specifically exclude the kind of civil disobedience we engaged in during the 1967 march on the Pentagon. My own feelings were with the Trotskyites as to the locus of our action — Washington — but with Dellinger and Davis for trying to involve SDS. After heated debate on what to do, when it looked like we might wind up with two conferences, I put forth a simple motion that Mobe undertake both activities — in Washington and Chicago. The idea carried overwhelmingly, and though the Trotskyites demurred a bit they decided to go along. Fred Halsted, in his book on the antiwar movement entitled *Out Now,* sometimes praises me, sometimes taunts me for what he calls "Lens' penchant for patchwork unity," but it is a fact — perhaps due to so many years at the collective bargaining table — that I had a knack for suggesting compromise formulas. One of the Congressional internal security committees called me "the peacemaker of the peacemakers." It didn't mean I was even-tempered, but I was sometimes able to cool down the tempers of others — as in this instance. Doug Dowd, an economics professor at Cornell, who was also co-chair of Mobe, solved the problem of a new name by proposing we call ourselves the *New* Mobilization Committee to End the War in Vietnam.

The next day the conference itself adopted the proposals — but not without additional wrangling and still another "unity" resolution from my fertile ·pen. Jerry Gordon, chairing the final session on behalf of the host city, left us all with a sour taste when he thanked me for the unity efforts, but denounced the rest of the leadership for conducting the meetings undemocratically. I reflected as I heard him that the movement usually comes through united for action, but only after leaving burrs on our psyches.

As it happened the Chicago action dribbled down to a minor affair. Dowd, Rennie Davis, Sylvia Kushner, and I met with Kathy Boudin and Terry Robbins of the Weathermen — as they were then called — to work out a common program for the planned demonstration in October, but it was clear from the outset we couldn't see eye to eye. They were decent people and not at all "riotous" in their personal relations, but what they were thinking about, as one of their Weathermen leaflets put it, was "recruiting an army . . . that's gonna fight against the pigs . . ." We were not only opposed to that sort of thing in principle, but we were mandated to organize a *large*, all-encompassing demonstration that was nonviolent. The Weathermen — in this and other meetings — indicated they wanted to build a select "anti-imperialist" movement, with the aid of black and third-world groups such as the Black Panther Party, Young Lords, and Young Patriots, whereas Mobe's objectives were to build an anti*war* movement, not necessarily limited to those who thought the war was "imperialist." SDS material called for "fighting in the streets," "busting people out of jail" under the theme "Bring the War Home." Even its style changed, with a liberal sprinkling of four-letter words.

The Weathermen held their "days of rage" from October 8 to 11, with 200 or 300 of them rampaging through an upper-class district in Chicago called the Gold Coast, smashing automobile windshields, tossing rocks at windows, over-turning trash cans. The next day an even smaller number gathered at Haymarket Square, site of the 1886 bombing during a working-class meeting that is commemorated all over the world as May Day; they marched a mile or two, then tried to break through police lines to commit more vandalism. I spoke to some of the young women afterward; they were in tears and absolutely terrified — it was their first attempt at "revolutionary violence." All-told there were a couple of hundred arrests (with a total bail set at about $2 million), many people beaten up, and absolutely nothing accomplished. I remonstrated with two of the participants "you broke the windshields of a number of Volkswagens; were they the limousines of the big bourgeoisie you were after?" In the aftermath some of the Weathermen leaders under indictment for rioting went underground to establish an illegal organization; except for a few that have come up to face trial and return to a normal life, they are still there as this is written. Allegedly, Terry Robbins was blown up while fabricating bombs at someone's home.

New Mobe's only action in Chicago that fall was on October 25 when we held a rally at Civic Center in support of the Chicago 7, on trial at the federal court house a few blocks away. It, by the standards of the day, was a relatively small affair, with perhaps 5,000 in attendance. I chaired the meeting and most of the conspiracy defendants came to speak during the luncheon recess in the court room. Fred Hampton, of the Black Panther Party in Chicago, substituted for Bobby Seale; this was, I believe, the last time he spoke publicly before being gunned down by Chicago police while he was asleep in his apartment in the predawn hours December 4. The incident remains a cause celebre, for although the police were freed of criminal charges, a civil suit for millions in damages is still pending.

The focus of New Mobe's organizing efforts in 1969 turned to the fall offensive — October 15 and November 15. In July, at my insistence that the Washington project be directed by a pacifist, we designated Ron Young of the Fellowship of Reconciliation for the job. Tall, handsome, dedicated, Ron was an excellent choice. He had initiative and he got along well with almost everyone. He moved to Washington to take on his new duties, joined in the ensuing weeks by Sid Peck, Dick Fernandez (founder of Clergy and Laymen Concerned), Trudi Young, Rennie Davis, Brad Lyttle, Fred Halsted, Stewart Meacham, and Susan Miller (who headed up a special staff organizing the March Against

Death), and in the last few weeks myself and a few others, supplemented by Abe Bloom, Alice Arshak, and a host of people from Washington, D.C.

III

From October 15 through November 15 — just one month — more people in the United States demonstrated against war than at any time in American history. The people who had been willing to give Nixon a chance earlier in the year were now out of patience. So deep did the disaffection go that it even penetrated the sport of football. One of our Mobe leaders in Ann Arbor, Michigan, Gene Gladstone, told me one day that there was going to be an antiwar action at the next University of Michigan football game. I didn't think football and peace were natural allies, but sure enough 15,000 people leaving the game that day joined in a march from the stadium to the campus where they heard speeches by Dave Dellinger and Sid Peck. The same spirit evidently caught on with the whole liberal milieu. The protest forces were now ready and willing; they only had to be mobilized. At our July conference a young man named David Hawk reported to the delegates about a pending Vietnam Moratorium — and asked for Mobe's endorsement and participation. It was an ingenious proposal, suggested in late spring by a long-time Boston peace activist, Jerome Grossman, to declare a moratorium on "business as usual" Wednesday, October 15, then increase it to two days in November, three days in December, and so on, "in order that students, faculty members, and citizens can devote time and energy to the important work of taking the issue of peace in Vietnam to the larger community." Most demonstrations were held on weekends, to ensure the largest possible turnout. But the Moratorium was scheduled for midweek when everyone would be at school or at work, requiring in effect that participants engage in a strike. Many unions that supported the Moratorium decided to "strike" symbolically, for a few minutes, or by conducting a meeting during lunchtime, or "by observing a one minute silence for peace." But at colleges and high schools the strike was to be real. Among the suggested activities for these strikers were "town meetings, debates, anti-war rallies," canvassing of homes, talks with "opinion-makers," leafletting, vigils, study groups in churches or homes, showing of antiwar films in downtown theaters, petitions, teach-ins. Businessmen and professionals were asked to "give employees an hour off for peace," observe a minute of silence, talk with other businessmen, "run ads in papers stressing the economic impact of war." The proposal was so simple and so direct it caught on like prairie fire.

The four young people who took charge of the Moratorium program were veterans of the presidential campaign of Senator Eugene McCarthy in 1968, and remarkably competent. Hawk had been a student at Union Theological Seminary and a staff member of the National Student Association so that he had many hundreds of contacts in academia. Sam Brown (later an official in the Carter administration) had also been a divinity student at Harvard. He was the one approached by Grossman, and he usually acted as Moratorium's spokesperson. Marge Sklencar, a truly fine administrator, had been president of a student union at — I believe — a Catholic college in the Chicago area. David Mixner, the fourth member of the team, came from a university back east and was then working with Senator George McGovern on the Democratic Party reform commission. They were a lively bunch, these four, particularly Hawk and Sklencar, of whom I was especially fond, and I'm sure they had pushed McCarthy a few notches further to the left than he originally intended to go. None had been active with Mobe — though Hawk participated in the 1968 Chicago action — but life was pushing them toward a position similar to ours. "Ending the war in Vietnam," said the Call for a Vietnam Moratorium, "is the most important task facing the American nation. . . . Few now defend the war, yet it continues. Death and destruction are unabated; bombs and fire continue to devastate South Vietnam. Billions of dollars are spent on war while the urgent domestic problems of this country remain unattended. Moreover, the war has had a corrupting influence on every aspect of American life, and much of the national discontent can be traced to its influence."

The Moratorium staff, unlike Mobe's, was not responsible to any steering committees or conferences; it was a movement, so to speak, unto itself. But it had links to the entire liberal community, including the Americans for Democratic action, Walter Reuther and the UAW, senators like McGovern, representatives like Don Fraser; and, though Sam Brown always seemed to be uneasy with Mobe, it utilized our resources to the fullest. In scores of cities we and the Student Mobilization Committee (SMC) were all there was of Moratorium, and in many others, as in Chicago, we were its linchpin. Prior to October 15 — throughout September — Ron Young, Sid Peck, Dick Fernandez, and myself spoke at universities in sixty cities, coast to coast, mobilizing for both autumn actions. (Indicative of the change in mood on the campus by then was a comment by right-wing commentator M. Stanton Evans during a debate with me at one of these colleges: "I know everyone here will agree with Mr. Lens; I simply appeal to you to give my point of view a fair hearing." How times had changed! Earlier in the decade — when I debated Buckley for instance — peaceniks were as rare at such meetings as needles in haystacks. Now it was the other way around; it was hard to find a hawk in most schools.)

On the appointed day, the response to the Moratorium was phenomenal. As *Life* put it "a display without historical parallel, the largest expression of public dissent ever seen in this country." No one kept a tally but there must have been demonstrations and school strikes in at least a thousand communities, perhaps more; and the number of participants, we estimated at the time, was 2 or 3 million. Even in Salt Lake City, by no means a liberal mecca, 5,000 people showed up for a rally; in Boston 100,000; in New York — for various actions — at least twice that number; in Chicago — where a state legislator, Robert Mann, and I chaired the rally at the civic center — about 10,000.

Numbers alone can't convey the significance of this event. Nixon's henchmen were wont to disparage our numbers (even if we brought a million people to the streets, they said, it was only half of one percent of the population). But there was in addition to the size of the crowds the *quality* of commitment, the faces of young men and women looking toward the beautiful tomorrow. Even in strict numerical terms the Moratorium was something of a miracle if you consider that the vast portion of the population never takes a political position. On November 3, Nixon referred to a "silent majority" that supported his war effort, but if it were really true that most Americans were quiescent it certainly wasn't because they favored the war. One could tell from a hundred different things that the antiwar sentiment had permeated a decisive part of the population. There was the philosophy professor at a New York university who told me he began every class with a fifteen-minute discussion of Vietnam; there were the Moratorium committees formed at every major newspaper in New York, at TV stations, publishing houses, among secretaries and lab workers at the Massachusetts Institute of Technology, workers throughout government agencies in Washington. There were the antiwar buttons on scores of thousands of lapels and dresses, the peace symbols on automobiles. There were the many actors, actresses, singers, entertainers, artists — from Leonard Bernstein to Candy Bergen — who were willing to perform gratis for the movement. Very few of such people were political pundits, but they had sensitive emotional antennae that picked up the national mood. Candy Bergen, for instance, was the star attraction for our money-raising affair at Hugh Hefner's mansion in Chicago the evening of the Moratorium, aimed at bailing us out of a deficit. (Alas, I personally couldn't attend because feminists had put a picket line around the place in protest against the sexism of Hefner and his *Playboy* magazine. Though I disagreed with that tactic, particularly for that occasion, I wouldn't cross a picket line.) At every one of our affairs now there were nationally known entertainers — Phil Ochs; Peter, Paul and Mary; Mitch Miller; Shirley MacLaine; Tony Randall; Janis Joplin. Only self-delusion accounted for

Nixon's belief that he still had a mandate to carry on hostilities.

IV

On the morrow after the Moratorium Monsignor Charles O. Rice, Stewart Meacham, and I, as the labor committee of Mobe, sent a letter to dozens of leading unionists around the country urging them to bring their members to Washington November 13 to 15, and above all to send "desperately needed funds." We were heartened by the events the day before but we couldn't be sure how the next action would turn out. It was, to begin with, a far more complicated affair logistically. The Moratorium took place where the participants lived. But a Mobilization in Washington with people coming from all fifty states required extensive travel — 4,000 chartered buses, in addition to trains, and many thousands of automobiles. Hundreds of thousands of dollars had to be raised in the communities to finance those who couldn't afford to pay their own way. Thousands of housing units had to be found for those who intended to come early for the March Against Death and stay over for the big rally. Then there was the recruiting and training of 4,000 marshalls — responsibility of Brad Lyttle and Fred Halsted — a staggering task. So was the installation of public address systems, rental alone costing $10,000. Hundreds of money collectors had to be selected, trained, and provided with boxes. Then there were such mundane problems as portable toilets for a crowd expected to be a quarter of a million (rental of so many units would have bankrupted us; the government was finally forced to provide them), walkie talkies (twenty-four of them) to facilitate communication between chief marshalls, twenty-four bull horns, and the painting of thousands of banners, signs and placards. To a lesser extent, all this had to be duplicated in San Francisco where Mobe was holding a second parade and rally for those who didn't want to travel cross country.

Another factor we had to consider was whether popular enthusiasm for a second major antiwar action could be regenerated in so short a period, thirty days. We had never done it before; the time gap was usually four to six months. On the other hand we had more momentum to build on than in previous years — especially if we could enlist the help of the Vietnam Moratorium team. They had headquarters in the same building as Mobe — 1029 Vermont Avenue in Washington — and of course we knew them well. But the first joint meeting with the four young people and some of their older supporters failed to win an endorsement for November 15. Stewart Meacham gave me the impression it had been a wild session; he asked me to come to the second one to massage injured egos. The Moratorium leaders were worried about the "tone" of our rally, its radicalism, the danger of violence — essentially, that Mobe might offend the middle class audience they were currying to. I pointed out they they would have speakers representing their view, would carry their own posters, and could be as moderate as they liked. I also told them that groups that might be prone to violence had given us assurance they would not embarrass Mobe.

After a while, just as in collective bargaining negotiations, I could "feel" Joe Duffy of Americans for Democratic Action and Congressman Don Fraser (D.-Minn.) coming around. I typed up a brief memo in which each side agreed to support the actions of the other and establish committees of liaison to "make both sets of action monumental successes." The New York *Times* reported next day that "the leaders of the two antiwar organizations that are planning separate demonstrations for mid-November [Moratorium, it will be recalled, projected a two-day "strike" for the second month] endorsed each other's plans today and pledged that their protests would be 'legal and nonviolent.'"

Moratorium unfortunately never did organize any further actions (it dissolved in April 1970); the center of attention was on the March Against Death on November 13 and 14, and the big parade and rally the next day. The March Against Death was organized by Meacham, Susan Miller of the Episcopal Peace Fellowship, and a small staff, capitalizing on the growing antiwar sentiment in churches and synagogues throughout the country. As finally projected 45,000 people would walk single file from Arlington National Cemetery across Memorial Bridge to the White House and Capitol. The parade and rally was to be in the traditional mold, from the Capitol to the White House to the Washington Monument, where the entertainment and speeches would take place.

First soundings after Moratorium gave the event its blessings were excellent. Our ranks were firm and united. Symptomatic of that unity was the unanimous approval of "A Call to the Fall Offensive to End the War," a 1,500-word tract I wrote that served as Mobe's basic political document. What was surprising about it was that representatives of churches and moderate organizations, on the one hand, and those of leftist and ultraleftist persuasion on the other, agreed to a document that was explicitly anti-imperialist. It put the Vietnam war within the context of America's foreign policy generally. "The American Empire," it said, "has no intention of giving up its 429 world wide bases . . . nor its policing of the world against national revolution. The United States has treaties to defend forty-two nations, and secret military agreements to defend two dozen more, including fascist and semifascist governments such as those in Spain, South Korea, Greece, Thailand, Bolivia, Jordan, Brazil, Iran, Taiwan. . . . The fact is that the United States has become the bastion of counter-revolution, the ally of scores of corrupt and reactionary regimes. . . . Why is Washington so interested in these dictatorial governments around the world? The answer lies in trade and investment." The tract, distributed in scores of thousands of copies, called on America to "Stop the War," "Stop the War Machine" by ending the arms race, and "Stop the Death Machine" by aiding "the poor and hungry, the Black and Brown communities, the sick, the cancer victims of air pollution, the accident victims of automobiles — free us all to live, to love, and to run our own lives."

At the office on Vermont Avenue things were running smoothly — as smoothly as they can in the chaos of incessant telephone rings, committee meetings, cranking mimeograph machines, arrivals and departures of friends from Bloomington and Madison. Fred Halsted and Brad Lyttle were arranging the logistics. Ron Young, Sid Peck, and Dick Fernandez were negotiating for permits (with the help of Lyttle and Halsted), as well as handling routine matters such as responding to out of town requests and raising money. Cora Weiss, with the help of Peter Yarrow of Peter, Paul, and Mary, was assembling an outstanding corps of entertainers. It all seemed to be going quite well. But two dark clouds began to hover over the undertaking. One was the issue of violence. White House aide Dwight Chapin prepared a long memo for Nixon laying out the scenario for checkmating Mobe, "to isolate the radical leaders of the 'Moratorium' event and the leaders of the 'Mobilization' committee. They are one and the same and their true purpose should be exposed." Leaving aside the infantile reading of the politics of our two antiwar forces, the administration was determined to "isolate" us. Among the techniques Chapin worked out for the president was to approach Congressional moderates asking them to withhold endorsement of the November events — a ploy that worked exceptionally well. Until almost the end only one representative, Allard Lowenstein, sanctioned the use of his name — sixty-five had done so for the Moratorium. Senator George McGovern did not decide to participate in the Mobilization until November 10, five days before it took place.

The major reason for standing aloof was the universal fear that the rally would end in tempestuous violence. At every step of the way the administration and members of the press spread the word, directly or by innuendo, that Mobe could not control the forces in its ranks who intended to explode on November 15. It reached the point where every press conference we held — usually daily — was dominated by questions such as "How can you guarantee that your followers won't cause riots over the city?" On November 10, we flew in Dellinger, Rubin, and Abbie Hoffman from the Chicago trial to counteract, at a press conference, the "fears of violence raised by Attorney General Mitchell" and his staff. They gave assurances that a small demonstration they intended to hold at the Justice Department "will conform to the legal and nonviolent discipline the anti-war coalition has established." We even had a Weatherman leader advise all and sundry "that we intend to abide by the non-violent principles you [New Mobe] have established for your November 13–15 actions." None of this, however, did much good; the question of violence kept coming up at press conferences and in news stories that emanated from the conferences — all I'm sure orchestrated from the White House and Justice Department. At one press meeting — held at the Ambassador Hotel on 14th and K — I burst into anger at Clark Mollenhoff of the Des Moines *Register:* "Why the hell don't you ask the man who is really committing violence, Richard Nixon, whether he intends to continue the massacres in Vietnam? If all of us on this podium lived a thousand years we couldn't perpetrate as much violence as Nixon does in one day. Ask your questions of him, not us." We cut off all queries on the subject from then on, but an insidious thought was planted in millions of minds, that it was dangerous to come to Washington. (Strangely enough this was at approximately the time that Seymour Hersh, a free-lancer who wrote for a publication to which I also contributed, the *National Catholic Reporter,* exposed the massacre at My Lai, where most of the 739 men, women, and youngsters rounded up were slaughtered point blank by American GIs for no apparent reason.)

Still the effort to picture Mobe's leaders as raving and irresponsible revolutionaries continued to the end. On October 30, Vice President Agnew read us out of polite society: "When the President said 'bring us together' he meant the functioning, contributing portions of American citizenry," which presumably we weren't. Mitchell appeared on TV to defend Agnew's characterization of antiwar demonstrators as "effete snobs," and defined them as "active militants who want to destroy . . . some of the institutions of our government." On November 3, Nixon made his long-expected TV appearance; this was to have been the occasion for announcing escalation of the war. Instead he fed the nation rhetorical fare for avoiding "defeat and humiliation." The "popular and easy course," he said, would be to get out, but that would "inevitably" be followed by "massacres" by the communists throughout the world. And in conclusion the President warned that there were two types of Americans, a "minority" who were trying to force their views on the nation "by mounting demonstrations in the street" and a "silent majority" who supported his as yet unrevealed plan for peace. I wrote a press release in answer to Nixon, and as I typed away I was confident the speech had helped us. As it turned out, however, it did considerable harm, for it portrayed the movement as flaunting majority will.

A second problem was the impasse our people were having with Attorney General Mitchell and his staff in securing a permit to march on Washington's main artery, Pennsylvania Avenue. Mitchell was willing to let us parade on streets where no one would see us, but he, Kleindienst, and John Dean were adamant about Pennsylvania Avenue. Every day or two, our attorney Phil Hirschkop and Ron Young would report no progress, and the mere hint that there was trouble about the parade route fed anxieties outside Washington about violence. In the early days it seemed that we would have to scrape for buses to bring people to the city. I called Harold Gibbons of the teamsters and asked if he couldn't use his influence with bus companies to get us more vehicles. We thought then that our goal of assembling a quarter of a million people could be met handily. But as the insinuations of violence continued, inflamed further by the controversy over permits, we received calls from our constituencies outside Washington advising of cutbacks and cancellation of buses. The mood at the office turned from radiant to apprehensive.

Mitchell, however, stuck to his guns too long; he turned out to be our best ally, for in the minds of hundreds of thousands — including some of the timid figures in Congress — the issue was no longer simply antiwar, but in addition civil liberties. Some respectable people might hesitate about linking themselves to radicals to protest against a war, but they would rise to the occasion in defense of constitutional guarantees of freedom of assembly. Overnight the mood turned around full circle. Dozens of prominent citizens came to our defense, scores of members of Congress added their names to our lists and sought passes to the 2,000 seat VIP section we erected at the rally site. George McGovern, Gene McCarthy, Senator Charles Goodell, a Republican, closed ranks behind us, as did thirty-eight prominent people, including John Kenneth Galbraith, Arthur Schlesinger, Jr., Henry Steele Commager, Mary McCarthy, Lewis Mumford, and Hannah Arendt, who placed an ad in the New York *Times* of November 12 condemning "suggestions emanating from the Administration that exercise of these constitutional rights [of assembly and petition] is an irresponsible means of influencing policy. . . . We believe that the obligation of the American government is to protect these American citizens in their desire to protest lawfully and peacefully." Attorney General Mitchell's blunderbuss tactics had turned things around for New Mobe. We fielded phone calls from supporters again begging for buses; the whole situation was reversed. During one of those hectic times when our telephones were hours from being cut off (because we were tens of thousands of dollars behind in our payments) Fernandez, Peck, and I got on long distance and raised $45,000 in half an hour.

Even the media gave us more sympathetic attention. A piece in the November 13 New York *Times* began with a prophetic call by me for Nixon's impeachment: "If there were a Congressman Thaddeus Stevens alive today, President Nixon would be impeached, Sidney Lens told a group of reporters today in the ninth-floor headquarters of the New Mobilization Committee to End the War in Vietnam." That was an idea we wanted very much to put across, that Nixon was in violation of the Constitution. *Newsweek* ran a piece correctly picturing us as "more radical than the organizers of last month's moratorium," but conceding that we had subordinated "ideology to the larger goal of staging the big parade." That too was an image we wanted to project. The picture of Cora Weiss, Ron Young, Sid Peck and myself that went with the article conveyed the same impression, that we were a sane and sensible group, not at all like the bomb throwers and rock throwers we had been portrayed as before.

V

At 6 P.M. on Thursday, November 13, Judy Droz of Columbia, Missouri, widow of Navy Lieutenant Donald Droz, killed in action in the Mekong Delta seven months before, conducted a memorial prayer to begin the March Against Death. Twelve widows and next of kin as well as thousands of others lined up behind Ms. Droz — a beautiful woman with a round, solemn face — each wearing a placard with the name of someone killed in action or a devastated Vietnam village, and walked quietly, single-file, lighted candles in their hands, through the Washington mist. Two and a half hours later the first contingent, having passed the White House and called out the names on their placards, presumably to get the message to President Nixon, were at the end of the trail, at the Capitol. There they deposited the name cards in twelve big caskets that would be carried in the parade Saturday. Not far from Ms. Droz were Ben Spock and Rev. William Sloan Coffin, who were scheduled to chair the rally November 15. I waited with Steward Meacham and Susan Miller for a couple of hours before joining the procession that moved along a four-mile route, involved 45,000 people and took forty hours to complete. It was the most moving antiwar action I have ever been in; hundreds of people dabbed tear-stained eyes, as the silence of the march evoked memories of lost husbands, fathers, children, or the toll of dead in a faraway country. The March Against Death ended as the parade was about to begin.

Bright and early Saturday, November 15, I arrived at a relatively empty Mobe office to prepare for the festivities that day. Bernard (Bud) Nossiter, a Washington *Post* reporter whom I had met at the home of I. F. (Izzy) Stone, the legendary left-wing journalist, was waiting for me. Sylvia

Kushner, secretary of the Chicago Peace Council, was also waiting. I asked her to mind the office, assisted by Pat Richartz, also of Chicago, as Nossiter (who was assigned to traipse after me) and I went to pick up another Mobe co-chair, Doug Dowd — one of those good-humored people who exudes joy. Doug and his wife had come in only the night before, and though he wanted to see the festivities, he agreed readily when I asked him to monitor events at a government building — I think it was the central police station — along with representatives of the White House. They were to receive reports from police and others, and Doug was to communicate anything untoward to me. As much as I hated to confine Dowd it was a fortunate choice that may have prevented another of those police riots for which the 1960s became famous.

At the assembly site near the Capitol, large numbers of people were already milling about, indicating that despite temperatures in the low 30s the crowd would exceed our expectations by a wide margin — as the Washington *Post* put it, "easily the largest antiwar crowd ever assembled in the United States." The March Against Death ended at 8:30 A.M. and a brief memorial service was held. Eugene McCarthy gave a short talk and we lined up for the parade. Leading us in a dazzling white suit was Cora Weiss, marching backward, giving instructions to marshalls. In the first row was Coretta Scott King, flanked by McGovern and Goodell (who were less shy about coming to the fore now), myself, Dave Hawk, and Stewart Meacham. Behind us was a mass of humanity, intense, eager, determined, yet good-natured, carrying banners and signs by the scores of thousands, shouting slogans when called upon by the marshalls. "One, two, three, four — Tricky Dick, end the war"; "Ho, Ho, Ho Chi Minh, NLF is gonna win." The signs reflected the spontaneous ingenuity of youthful minds: PEACE IS PATRIOTIC, ANOTHER SILENT AMERICAN FOR PEACE, SPIRO EATS GRAPES, HO CHI MINH WAS A JEFFERSONIAN DEMOCRAT, I'M A SPOCK BABY, NOT ONE MORE DEAD, THE WORLD WILL LONG REMEMBER WHAT WE

DO HERE TODAY, PULL OUT, TRICKY DICK, THIS WAR IS UNHEALTHY AND INSANE, PEACE, PEACE, PEACE, SEND SPIRO BACK TO GREECE. The contingents represented cities, functional groups such as unions (and Business Executives Move for Peace in Vietnam), colleges, leftist political parties, the Student Mobilization Committee, Veterans for Peace, Vietnam Vets for Peace. Up front were the twelve caskets, carried by pallbearers, and somewhat further back a handsome black man weighted down by a big cross.

So massive was the crowd that there were still tens of thousands waiting to parade when the rally was set to begin; they were asked to come directly to the thirty grassy acres at the Washington Monument. It was impossible to find anyone once you lost sight of him or her, or to get to the front where improvised stands housed VIPs, newspeople, and others with passes. It took Shirley more than an hour to get there, and my teen-age cousin, Louis Okun — treasuring the pass I had given him — never made it at all.

We had the usual four or five brigades of speakers — Coretta King; Goodell; McGovern; Gibbons; Dave Dellinger; David Hawk; Julius Hobson; Ossie Davis; Howard Samuels; Nobel laureate George Wald; some GIs; three or four leftists of various hues; and three chairpersons, Coffin, Spock, and Dr. George Wiley of the National Welfare Rights Organization. But Cora and Peter Yarrow had put together a package of entertainment that made even a few of the duller speeches tolerable. There were four casts of *Hair;* John Denver; Dick Gregory; Mitch Miller; Arlo Guthrie; Pete Seeger; Peter, Paul, and Mary. Every so often Mitch Miller or Pete Seeger would lead the hundreds of thousands in song. It was weeks before I stopped humming the tune "Give Peace a Chance." The mood was at once serious and electrifying; everyone, I'm sure, felt a unique sense of community. Even Jack Mabley, the *Chicago Today* columnist who had written a scurrilous column about me in 1962, told me later he had been immensely moved. Richard Nixon's press agents let it be known that the president was too busy to watch the festivities, but he too must have gotten the message. "It was the best, it was the biggest, it was the last of the antiwar demonstrations," wrote Nicholas von Hoffman in his syndicated column. "If it cannot convince the men who make war and peace they can't safely go on with the conflict, then no amount of marching, praying or singing will change their minds." Alas, it wasn't the last, but it was certainly the biggest. Our estimate — made by Brad Lyttle from airplane pictures — was that 800,000 people were present. Mabley told me later that the Air Force had made a scientific count from their own photos of 780,000. Columnist Mary McGrory called it "the greatest gathering in American history"; Attorney General Mitchell, according to wife Martha, said it reminded him of the Russian Revolution.

Late in the afternoon, while another *Hair* cast was entertaining, I called Doug Dowd from my direct line below the stage to find out if it were safe to send everyone home. There were still a few hundred thousand people present. Dowd said there was a problem. A couple of thousand people, led by Dellinger, Jerry Rubin, and Abbie Hoffman, had assembled at the Department of Justice to protest the conspiracy trial. Mobe had been wary of this plan throughout — fearful that despite Dellinger's best efforts there might be a small riot — and therefore had refused to endorse or organize it, though we did assign marshalls to protect it. The number wasn't large, considering what it had to draw from, and it was not unruly except for a handful who broke a few windows, threw a paint bomb, and ran a flag up the Justice Department's flagpole. Had the police left it to Mobe's marshalls it would easily have been contained. The men in blue, however, tossed tear gas at the crowd sending it scurrying hither and yon. If the hundreds of thousands still at the Washington Monument were to be dismissed at this point, both Doug and I feared there would be a major confrontation and perhaps a police riot. I went back to the stage and asked the *Hair* cast to continue singing for another thirty or forty minutes — until Doug gave me the all-clear sign.

As dusk settled over the city we all dispersed, tired but

euphoric. There had been hundreds of demonstrations in synchronization with the one in Washington, all over the world, some large like the one in San Francisco (100,000 people), some smaller like the one in London which drew a thousand people, some tiny like the one in Wheaton, Illinois, where 200 gathered. A poll of 17,128 persons by the Chicago *Sun-Times* in the Chicago area — hardly a bastion of liberalism — showed that 59.4 percent wanted the U.S. to get out of Vietnam by December 1970, 19.2 percent to "withdraw our troops as the South Vietnamese appear ready to carry on the fighting," 2.4 percent to continue as at present, and only 18.7 percent to step up military pressures.

VI

As the 1970s opened, both the Nixon administration and the antiwar movement were carried by previous momentum toward another inevitable clash. Unbeknownst to the public the Pentagon had conducted 3,630 B-52 bomber raids on a neutral country, Cambodia, in the fourteen months after March 1969, in an effort to destroy what it claimed was the command center of the NLF — the Central Office for South Vietnam (COSVN). The original project, suggested by General Creighton Abrams based on "hard intelligence" that COSVN headquarters were "in Base Area 353," contemplated 60 sorties, which by ordinary standards was more than enough to put the central office out of existence. But the idea was evidently so appealing — bombing defenseless areas — that Operation Breakfast was followed by operations "lunch," "snack," "dinner," "dessert," "supper" until it was a mammoth undertaking, requiring a complex procedure to hide it not only from the public but from top military and government officials.

On April 29, 1970, the coordinating committee of Mobe was meeting in the living room of Cora Weiss's home in the Riverdale section of New York, when Cora excused herself to take a call from someone on the New York *Times.* We were considering Mobe's winter-spring offensive, based on a draft plan I had written which decentralized activities, focussing on the communities (rather than Washington) and at a different target every month. The information Cora transmitted from her newspaper source, however, pushed the decentralized campaign into the background. Nixon, she was told, would announce an invasion of Cambodia by American and South Vietnamese forces the next day. Just a week and a half earlier he had said he would withdraw another 150,000 troops within the next twelve months. A stunned Mobe coordinating committee voted to conduct a protest rally at the White House on May 9, ten days away.

When Nixon announced the invasion of Cambodia on April 30, 1970, the campuses erupted as never before. According to a study by the Carnegie Commission of Higher Education, 350 colleges and universities were closed down by student-faculty strikes, and 200 more by action of their presidents. Four million students — more than half the nation's college enrollment "hit the bricks," so to speak, not to mention high school and grammar school pupils. After the Ohio National Guard murdered four students and wounded eleven more at a Kent State antiwar rally on May 4, clashes with the authorities reached such proportions that the National Guard was called out to quell disturbances at twenty-one institutions of higher learning. A thousand lawyers, many from solid Wall Street houses, made the pilgrimmage to Congress to press the case for peace. No one had taken to the barricades and the demonstrations were still educational, not revolutionary, yet as Max Frankel observed in the New York *Times:* "America was a nation in anguish last week, her population divided, her campuses closed, her capital shaken, her government confused, her President perplexed." Thirty-seven school presidents sent Nixon a letter pleading that he end hostilities.

Within the administration, Secretary of the Interior Walter Hickel compared Nixon to King George of England, who, in 1776, also refused to listen to "youth in its protest." Two hundred and fifty State Department employees signed a petition to Secretary of State William Rogers decrying the invasion, and James Allen, Commissioner of Education, was applauded by 400 of his employees when he openly criticized the president's Cambodia decision. The night of the Kent State killings Nixon was so anguished over the state of affairs in his government he made fifty-one phone calls from 9 P.M. to 5 A.M., eight of them to Henry Kissinger. Kissinger later commented that the president had been "on the edge of nervous breakdown." It is an axiom of the American form of government that when a president loses popular support he loses leverage with Congress, and his ability to rule is hobbled. Letters, phone calls, petitions to members of Congress gave them pause about following the president blindly, and encouraged them to chart an independent path. Nixon's anxiety flowed from an understanding of this process.

I didn't attend the May 9 demonstration — I left for Paris to speak at a similar event — but I helped Peck, Lyttle, Halsted, Ron Young, Trudi Young, and others prepare for it. In the process, I wrote two statements to be read from the podium, a Bill of Indictment and a Pledge of Action, which I think reflected the embittered mood of the protestors and most American youth. "We who assemble here in Washington on May 9th, representing the majority of democratic opinion in the United States," said the indictment, "charge Richard Nixon and the Nixon Administration, with the following crimes, malfeasances, misfeasances, and misdemeanors." Then followed the specific items: "violation of Article 1 Section 8 of the Constitution (placing the right to declare war in the hands of Congress alone), violation of Article 2 Section 4 of the U.N. Charter," "violating the Geneva Agreements of 1954 and 1962 . . . by bombing Laos, sending in more than a thousand troops and advisors," "financing the Khmer Serai and other rightist forces in the Republic of Cambodia," invading Cambodia, "imposing a fascist regime on South Vietnam," repressing dissent, subverting democracy at home, imposing "involuntary servitude" on 3.5 million members of the armed forces "for the sole purpose of defending the interests of the military-industrial complex, and to further imperialist expansion." It concluded with a demand "that you, your vice-president and your cabinet resign immediately and place yourself before the bar of American opinion for appropriate action." The Pledge of Action stated that "We, who assemble here in Washington May 9th . . . will under no circumstances serve in the war in Indochina, and if we are not subject to the draft we will advise all young people of their right to refuse such service." We also pledged to work for a cut-off of funds for the war, to boycott the class of any professor associated with the Pentagon, AEC, NASA, CIA, "or any private corporation associated with the war machine."

From all reports there were between 100,000 and 125,000 people present and things went smoothly, except that the planned civil disobedience at the White House by a couple of thousand participants was poorly organized because of internal friction and resulted in minor violence and a few hundred arrests. There were considerable numbers of people protesting elsewhere in the United States and, in fact, throughout the world. I was one of the main speakers at the great rally just outside Paris that was twice the size of the one in Washington — 200,000 people. (I intended to read the speech in French, but everyone agreed my accent was so unique few people would understand me. Instead I read the first paragraph in English, an interpreter read the full text in French, and I finished with the last paragraph in English.) On the program, too, was Xuan Thuy, North Vietnamese ambassador to the peace talks with the United States; when the two of us embraced there was an explosion of whistles, cheers, and clicking of cameras. This was a symbol of what the world wanted — peace between two peoples.

The assemblage in Washington at the time of the Cambodian invasion was the last large one in 1970. Even before it took place, Nixon announced that the allied incursion would be limited to twenty-one miles beyond the border, and that the troops in Cambodia would be withdrawn within three to seven weeks. The national temper cooled slightly with this definition of objectives, and, while it did not prevent the outpouring of May 9, it narrowed the focus of hostility subsequently. Moreover this was the midterm Congressional election year, which soaked up energies that would otherwise have been used in antiwar work.

It would be wrong to measure the effectiveness of the peace movement in terms of its big Washington demonstrations. A sampling shows an enormous amount of small actions, some involving a handful of people, some a few thousand. There were a dozen defense committees at work at any given time, defending freedom for the Seattle Eight, for instance, charged with conspiracy to provoke riots; or a Committee for the Defense of Professor Sidney Peck, who was accused of two counts of aggravated battery and two counts of resisting arrest for his role in the 1968 Democratic Party events and faced twelve years in jail and $20,000 in fines. Amongst the most publicized cases were those of Catholic activists who poured blood on draft records or burned them — the Berrigan brothers (Phil and Daniel — both priests), Jane Kennedy, the Milwaukee 14. In early 1972, the federal government brought to trial Phil Berrigan, his future wife, Elizabeth McAlister, Eqbal Ahmad — all friends of mine — and four others on the ludicrous charge of plotting to kidnap Henry Kissinger and bomb government underground facilities in Washington to put the city out of commission. (The vast majority of civil liberties cases, incidentally, turned out in our favor.) Then there was a significant increase in activities by second-level trade unionists: 100 union members in San Francisco placed ads in the newspapers calling on colleagues to "stop work, stop war" on Wednesday April 15, 1970. Dick Liebes of my national union (Building Service) and Anne Draper of the Amalgamated Clothing Workers, an old friend of mine, formed a particularly effective San Francisco–Bay Area Labor Assembly for Peace, and their efforts were duplicated — though not quite as successfully — in a dozen other communities. Labor Against the War in Minneapolis held a public indoor rally with me giving the main talk. A Teachers Committee for Peace in Vietnam was formed in New York. Dave Livingston and Al Evanoff of District 65, and Moe Foner and Leon Davis of Local 1199 in New York were conducting a host of antiwar educational activities for their members.

Unlike the Old Left of the 1930s we didn't establish schools to study peace issues, but we did publish ads in newspapers (a Sunday New York *Times* full-pager, June 7, 1970, was headlined IT'S 11:59 P.M.), and innumerable brochures and leaflets. Material prepared by Harry Chester of the UAW for Mobe's labor committee (Lens, Meacham, Peck) was transformed into leaflets and distributed to tens of thousands of workers. It made graphic what the war was costing each community: "As an example, the figures show that metropolitan New York has 11,450,000 people . . . and that it contributed more than a billion and three-quarters dollars for the Vietnam war each year. With that money the people of New York could have built 88 fully-equipped hospitals with 88,000 beds; or 125,000 low cost housing units (at $14,000 a unit); or 44,000 school classrooms (at $40,000 a classroom)."

Then there was the continuing antidraft resistance — turning in of draft cards, picketing draft boards, sabotage of the registration process by sending all kinds of irrelevant material to be placed into individual draft files, or, on the more militant side, pouring blood and setting fire to draft records. There were campaigns by some in support of appropriation bill amendments by Senators Mark Hatfield and George McGovern to withdraw all American forces from Indochina by 1971, and there were attempts to put the issue of withdrawal on the ballot in various cities — as an expression of public sentiment. By the latter part of 1970, these referenda were turning decisively in the movement's favor: Detroit voted almost 2 to 1 for getting out; a complicated poll in Massachusetts showed absolute majority for planned withdrawal, more than a third for immediate withdrawal, and a bare 15 percent for fighting on. An immediate withdrawal proposal carried in San Francisco by 108,000 to 103,000, and in Marin County by a slightly better margin.

On Hiroshima Day — August 6 — there was the usual

spate of small vigils and rallies commemorating the first nuclear tragedy. I took advantage of the fact that this was the twenty-fifty anniversary of the destruction of Hiroshima, to pressure President Nixon to declare August 6, "a national day of mourning and concern." It received considerable publicity, but no response from the president. Then there were the press conferences and statements in response to government harassment. In December an undercover agent of the U.S. army, John M. O'Brien, admitted spying on a dozen people, among them Senator Adlai Stevenson, former Governor Otto Kerner, Jesse Jackson, Staughton Lynd, Bobby Rush of the Black Panther Party, and me. We issued a few statements and conducted a number of small protests. Then of course there were the picket lines placed around Nixon and Agnew wherever they went. We had at least three or four in Chicago that year, at one of which I was arrested for leading pickets onto a forbidden street. There were, in addition, actions to keep alive the memory of Martin Luther King. One year Jack Spiegel and I teamed up with the Reverend Jesse Jackson of Operation PUSH to organize a parade on Chicago's State Street commemorating the date of King's assassination. A majority of America was clearly opposed to the war by now, and a good part of that majority was showing its displeasure in a hundred different ways.

Still, Nixon and Kissinger (who had been meeting secretly with the Vietnamese adversary since 1969) were determined to continue the war until they could arrange a solution without American "humiliation" and without defeat. The Vietnamese, I'm sure, wanted as desperately as Kissinger to find a facesaver for Washington. On February 8, 1971, I had a private three-hour meeting in Paris with Xuan Thuy, one of the two North Vietnamese peace negotiators, and one of the items we discussed was this question of saving face. The ambassador had just received separate communications, he told me, from the two best-known American senators, suggesting that Hanoi ship American prisoners of war to a neutral country, such as Sweden, as a gesture of good will. What did I think of the request, Thuy wanted to know. "If we do it," he asked, "will that make it easier for the American administration to come to an understanding?" Over and over he stressed that Hanoi did not want to demean the United States; I think he recognized that if it did, the time would come when Washington felt so shamed it would be *unable* to retreat. Under any circumstances, Thuy stated — as I paraphrased it in a press conference when I returned home — "We have tried to do good on the prisoners of war issue, and every time we have been castigated for it. We released nine prisoners. Later, when there was a clamor to issue the names of the prisoners, we issued the names through leaders of the antiwar movement. . . . Then we released the names through Sen. Edward Kennedy and Sen. J. William Fulbright, and were charged again with bad faith." Yet Hanoi was ready, I'm convinced, to do any number of things to guarantee withdrawal without humiliating the United States. My advice on the prisoners was that Hanoi ought first to get an assurance from Nixon that this would lead to the end of the war — "otherwise you're giving up a queen without getting so much as a pawn." He thought about that for a while and changed the subject, but I think North Vietnam would have eagerly complied with the senators' request if it could have been convinced that it would shorten hostilities.

VII

At home, meanwhile, a split took place in the peace movement. Perhaps it was frustration, perhaps impatience, perhaps a sectarian bent on the part of some, but toward the middle of 1970 a schism became apparent in the ranks of New Mobe. One segment — a majority that included Peck and Dellinger — held that Mobe should transform itself into a multi-issue movement, seeking thereby to incorporate into the coalition black civil rights organizations, consumer associations, welfare groups, feminist forces, unions, and others. This was a natural extension of the "working proposal" I had written after the November demonstrations, which stated that "instead of appealing to an undifferentiated mass on a high political level, New Mobe in addition will appeal to specific major constituencies on a self-interest level. Those constituencies will include GIs, workers — in and out of trade unions — consumers, the student-scientific milieu, political prisoners." As a corollary — to shake the tree more — it also favored a step-up in civil disobedience. Within this element stood Rennie Davis — a bit off to the side but with a large following on the campuses — who felt that the movement should actually try to prevent Washington from functioning if it didn't stop the war. Rennie was not talking violence or revolution, but his outlook called for something more than traditional civil disobedience. On the other side stood Jerry Gordon and the Trotskyites who felt Mobe should remain an antiwar group and continue to assemble big demonstrations as a combined tool for education and protest.

Politically I was with Peck and Dellinger — we ought to try, I felt, to broaden the coalition, even though experience showed that the domino theory didn't always work in protests. I favored experimenting with the multi-issue approach, while continuing with large nonviolent antiwar demonstrations. I certainly didn't think a split in New Mobe was necessary and it probably would not have taken place but for the manipulative manner in which the Trotskyites functioned. In any case, by September 1970 there were two organizations in existence, one to which I subscribed, with the unwieldy name, National Coalition Against War, Racism and Repression (NCAWRR), and the other, presided over by five coordinators, with Jerry Gordon as its key figure, called National Peace Action Coalition (NPAC). Gordon wrote me a three-page letter and spoke to me privately about taking on the task of trade union coordinator for NPAC, but while I could have been comfortable being in both coalitions I couldn't repudiate old friends and comrades. I went back to my unofficial role as peacemaker. I attended NPAC conferences, took the floor, spoke primarily to their leaders, and on a number of occasions was able to smooth over differences with our group. In the end NPAC and NCAWRR (which changed its name to Peoples Coalition for Peace and Justice) joined hands in the biggest action of the next two years, another turnout in Washington late in April 1971.

In the prelude to this new outburst, Nixon first tamped down protest — then inflamed it. In addition to withdrawing troops he made still another peace offer on October 8, 1970, reshuffling the language but adding nothing new to previous so-called peace offers. North Vietnam and the Viet Cong — which Nixon, like Johnson, always referred to as part of the North Vietnamese forces — would withdraw above the dividing line, leaving the country to the tender mercies of General Thieu and American "advisors," while negotiators continued talking — perhaps for twenty years or more, as in Korea. Nonetheless the proposal did have an impact on many Americans. Nixon could say he had made offer after offer but the other side wasn't bending. Within a few weeks, however, the pendulum began swinging the other way. On November 20, the administration resumed bombing North Vietnamese cities. In early February 1971, almost concurrent with the third American landing on the moon, an invasion of Laos was executed by the South Vietnamese army, aided by American air strikes, including B-52s to "interdict" Hanoi's supply routes. This was to be a test presumably of "Vietnamization," but alas it turned into a fiasco. By mid-March the Saigon forces had been disgracefully routed, hundreds of American helicopters had been lost, and for the third spring in a row an American-inspired offensive had failed.

This glaring setback was a major factor, I believe, in the enormous outpouring of people for the Washington demonstration of April 24. Jerry Gordon, functioning out of an eighth-floor office at 1029 Vermont (ours was on the ninth), did an excellent job of pulling the forces together. PCPJ (Peoples Coalition for Peace and Justice — the group I was with) was a partner in the undertaking and was the primary planner of the peripheral activities, such as demonstrations at the Department of Justice and helping the recently formed Vietnam Vets Against the War. But NPAC (Gordon's organization) had the main responsibility for the big event. Communication between the two floors was not always cordial; there were the inevitable disputes over speakers, program, chair, finances, but this time there were two separate organizations, making resolution more difficult. Nonetheless, the more than half a million people who attended thrilled to an inspiring event. There were considerably more unionists present this time than two years previously, as punctuated by the fact that two labor officials, Abe Feinglass of the Amalgamated Meatcutters and Dave Livingston of the Distributive Workers, acted as co-chairpersons. There were also more minority groups and veterans on hand. Entertainment was trimmed down a bit, but speeches by the likes of Bella Abzug, Coretta King, Ralph Abernathy, Harold Gibbons, Puerto Rican socialist Juan Mari-Bras kept the adrenalin flowing. I never did get a clear report of what happened in San Francisco but as I understand it a quarter of a million showed up there in what was indisputably the biggest antiwar manifestation the city had ever seen.

Preceding April 24, for five days, Vietnam veterans held the media's attention. Organized into a new group called Vietnam Veterans Against the War (VVAW) more than a thousand ex-soldiers engaged in a project they called Operation Dewey Canyon III, a mocking parody on the Laotian invasion that the Pentagon had dubbed Operation Dewey Canyon II. Ragged, dressed in fatigues, bearded, encamped a hop and skip from the Capitol they slushed through the halls of Congress telling members about war crimes they themselves were involved in; they play-acted "search and destroy" missions with dummy guns; held a silent march led by legless veterans; and in an exceptionally moving performance one day hurled medals and decorations they had won in combat at the domicile of America's legislative branch. They were a colorful lot, shouting, yelling, crying, and they received reams of publicity. One of their leaders was a clean-cut young chap named John Kerry, a former navy lieutenant, whom I had met in Chicago while helping Murray Finley organize a meeting in Chicago on his behalf. Speaking to a congressional committee he expressed the hope that Vietnam, instead of being an "obscene" memory, might turn America around to a new course.

In the aftermath of April 24, the stage was set for Rennie Davis and the May Day Tribe "to stop the government." In collaboration with the PCPJ, the action began on Saturday May 1 with sit-downs and sit-ins by groups of a few hundred (mostly pacifists) at Selective Service, HEW, and the Justice Department, leading to the usual arrests. In the evening there was a thundering rock concert that attracted a crowd of 50,000 young people. The main event, however, was on Monday, May 3, with about 16,000 participants. The PCPJ contingent walked toward the Pentagon prepared for arrest there — but they never got across the 14th Street Bridge. The police attacked and the crowd disintegrated. The May Day Tribe, however, along with some PCPJ adherents, dispersed into mobile units, each trying to block traffic on a pivotal artery. Seven thousand people were arrested that morning, many of them simply snatched off the streets because they looked young — including, according to Fred Halsted, "an army lieutenant, an off-duty cop, a law professor, a Washington *Star* reporter, numerous businessmen, and even a couple on their way to get married." David McReynolds of the War Resisters League described the scene to Halsted this way: "There was tear gas all over the city, there were helicopters flying around. The May Day action was totally ineffective but the police managed to gas a large part of the population of Washington."

Thousands more were hauled off to jail the next day when PCPJ held a noon rally at the Justice Department. Years later the courts would rule this roundup of 12,000 citizens illegal and order payment of damages, but even though Rennie's planning left much to be desired, the government's response alienated millions of liberals who took the Constitution seriously. Davis and John Froines were indicted for conspiracy again, but nothing came of that. A few years later Rennie left the movement to join the religious cult of Maharaj Ji. I liked Rennie, but I'm afraid he had a messianic notion of what we could accomplish in 1971. (In an inscription to a book on Guru Maharaj Ji he gave me in October 1973, he wrote: "Sid, no one knows better than I how incredible this all sounds. 'The Lord is on the planet and we're about to see the greatest change in human history.' It's totally unthinkable. But really, this is something you should stay open to.")

Though local antiwar actions continued to attract 5,000, 10,000, 25,000, 40,000 (in November 1971, for instance), the movement never mended its rift and never again brought large numbers of people to the streets — on the scale of November 1969 or April 1971 (though a Counter-Inaugural on January 20, 1972, still drew 100,000 or more). But the virus of "creative discord" had now penetrated the military goliath itself. The American armed services, as Stuart Loory and David Cortright showed in their books on the subject, were undermined from within. Their morale deteriorated; large numbers — many hundreds of thousands — became addicted to drugs; "fragging" of officers occurred so frequently it could no longer be considered incidental.

Throughout the year 1972, tensions mounted and tempers flared, in tempo with what can only be considered political hysteria on the part of Richard Nixon. To be sure, he gained immeasurably and was assured re-election by his visit to China that year — after twenty-three years in which the State Department refused to acknowledge the existence of that august land. But the mining of the harbor of Haiphong, the off and on aerial bombing of Hanoi, including the most vicious attack of all, after Henry Kissinger had made his famous statement during the election campaign that "peace is at hand" — all this reflected vengefulness more than strategy. The administration was, for all practical purposes, simply striking out blindly, trying to check a debacle. To all this both Hanoi and the NLF responded militarily and PCPJ and NPAC (sometimes separately, sometimes in unison) responded with habitual demonstrations — including a march in Washington after the mining of Haiphong.

In the end Nixon had to get out anyway. The terms of the

agreement negotiated by Kissinger with Le Duc Tho and Xuan Thuy were somewhat worse than the offer I had brought home from the Vietnamese in Stockholm back in 1967. American troops were totally withdrawn in exchange for prisoners held by Hanoi. But North Vietnamese troops remained on South Vietnamese soil, along with the NLF; and a few years later they took over the whole country. At the same time, the Lon Nol client regime was ousted by the Khmer Rouge in Cambodia. The United States had lost the war, completely and abysmally. Worse still, the war had brought to the surface a metastasizing cancer that had previously festered subsurface — the cancer of an empire in dissolution.

Chapter 12
Trauma of the 1970s

I

The two spates of radicalism in my lifetime have spurted in response to crisis issues — an economic depression in the 1930s and an unpopular war in the 1960s. When the pall of the Great Depression began to lift, the American left, with the exception of the communists who carried on for another decade, disintegrated. (The communists were a special case, in that they metamorphosed from ultraleftism, to piggy-back reformism — on Roosevelt's back — and then turned into active advocates of a popular war.) Similarly, the radicalism of the 1960s fattened on an unpopular war (and to an extent on the civil rights crusade); but once the war was over fell into steep decline. In radical politics, a single issue can act as a fuse. But when the fuse burns out, so does the radical movement. The American spirit is pragmatic, not philosophical; perhaps that is true of all countries but it definitely is here.

When the Vietnam war ended, the ranks of the Peoples Coalition for Peace and Justice melted away. "There is need for PCPJ to exist in this crucial period when we are faced with the bloated military budget, the corruption in government, growing inflation and the relation of all these issues to the vital needs of the American people who are angry and looking for solutions," lamented the PCPJ interim committee when it dissolved on April 30, 1974. "But, in spite of many appeals, we have not received the necessary funds and personnel to keep the organization going. . . ." It became apparent that what we called "the antiwar movement" was really a melange of three elements — a relatively small number of leftists, old and new; a larger number of young people of the counterculture who reacted to events emotionally, not politically; and tens of millions who were antiwar because the United States was losing. When the war was over, the third group just dropped away; the second either melted into the established order or went back to the independent existence — and hedonism — of its predecessor of the 1950s, the beatniks. Only the first group remained, but its ranks too were decimated by weariness and the usual schisms that have harried the Leninist left in times of regression — much like the breakaways within Trotskyism in the 1930s. There must have been at least a dozen splits in American Maoism alone, perhaps twice that many; and there were not a few of our anti-Vietnam activists, like Tom Hayden and Jane Fonda, who decided that social change would have to come from within "the system," rather than from without.

After January 27, 1973, when an agreement was finally signed between the adversaries in Vietnam, the leading figures who had sired New Mobe, PCPJ, and NPAC dispersed to the four winds. Most of them remained in what is loosely called the movement, but not as a unified force. Ron Young left the Fellowship of Reconciliation, where there had been friction over his position for unqualified American withdrawal, to become national peace secretary of the American Friends Service Committee — a promotion of sorts. His predecessor in that job, Stewart Meacham, accepted AFSC assignments in Asia for a few years, then retired to Honolulu. Dave Dellinger, after winning reversal of the conspiracy case decisions, began publishing, with a few associates, another movement magazine, *Seven Days.* Sid Peck resumed teaching sociology in Boston and Doug Dowd, economics in the San Francisco area. Norma Becker and Dave McReynolds remained in place as guiding forces of the War Resisters League, but the Fifth Avenue Peace Parade Committee, which Norma headed, faded away. Cora Weiss, after a while, put her considerable energies to work raising funds, through an organization called Friendshipment, to aid the people of Vietnam. Dick Fernandez went to work for religious and community institutions. Jerry Gordon left the legal profession to become a full time union organizer. Brad Lyttle returned to Chicago to earn a Ph.D. Richie Rothstein and Paul Booth went to work for unions. Fred Halsted stayed where he was in the top echelons of the Socialist Workers Party. Rennie Davis, as already related, joined the cult of an Indian guru. John Froines took a state, then a federal, job in his scientific field. Dave Hawk wound up with Amnesty International and Sam Brown as state treasurer in Colorado, then as director of ACTION in Washington. Tom Hayden moved to the West Coast, married Jane Fonda, and made an unsuccessful — but surprisingly strong — run for the U.S. Senate. Hayden's comment that "the radicalism of the 1960s is the common sense of the 1970s" was obviously self-serving, but it represented the view of a fair number of his peers — though not mine.

My own life changed minimally. I was still employed part-time by my union — until the beginning of 1976 when my local merged with another and I retired. I continued to publish books and articles; I traveled a little outside the country, but extensively on lecture engagements inside; and I sponsored or formed a number of groups to grapple with what I felt were America's most urgent problems.

The 1970s, like the 1950s, were a period when a radical could only hold on and wait for the next leftist surge. It was not so difficult this time, however, because there was no revival of McCarthyism; on the contrary America won the fight against an incipient dictatorship by driving Richard Nixon from office.

II

My writing in the eleven years from 1969 through 1979 focused on ideological and strategical items I felt the left had long neglected. Of the seven books I published in that period four were on what I called "the underside of American history," two on the arms race, and one on the strategy of revolution. What prompted the volumes on the "underside" of U.S. history was the realization that the Old Left had saturated Americans with foreign heroes and ideas originated by foreigners, leaving the impression there was nothing revolutionary worth emulating in the American past. How much easier would it be to proselytize, I thought, if the left hailed heroes of the American underclasses and ideas born in the United States. Our forebears, for instance, had fought for a half or three quarters of a century against the chartering of limited-liability companies (corporations); why not refer to that element in the American tradition as one of the justifications for challenging capitalism rather than, or in addition to, the rational critique of *Das Kapital*? Another example: the Old Left always pointed to Lenin and the Russian Revolution as the broad guideline for future revolutions elsewhere, but never adopted Sam Adams and the American Revolution as examples to emulate. Yet there was little difference between Lenin's and Adams's strategy — if it weren't for the fact that Lenin probably hadn't heard of Sam Adams one could even say that the father of the Russian Revolution had cribbed from the father of the American revolution. Adams believed in working both inside and outside the established order — he ran for the House of Burgesses but also formed "committees of correspondence"; so did Lenin, his followers stood for the Duma but also built Workers Councils (Soviets). Adams created a dual army, the Minutemen; Lenin had his Red Guards. Adams formed a dual government — the Continental Congress; Lenin, a Congress of Workers and Soldiers Soviets. In all the years I have been in the American radical movement, I have seldom heard anyone in the left refer favorably or even unfavorably to Sam Adams.

There was still another reason for publishing four books on the "underside" of American history. The two postwar generations, it seemed to me, had a weak appreciation of the past — and that includes those who were radicalized. I was flying to a demonstration in Washington one day seated alongside a college student going to the same demonstration who was reading, of all things, a magazine of which I was an editor, *Liberation*. I introduced myself, asked if he read the magazine regularly. Fairly so, he said. Had he ever heard of A. J. Muste, its founder and the "father," so to speak, of the present antiwar movement? No, he hadn't. Norman Thomas? No. Eugene V. Debs? No. He was a history major but he knew nothing of the Molly Maguires (this was before the movie about them came out), the railroad strikes of 1877 and 1894, the Wobblies, only vaguely about Sacco and Vanzetti. For many of the postwar youth, the past was irrelevant; there was no sense of identification with the heroic figures who fought for the injured and oppressed of yesteryear, and little desire to learn any lessons from their struggles. It was as if history was beginning just now, today.

With all this in mind I published four books on the segment of history traditional historians seldom deal with, each from a different angle. The first, *Radicalism in America*, a history of the left in the United States from 1620 to modern times, appeared in 1966 and has been republished a number of times since. The second was a volume entitled *Poverty: America's Enduring Paradox*, which came out early in 1969. It described a twin saga of poverty and the antipoverty programs — which never seemed to catch up with it. I traced antipoverty programs from Queen Elizabeth's poor laws, to the settlement of America by those trying to escape the poverty of Europe, William Penn's Holy Experiment in Pennsylvania, the land distribution during and after the American revolution, the crusade against slavery, the charity and prohibition movement, up to and including the reforms of the New Deal and Lyndon Johnson's War on Poverty. And I indicated throughout that despite all these efforts poverty was still with us, that as one form of poverty faded another came to the fore, as one group of people escaped economic misery another was plunged into it. "There are very few excellent books that contribute significantly to our historical knowledge of poverty in America," wrote Professor Milton R. Konvitz in the *Saturday Review*. "Now we can add to this sparse list *Poverty: America's Enduring Paradox* by Sidney Lens. . . . His book is competently done in a workmanlike style, free of sentimentality or sermonizing, for he knows that the facts are their own sermons." I received the Patron Saints award of the Midland Authors for this work the following year — a check and a plaque for "his social conscience in his writing and personal involvement."

Two years later, in 1971, Thomas Y. Crowell Company brought out the third volume in this series, *The Forging of the American Empire*. It was a chronicle of intervention and planned intervention beginning with Alexander Hamilton's dream of seizing a large chunk of Latin America in the 1790s; the wars against Indians; the snatching of Florida and the attempted acquisition of Canada in 1812; the theft of half of Mexico; the war against Spain; gunboat diplomacy; the two world wars; up to and through Vietnam — all told 160 major and minor wars. It was meant as an antidote to the conventional wisdom that the United States, unlike Britain and France, eschewed imperial expansion.

Understandably, I hit a raw nerve with anti-communist liberals like Arthur Schlesinger. "Suppose," argued Schlesinger in the *Saturday Review*, that "America from the start had been a communist nation . . . does Mr. Lens seriously think there would have been no westward expansion, no slaughter of the Indians, no Monroe Doctrine, no advance into Latin America and the Pacific, no expulsion of threatening nuclear missiles from Cuba." In a letter of rebuttal I wrote: "This scatter shot critique is an interesting defense of imperialism by vulgar anti-communists. The United States is not so bad because the communists would have done the same thing. There is no central focus to our slaughter of the Indians, our 160 major and minor wars, our CIA machinations, our interventions in Cuba, the Dominican Republic and Indochina. Occasionally our motives have been less than exemplary (all nations presumably make *some* mistakes), but essentially we have had to do what we did to keep other greater powers from expanding, and thereby threatening our security. . . . This has always been the apologia for imperialism — though not as well embroidered with 'scholarly' erudition. Senator Lodge, Sr., was more honest with us when he said that 'commerce follows the flag'; and Cordell Hull and Dean Acheson when they said that our problem is how to get rid of our 'surplus' goods and capital; and Ike Eisenhower when he lamented that we might lose the 'tin and tungsten' of Southeast Asia if Indochina went communist."

I wish this sort of debate could have been pursued for it is central to the myth of morality by which many Americans justify wars like Vietnam or the dispatching of marines to the Dominican Republic.

The two other books in this series, both published in 1973, did not stir so much controversy. *Poverty, Yesterday and Today* was a juvenile version of *Poverty: America's Enduring Paradox* for high school students. *The Labor Wars,* commissioned by Doubleday, traced the bitter struggles of the trade union movement from the Molly Maguires of the 1870s to the sit-down strikes of the 1930s. Monsignor Charles Owen Rice, after paying tribute to me personally as a "fine journalist, a rough and ready scholar, and to this day an activist," called *The Labor Wars* "a work of piety, written to show the radical youth of today, that the working class and organized labor met and surmounted even more injustice and violence than the resisters of today There were many Kent States for labor, and when they were over, surviving victims were imprisoned and sometimes hanged for their resistance against tyranny." That was exactly the message I was trying to get across; it was music to aging ears.

III

As of 1973, the American public was no longer responding in significant numbers to the books, articles, vigils, and implorations of the disparate forces called The Left. The one big issue that had excited their interest, Vietnam, was low on their list of concerns. Yet the trauma of America did not abate; it was like a running sore that would not heal.

To begin with there was the economic crisis. The wage and price controls that had been instituted by Nixon in response to a gold drain, a near-record $23 billion budget deficit, and the first trade deficit with foreign countries in more than eight decades, were still in effect; and workers were chafing at the bit because, despite "controls," prices were going up more rapidly than wages. By June 1974, take home pay of a worker with three dependents was five dollars a week less than in 1972 and almost identical to what it had been in 1965. To make matters worse America was experiencing shortages of dozens of items — eggs, steak, gas, blue jeans, candles, freezers, wheat, leather, air conditioners, sardines, paper — as the dollar declined and it became more profitable for foreigners to buy U.S. goods and for American business-people to sell overseas where there were no controls. Large companies, according to *Business Week*, were "seeking alternatives for practically everything — General Foods needs a sugar substitute. Clorox has to find a replacement for soda ash in bleach and so on . . . " Controls had plunged the country into what I called in a *Progressive* article "a shortage economy." "There's a shortage of gas, a shortage of wheat, a shortage of paper," said comedian Frank Darling, "and the greatest shortage of all is the shortage of truth."

The economic trauma was not what the economists call a "readjustment" but a manifestation of structural weaknesses that was long-term. In good times and in bad there was now permanent inflation, unlike the nineteenth century when prices at the end were not much more than at the beginning, and unlike the pre–World War II period when there were still occasional annual drops in living costs. As of 1973, consumer prices had gone up every single one of the previous eighteen years. A combination of administered prices — prices raised in concert by the three or four largest companies of industries such as auto, steel, cereal, rubber — and budget deficits, caused by bloated military expenditures, fed the nation a bitter diet of unending price increases, sometimes running into double-digit figures. Unable to achieve stability, the American economy was becoming what *Business Week* called "The Debt Economy." We were mortgaging the incomes of our children and grandchildren to pay for our own follies today. "The U.S. economy," wrote *Business Week*, "stands atop a mountain of debt $2.5 trillion high," a trillion in corporate debt, $600 billion in mortgage debt, $200 billion in consumer debt—all figures that have increased vastly since then. Keynesian economics, which had ministered to America's economic ills for four decades, had clearly run out of gas. The price of gold—measuring rod of the value of the dollar—which had been $35 an ounce in 1971, had doubled to $70 an ounce in August 1972, and doubled and redoubled again so that by the end of the decade it was ten times as high as it was at the beginning of the decade. Unemployment of 5 or 6 percent of the workforce was now considered "normal"—usually it was higher. By mid-1974 the American economy was experiencing its worst slump since 1938. "Nothing in the years since the end of World War II," commented Nat Goldfinger of the AFL-CIO, "approaches the sharp, precipitous drop in workers' buying power of 1973 and 1974." Richard Nixon, trying to regain a measure of popularity during the Watergate crisis, boldly proclaimed that "there is not going to be a recession," but in 1974 the percentage of unemployed had climbed to 6.1 percent of the workforce and in 1975 to 9.1 percent. And, to confound all the laws of capitalist economics, in the midst of this precipitous downturn prices continued to shoot skyward; they were up more than 10 percent. The economists coined a new word, *stagflation*, to depict the unusual phenomenon of economic stagnation and inflation existing concurrently—a defiance of everything Adam Smith and the classical economists had taught us.

In the summer of 1974, I suggested to Norma Becker, Dave McReynolds, and Bill Douthard of the War Resisters League that the old peace forces ought to do something about the economic crisis. Thus, under their tutelage was born still another of our coalitions, the Coalition on the Economic Crisis. Included in its ranks were not only the traditional peace groups (Clergy and Laity Concerned, Fellowship of Reconciliation, Catholic Peace Fellowship, Women Strike for Peace), but a good sprinkling of others — Barbara Ehrenreich representing the New American Movement; Ben Spock, the People's Party (with which I was also associated); Reverend Bernard Lee, the Southern Christian Leadership Conference; Maggie Kuhn, the Gray Panthers; and a few trade unionists such as Jim Haughton of New York and my old campaign manager when I ran for Congress, Al Kaplan, who was now a national vice president of the American Federation of Government Employees. The Coalition declared its ultimate hope for "changing a system whose primary objective is the maximizing of corporate profits." On the immediate side, plans were formulated for local actions such as town meetings, teach-ins, petitions, street-corner forums, hearings, a national education campaign. Some of these were partly implemented, and many of our people participated in a large Washington rally sponsored by the Industrial Union Department of the AFL-CIO. But we found that neither the working class nor the middle classes felt sufficiently under siege to shake the rafters. Their psyches were not yet saturated with desperation — the "saturation process" I had referred to in my first book, *Left, Right, and Center,* was not yet in play.

The Middle East War which began on October 6, 1973 (on Rosh Hashanah, the Jewish Day of Atonement), when Egypt and Syria attacked across the Sinai and the Golan Heights, revealed two other aspects of the trauma of the 1970s. One was the trigger-close proximity to nuclear war that overlay relations between the superpowers. A dispute over cease fire almost plunged the world into that maelstrom it had been trying to avoid for three decades. The war didn't go too well for the Israeli at first, but sixteen days after hostilities were initiated they finally turned things around, surrounded 100,000 Egyptian troops in the Sinai, and threatened them with annihilation. At this point the Soviets demanded that

Israel observe a cease fire, and when the demand was disregarded, they dispatched ships and planes with nuclear weapons to the scene.

The United States responded on October 24 by placing its armed forces on a worldwide DefCon 3 Alert. DefCon (Defense Condition) 5 is the peacetime condition, DefCon 1 is war. But in the Mediterranean, the Sixth Fleet was placed on DefCon 2, just one step from what could have been World War III, nuclear bombs and all. Americans, by and large, didn't appreciate the danger in the October 1973 crisis — it wasn't as frightening as October 1962 because it ended quickly. But it indicated again how thin was the shield between peace and nuclear engagement.

More visible to the general public at the time was the oil embargo that resulted from the Israeli-Arab war. Five days before the fighting ceased on the Sinai, Arab oil ministers meeting in Kuwait used their leverage against Israel's allies by cutting production 15 percent and threatening to cut it by additional 5 percent increments each month until the Israeli withdrew from the territories seized in 1967. They also imposed an outright embargo on exports to the United States (and the Netherlands).

There had been gratuitous hints emanating from Washington from time to time that the United States would send in the marines if ever its supply of oil were endangered. Certainly Kissinger would not have shrunk from such a move — he later made the threat himself. But with Indochina still in the forefront of national anxiety another invasion would have fired domestic fuses that the Nixon administration might not have been able to contend with. Kissinger's effort to mobilize the industrial states for a buyers' strike were similarly abortive; the Western powers simply refused to hang together on this issue, each trying to run around the other to work out a deal on its own, few willing to make up the shortfall, for instance, for the Netherlands. In the face of American weakness, then, the Organization of Petroleum Exporting Countries, formed in 1960 and only moderately effective until then, took the initiative to extract tribute on a scale never before seen. They increased the posted price by 70 percent in October 1973, another 128 percent on Christmas Eve, and more as the months went by. For a barrel that cost 10 to 20 cents to produce in Saudi Arabia, the world was soon paying $12 or $13, four times what it had been paying previously. Arthur F. Burns, chairman of the Federal Reserve Board, estimated in 1974 that "oil revenues of the OPEC nations will amount to something in excess of $100 billion per year, if their current oil exports and prices are maintained. This is four times as large as the figure for 1973." The enormous drain of income from the industrial states to the less-developed oil producing states (and the multinational oil companies, incidentally) meant that America (and other Western states) would have to produce that much more simply to maintain the old standard of living, and might, in fact, have to submit to a slow decline.

In the United States the embargo and price increase manifested itself in long lines at the gasoline pumps — and bloated profits in the countinghouses of the Seven Sisters (for the first nine months of 1973 Exxon's earnings jumped 59.4 percent, Mobil's 38.4 percent, Texaco 34.8 percent, Standard of Ohio 92.6 percent). Inquiry revealed that the embargo was not as effective as generally thought: the shortfall was merely 3 or 4 percent, easily recuperable from stockpiles. American Petroleum Institute figures, according to the Philadelphia *Inquirer,* showed that from October through December 1973 both crude oil and refined products "were running ahead of the same months in 1972 . . . " But the oil companies exploited the embargo to raise prices, as they were to exploit the Iranian crisis six years later for the same purpose.

Shirley, a few friends, and I — outraged like everyone else — formed a group in Chicago called Citizens Committee on the Energy Crisis. We distributed circulars, put a picket line around Standard Oil of Indiana offices, and published a full-page ad in the Chicago *Sun-Times,* appealing to the American people: "Don't Let Oil Companies and Richard Nixon Make a Sucker Out of You!" Scores of prominent people, including Pat Gorman and Studs Terkel appended their names to an ad that called for nationalization of the industry, and it received an excellent response. It wasn't difficult convincing people in 1973–74 that the oil corporations had manipulated domestic production and had allowed oil refinery capacity to languish in order to bludgeon extra billions from the consumer pocketbook. Unfortunately when the lines tapered down and supplies became adequate Americans adjusted to higher prices, and the Citizens Committee on the Energy Crisis closed its tent. Six years later independent truckers, dismayed over diesel prices and 55-mile-an-hour speed limits, raised the same banner for a government takeover of the oil industry, and in August 1979 the AFL-CIO, no bastion of radicalism, seemed to be leaning in the same direction. Government ownership was fast approaching an idea whose time had come, especially since the energy crisis remained part of the American malaise throughout the decade.

A third element in the trauma of the 1970s was a development that to most people seemed aberrant, unrelated to systemic defects in the postwar system. Watergate was viewed as an unconsummated burglary of Democratic Party headquarters in June 1972, during the Nixon-McGovern electoral contest, compounded by an amateurish criminal cover-up that ultimately caused Nixon to resign rather than face certain impeachment and conviction. For us on the left, however — as I wrote in a memo for the Impeach Nixon Committee, of which I was chairperson — "the burglary and the cover-up were simply a wedge that helped pry open far more serious abuses of the Constitution and our underlying principle of 'government by consent of the governed.' To put it bluntly, the issue of Watergate — the totality of Watergate — was whether the Presidency shall accrue to itself illegal, extra-legal and dictatorial powers." Endemic to Watergate, we felt, was that syndrome of illegality that had marked the behavior of the national security state since its origins in the latter half of the 1940s — the violation of other people's rights by the CIA (in defiance of Article 2, Section 4, of the

UN charter), the violation of its own charter limiting it to activity on foreign soil, and the violation of the rights of American citizens by the FBI, NSA, the post office, the military, through such machinations as COINTELPRO, illegal opening of mail, spying, and similar malfeasances.

"Watergate, in this broader and true sense," I wrote, "revealed that the incumbent President was in the process of establishing a secret police with the power to commit illegal acts (the Tom Charles Huston Plan), that in fact when the Huston Plan was partially pigeonholed, its functions were taken over by the Plumbers. Watergate revealed a whole pattern of 'government by men' — the President and his men — rather than our vaunted principle of government by law. There was the 'enemies' list and IRS approval of Nixon's income tax (which it was later forced to rescind), the deals with International Telephone and Telegraph and the milk producers (trading campaign contributions for political favors). It revealed as well that the Presidency was working feverishly to nullify the other two branches of government — by its secret war in Cambodia (without the knowledge of Congress), by the impounding of funds, by its refusal to divulge evidence on the spurious ground of 'national security' and 'executive privilege.' "

People were a bit puzzled to learn on June 18, 1972, that five men had been arrested for a botched burglary of the Democratic Party headquarters the day before. The New York *Times,* true to its tradition of not sensationalizing news of crimes, buried the story on page 30. As the details of the incident came out — that the burglars had rented rooms in the nearby Watergate Hotel, where $3,200 in hundred dollar bills and a notebook with the name "E. Hunt" (E. Howard Hunt) and the initials "W.H." (White House) were found — some eyes boggled. Despite the best efforts of the Democrats, however, the burglary did not become an issue in the campaign, certainly not enough to make any difference. Nixon's trips to Peking and Moscow and the assurance by Kissinger that "peace is at hand" won the

President a lopsided victory; McGovern carried only Massachusetts and the District of Columbia.

But in the ensuing months many titillating facts came to light about the burglary — transcripts of bugged conversations at the Democratic Party headquarters were carried to an official of the Committee for the Reelection of the President; Hunt and G. Gordon Liddy, implicated with the burglars (four of whom were of Cuban birth), had been employed at one time by the White House; and $25,000 that had been contributed to the Nixon campaign had somehow wound up in the bank account of the chief burglar, Bernard Barker. In January 1973, the Watergate trial began in the U.S. District courtroom of Judge John Sirica, with five of the seven defendants pleading guilty, and the Justice Department dragging its feet on trying to connect the burglary with someone higher up than the burglars themselves. On March 20, 1973, however, James W. McCord, Jr., a former CIA agent like all of the burglars, delivered a letter to Judge Sirica charging that perjury had been committed, evidence suppressed, and political pressure applied on the defendants. It blew the case sky high. Meanwhile — in February — the Senate had voted unanimously to set up a Select Committee, headed by a conservative but charismatic senator from North Carolina, Sam Ervin, to probe abuses during presidental campaigns, including Watergate. For weeks the televised hearings, supplemented by the revelations of two Washington *Post* reporters, Bob Woodward and Carl Bernstein, and the testimony of former White House counsel, John Dean, cast a black cloud over White House disclaimers of criminal involvement, but there were not many people as yet who believed Nixon could be driven from office. It had never happened before, and the general feeling was that Nixon was too slippery to be caught in the net.

While this big drama was being enacted in Washington, a social worker in Chicago, Steve Simon, was circulating a petition calling for Nixon's impeachment. Steve, a cleancut man with an artistic flair, had a penchant for one-man projects. When I saw the petition, I decided to organize a committee to expand what Steve was doing into an areawide effort. I was involved at the time in still another organization I had formed, Chicago Tomorrow, whose purpose was "to initiate actions in solidarity with our Chicago radical and populist community." It was planned to be, as I had conceived it, a Midwestern edition of the Institute for Policy Studies in Washington — doing research, writing, and publishing on the one hand, and conducting teach-ins, forums, and "mass activities," on the other. To house Chicago Tomorrow, its classes and forum, John Rossen (one of the organization's founders) provided us with a large second-floor loft on Lincoln Avenue, rent-free; and here too we set up shop for the Illinois Impeach Nixon Committee. The founding session in the summer of 1973 drew four dozen enthusiastic persons from many milieus. I was chosen as chairperson, Simon as director, and we set ourselves at first the simple task of distributing circulars and soliciting signatures for the impeachment petition. After a while, we formed a group of ten sponsors — among them Al Raby (Chicago's civil rights leader at one time); A. A. Rayner, a former alderman; Don Rose, who years later would manage the successful campaign of Jane Byrne for mayor; Jesse Prosten of the meat cutters union — and published ads in newspapers explaining why Nixon ought to be impeached. Many of my friends felt this was another woolly expedition: "Congress isn't going to impeach a sitting president no matter how crooked he is," they said. "You're just wasting time and money." My feeling was that even if we didn't win the effort had to be made, if only to educate Americans about the illegalities committed by the presidency in their name. As it happened, we were able to do much more than that, and the campaign we undertook in the districts of two Republican members of the House Judiciary Committee, Tom Railsback and Robert McClory, had some influence, I'm sure, on their final vote for impeachment.

Every day or two some of us would take clipboards and petitions to State Street or "New Town," where many young people lived, or Hyde Park, the intellectual mecca of Chicago, to test sentiment; while hundreds of people signed — even lined up, waiting for the opportunity — there were not a few who still hurled insults at us and occasionally threatened to punch us in the nose. But the noose was tightening on Nixon and with each pull sympathy for impeachment grew until it finally seemed to be — even to those who had said we were wasting our time forming a committee — a viable possibility. In May 1973, Congress had confirmed a special prosecutor, Harvard law professor Archibald Cox, to investigate the Watergate crimes. In July Alexander Butterfield, a former White House aide, made the sensational disclosure that Nixon had been taping presidential conversations in the White House from 1971 on, so that there was electronic proof of whatever had happened. Both Cox and the Ervin committee were rebuffed when they tried to secure the relevant tapes from the White House, and when Cox took the issue to court he was fired by Nixon. Attorney General Elliot Richardson and Assistant Attorney General William Ruckelshaus resigned in protest. This "Saturday Night Massacre" evoked a half million bitter telegrams to members of Congress that week, and a wave of protest such as the nation had seldom seen before. The House Judiciary Committee began to seriously consider impeachment hearings, and in the Chicago area the Impeach Nixon Committee was inundated with requests for speakers, leaflets, petitions, buttons, bumper stickers, T-shirts, prepaid postcards, and what have you. At Queens College students organized an Impeachment Fair. New Yorkers held a Screeching Impeach-In — dispersing through the crowd at Times Square on New Years' Eve, shouting "Impeach, Impeach." In Philadelphia there was a tape-in, citizens being interviewed in the streets about their opinion on impeachment, the tapes then sent to Chairperson Peter Rodino of the House Judiciary Committee. Everywhere people signed petitions; in the Chicago area we garnered tens of thousands of names. A month later a national impeachment committee came into existence under the leadership of Ted Glick, one of the people indicted with

Father Phil Berrigan in the Harrisburg case; Kitty Tucker, who would later play a role in the antinuke movement; and Brian Coyle of the New American Movement. Among its first activities were "local actions" January 20, hometown "impeach-ins" in the first half of February, and a Washington "lobby-in" February 4 through 8.

Our impeachment campaign in the Chicago area took on wings before the Saturday Night Massacre when Lynne Heidt, director of a peace center in suburban Evanston, volunteered to work full-time. Lynne was a woman of boundless energy. She transferred the Impeach Nixon Committee office to Evanston, organized scores of house meetings (with the help of Richard Criley of the Chicago Committee to Defend the Bill of Rights), arranged for scores of newspaper interviews, radio and TV appearances. She formed fifty-eight Impeach Nixon Home Headquarters throughout the state, in twenty-two of the twenty-four Congressional Districts, mobilized 2,000 volunteers, held areawide conferences, and led a contingent of delegates from each district to lobby every member of the House from our state in their Washington offices. As the Judiciary Committee hearings began, I solicited $1,500 from a peace-oriented couple back east and Lynne hired a half dozen university students to promote meetings and a letter-writing campaign in the Railsback and McClory districts. These two Republicans were pivotal, in a sense, for the outcome of the House Judiciary Committee proceedings, and, as I said, I think our efforts were useful.

Early in August 1974, Nixon resigned. I recall vividly watching him on TV addressing the White House staff on the morning he left for California. One thing particularly affected me: "My mother," he said, "was a saint." Back in 1963, some months after Nixon was defeated for governor of California and after he had made that famous remark to the press "you won't have Nixon to kick around anymore," I gave a talk at a church in Pasadena, under the auspices of the American Friends Service Committee. Reminding the audience that California had inflicted Nixon on the nation I made a number of disparaging comments about his red-baiting career and his general outlook on politics. Sitting in the front row, unbeknownst to me, was Nixon's mother. At the meeting of the Society of Friends the following Sunday a number of people took me to task in absentia for what I had said about the son of a Quaker. I was told that Mrs. Nixon made the strongest defense of my right to say what I pleased of anyone present. Richard Nixon's mother probably was a saint. I could see in him, as he spoke that morning, a tear forming in his eye, the man who came out of a pacifist background transformed by insecurity, ambition, and greed into a raging militarist and a would-be dictator. I couldn't like Nixon, but the remark about his mother helped me understand him.

IV

Watergate and the economic crisis were *visible* features of the trauma of the 1970s. Citizens were directly affected by them; they related them to their own future. But the most ominous element of that trauma was a danger that for most Americans was *in*visible, the arms race. No one could conjure in the mind's eye the death and devastation of an atomic explosion; and though the thought of one may have been present in the subliminal anxieties of the general populace, few felt there was anything imminent about the problem. No nuclear bombs had been dropped on people or cities since August 9, 1945; three decades of abstinence from nuclear war seemed proof enough that the threat of holocaust was too distant to worry about. As for the antiwar movement — or what was left of it — it was still preoccupied as late as April 1975 with Indochina, fearing a new dispatch of American marines, even as Lon Nol and Thieu were being ousted. Then in mid-May, the new Cambodian regime seized an American container ship, the *Mayaguez,* presumably in Cambodian waters. As usual in periods of tension, Kissinger feared for America's "credibility," and to prove that there was still manhood in the old body, he and President Ford decided to punish the communist regime by indiscriminate sinking of boats around the island of Koh Tang and B-52 bombings of Kompong Som — all but destroying the port, the oil refinery, the airfield and the railroad yard, and hundreds of buildings at a naval base. Some of us were concerned that this might be the prelude to another American landing and we held meetings to prepare protests. Fortunately the *Mayaguez* incident ended quickly with the release of the sailors but not before the Pentagon had lost forty-one men, and forty-nine more wounded in defense of forty sailors who were freed anyway.

Indochina, in a sense, had deflected the antiwar movement from its primary objective — terminating the nuclear arms race — for about a decade. It was only in 1975 that my own energies turned back to that issue. I had been busy with the Impeach Nixon Committee until mid-1974, then with the Coalition on the Economic Crisis, along with a Chicago group in defense of the Angolan revolution, and, of course, the usual articles and books, the normal union activities, and episodic undertakings like raising a few thousand dollars (with the help of Studs Terkel) for Jane Kennedy who was defending herself against the charge of destroying draft records. I wrote some pieces on Mayor Daley, on "socialism for the rich" (outlining the $100 billion plus annual tax breaks and "welfare" benefits for the upper classes), on labor and the CIA, a regular column for the *National Catholic Reporter,* and a theoretical book, *The Promise and Pitfalls of Revolution.* But I wasn't traveling abroad so much anymore — my most recent trips were for a few days in Italy and a week in Kuwait. I had time to ruminate about the arms race — and catch up with my research.

I knew something of the subject, of course. In 1970 I had written a long series of articles for the *National Catholic Reporter* on the "Military-Industrial Complex" and had expanded it into a book by the same title, which was published in a number of countries and had an especially good sale in Japan (it was banned by Franco in Spain). In a page-one review in the New York *Times* book section Harrison Brown called it "a masterful job of describing the diverse elements of the complex . . . which I hope receives the widest possible circulation." But the *Military-Industrial Complex* dealt primarily with the purposes of the arms race and the role of the constituencies that promoted it — the Pentagon, business, academia, labor's hierarchy. It dealt with the nuclear issue only peripherally.

Now in 1975, as I dug into the role of the atom in warfare I realized that I myself, and the movement even more, didn't have a proper appreciation of the urgency of the matter. I mimeographed fifty letters to the key activists I had worked with during the Indochina war — Dellinger, Peck, Norma Becker, Dave McReynolds, Doug Dowd, Art Waskow, Ben Spock, Phil Berrigan, Sandy Gottlieb of SANE, Brad Lyttle, and others. "It seems to me," I wrote, "that in the wake of the administrations's defeat in Indochina, Messrs. Kissinger, Ford, and [James] Schlesinger have developed a new strategy for 'defense' which is more frightening than anything we have ever confronted." The year before, Schlesinger as Secretary of Defense had proclaimed as American policy "restrained counterforce" — or, translated into traditional English, a limited nuclear attack next time there was a "small" war. And there were some in the Pentagon and elsewhere who were beginning to think that with a few new technological breakthroughs (such as a "graser" to intercept Soviet missiles), the United States might be able to mount a full-scale nuclear war against the Soviet Union — and win, if by win was meant a loss of "only" 10 or 20 million Americans. I pointed this out in my letter, as well as the fact that while we had "spent ten years trying to terminate a 'small' war, the bigger problem of the arms race and nuclear incineration had grown far more alarming. The mystique of militarism, far from being damaged, has been enhanced by the defeat in Indochina." I asked each recipient if he or she agreed and was willing to attend a preliminary meeting to reorganize our forces. Virtually all did, though not all could come on the date set by Gottlieb and Ethel Taylor of Women Strike for Peace, who undertook organizational arrangements for the meeting. Seventy or eighty people attended on

September 20; Herbert (Pete) Scoville, once a top official of the Defense Department and the CIA (turned peacenik) made the opening address. He was an exceptionally well informed person (I gained greatly from talking with him when I wrote my book on the arms race later on), but his position was very moderate — he suggested as a major goal working for a "no first use" resolution, for instance. Then again the attendance, while adequate enough, was not "heavy" enough; the main figures who could have formed a new antiwar organization were not present. The effort proved unproductive.

I attacked the problem from a different angle; I started teaching a class on revolution and the arms race at Roosevelt University (and a few sessions of a labor history course at the University of Illinois) while researching one of the most important articles I've ever written. In February 1976 the *Progressive* came out with "The Doomsday Strategy," a 20,000-word piece which I expanded into an 80,000-word book, published by Doubleday the following year. There was really not much up-to-date material, I found, on the nuclear race at that time. Swedish diplomat Alva Myrdal and William Epstein (who had worked for the UN) published excellent volumes on the subject before mine appeared. But "The Doomsday Strategy," and the book based on it, injected two basic ideas that were new to the discussion.

First was the concept that the nuclear race was self-propelling, drawn along on its own momentum. It was an impersonal process — engineers and scientists inventing and developing ever more efficient instruments of horror, heedless of political, personal or other consequences; numerous constituencies (the Pentagon, academe, defense contractors, certain members of Congress, the labor hierarchy) all with a stake in the race, defending and promoting it; think-tanks and intellectuals, subsidized by the Pentagon and big business, developing sophisticated rationales for continuation of the Cold War and infusing it into the mass media; and finally the overplayed sing-song of anti-communism "scaring the hell" out of the American people — as Senator Arthur Vandenberg once put it — that if they didn't spend mountains more on "defense" the Russians would take our country over. It was a self-enclosed system pushing the level of atomic armaments on both sides furiously upward. The end result was bound to be, as C. Wright Mills noted, that the preparation for war could be the cause of it. No single individual now could halt the nuclear arms race, not even the president — it was just too deeply embedded in the system. Only a sustained outpouring of protest by the American citizenry could reverse matters.

The second concept I added to the nuclear probe was that the United States was not seeking, as its government claimed, a stalemate — or what was called "mutual assured destruction" or "balance of terror" — but was still feverishly trying to find a way of achieving total victory. Americans were being told that Washington wanted nothing more than to "deter" the Soviets — "we" have enough weapons to destroy them, "they" have enough to destroy us, and in that balance of terror neither will dare attack. In fact, however, this image of "deterrence" was a fiction. Otherwise why would the United States need 31,000 warheads with the firepower of 635,000 Hiroshima bombs to destroy only 218 Russian cities with a population of 100,000 or more? And why was it manufacturing three new ones every day? The answer was that while Washington talked of stalemate it was seeking a way of winning. What was lacking in the missile age was a means of defense — there was no way to limit casualties to a few million at a time when Soviet missiles could hit American targets in thirty minutes, and vice-versa. Washington was researching furiously to find a defensive system — at the same time developing offensive weapons of great accuracy, like the MARV, the cruise missile, the Mark 12-A warhead that were suited for a "first strike," a surprise attack, but were only minimally necessary for a "second strike," a retaliatory attack. Meanwhile the active component of Washington's nuclear strategy was, as James Schlesinger had proclaimed in 1974, for a *limited* nuclear war in the next military crisis.

"The Doomsday Strategy," it is generally admitted, was

the seed for a new antiwar coalition. "Sid Lens started the process of forming the Mobilization for Survival," wrote Tom Cornell in the Fellowship of Reconciliation magazine, "with the publication of 'The Doomsday Strategy' . . . Gadfly Lens gave peace movement leaders little peace until informal organizing meetings were held of representatives of various segments of the activist peace movement, starting in the spring of 1976 and culminating in a national conference in Chicago, December 2–4, 1977." The article was reprinted in larger numbers than any other *Progressive* piece, except for one on McCarthyism in the 1950s; it was commented on by a number of national columnists and as one of its welcome side benefits, brought me a packet of lecture invitations. (I used it as my theme also when I spoke at the massive rally organized by the Peoples Bicentennial Commission on July 4 that year, to commemorate the nation's 200th birthday.) Propitiously, the article appeared around the time that young pacifists were walking cross-country in the Continental Walk for Disarmament and Social Justice. Small groups, sometimes a dozen or two, occasionally a hundred, traipsed along highways, held meetings in cities and small towns, slept in churches, and then coagulated into a few parades involving 2,000 people in Washington, mid-October 1976. My role in this affair, conducted primarily by the War Resisters League, was limited to marching and speaking in Chicago and at the main rally in Washington. But I was told that many walkers were reading my Doomsday piece as they marched in the hinterlands.

I had the feeling, as I walked with Dave Dellinger the last few miles of this small but moving event, that there was strong sentiment for a rebirth of the disarmament movement we had left in limbo during the decade of the Indochina War. The Washington *Post* reporters who covered the event also sensed that the movement was reassembling. "When the walk reached the Sylvan Theatre," they wrote, "the crowd witnessed something of a reunion of the antiwar left — Sidney Lens, Daniel Ellsberg, David McReynolds, Dave Dellinger and

Cora Weiss. All were on the program along with activist comedian Dick Gregory."

A month later, while on a speaking date at a church in Boston, I called Sid Peck, who lived in nearby Cambridge, and asked him to bring together a few peaceniks to discuss the nuclear issue. About twenty-five came, including Marjorie Swann of the American Friends Service Committee and two Nobel laureates, George Wald and Salvador Luria, whom I had met years before when I spoke at the University of Illinois. The Boston meeting sparked another meeting of fifty or sixty people — this one organized by Norma Becker, with Peck's help, in New York — and then another meeting in Philadelphia of a couple of hundred, out of which came the Mobilization for Survival. Most of the faces were new, but they were indistinguishable from those that had followed behind A. J. Muste in the protest we held at the Pentagon in the summer of 1965 or the national assemblage that Peck brought to Cleveland to form the first Mobe a year or so later. They were young, eager, idealistic. Only a minority were veterans of the older struggle — like Peck, Dellinger, McReynolds, Norma Becker, and Sam Lovejoy who had caused a national stir by pulling down a tower at a nuclear reactor site in New Hampshire and forming the Clamshell Alliance.

Mobilization for Survival was designed around four slogans — Zero Nuclear Weapons, Ban Nuclear Power, Stop the Arms Race, and Fund Human Needs. In its first year, it set dates for four activities — demonstrations around Hiroshima Day, August 6, 1977; a month and a half of teach-ins in late fall; a "fund human needs" day in the spring of 1978, calling on the nation to divert military expenditures to human needs; and a culminating activity, a demonstration on May 27, 1978, coinciding with the much awaited United Nations disarmament conference. The human needs affairs didn't come off too well, essentially because not enough unions were prepared to join us, but the others went moderately well. There were more and larger Hiroshima Day marches and vigils that year than there had been for a long time. Scores of teach-ins were held throughout the country, with Dan Ellsberg and myself carrying the largest load as speakers, but with many others involved as well, Barry Commoner, Phil Berrigan, Ben Spock, and most of the old timers. The May 27 demonstration attracted 25,000 people at the UN, including 600 or 700 Japanese and their top union leaders, and a few dozen people from Europe. At a conference held sometime later, Terry Provance, one of three coordinators, reported that Mobilization for Survival (Mobe) had 280 affiliates, most of them local branches, but also forty national and regional groups, as well as sister movements in Japan and Western Europe who were part of the *International* Mobilization for Survival.

In promoting the crusade against nuclear and conventional armaments, Mobe was only a modest success. The danger, as I have already noted, was an invisible one, one that was difficult to make graphic or real. But the campaign against nuclear energy, endemically related to the nuclear bomb, did impinge itself on the national consciousness and Mobe did play a role in that. Most Mobe adherents were pacifists, preoccupied with the problem of nuclear war; but they soon realized that the reactor and the bomb were brothers, or, at the least, cousins. Both were part of a single process that began with uranium mining, milling, enrichment, and diverged only in the final stages when uranium with a 3- or 4 percent content of radioactive U-235 was made into pellets for reactors, and uranium with a 90 percent U-235 content (or plutonium) was made into bombs. Every reactor, just like every atmospheric bomb test, moreover, spewed radiation into the biosphere, causing cancer and death. Both segments of the nuclear industry were jointly responsible for the "waste" problem, the radioactive waste that will torment humankind for thousands of years. Worst of all each of the approximately 200 reactors around the world was a vehicle for nuclear proliferation. From the 500 pounds of plutonium in its waste every year it was theoretically possible to produce twenty-five bombs like the one that fell on

Hiroshima. As nations acquired "reprocessing" facilities to separate the plutonium from the waste — something that is already technologically feasible — more and more would join the "nuclear club." President Ford predicted that by 1985 forty nations would have access to the plutonium and would have the know-how to make nuclear bombs. Thus the "peaceful" reactor was the handmaiden for nuclear proliferation.

All of this suggested both to the antimilitarism and the antireactor forces that they had a common purpose, and while there existed a rapidly growing, separate antinuke (antireactor) movement, Mobe supporters were involved in most of its protest actions, often joining hands for a common demonstration — as for instance in the rally of 100,000 people in Washington after the Three Mile Island reactor accident near Harrisburg in 1979. Mobe supporters in sizable numbers joined in the Clamshell Alliance campaign at Seabrook, New Hampshire. Many environmentalists came to the demonstrations conducted by Mobe at Rocky Flats near Denver, where the triggers were being manufactured for nuclear bombs. Accidents and emissions at this facility made the area far more radioactive and dangerous than it would have been under normal circumstances. As revelations came forth that soldiers were dying of leukemia because they were marched within a few thousand yards of a nuclear test at Yucca Flats, Nevada, in 1957 and that a proportionately large number of people were dying in Utah because of tests in nearby Nevada, radiation became a real and visible threat for Americans — and the antinuke movement grew apace. So strong was the opposition to "nukes" that California and one or two other states practically illegalized the construction of new reactor facilities; many states forbade transportation or storage of waste in their confines; and there was pressure within Congress for a moratorium on nuclear energy. To that extent at least Mobilization for Survival is part of the historical mainstream. Hopefully, it will also be able to place The Bomb in the forefront of national consciousness in the not too distant future.

This book, like life itself, ends in mid-air. As I write there are hundreds of mementos of the near-past or of ongoing activities that would crowd this personal saga beyond need — the special issue of *National Catholic Reporter* I edited under the headline THE NUCLEAR ARMS RACE—A TICKET TO HELL; my interviews with Earl Browder, former head of the Communist Party, and James P. Cannon, former head of the Trotskyites, a few weeks before each of them died, for a book on the "Old Left and New Left" that I ultimately discarded; a trip I made to Puerto Rico to write an article, and trips to Iran and Nicaragua I had to cancel; a highly satisfying well-attended dinner in June 1977 which honored me "in appreciation for his written and spoken words and courageous deeds in behalf of world peace and human survival"; the Coalition Against Registration and the Draft I helped John Rossen organize; the demonstration of 2,500 students at the University of Chicago at which Dellinger, Studs Terkel, Eqbal Ahmad, and I spoke in protest against the award of $25,000 to Robert McNamara; my role in the campaign of the *Progressive,* of which I was a contributing editor, to publish an article on "The Secret of the H-Bomb," which a politically near-sighted judge in Milwaukee temporarily banned; my promotion of a "nuclear moratorium" amendment to the SALT II treaty calling for an immediate halt to further research, development, testing, manufacture, and deployment of nuclear weapons and launchers; and many I'm sure I've forgotten. None of this is important in itself, except to indicate, as a Chicago *Sun-Times* article on me some years ago put it, "He's Still At It." I hope I can continue to be "at it," for I'm as convinced today as I was in the early 1930s that social revolution is both desirable and all but inevitable.

At a meeting and concert of 3,000 people in Madison, Wisconsin, during July 1979, called to protest banning a planned *Progressive* article by Howard Morland on secrecy, George Wald scanned the crowd silently for a moment, and said slowly: "I think I see a movement again." I do too. One could see it in the standing ovations the students gave Wald and myself that evening, and in the absolutely wild response to Pete Seeger and his songs — including a rendition of "The International" in French. One can hear it at every rally when someone cries out "no nukes." The trauma of the 1970s, unless I'm mistaken, almost surely will lead to a new New Left in the 1980s. For it is clear that humanity cannot solve its economic problems within this system of capitalism, nor can it prevent a nuclear holocaust. Capitalism, to be fair, has added a bit of humanism to its facade with welfarist measures in the last four decades, but it is still based on greed, social Darwinist hostility toward the underclasses, and planlessness. It must give way in the end to a system that is international in character, that divides income and wealth equitably, that plans the conservation and utilization of dwindling resources.

I know today, just as I knew in the 1930s, that all this must come — if humanity is to survive. What I don't know for certain (though I did feel I knew it in the 1930s) is how it will come about. In a book I published in 1974, *The Promise and Pitfalls of Revolution,* I offered some thoughts on revolution I think remain valid today. It occurs to me, to begin with, that the struggle against nuclear war is a social revolution in itself. Neither capitalism nor the present forms of communism (nationally oriented as they are) can survive the nuclear age. If a total war is to break out between them it will mean the end of their civilizations. And if war is to be avoided they must not only disarm, but establish a worldwide mechanism for containing conflict before it evolves into military violence. They must move, in other words, toward a single sovereignty. Theoretically, it is possible for a single country to conquer all others — as Lord Cecil Rhodes (for whom Rhodesia was named) envisioned for Britain in the nineteenth century. In practice, however, internation-hood will be feasible only to the extent that the rich are willing to share with the poor, and the powerful to plan a worldwide economy with the powerless. Without egalitarianism — the kind preached by religious and lay prophets since time immemorial — an international society is impossible, and without an international society, or major steps in that direction, nuclear holocaust is inevitable.

The question then is how will this social revolution come about. No one really knows and no one can really be as certain as we were in the 1930s. Marxism was based on the assumption that it would be repeatedly updated. In an era that has provided us with such technological changes as the atom, the computer, automation, and with myriad problems resulting from the fact that "the revolution" came first to underdeveloped countries, rather than to the highly developed ones, Marxism obviously needs so total a refurbishing it will hardly be recognizable. Just as the "utopian" theories of socialism in the first part of the nineteenth century (those of Robert Owen, for instance) were replaced by Marx's mature and coherent concepts, so a new strategy for revolution awaits elaboration today.

My *Promise and Pitfalls of Revolution* attempted to add a few fragments to the discussion of a new strategy. It is not at all preordained, I think, that the revolution on history's agenda for the Western World must be like 1917 or 1789 — a revolution that peaks in one burst of violent activity, and places centralized political power in a few hands. It can be like the bourgeois revolution in Denmark which spanned seven or eight decades relatively peaceably — a revolution in stages — or like the Meiji Restoration in Japan in 1868, where the feudal class itself overthrew feudalism and established a capitalist society. A revolution in stages is desirable, if it is possible, because there is a minimum of bloodshed and political power remains dispersed. In a violent revolution there is a tendency for such power to be centralized in a single person or a small group; that is the kind of situation that lends itself to authoritarianism, whether in a capitalist or a socialist society. It becomes very difficult for a leader under those circumstances to disgorge himself of the total power in his hands; only a few socialist leaders have had moderate success in that regard. It is much better for a revolution to proceed in stages, and I think that it is possible in the United States and Western Europe today. I listed in *Promise and Pitfalls* a number of radical-reforms whose promotion would bring about the revolution in stages — ranging from a 100-percent inheritance tax above a modest level, to public acquisition of corporations, national indicator planning, nationalization of banks, oil companies, utilities, a national ecological plan, to a dozen forms of neighborhood and regional control of political leaders, a program for disarmament, and steps to liquidate the military-industrial complex.

Is all this feasible? I'm not certain, but I think it is. If anyone has a better scenario, or if events dictate another course, I'll be happy to follow him, her, or it. In any event I do not repent for a moment a half century of radicalism.

Indeed, I take pride in it.

Index

Brennan, Ray, 238
Bridges, Alfred Renton
  ("Harry"), 63, 64, 70, 106,
  109, 253
Britain: in World War II, 86, 87,
  89–90; postwar economy of,
  129, 131
British Guiana, 281–282
Brockway, Fenner, 182, 185
Brooks, George, 114
Brookwood Labor College, 32
Brophy, John, 72, 77
Browder, Earl, 23, 40, 85–86,
  87, 404; attitude toward New
  Deal, 38, 39; persecution of,
  during World War II, 90, 91
Brown, George, 272
Brown, Harrison, 396–397
Brown, Irving, 194, 195
Brown, Sam, 325, 349, 350,
  379
Buckley, William, 28, 267–268
Budenz, Louis F., 33, 203
Bukharin, Nikolai I., 81
Bunker, Ellsworth, 324
Burke, Tom, 143
Burnham, Forbes, 282
Burnham, James, 33
Burns, Arthur F., 388
Buschmann, Hugo, 194
Butterfield, Alexander, 393
Byrnes, James F., 127

C

Caballero, F. Largo, 82
Cab drivers, Washington,
  unionizing of, 48

Cabell, C. P., 240
CADRE (Chicago Area Draft
  Resisters), 294
Caldera, Rafael, 220
Caldwell, Max, 99–105
Calverton, V. F., 48
Cambodia, 126; U.S. invasion of,
  363–364, 390; and *Mayaguez*
  incident, 395–396
Campos, Pedro Albizu, 224
Canaris, Adm. Wilhelm, 89–90
Canh, Do Xuan, 317
Cannon, James P., 20, 26, 84,
  404; and formation of Com-
  munist League of America,
  26–28; and Workers Party,
  30, 33–34; and Socialist
  Workers Party, 42, 44;
  schism with Shachtman, 44;
  persecution of, during World
  War II, 90–91
Capone crime syndicate, in
  labor unions, 96–97, 98,
  99–105, 119
Capote, Truman, 241
Carey, Archibald, 155
Carey, James B., 70, 252
Carmichael, Stokely, 225, 226,
  278, 314
Carstens, Art, 161
Carter, Jimmy, 163
Casey, Michael, 64
Castro, Fidel, 173, 178, 263;
  and Cuban Revolution,
  238–244; and October
  missile crisis, 275–277
Castro, Raul, 238
Chambers, Whittaker, 166

Chamberlain, Neville, 89
Chamoun, Camille, 217
Chapin, Dwight, 355
Chavez, Cesar, 106
Chester, Harry, 368
Chiakulas, Charles, 151, 157, 158; and Hickman Defense Committee, 151, 154, 155; labor activities of, 155, 205–206, 211; and peace movement, 251, 252, 253
Chiang Kai-shek, 25, 202, 338
Chicago *American,* 172, 279
Chicago Council on Foreign Relations, 157, 267
Chicago *Daily News,* 246–247, 249, 259, 280, 283
Chicago Federation of Labor, 32, 100, 142, 212
Chicago Industrial Union Council, 109, 110
Chicago *Maroon,* 274
Chicago *Sun-Times,* 153, 174, 238, 240–241, 246, 247, 260, 262, 363, 388, 404
Chicago Tomorrow, 392
Chicago *Tribune,* 102, 153
Chile, 220–221
China: revolution in, 126, 195, 202, 284–285; and Korean War, 203, 337, 338
Chomsky, Noam, 322
Church, Sen. Frank, 164
Churchill, Winston, 256
CIA, 132, 174; formation of, 130, 164. *See also* Militarism, U.S.

CIO (Congress of Industrial Organizations), 32, 56, 63, 77–78, 97; organizing of steel workers, 55, 72, 77; formation of, 69–70; role in rubber plant strikes, 71–72; role in auto workers' strike, 73–77; attitude toward World War II, 86; Lens as director of Local 329 of, 103–104, 117–124; building trades campaign of, 107–108; and Montgomery Ward strike, 110; weak bargaining power of, 134, 136–137; during McCarthy era, 175; merger with AFL, 227–228; affiliation with ICFTU, 260. *See also* AFL-CIO
Citizens Committee on the Energy Crisis, 388–389
Civil rights movement, 155, 221, 223, 224–226, 278–279, 291, 314
Clamshell Alliance, 401, 403
Clayton, William, 130
Clement, Travers, 221
Clergy and Laity Concerned, 386
Clifford, Clark, 127
Clinton, Stanford, 118, 136, 138–139, 141
Coalition Against Registration and the Draft, 404
Coalition for an Anti-Imperialist Movement (Co-Aim), 342
Coalition on the Economic Crisis, 386

Cochran, Bert, 70, 230, 233
Coffin, Rev. William Sloan, 305, 320, 359, 361
Cohen, Fannie, 32
Cold War, 38, 174–175, 183, 195, 260. *See also* Militarism, U.S.
Coleman, David, 150–151
Coleman, McAlister, 72
Commager, Henry Steele, 229, 358
Committee for Independent Political Action, 304
Committee for Industrial Organization, 69. *See also* CIO
Committee for Nonviolent Action, 255, 299–301
Committees of Correspondence, 254–255
Commoner, Barry, 402
Communist League of America, 24; formation of, 26–29; union organizing of, 28, 29–30; merge with American Workers Party, 30, 33; anti-French turn faction of, 41–42. *See also* Socialist Workers Party
Communist League of Struggle, 43
Communist Party, American, 21, 32, 60; during Depression years, 19–20; and Stalin's Third Period, 23–25; Communist League of America's opposition to, 26–29; attitude toward New Deal,

38–39; reformism or Americanization of, 39–40; working within unions, 69–70, 120–122; reactions to World War II, 86–87; antilabor sentiment of, during war, 109–111, 120–122; during McCarthy era, 156–157, 164–166; effect of anti-Stalinism sentiment on, 203–204, 206; New Left's rejection of, 227; attitude toward Khrushchev, 230–232
Conference for Progressive Labor Action (CPLA), 20, 33
Congress, peace supporters in, 249–251, 265, 271–275, 289
Congress of Industrial Organizations, *see* CIO
Connor, Bull, 279
Continental Walk for Disarmament and Social Justice, 400
Coolidge, Pres. Calvin, 157
Cornell, Tom, 400
Cortright, David, 375; *Soldiers in Revolt*, 306
Cosbey, Robert C., 272, 275
Coser, Lewis, 221
Coulter, C. C., 102
Counterinaugural, antiwar movement's, 341–342
Cousins, Norman, 255, 256
Cox, Archibald, 393
Coyle, Brian, 394
Crossman, Richard, 182
Crozier, Michel, 182
Crystal Tube plant strike, 143–144

Humphrey, Sen. Hubert, 165, 175, 323, 334
Hunt, E. Howard, 390, 391

I

Illinois Workers Alliance, 45
Impeach Nixon Committee, 392–394
Independent Socialist League, 44, 206
India, 218–219, 284
International Confederation of Free Trade Unions (ICFTU), 186, 260
International Ladies' Garment Workers' Union (ILGWU), 176
International Longshoremen's Association, 106
International Longshoremen's Union, 63
International News, 47
Inter-University Committee for Debate on Foreign Policy, 310–311
Iran: CIA intervention in, 132, 218, 284, 295; Mossadegh as Prime Minister of, 217–218
Italy: communism in, 125, 130; U.S. political financing in, 164, 189

J

Jack, Homer, 155, 157, 255
Jackson, Jesse, 369
Jacobs, Paul, 29, 223, 307

Jacobson, Jules, 267
Jagan, Cheddi, 281–282
James, William, 31
Jewish Labor Committee, 204
Johnson, Arnold, 318
Johnson, Byron, 249, 250
Johnson, James, 306
Johnson, Pres. Lyndon B., 225, 248, 281, 295, 323; presidential campaign of, 284, 288–289; and Vietnam War, 285, 286, 287, 289, 296, 297, 317–318, 339
JOIN (Jobs or Income Now), 304
Joplin, Janis, 351
Jumblatt, Kamal, 217

K

Kadar, Janos, 232, 329
Kahan, Seymour, 212
Kamenev, Lev Borisovich, 80, 81
Kampelman, Max, 170
Kantorowicz, 193
Kaplan, Allan, 272, 273, 386
Kasavubu, Joseph, 258
Katzenbach, Nicholas de B., 289
Keating, Sen. Kenneth, 275
Kelly, Mayor Ed, 45
Kempton, Murray, 267
Kennedy, Sen. Edward, 272, 370
Kennedy, Jane, 367, 396
Kennedy, Pres. John F., 275, 278; and Bay of Pigs, 244–246, 279; assassination of, 247–248, 264; presidential